Modern Chinese Lexicology

Centring on "words" which connect vocabulary and semantic morphemes, this book makes a systemic and in-depth analysis on the study of modern Chinese lexicology.

Firstly, it clarifies the definitions and properties of vocabulary, words and semantic morphemes in Chinese. Then the structure forms of Chinese words are examined. It is worth noting that this research is one of the first to distinguish word formation and lexical morphology. It observes that word formation studies how neologisms are coined, while lexical morphology refers to the ways in which semantic morphemes are combined with each other. On word meaning and its clustering, it discusses the relationship between word meaning and concept, as well as the criteria and principles of the clustering. Specifically, it studies monosemes, polysemes, synonyms, near-synonyms, antonyms, etc., including their characteristics and types. Lastly, it explores the evolution of word meaning and its laws, as well as the dynamic form of vocabulary.

This book will be a valuable reference for scholars and students in linguistics, especially in Chinese lexical studies.

Ge Benyi is a professor and PhD supervisor of Chinese Linguistics at the School of Chinese Language and Literature, Shandong University. She is mainly engaged in the teaching and research of Chinese linguistics with a special preference for Chinese lexicology.

Chinese Linguistics

Chinese Linguistics series selects representative and frontier works in linguistic disciplines including lexicology, grammar, phonetics, dialectology, philology and rhetoric. Mostly published in Chinese before, the selection has had far-reaching influence on China's linguistics and offered inspiration and reference for the world's linguistics. The aim of this series is to reflect the general level and latest development of Chinese linguistics from an overall and objective view.

Titles in this series currently include:

Modern Chinese Lexicology
Ge Benyi

Modern Chinese Parts of Speech
Systems Research
Guo Rui

Modern Chinese Parts of Speech
Classification Theory
Guo Rui

Prosodic Syntax in Chinese
Theory and Facts
Feng Shengli

Prosodic Syntax in Chinese
History and Changes
Feng Shengli

The Experiential Guo in Mandarin
A Quantificational Approach
Ye Meng

Research on Functional Grammar of Chinese
Information Structure and Word Ordering Selection
Zhang Bojiang, Fang Mei

Research on Functional Grammar of Chinese
Reference and Grammatical Category
Zhang Bojiang, Fang Mei

For more information, please visit https://www.routledge.com/Chinese-Linguistics/book-series/CL

Modern Chinese Lexicology

Ge Benyi

First published in English 2018
by Routledge
2 Park Square, Milton Park, Abingdon, Oxon OX14 4RN

and by Routledge
711 Third Avenue, New York, NY 10017

Routledge is an imprint of the Taylor & Francis Group, an informa business

© 2018 Ge Benyi

Translated by Xu Dekuan

The right of Ge Benyi to be identified as author of this work has been asserted by her in accordance with sections 77 and 78 of the Copyright, Designs and Patents Act 1988.

All rights reserved. No part of this book may be reprinted or reproduced or utilised in any form or by any electronic, mechanical, or other means, now known or hereafter invented, including photocopying and recording, or in any information storage or retrieval system, without permission in writing from the publishers.

Trademark notice: Product or corporate names may be trademarks or registered trademarks, and are used only for identification and explanation without intent to infringe.

English Version by permission of The Commercial Press.

British Library Cataloguing-in-Publication Data
A catalogue record for this book is available from the British Library

Library of Congress Cataloging-in-Publication Data
A catalog record for this book has been requested

ISBN: 978-1-138-57661-2 (hbk)
ISBN: 978-1-351-26952-0 (ebk)

Typeset in Times New Roman
by Apex CoVantage, LLC

Contents

Preface to the third Chinese edition vi
Preface to the first Chinese edition vii
Preface to the revised Chinese edition viii

1 Vocabulary revisited   1

2 Words and semantic morphemes   27

3 The emergence and structural forms of words   55

4 Word meaning   110

5 Word meaning clustering   123

6 The evolution of word meaning and its laws   169

7 Exploring the dynamic form of vocabulary   189

   References   215
   Index   227

Preface to the third Chinese edition

The first edition of *Modern Chinese Lexicology* was published in 2001, and its revised edition was published in 2004. After the publication of the book, strong supports from readers have been received and it has been reprinted eight times in ten years and the supply still falls short of demand up to now. Apart from being grateful, I am here only to express my deep respect and gratitude to my friends and readers who support me.

Now the Commercial Press is taking over publishing the book, so I took advantage of this opportunity to make further revisions as much as I could for the sake of perfection. The major revisions include but are not limited to:

- First, necessary supplements were made to the points which had not been thoroughly discussed before.
- Second, improper examples were replaced as much as possible.
- Third, modifications to the elaborations that were not clear enough and corrections to the occasionally few typos were made.
- Fourth, some major references were supplied at the request of the readers. The references are listed in chronological order, the purpose of which is just to let the readers know that it is in this process that I learned and studied Chinese lexicology, and it is in the nourishment and inspiration of these works that I keep moving forward.

It was another revision, though, I don't think it is possible to reach the acme of perfection in learning, and I still sincerely wish that all my friends and readers will continue to make valuable comments.

Ge Benyi
Shandong University
June 2012

Preface to the first Chinese edition

The present little book, *Modern Chinese Lexicology*, is an integration of my former book, *A Study on Chinese Vocabulary*, and the researches, thinking and writings of more than ten years in the past. It may also be said a monograph to have ensembled my current researches on Chinese vocabulary.

I began to be interested greatly in vocabulary while I was teaching the course "introduction to linguistics" after my graduation and was enrolled as a teacher by my Alma Mater in 1955. Since then, I have been consciously or unconsciously willing to learn, observe and think about problems in Chinese vocabulary. During the long fifty years or so, I have not only enjoyed myself but also gained a lot from it. My book *Vocabulary of Modern Chinese* was published in 1961. Although this little book was only one of my works of apprenticeship, its publication gave me invaluable encouragement and confidence. I began to do my own studies: on the basis of learning the research findings of former and contemporary scholars, I began to go my own way and learn to speak my own words.

A Study on Chinese Vocabulary was published in 1985. Due to the limitations of the academic level and conditions of study at that time, it was a little bit simpler because some problems have not even been mentioned. But I am still consenting to the many points of view in that book at present; therefore, I will continue to use them in this book, except that some new ones are to be added and others are to be modified to a certain extent. Furthermore, some new ideas and contents are to be added and some new questions are to be discussed.

Whichever academic research field is a colourful world; whichever researcher can investigate and explore in this world by his own strength; at the same time, on whichever problem one can put forward his own views according to the specific practice of himself. Whether this view is appropriate or not, whether it is correct or not, of course, would depend on the test of the reality and the judgement of the academic community. It is with such an idea that I am engaged in research and writing. Therefore, after the publication of this book, I still hope to get help and criticism from everybody.

Ge Benyi
Shandong University
May 2000

Preface to the revised Chinese edition

The book *Modern Chinese Lexicology* was published by Shandong People's Publishing House in April 2001. It has been well recognized and accepted after its publication and was printed for the second time in March 2002 in line with the social needs. The distribution of the book is gratifying, but I find many viewpoints in the book unsatisfactory whenever I read the book. This is mainly reflected in that the discussion on some issues is too simple and therefore not complete, and it is not detailed and lucid enough for the explanation of some new theoretical points of view. There are also some omissions and instances of negligence in the text. Now Shandong People's Publishing House will reprint the book, and I have decided to take this opportunity to revise the book. In addition to supplement some necessary new contents, I will make up some deficiencies that have been noticed so as to enrich and improve the book.

In October 2002, *Chinese Lexicology* (six volumes), of which I am editor-in-chief, was published by Shandong University Press. In addition to making everyone feel happy, the publication of the book also baffled and confused my friends by mainly the following two issues:

- First, by baffling it is meant that, in the book, especially in the first volume, a number of well-known scholars are criticized. I never criticized others in my works in the past, so that baffled everybody. I, without any doubt, am not in the least favour of such criticism in the book, which is very inconsistent with my usual principles and academic style, not to mention that among the criticized are the respected scholars with whom I am familiar and quite not a few have been good friends of mine for years. The reason why I kept the passage lies in that the book was authored by division of labour and I myself have also been criticized in that very volume. In order not to suppress criticism, especially the criticism to my own, and to give others freedom of opinion and expression, I kept the passage as it was. What needs to be explained here is that my own scholarly philosophy remains unchanged as ever.
- Second, by confusion it is meant that I myself was criticized in the book that I edited myself; thus, my friends and students who had read my writings were so confused that they couldn't help asking if my viewpoints have changed. I have already explained the reasons for retaining that passage above, so here

I can say with certainty that my academic viewpoints have not been changed. From *A Study on Chinese Vocabulary* to the first edition of *Modern Chinese Lexicology*, up to this revised edition, there is no contradiction among the theoretical viewpoints, and if there is any difference, it is only that I try to revise the contents of later editions so that the latter is more perfect than the former. Therefore, it can be said that the revised edition of *Modern Chinese Lexicology* now published is the most representative of my current academic thinking.

Great gratitude to all those concerned about this issue, and I hope that everybody can understand this.

Ge Benyi
Shandong University
May 2004

1 Vocabulary revisited

Section 1 What is vocabulary?

I Definition and properties of vocabulary

What is vocabulary? There exist many casual and self-sustaining definitions, such as "all the words in a language taken together constitute what is known as its vocabulary" (Josef Stalin), "All the words used in a book are called vocabulary", or in general, "Vocabulary is a generic term for words", and so on and so forth. Such interpretations are common in literature and they are justified in certain contexts, because vocabulary is indeed a collective concept referring to words and it is used to denote the sum total of words. However, those definitions are not so exact and correct from the point of view of linguistic studies, against the requirements for scientific terminology in lexicology. To correctly define vocabulary, we need to start from the properties of vocabulary.

As early as in the 1950s Josef Stalin pointed out that:

> however, by itself, the vocabulary does not constitute the language – it is rather the building materials of the language. Just as in construction work the building materials do not constitute the building itself, although the latter cannot be constructed without them, so too the vocabulary of a language does not constitute the language itself, although no language is conceivable without it. But the vocabulary of a language assumes tremendous importance when it comes under the control of grammar.[1]

Although the remarks by Stalin are not without shortcomings, they put forward some basic properties and functions of vocabulary.

We should note that what can serve as building materials of language abounds and what matters is what they construct, within what range and under what conditions. For example, phones, which serve to form phonemes, are only building materials for syllables; and semantic morphemes are just building materials for words and so on. As for vocabulary, it is building materials for sentences. In other words, vocabulary serves to form utterances for communication. Therefore it is the function and property of vocabulary to serve as sentence-making materials. In accordance with such a conclusion, we should acknowledge that all language elements with this function and property belong to vocabulary. For example, although they themselves are composed of words, idioms and formulaic expressions are building blocks for sentences and possess the same property and function as words. Therefore, such elements should not and cannot be excluded from vocabulary. In conclusion, we hold that vocabulary is the aggregate of all the words and all the fixed structures equivalent to words in one language. In other words, vocabulary in a language consists of two fundamental components – all the words and all the fixed structures equivalent to words in that language.

II Components of vocabulary

As was noted above, vocabulary consists of two fundamental components: words and fixed structures equivalent to words in function. Therefore we will discuss and analyze the two related but distinctive components respectively in this section.

(I) The aggregate of words

All the words in one language constitute the aggregate of words of the language concerned, which can be divided into two parts: basic vocabulary and common vocabulary.

1 BASIC VOCABULARY

Basic vocabulary, which is a principal and indispensable part of vocabulary, is the aggregate of all the basic words in a language. Basic vocabulary and syntax together shape the foundation of a language. Logically if the basic vocabulary of a language changes completely or vanishes altogether, it will mean that the relevant language is no longer in existence.

The words in basic vocabulary are called basic words, which denote the most necessary objects and concepts in everyday life of human beings so they are extremely closely related to the life of people and they are the lexical components which people from all walks of life can hardly do without. Language learning begins from acquiring basic words, for they express the names of the objects and actions which people need most. Therefore without basic words, it is impossible for a person to communicate.

Basic words in Chinese include:

> 天 (*tian*, "sky") 地 (*di*, "ground") 山 (*shan*, "mountain") 水 (*shui*, "water") 人 (*ren*, "people") 鸟 (*niao*, "bird") 牛 (*niu*, "cow") 羊 (*yang*, "sheep; goat") 风 (*feng*, "wind") 雨 (*yu*, "rain") 阴 (*yin*, "cloudy") 晴 (*qing*, "sunny") 花 (*hua*, "flower") 草 (*cao*, "grass") 江 (*jiang*, "river") 河 (*he*, "river") 树木 (*shumu*, "trees") 道路 (*daolu*, "road") 天气 (*tianqi*, "weather") 阳光 (*yangguang*,

"sunshine") 白云 (*baiyun*, "clouds") 空气 (*kongqi*, "air") 太阳 (*taiyang*, "sun") 月亮 (*yueliang*, "moon") 石头 (*shitou*, "stone") 沙子 (*shazi*, "sand")

爷爷 (*yeye*, "grandpa") 奶奶 (*nainai*, "grandma") 父亲 (*fuqin*, "father") 母亲 (*muqin*, "mother") 爸爸 (*baba*, "daddy") 妈妈 (*mama*, "mom") 姐姐 (*jiejie*, "elder sister") 弟弟 (*didi*, "younger brother") 叔叔 (*shushu*, "uncle; father's younger brother") 姑姑 (*gugu*; "aunt; father's sister") 舅舅 (*jiujiu*, "uncle; mother's brother") 姨妈 (*yima*, "aunt; mother's sister")

头 (*tou*, "head") 手 (*shou*, "hand") 嘴 (*zui*, "mouth") 腿 (*tui*, "leg") 脚 (*jiao*, "foot") 心 (*xin*, "heart") 肺 (*fei*, "lung") 肝 (*gan*, "liver") 眼 (*yan*, "eye") 牙 (*ya*, "tooth") 耳朵 (*erduo*, "ear") 鼻子 (*bizi*, "nose") 胳膊 (*gebo*, "arm") 指头 (*zhitou*, "finger") 头发 (*toufa*, "hair")

书 (*shu*, "book") 笔 (*bi*, "pen") 纸 (*zhi*, "paper") 墨 (*mo*, "ink") 车 (*che*, "car") 船 (*chuan*, "ship") 布 (*bu*, "cloth") 线 (*xian*, "thread") 锅 (*guo*, "boiler") 碗 (*wan*, "bowl") 灯 (*deng*, "lamp") 门 (*men*, "door") 墙 (*qiang*, "wall") 窗户 (*chuanghu*, "window") 房子 (*fangzi*, "house") 桌子 (*zhuozi*, "table") 椅子 (*yizi*, "chair") 刀子 (*daozi*, "knife") 绳子 (*shengzi*, "rope") 电话 (*dianhua*, "telephone") 电视 (*dianshi*, "television") 汽车 (*qiche*, "automobile") 衣服 (*yifu*, "clothes") 邮票 (*youpiao*, "stamp") 学校 (*xuexiao*, "school") 老师 (*laoshi*, "teacher")

米 (*mi*, "rice") 面 (*mian*, "flour") 粮 (*liang*, "grain") 油 (*you*, "oil") 盐 (*yan*, "salt") 菜 (*cai*, "vegetable") 糕 (*gao*, "cake") 饼 (*bing*, "pancake") 鱼 (*yu*, "fish") 肉 (*rou*, "meat") 虾 (*xia*, "shrimp") 饭 (*fan*, "food") 粥 (*zhou*, "porridge") 馒头 (*mantou*, "steamed buns") 米饭 (*mifan*, "rice") 面条 (*miantiao*, "noodles") 饺子 (*jiaozi*, "dumplings")

走 (*zou*, "walk") 跳 (*tiao*, "jump") 看 (*kan*, "look") 想 (*xiang*, "think") 生 (*sheng*, "alive") 死 (*si*, "die") 睡 (*shui*, "sleep") 醒 (*xing*, "wake up") 买 (*mai*, "buy") 卖 (*mai*, "sell") 来 (*lai*, "come") 去 (*qu*, "go") 学习 (*xuexi*, "study") 工作 (*gongzuo*, "work") 休息 (*xiuxi*, "rest") 劳动 (*laodong*, "work") 成功 (*chenggong*, "succeed") 失败 (*shibai*, "fail")

红 (*hong*, "red") 白 (*bai*, "white") 甜 (*tian*, "sweet") 苦 (*ku*, "bitter") 方 (*fang*, "square") 圆 (*yuan*, "round") 厚 (*hou*, "thick") 薄 (*bo*, "thin") 大 (*da*, "big") 小 (*xiao*, "small") 长 (*chang*, "long") 短 (*duan*, "short") 高 (*gao*, "high") 低 (*di*, "low") 深 (*shen*, "deep") 浅 (*qian*, "shallow") 多 (*duo*, "many") 少 (*shao*, "little") 美丽 (*meili*, "beautiful") 漂亮 (*piaoliang*, "pretty") 轻快 (*qingkuai*, "brisk") 沉重 (*chenzhong*, "heavy") 丰富 (*fengfu*, "rich") 干净 (*ganjing*, "clean") 团结 (*tuanjie*, "united") 健康 (*jiankang*, "healthy")

上 (*shang*, "up") 下 (*xia*, "down") 前 (*qian*, "front") 后 (*hou*, "back") 左 (*zuo*, "left") 右 (*you*, "right") 春 (*chun*, "spring") 夏 (*xia*, "summer") 秋 (*qiu*, "autumn") 冬 (*dong*, "winter") 东 (*dong*, "east") 西 (*xi*, "west") 南 (*nan*, "south") 北 (*bei*, "north")

一 (*yi*, "one") 二 (*er*, "two") 三 (*san*, "three") 四 (*si*, "four") 十 (*shi*, "ten") 百 (*bai*, "hundred") 万 (*wan*, "ten thousand") 你 (*ni*, "you") 我 (*wo*, "I") 他 (*ta*, "he") 谁 (*shui*, "who") 这 (*zhe*, "here") 那 (*na*, "there") 再 (*zai*, "again")

. . .

4 *Vocabulary revisited*

Basic vocabulary possesses the following characteristics:

- First, universality. Basic vocabulary is extremely closely related to people's life. Therefore it is indispensable to the people of any trade, so it is widely used by all the people with the most extensive coverage and highest frequency of use.
- Second, stability. As the basic words are used by all speakers, they tend to be long-standing and pass from generation to generation. Therefore they are unlikely to change. In other words, the vast majority of basic words are ones that come to be after long-time usage. While being widely accepted by the speech community, basic words possess great stability.
- Third, basic vocabulary is the foundation for neologism creation. This property was previously referred to as "productivity" in my book *Studies on Chinese Vocabulary*. Afterwards I began to realize that "foundation for neologism creation" is a more proper term, because basic words are words themselves, and therefore incapable of producing new words (neologisms). However, basic words can be the foundation for neologism creation, in two ways: first, basic words can serve as semantic morphemes for simple basic words. In this case, the basic word and the semantic morpheme are identical in form. A simple word comes into being at the same time with the simple semantic morpheme making up it, and they exist in one and the same form with completely different property and function. Therefore, while a basic word is in common use and possesses stability, the semantic morphemes that make up the word obtain a strong word-formation ability. Take "人 (*ren*, 'people; human')" for example. As a semantic morpheme, it constitutes a basic word "人" and at the same time, it can be used to form many other compound words; thus it has high productivity. Second, as for compound basic words, when basic words of this type are widely used and possess stability, they are transformed into compounding semantic morphemes as a whole and can be used to create neologisms. For instance, "工作 (*gongzuo*, 'work')" is a compound formed by two semantic morphemes: "工 (*gong*, 'work')" and "作 (*zuo*, 'engage in certain activity')". But when the compound word "工作" is established as a basic word by the language community and is widely in use, the language form "工作" will turn into a compounding semantic morpheme as a whole and will be used to create neologisms, such as "工作服 (*gongzuo-fu*, 'work clothes')", "工作帽 (*gongzuo-mao*, 'work helmet')", "工作台 (*gongzuo-tai*, 'worktable')", "工作日 (*gongzuo-ri*, 'working day')", etc. That is to say, because "工作" is a basic word, it is more likely to become a semantic morpheme to form a new word. Thus "工作" becomes the foundation for neologisms with the status of a word. Many compound basic words are of the similar nature. Of course, when a compound word is used to form neologisms as a compounding semantic morpheme, this lexical component has two distinct functions and characters: when it is used to make a sentence, it is a word, and when used to form a neologism, it is a semantic morpheme; this is the case with "工作".

The three characteristics of basic words are interconnected, and "universality" is the most fundamental. A word becomes stable only if it acquires the property of universality, which enables it to become the foundation for neologism creation.

Please note that stability of basic words should not be confused with a long history of words, because non-basic words may also have a long history. But without universality, words of long history still do not become basic vocabulary. For example, the word "诗经 (*Shijing*, 'Book of Poetry')" has a quite long history, but since it does not acquire universality, it belongs to common vocabulary. On the other hand, if a word with only a brief history acquires universality and thus becomes stabilized, it may well have a chance to become a basic word. "电视 (*dianshi*, 'television')" has comparatively a short history, but owing to its universality, it gets stabilized. Therefore, it has been established as a basic word in the contemporary Chinese language. After acquiring universality and stability, a basic word will certainly become the foundation for neologism creation of a language community.

Please also note that, the characteristic that basic words are the foundation for neologism creation is defined for the total of basic vocabulary. As a matter of fact, certain basic words, such as "你 (*ni*, 'you')", "谁 (*shui*, 'who')" are weak in creating neologisms. Despite this fact, they are still basic words, for they have the properties of universality and stability.

2 COMMON VOCABULARY

The aggregate of words other than basic vocabulary in one language is the common vocabulary of that language. Compared with basic vocabulary, common vocabulary is used less widely and with low frequency. Common vocabulary is much weaker than basic vocabulary in stability and in being the foundation for neologism creation. However, common vocabulary has its own characteristics: it is extremely sensitive in reflecting social changes and developments and such characteristics as "the development of vocabulary is much faster than that of sound and grammar" and "the development of vocabulary reflects the face of social development to some extent" are more prominent and evident as far as common vocabulary is concerned. Common vocabulary is rich in content. Therefore one must learn and acquire common vocabulary of a language in addition to basic vocabulary in order to learn and use that language more competently.

Common vocabulary, large in number and extensive in coverage, has the following components:

> First, inherent words passed down from history. These words were already in existence in the past and some of them had a quite long history and others were passed down and stabilized in various historical periods. These words have been used from generation to generation by people after their formation, but they have not acquired universality and cannot be used as

the foundation of neologism creation. They therefore belong to common vocabulary. For example,

> 夫人 (*furen*, "lady") 儒家 (*rujia*, "the Confucian school") 诞辰 (*danchen*, "birthday") 逝世 (*shishi*, "pass away") 颜面 (*yanmian*, "face; prestige")
> 饮食 (*yinshi*, "diet") 居留 (*juliu*, "residence") 界限 (*jiexian*, "limit") 借鉴 (*jiejian*, "draw lessons from") 编纂 (*bianzuan*, "compile")
> 别号 (*biehao*, "alias") 彩霞 (*caixia*, "rosy clouds") 拜访 (*baifang*, "pay a visit") 残忍 (*canren*, "cruel") 沉浮 (*chenfu*, "ups and downs")
> 晨曦 (*chenxi*, "dawn") 错综 (*cuozong*, "intricate") 胆寒 (*danhan*, "appalled") 底稿 (*digao*, "manuscript") 论题 (*lunti*, "topic")
> 独裁 (*ducai*, "dictatorship") 封锁 (*fengsuo*, "blockade") 风采 (*fengcai*, "graceful bearing") 风云 (*fengyun*, "wind and cloud; a stormy or unstable situation") 璀璨 (*cuican*, "bright")
> 灿烂 (*canlan*, "brilliant") 感慨 (*gankai*, "sigh with emotion") 激烈 (*jilie*, "fierce") 昂扬 (*angyang*, "high-spirited") 珍爱 (*zhen'ai*, "cherish")

Second, neologisms created in line with the need of social communications. Neologisms are newly coined words or words with a short history. Time is an important element in defining neologisms. That is to say, we should define neologisms within a certain time span. If we take the Tang Dynasty (618–917) as the point of reference, words coined at the beginning of the dynasty would be neologisms without doubt. Those words certainly should not be treated as neologisms by the time of the Song Dynasty (860–1279). In the same way, words created at the beginning of new China (1949–) should not be considered neologisms by the time of Reform and Opening-Up in 1978. Therefore neologisms are newly created words accepted by the society in a certain period.

After their creation, a small number of neologisms may become basic words and part of the basic vocabulary by conventionalization after repeated use in the linguistic community. This is a necessary law governing the constant replacement and development of basic vocabulary. For example, in the contemporary Chinese language, such words as "塑料 (*suliao*, 'plastic')", "电视 (*dianshi*, 'television')", "家电 (*jiadian*, 'home appliances')", "法制 (*fazhi*, 'legal system')", "民警 (*minjing*, 'policeman')" and "小康 (*xiaokang*, 'relatively comfortable life')" and so on are taken as basic words. Yet a far larger number of neologisms belong to common vocabulary as general words. At the present time neologisms in the contemporary Chinese language are numerous. For instance,

> 离休 (*lixiu*, "retire [for those employed before 1949]") 退休 (*tuixiu*, "retire") 录像 (*luxiang*, "video recording") 展销 (*zhanxiao*, "sales exhibition") 网友 (*wangyou*, "netizen") 视频 (*shipin*, "video") 考评 (*kaoping*, "examine and evaluate") 挂靠 (*guakao*, "be attached or affiliated to")
> 手机 (*shouji*, "mobile phone") 光盘 (*guangpan*, "optical disc") 评估 (*pinggu*, "evaluate") 法盲 (*famang*, "law-ignorant person") 档次 (*dangci*,

"level") 牵头 (*qiantou*, "take the lead") 联手 (*lianshou*, "work in unison") 网吧 (*wangba*, "cybercafé")

环保 (*huanbao*, "environmental protection") 创收 (*chuangshou*, "income generation") 定岗 (*dinggang*, "to settle the number of working staff") 下岗 (*xiagang*, "be laid off") 反思 (*fansi*, "reflection") 乒坛 (*pingtan*, "the table tennis circles") 香波 (*xiangbo*, "shampoo") 减肥 (*jianfei*, "slimming; weight reduction")

透明度 (*toumingdu*, "transparency") 公务员 (*gongwuyuan*, "civil servant") 牛仔裤 (*niuzaiku*, "jeans") 关系学 (*guanxixue*, "connectionology; favouritism through connections") 乌发乳 (*wufaru*, "shampoo to make hair dark") 显像管 (*xianxiangguan*, "picture tube")

太阳能 (*taiyangneng*, "solar energy") 摄像机 (*shexiangji*, "video camera") 录像机 (*luxiangji*, "video recorder") 电子琴 (*dianziqin*, "electronic organ") 计算机 (*jisuanji*, "computer") 扫描仪 (*saomiaoyi*, "scanner")

立交桥 (*lijiaoqiao*, "overpass bridge") 软包装 (*ruanbaozhuang*, "flexible package") 追星族 (*zhuixingzu*, "idolater; fan") 宇航员 (*yuhangyuan*, "astronaut") 双职工 (*shuangzhigong*, "working couple") 志愿者 (*zhiyuanzhe*, "volunteer")

Third, archaic words re-employed for special needs. Archaic words usually refer to those that were used in the past but are out of use today. Out of communicative needs, people may well re-employ some archaic words to allow them to return to common vocabulary for a certain period of time. Therefore, the concept of archaic word has two implications. From a diachronic point of view, archaic words in Chinese vocabulary are those that were once used in history but have become obsolete today. Some of the archaic words may be re-employed out of social needs and others may be out of use for good. From a synchronic point of view, the concept refers to the archaic words included in the vocabulary in a certain historical period, i. e., the archaic words re-employed in that period. The archaic words in this sense are organic elements of the relevant synchronic lexical system concerned. Therefore the so-called archaic words from the synchronic point of view are the archaic words re-employed by the synchronic community.

Archaic words in the contemporary Chinese language are archaic words used by people in contemporary society and are elements of the lexical system of the contemporary Chinese language. Archaic words in the contemporary Chinese language are of two types: words referring to the objects and phenomena that existed in history and words that appeared in ancient myths and legends. "县官 (*xianguan*, 'county magistrate')", "保长 (*baozhang*, 'magistrate of *bao* (administrative system organized on the basis of households in ancient China)')", "宰相 (*zaixiang*, 'prime minister in feudal China')", "青楼 (*qinglou*, 'brothel')", "书童 (*shutong*, 'page-boy; a boy serving in a scholar's study')", "巡捕 (*xunbu*, 'police or policeman (in former foreign concessions)')", "上朝 (*shangchao*, 'go to royal court')" and "接旨 (*jiezhi*, 'respectfully awaiting a royal decree')", etc. are examples of the former, which can also be called historical words. "天宫

(*tiangong*, 'heavenly palace')", "龙王 (*Longwang*, 'the Dragon King')", "天王 (*Tianwang*, 'the Sky King')", "王母 (*Wangmu*, 'the Queen Mother of the Western Heavens')", "天将 (*tianjiang*, 'senior generals in the heaven')", "龙女 (*longnü*, 'dragon lady')", etc. are examples of the latter. The characteristics of such words are: they are all closely related to the historical objects or ancient myths and legends, and must be used when people learn history or tell historical stories or myths and legends. Even though the objects and phenomena referred to by those words and expressions are no longer in existence now, their use has been uninterrupted not even for a moment because the learning and telling of history and fairy tales never ceased. Consequently those words and expressions are frequently or even constantly employed by people from generation to generation and they are of a positive function in understanding history and narrating the past. At any stage of the development of vocabulary, this type of words and expressions constitute a comparatively stable part of the archaic words in the common vocabulary. From this perspective, they are similar to the inherent words in that both of them are historically passed down. But they are of absolutely different types: the major difference lies in that the objects and phenomena referred to by archaic words only emerge in relating the matters in the past and are basically of no relation to the modern society otherwise, whereas the inherent words are closely linked to social life in the time of their own. The other case is that, some words which were once used in ancient Chinese are now generally no longer in use, but out of some communicative needs or for some rhetoric purposes, they are picked up by people. For example, "哉 (*zai*, 'a particle expressing surprise, admiration, etc. at the end of a phrase')" in "壮哉！刘公岛 (*Zhuangzai! Liugong Dao*, 'How impressive you are, Liu Gong Island')" (quote from a newspaper), "余 (*yu*, 'a term addressing oneself')" and "载 (*zai*, 'year')" in "余虚度年华五十余载 (*Yu xudu nianhua wushi yu zai*, 'I have been idled for more than fifty years')" (quote from a newspaper) all belong to this category. Such archaic words are more often in written Chinese language.

There are growing cases in which an archaic word is re-employed, but with a meaning different from its original one. For example, the original meaning of "乌纱帽 (*wushamao*)" is "a kind of hat worn by one holding an official post", now it is used to denote "holding an official post". A further example is "状元 (*zhuangyuan*)", whose original meaning of "the person with the best score in the highest imperial examination in ancient China" is altered to figuratively refer to "the very best in the field concerned". It is obvious that such a phenomenon is not only a way of re-employing an archaic word, but also closely related to the development of word meaning: that a new sense item is generated on the basis of the meaning of an old word is beyond any doubt one significant aspect of word meaning development.

Fourth, dialect words from dialects. Such dialect words are those originate from regional dialects. They are one of the components of the lexical system of the common language of the community and are completely different from the dialectal words existing in various regional dialects. For example, "搞 (*gao*, 'make')", "垃圾 (*laji*, 'rubbish')", "名堂 (*mingtang*, 'tricks')", "把戏 (*baxi*, 'tricks')",

"尴尬 (*ganga*, 'awkward')", "瘪三 (*biesan*, 'a city bum')", "二流子 (*erliuzi*, 'a habitual loafer')" and "亭子间 (*tingzijian*, 'a garret')", etc. are all words in Chinese common language coming from regional dialects of China. Although these words are also in existence and in service as dialectal words in relevant regional dialects, they are one of the indispensable components in the common vocabulary of Chinese common language. Compared with such words as "阿拉 (*ala*, 'I')" and "侬 (*nong*, 'you')", etc. in Shanghai dialect, because these words have not been assimilated yet into the vocabulary of Chinese common language, they are only words in the regional dialect of Shanghai instead of components of vocabulary in the modern common language of China.

Fifth, loan words coming into being under the influence of foreign languages. In the course of social development, the intercommunication between different countries and different ethnic groups will certainty bear impact on the mutual contact and absorption of the vocabulary between the ethnic groups concerned. A loan word is a word that comes into being in this way. However, one point must be made clear: the so-called loan words are those coming into being under the influence of a foreign language and they are by no means the original words in the relevant foreign language. The reason lies in that, when borrowing a word from a foreign language, there must be a process of reforming and re-creation on the basis of the original foreign word, whichever language it is. As far as Chinese is concerned, this is a word coinage process of reforming and Chinesization of turning an alien word into a loan word on the basis of the original. A loan word in Chinese must go through such a Chinesization process before being accepted. Therefore, the loan words in Chinese belong to Chinese vocabulary and are one component of the Chinese lexical system and they are related but not equal on any account to the respective alien words.

Loan words abound in the contemporary Chinese language and especially after 1980s large quantities of loan words spring up with unprecedented numbers, area of coverage and diversification in forms of formation. Currently, the ways of Chinesization of loan words are as follows:

(1) A neologism with a phonetic form directly imitating the foreign one but reformed with Chinese speech sound so as to conform to the characteristics and rules of the Chinese language. This type of words is usually referred to as phonemic loans. In written form they are represented with Chinese characters same or similar in pronunciation with the foreign words. For instance,

咖啡 (*kafei*, "coffee") 吉他 (*jita*, "guitar")
巴黎 (*Bali*, "Paris") 伦敦 (*Lundun*, "London")
白兰地 (*Bailandi*, "Brandy") 法兰西 (*Falanxi*, "France")
奥林匹克 (*Aolinpike*, "Olympics")

(2) A loan word directly borrows the alphabetical form in written form and is reformed with Chinese speech sound in pronunciation so as to conform to the characteristics and rules of the Chinese speech sounds. This type of words can be referred to as form-phonemic loans. The forms of most form-phonemic

loans are the abbreviated form of the original foreign words and others of such words directly borrow the abbreviated forms from the foreign language.[2] For instance,

CT – The original word is Computerized Tomography, and the phonetic form after Chinesization is *seiti*

CD – The original word is Compact Disc, and the phonetic form after Chinesization is *seidi*

MTV – The original word is Music Television, and the phonetic form after Chinesization is *ai·mu tiwei*

VCD – The original word is Video Compact Disc, and the phonetic form after Chinesization is *weiseidi*

DVD – The original word is Digital Video Disc, and the phonetic form after Chinesization is *diweidi*

(3) A new loan word is formed with the transliterated components that have been Chinesized combined with a Chinese semantic morpheme relating in meaning with the original foreign word. These words are usually referred to as phonemic-semantic loans. For instance,

啤酒 (*pijiu*, "beer") 咖啡茶 (*kafeicha*, "coffee")
芭蕾舞 (*baleiwu*, "ballet") 吉普车 (*jipuche*, "jeep")
坦克车 (*tankeche*, "tank") 巧克力糖 (*qiaokelitang*, "chocolate")

(4) A new loan word is coined with the letters representing foreign words, which are Chinesized with Chinese speech sound, combined with a relevant Chinese semantic morpheme. These words are named graphic-semantic loans. For instance,

B超 (*bichao*, "type-B ultrasonic") – The Chinesized sound of "B" is *bi*, plus a Chinese semantic morpheme 超 (*chao*, "ultra-")

BP机 (*bipiji*, "beeper") – The Chinesized sound of "BP" is *bipi*, plus a Chinese semantic morpheme 机 (*ji*, "machine")

γ刀 (*gamadao*, "γ knife") – The Chinesized sound of "γ" is *gama*, plus a Chinese semantic morpheme 刀 (*dao*, "knife")

(5) On the basis of the Chinesization of the sound of the foreign words, a Chinese character similar in sound and relevant in meaning is used to represent a syllable of the foreign word. Such Chinese characters bear a resemblance to the Chinese semantic morphemes composing the word. The loan words Chinesized in such a way of sound-meaning pairing are usually referred to as meaning-indicative phonetic transcription. For instance,

The word "绷带 (*bengdai*)" is an example of meaning-indicative phonetic transcription of the English word "bandage" Chinesized with Chinese characters "绷 (*beng*)" and "带 (*dai*)". The pronunciation of "绷" and "带" is extremely similar to their original syllable "ban" and "dage" respectively, and their meanings are associated to a certain degree with those of the original foreign elements respectively. The component "绷" means "to tighten" and "带" means "a long strip of cloth" and the two characters put together can be justified in indicating the original meaning "a strip of material used for binding round a wound or an injury" of the original foreign word "bandage".

Other examples of this kind are as follows:

拖拉机 (*tuolaji*, "tractor") – This word comes from the Russian word "трактор" with three meaning-indicative phonetic transcribed characters.

可口可乐 (*Kekou Kele*, "Coca-Cola"') – The word comes from the English word "Coca-Cola" with the four syllables of the original all transcribed in meaning-indicative phonetic forms.

In addition, some words are a combination of meaning-indicative phonetic transcriptions and phonemic-semantic loans. For instance, "霓虹灯 (*nihongdeng*, 'neon light')" comes from an English word "Neon". "霓虹 (*nihong*)" in "霓虹灯" are two characters of meaning-indicative phonetic transcription and "灯 (*deng*)" is a Chinese semantic morpheme of phonemic-semantic loan.

(6) A neologism is formed with Chinese semantic morphemes and Chinese morphologic rules with reference to the meaning of a foreign word. This type of words are usually known as semantic loans. Such words are usually not treated as loan words. For instance,

民主 (*minzhu*, "democracy") 足球 (*zuqiu*, "football") 铁路 (*tielu*, 'railway') 电话 (*dianhua*, "telephone") 煤气 (*meiqi*, "coal gas") 水泥 (*shuini*, "cement")

维生素 (*weishengsu*, "vitamin") 扩音器 (*kuoyinqi*, "microphone") 收割机 (*shougeji*, "combine") 无产阶级 (*wuchan jieji*, "proletariat")

Most of the semantic loans of this type took the form of phonemic loans when they came into the Chinese community and later on they were replaced by semantic loans. This is due to the fact that people get accustomed to using the linguistic forms of their own ethnic groups.

Phonemic loans as one form of loan words will always remain in the lexical system. Yet it can be argued that the fact that some phonemic loans will gradually be replaced by semantic loans is among the laws of the development of Chinese loan words. For instance, since China's reform and opening-up (1978), such phonemic loans as "克力架 (*kelijia*, 'cracker')" was replaced by "饼干 (*binggan*, 'cracker')", and the frequency of "超短裙 (*chaoduanqun*, 'mini-skirt')" and "洗发水 (洗发剂) (*xifashui/xifaji*, 'shampoo')" exceeds far and away that of "迷你裙 (*miniqun*, 'mini-skirt')" and "香波 (*xiangbo*, 'shampoo')" respectively. These best illustrate the above-mentioned law of vocabulary development in Chinese.

All the words mentioned in this section are formed with foreign words as base form. They are all Chinese words coming into being under the influence of foreign words and are all non-negligible ingredients in Chinese vocabulary.

Sixth, words in social dialects. Social dialects are branches of the national language, catering for the communicative needs of different trades and groups in society. Different from regional dialects, social dialects only have certain words and expressions gearing to the communicative needs of the trade and group concerned, without distinctive basic vocabulary and syntactic structure of their own, letting alone the sign system of their own. Such words come into being out of the differences in social division of labour and living conditions etc. and they are all organic ingredients of the national vocabulary. Such words are seldom used by people outside of the trade or group concerned, though there is no secrecy at all for them and whoever needs them can contact, understand and acquire them. Specifically, social dialects include the following parts:

Jargon is one of the principal parts of social dialects. Jargon refers to the words used by various trades and groups due to social division of labour. For example, in education, we have "答疑 (*dayi*, 'answering question'), 自习 (*zixi*, 'self-study'), 教室 (*jiaoshi*, 'classroom'), 教具 (*jiaoju*, 'aids'), 课桌 (*kezhuo*, 'desk'), 学分 (xuefen, 'credit'), 课程 (*kecheng*, 'curriculum'), 选修 (*xuanxiu*, 'take as an elective course'), 基础课 (*jichuke*, 'basic course'), 课程表 (*kechengbiao*, 'class schedule'), 课堂讨论 (*ketang taolun*, 'class discussion')", etc. ; in medical sciences, we have "内科 (*neike*, 'internal medicine'), 外科 (*waike*, 'surgery'), 眼科 (*yanke*, 'ophthalmology department'), 中医 (*zhongyi*, 'Chinese medicine'), 西医 (*xiyi*, 'western medicine'), 医生 (*yisheng*, 'doctor'), 护士 (*hushi*, 'nurse'), 门诊 (*menzhen*, 'outpatient department'), 处方 (*chufang*, 'prescription'), 诊断 (*zhenduan*, 'diagnosis'), 治疗 (*zhiliao*, 'treatment'), 病房 (*bingfang*, 'inpatient ward'), 针灸 (*zhenjiu*, 'acupuncture'), 推拿 (*tuina*, 'massage'), 注射 (*zhushe*, 'injection'), 开刀 (*kaidao*, 'surgery'), 手术 (*shoushu*, 'operation')", etc. ; and in drama, we have "主角 (*zhujiao*, 'protagonist'), 配角 (*peijiao*, 'supporting actor'), 演员 (*yanyuan*, 'player'), 布景 (*bujing*, 'scenery'), 道具 (*daoju*, 'prop'), 台词 (*taici*, 'lines'), 龙套 (*longtao*, 'utility man'), " and the words indicating different roles "青衣 (*qingyi*, 'the demure middle-aged or young female character'), 花旦 (*huadan*, 'a young female character'), 武旦 (*wudan*, 'a female character type versed in shadowboxing, swordplay, etc.'), 武生 (*wusheng*, 'an actor playing a martial role'), 小生 (*xiaosheng*, 'young male character'), 须生 (*xusheng*, 'an elderly male character'), 花脸 (*hualian*, 'male character with a painted face')" and so on and so forth. Every trade has the jargon of its own. A certain person with a certain vocation will acquire the jargon in the relevant vocation out of the communicative needs within the vocation.

Although jargon is special vocabulary used by the group of a certain vocation, the range of use of some members of jargon may be enlarged more or less with the development of science and culture or the development and change of the words and expressions themselves. For example, with the improvement of people's life and the advances of science and culture, more and more people acquire opportunities to watch drama; therefore some words in drama are employed by more and more people due to the enlargement of the range of their use. In addition, with the popularization of pedagogical activities and medical enterprises, the scope of application of some parlances in these vocations will consequently be enlarged gradually.

For other members of jargon, some new sense items will be generated due to associations in the course of development and the new sense items will be used by people in other occupations even by all the people, with the words as a whole turning into polysemes from monosemes. At the same time, the range of use of some words will be gradually enlarged due to the universality of such words. Take "战士 (*zhanshi*)" as an example. It was originally a military term meaning "grass-rooted members in the military", and later on, it became a polyseme "generally referring to persons who take part in some just struggles or undertake some just cause", as in such phrases as "白衣战士 (*baiyi zhanshi*, 'warrior in white')" and "文化战士 (*wenhua zhanshi*, 'the culture warrior')", etc. Such a change makes that "战士" is not only a military term, but also a general word. It is obvious that the scope of application of "战士" is extended. Words such as "战线 (*zhanxian*, 'front')", "阵地 (*zhendi*, 'position')", "攻克 (*gongke*, 'conquer')", "尖兵 (*jianbing*, 'vanguard')", "麻痹 (*mabi*, 'paralysis')", "解剖 (*jiepou*, 'anatomy')", "角色 (*jiaose*, 'role')", "后台 (*houtai*, 'backstage')", "堡垒 (*baolei*, 'fortress')" and "舞台 (*wutai*, 'stage')" are all cases in point.

Another content of social dialect refers to the peculiar words and expressions used by children, students, cadres and elderly persons. Such words and expressions are community parlance coming into being due to such factors as differences in age, living conditions and psychological makeup, etc. For example, such words as "碗儿碗儿 (*wanr wanr*)" for 碗儿 (*wanr*, "bowl"), "球球 (*qiuqiu*)" for 球 (*qiu*, "ball") and "鞋鞋 (*xiexie*)" for 鞋 (*xie*, "shoe"), etc. are in children's speech. Primary pupils like to use "来的 (*laide*)" to mean "一块玩 (*yikuai wan*, 'play together')" while playing games, e. g., "咱们来的, 好吗？ (*Zanmen laide, haoma*?, 'Let's play together, shall we?')" Other examples are when a student uses "开夜车 (*kai yeche*)" to mean "book-reading at midnight", an elder uses "后生 (*housheng*)" to address a youngster and uses "老伴 (*laoban*)" to denote his/her wife/husband and so forth. Although small in number, these words and expressions can reflect the fact that people use different words due to differences in age, living conditions and educational level, etc.

The primary reason for dividing common vocabulary into the above six types lies in the sources and properties of the words concerned. As a matter of fact, there exist complicated relations and connections between the six types of words. Take neologisms as an example: in addition to common neologisms, a considerable number of neologisms originate from loan words, dialect words and social dialect words. After coming into being, some of these new elements become common neologisms in common use by the linguistic community, while others become social dialect words, especially new components in jargon. Some of neologisms can enter into the scope of inherent words or basic words after a period of application since its birth. Consequently, when we talk about common vocabulary, we should not only realize the different properties of various words and their distinctions, but also take into account the interconnections between them and their development in common.

3 THE RELATION BETWEEN BASIC VOCABULARY AND COMMON VOCABULARY

Basic vocabulary and general vocabulary have their own characteristics, so they are two entirely different parts of vocabulary. At the same time, basic vocabulary and common vocabulary are closely connected: they are in mutual dependence and develop hand in hand, and both are indispensable to vocabulary.

Basic vocabulary is the base of language and also the base for common vocabulary to come into being. Most words in common vocabulary come into being on the basis of basic vocabulary.

Common vocabulary is extremely sensitive in reflecting social development: it is in unceasing motion therefore new elements more often than not appear in common vocabulary and then certain particular elements go into basic vocabulary resulting in the development of basic vocabulary. From this point of view, common vocabulary is also the source of the development of basic vocabulary.

In addition, a few elements in basic vocabulary and common vocabulary are interchangeable. During the development of vocabulary, certain basic words are likely to turn into common words with the change of demand in social communications and vice versa. For example, "鬼 (*gui*, 'ghost')", "神 (*shen*, 'god')" and "野菜 (*yecai*, 'wild vegetable')", even "窝窝头 (*wowotou*, 'steamed corn bread')", etc. were basic words in the past, whereas they have turned into common words because the relation between these words and people's daily life went away. Such basic words as "当 (*dang*, 'pawn')", "当铺 (*dangpu*, 'pawnshop')" and "保长 (*baozhang*, 'magistrate of *bao* (administrative system organized on the basis of households in ancient China)')", etc., which were basic words, have become historical words (i. e., members in common vocabulary with the extinction of the things they denote). In contrast, "党 (*Dang*, 'the Party')", which was a common word, has become a basic word since it is a short form of "共产党 (*Gongchandang*, 'Communist Party')" and with the strengthening of the status and function of Communist Party in people's life. Other cases like "书记 (*shuji*, 'secretary')", "科技 (*keji*, 'science and technology')", "改革 (*gaige*, 'reform')" and the abovementioned "电视 (*dianshi*, 'television')", "塑料 (*suliao*, 'plastic')", "民警 (*minjing*, 'policeman')", etc. are nowadays also basic words.

Basic vocabulary and common vocabulary develop and abound together under such a mutual dependence and continual inter-converting. Their development in turn leads to the abundance and development of vocabulary as a whole.

(II) The aggregate of fixed structures equivalent to words in function

The fixed structures equivalent to words in function in Chinese are referred to as idioms in general. They mainly include idioms, formulaic expressions, proverbs, two-part allegorical sayings and proper nouns and so on. These fixed structures are all conventionalized set phrases and sentences coming into being in the long-term application of language. They all possess the following three common characteristics:

First, they are set constructions. These fixed structures take on the form of integral set constructions with a certain stability in language use.

Second, they are integral in meaning. Most of the meanings expressed by these fixed structures are abstract and generalized instead of being the simple summation of the literal meanings of their components thus the meanings of the fixed structure always appear as specific and holistic ones.

Third, they are building blocks in language. These fixed structures are all building materials functioning as words when they are put into use in linguistic activities.

Furthermore, the sub-groups of these fixed structures have characteristics of their own so as to form various distinct clusters with different characteristics.

1 Idioms

An idiom is a fixed phrase with a fixed configuration and a holistic meaning. For instance,

水落石出 (*shui luo shi chu*, "when the water subsides the rock emerges")
狐假虎威 (*hu jia hu wei*, "the fox assuming the majesty of the tiger")
望梅止渴 (*wang mei zhi ke*, "to quench one's thirst by thinking of plums")
千锤百炼 (*qian chui bai lian*, "thoroughly tempered")
胸有成竹 (*xiong you cheng zhu*, "to have a well-thought-out plan")
刻舟求剑 (*ke zhou qiu jian*, "to carve on gunwale of a moving boat")
比比皆是 (*bi bi jie shi*, "to meet the eye everywhere")
本末倒置 (*ben mo dao zhi*, "to have the order reversed")
波澜壮阔 (*bo lan zhuang kuo*, "to surge high and sweep forward")
沉鱼落雁 (*chen yu luo ya*n, " (a dazzling beauty that) makes the fish sink and wild geese fall")
初出茅庐 (*chu chu mao lu*, "just come out of one's thatched cottage")
打草惊蛇 (*da cao jing she*, "to beat the grass and frighten away the snake")
根深蒂固 (*gen shen di gu*, "to have a firm foundation")
排山倒海 (*pai shan dao hai*, "to topple the mountains and overturn the seas")
鲸吞蚕食 (*jing tu can shi*, "to swallow like a whale and eat like a silkworm")
借花献佛 (*jie hua xian fo*, "present Buddha with borrowed flowers")
顺水推舟 (*shun shui tui zhou*, "to push the boat along with the current")
朝三暮四 (*zhao san mu si*, "blow hot and cold")

Idioms abound in Chinese, and many of them are handed down from ancient Chinese with great vitality. They are concise in form, comprehensive and profound in meaning with expressiveness beyond general words and expressions.

As far as the form is concerned, idioms possess a prominent characteristic in being fixed in construction. Most idioms in Chinese have four syllables and one cannot change any element in an idiom or the order of it at will. For instance, "大公无私 (*da gong wu si*, 'selfless')" cannot be changed into "大公没私 (*da gong mei si*)", "大公和无私 (*da gong he mei si*)", or "无私大公(*wu si da gong*)"; "叶公好龙 (*Ye Gong hao long*, 'Lord Ye professed to love dragons')" cannot be changed into "李公好龙 (*Li Gong hao long*)", "叶公喜龙 (*Ye Gong xi long*)" or "叶公爱龙 (*Ye Gong ai long*)" and so on and so forth. The structural characteristics of Chinese idioms lead to their unique style of being regular in number of characters (usually four) and concise in form.

The meaning of an idiom is concise and condensed, and as a result, it is holistic and abstract in general. For some idioms in Chinese, such as "恋恋不舍 (*lian lian bu she*, 'to have great attachment for')", "两全其美 (*liang quan qi mei*, 'to be complete in both respects')", "惹是生非 (*re shi sheng fei*, 'to ask for trouble')", "普天同庆 (*pu tian tong qing*, 'the whole world joins in the jubilation')", "门庭若市 (*men ting ruo shi*, 'the courtyard is like a fair')" and "大快人心 (*da kuai ren xin*, 'affording general satisfaction')", etc., their meanings are equivalent more or less to the meanings of their components; thus one can know their meanings literally from their components. However, more often than not, the meanings of Chinese idioms are abstract and generalized ones on the basis of their components. It is difficult to know exactly the meanings of such idioms just from the literal meaning of their components. Take "九死一生 (*jiu si yi sheng*)" as an example: it means "narrow escape from death; survival after many perils"; it does not in the least simply mean "one escape out of nine deaths". The idiom "千方百计 (*qian fang bai ji*)" means "by every possible means" instead of "one thousand of methods and one hundred of strategies". It is the case with such examples as "犬马之劳 (*quan ma zhi lao*, 'to serve like a dog or a horse')", "昙花一现 (*tan hua yi xian*, 'a flash in the pan')", "中流砥柱 (*zhong liu di zhu*, 'mainstay')", "赴汤蹈火 (*fu tang dao huo*, 'to go into boiling water and walk on fire')", "枯木逢春 (*ku mu feng chun*, 'to be like a dry tree which again sprouts leaves in the spring')" and "骑虎难下 (*qi hu nan xia*, 'to ride a tiger and find it hard to get off')" and so forth.

A good number of Chinese idioms have special origins. Some originate from ancient fables, such as "愚公移山 (*Yu Gong yi shan*, 'the Foolish Man removing the mountains')", "鹬蚌相争 (*yu bang xiang zheng*, 'the snipe and the clam grapple')", "黔驴技穷 (*Qian lü ji qiong*, 'the Guizhou donkey has exhausted its tricks')", "揠苗助长 (*ya miao zhu zhang*, 'to try to help the shoots grow by pulling them upward')", "守株待兔 (*shou zhu dai tu*, 'to wait every day under the tree, in the hope that a hare would kill itself by crashing into a tree trunk')", "刻舟求剑 (*ke zhou qiu jian*, 'to carve on gunwale of a moving boat')" and so on. Others originate from myths and legends, such as "夸父逐日 (*Kua Fu zhu ri*, 'Kua Fu Chases the Sun')", "精卫填海 (*Jingwei tian hai*, 'Jingwei fills up the sea')", "开天辟地 (*kai tian pi di*, 'when heaven was separated from earth')" and "八仙过海, 各显神通 (*Baxian guo hai,ge xian shen tong*, 'when the Eight Immortals crossing the sea, each one shows his or her special prowess')", etc. Some originate from historical stories, such as "草木皆兵 (*cao mu jie bing*, 'every bush and tree looks like an enemy')", "望梅止渴 (*wang mei zhi ke*, 'to quench one's thirst by thinking of plums')", "完璧归赵 (*wan bi gui Zhao*, 'to return the jade intact to the State of *Zhao*')", "四面楚歌 (*si mian Chu ge*, 'to be besieged on all sides')", "负荆请罪 (*fu jing qing zui*, 'bearing the rod and willingly taking the punishment')", "卧薪尝胆 (*wo xin chang da*n, 'to sleep on the brushwood and taste the gall')" and so on. Still others come from literary works, such as "豁然开朗 (*huo ran kai lang*, 'to suddenly see the light')", "妄自菲薄 (*wang zi fei bo*, 'to improperly belittle oneself')", "径情直遂 (*jing qing zhi sui*, 'to achieve what one wishes')", "实事求是 (*shi shi qiu shi*, 'to seek the truth from facts')", "土崩瓦解 (*tu beng wa jie*, 'to crumble')", and "见异思迁 (*jian yi si qian*, 'to wish to change one's work the moment one sees sth. different')" so on and so forth. For the above-mentioned idioms, a proper understanding and profound comprehension only comes after a thorough awareness of their origins.

2 Formulaic expressions

A formulaic expression is also a fixed phrase with fixed configuration and holistic meaning.

Most Chinese formulaic expressions are in three syllables. For instance,

敲竹杠 (*qiao zhu gang*, "take advantage of sb's being in a weak position to overcharge him")
拖后腿 (*tuo hou tui*, "to be a drag on sb.")
戴高帽 (*dai gao mao*, "to over praise; to praise to the skies")
扣帽子 (*kou maozi*, "put a label on sb.")
穿小鞋 (*chuan xiaoxie*, "give sb. tight shoes to wear – deliberately put sb. to trouble")
背黑锅 (*bei heiguo*, "to be unjustly blamed")
栽跟头 (*zai gentou*, "suffer a setback")
磨洋工 (*mo yanggong*, "loaf on the job")
炒冷饭 (*chao lengfan*, "flog a dead horse; rehash")
翻老账 (*fan laozhang*, "bring up old scores again")
碰钉子 (*peng dingzi*, "receive serious rebuff")
抬轿子 (*tai jiaozi*, "gang up on sb. in gambling")
咬耳朵 (*yao erduo*, "whisper in sb's ear")
梳辫子 (*shu bianzi*, "sort out")
灌米汤 (*guan mitang*, "bewitch sb. by flattery")
夹楔子 (*jia xiezi*, "wedge in")
绕圈子 (*rao quanzi*, "go round and round")
泼凉水 (*po liangshui*, "discourage; pour cold water on")
跑龙套 (*pao longtao*, "play a bit role; be a utility man")
下马威 (*xiamawei*, "severity and power displayed by an official upon taking office")

A few formulaic expressions are in four or more than four syllables. For instance,

捅马蜂窝 (*tong mafengwo*, "to stir up a nest of hornets")
唱对台戏 (*chang duitaixi*, "stage a rival show")
吃哑巴亏 (*chi yabakui*, "be unable to speak out about one's grievances")
钻牛角尖 (*zuan niujiaojian*, "get into a blind alley")
杀回马枪 (*sha huimaqiang*, "wheel around and hit back")
走下坡路 (*zou xiapolu*, "go from bad to worse")
快刀斩乱麻 (*kuai dao zhan luanma*, "cut a tangled skein of jute with a sharp knife – make a lightning decision")
皮笑肉不笑 (*pi xiao rou bu xiao*, "a foxy smile")
穿新鞋走老路 (*chuan xin xie zou lao lu*, "put old wine in new bottles – continue old practices in new situations")
好心当作驴肝肺 (*haoxin dang zuo lüganfei*, "mistake sb's goodwill for ill intent")

Although formulaic expressions have fixed structures, their constructions are much weaker in being fixed compared with those of idioms. It is often found that there are several different forms for one and the same formulaic expression. For example, instead of using "拖后腿 (*tuo hou tui*, 'to be a drag on sb.')", one can use "拉后腿 (*la hou tui*)" and "扯后腿 (*che hou tui*)", and one can say "戳马蜂窝 (*chuo mafengwo*)" etc. to mean "捅马蜂窝 (*tong mafengwo*, 'to stir up a nest of hornets')". Furthermore, one can change the word order or add some components to a formulaic expression in accordance with the need of expression or the habit of language use of one's own. For instance,

Instead of saying "戴高帽 (*dai gaomao*, 'make compliment')", one can say "戴高帽子 (*dai gao maozi*)" or "戴上个高帽 (*dai shang ge gao mao*)".
Instead of saying "背黑锅 (*bei heiguo*, 'to be unjustly blamed')", one can say "背了黑锅 (*bei le hei guo*)" or "背上了黑锅 (*bei shang le he guo*)".
Instead of saying "拖后腿 (*tuo houtui*, 'to be a drag on sb.')", one can say "拖谁的后腿 (*tuo shui de hou tui*)".
Instead of saying "磨洋工 (*mo yanggong*, 'to loaf on the job')", one can say "磨了半天洋工 (*mo ge ban tian yang tong*)".
Instead of saying "捅马蜂窝 (*tong mafengwo*, 'to stir up a nest of hornets')", one can say "捅了马蜂窝 (*tong le mafengwo*)".

While weaker in being fixed in construction, formulaic expressions are more free and flexible with a high adaptability in language use.

The meaning of a formulaic expression is an abstract and generalized one with metaphor or semantic extension on the basis of the meaning of its components. As a result, its meaning is a generalized and integral one instead of a simple addition of the literal meaning of its constituents. For example, "戴高帽 (*dai gao mao*)" does not in the least mean "to put a tall hat on one's head", but means "to over praise; to praise to the skies"; while "背黑锅 (*bei hei guo*)" does not mean "to put a black pan on one's back" at all, but means "to be unjustly blamed".

The meaning of whichever formulaic expression is abstract and generalized, or else it is a general phrase instead of a formulaic expression. For instance, "走后门 (*zou houmen*)" is a formulaic expression when it denotes "to get something done through some improper means", while it is a free phrase when it means "to come in or go out by the back door".

One can achieve vivid and rhetoric effects with an animated image and a humorous tone by using formulaic expressions because they are abstract and generalized in meaning, high in figurativeness and rich in livelihood. In addition, being more popularized and easy to understand, most formulaic expressions originate from daily parlance of people's life; therefore they have an extremely extensive range of use: whether in written language or in spoken language, formulaic expressions are widely used with a vivid and lively expressiveness.

3 Proverbs

A proverb is a sentence with a specific meaning and a fixed structure. It is a popular and terse ready-made sentence circulated in oral with profound implications.

In construction, all proverbs are in fixed sentential forms. Some are in single sentences, for instance:

千金难买寸光阴。(*Qian jin nan mai cui guangyin*, "A thousand pieces of gold cannot buy an inch of time.")
强扭的瓜不甜。(*Qiang niu de gua bu tian*, "Nothing forcibly done is going to be agreeable.")
细工出巧匠。(*Xi gong chu qiaojiang*, "Fine products come from slow work.")
人正不怕影子歪。(*Ren zheng bu pa yingzi wai*, "stand straight and never mind if the shadow inclines")
小树不砍不成材。(*Xiao shu bu kan bu cheng cai*, "Little trees that are not cut cannot shape up")

Others are in complex sentences, for instance:

岁寒知松柏, 患难见人心。(*Sui han zhi songbai, huannan jian renxin*, "Only when the year grows cold do we see the qualities of the pine and the cypress; calamity is the touchstone of man.")
山中无老虎, 猴子称大王。(*Shan zhong wu laohu, houzi cheng dawang*, "The monkey reigns in the mountains once the tiger is not there.")
知树知皮不知根, 知人知面不知心。(*Zhi shu zhi pi bu zhi gen, zhi ren zhi mian bu zhi xin*, "It is impossible to judge a tree's root by its bark and it is impossible to judge a man's heart from his face.")
不下水, 一辈子不会游泳; 不扬帆, 一辈子不会操船。(*Bu xia shui, yi beizi bu hui youyong; bu yang fan, yi beizi bu hui cao chuan*, "If you don't go into water, you can't swim for a lifetime and if you don't sail, you can't drive a ship for a lifetime.")

恼一恼, 老一老；笑一笑, 少一少。(*Nao yi nao, lao yi lao; xiao yi xiao, shao yi shao,* "A man is old when he is angry, and he who smiles is less.")

Their meanings are specific and holistic because proverbs are always used in an integral sentential form. For some proverbs, one can get their meanings from those of their components. For instance,

败子回头金不换。(*Baizi hui tou jin bu huan,* "A prodigal who returns is more precious than gold.")
不贵尺璧宝寸阴。(*Bu gui chi bi bao cun yin,* "Do not value treasures but value every minute")
上山容易下山难。(*Shang shan rongyi xia shan nan,* "It is easier to go uphill than go downhill.")
不吃苦中苦, 难得甜上甜。(*Bu chi ku zhong ku, nan de tian shang tian,* "No pains, no gains")
春送千担粪, 秋收万担粮。(*Chun song qian dan fen, qiu shou wan dan liang,* "To send thousands of manures in spring, and harvest ten thousand of grains in autumn.")

For others, one can only understand their comparatively abstract and generalized implications by semantic extension or in a figurative way on the basis of the literal meanings of their constituents. For instance,

众人拾柴火焰高。(*Zhong ren shi chai huoyan gao,* "When everybody adds fuel, the flames rise high.")
搬起石头打自己的脚。(*Ban qi shitou da ziji de jiao,* "Lift a stone to beat one's own foot.")
只要功夫深, 铁杵磨成针。(*Zhiyao gongfu shen, tiechu mo cheng zhen,* "Little strokes fell great oaks.")
留得青山在, 不愁没柴烧。(*Liu de qingshan zai, bu chou mei chai shao,* "As long as the green hills are there, one need not worry about firewood.")
种瓜得瓜, 种豆得豆。(*Zhong gua de gua, zhong dou de dou,* "As a man sows and so he shall reap.")

Although the above-mentioned are two different cases, all what they express in content is the summarization of the experience of people's long-time life. With the form of a sentence, a proverb either represents a judgement or an inference, or tells an inevitable reason or law through a semantic extension or a metaphorical process on the basis of vivid description, so the contents of proverbs are all rich and profound with philosophical implications in general.

Although proverbs are fixed sentences in form, they are building blocks of language just like words. In application, a proverb can be a syntactic constituent in a sentence, can be a single sentence, or can be a clause in a complex sentence. More often than not, proverbs are used as independent sentences or clauses because they are in sentential forms.

4 Two-part allegorical sayings

Two-part allegorical sayings are peculiar linguistic forms with specific meanings and fixed structures. They are also ready-made and conventionalized by the masses and are very closely connected to social life with a very strong life flavour.

The peculiarity of two-part allegorical sayings lies in that they are composed of two parts in structure. For instance,

> 哑巴吃黄连 – 有苦难言。(*Yaba chi huanglian – you ku nan yan*, "A mute eats coptis – it is hard to tell (the bitterness of coptis)")
>
> 鲁智深倒拔垂杨柳 – 好大的力气。(*Lu Zhishen dao ba chuiyangliu* – hao da de liqi, "Lu Zhishen pulls up a willow upside down – what a great strengh.")
>
> 千里送鹅毛 – 礼轻情义重。(*Qian li song emao – li qing qingyi zhong*, "A goose feather sent from a thousand *li* away – a small gift that conveys great affection.")
>
> 电线杆上绑鸡毛 – 好大的胆(掸)子。(*Dianxiangan shang bang jimao – hao da de dan (dan) zi*, "Tie a duster on a telegraph pole – what a big gall.")
>
> 四两棉花 – 谈 (弹)不上。(*Si liang mianhua – tan (tan) bu shang*, "Four grams of cotton – not to mention")
>
> 打破砂锅 – 问 (璺)到底。(*Da po shaguo – wen (wen) dao di*, "To break a marmite – insist on getting to the bottom of the matter")

From the point of view of meaning, the first part in a two-part allegorical saying is a semantic extension or metaphor of the meaning and the second part is where the true meaning of the semantic extension or metaphor lies. The two parts are connected into a whole by the semantic extension or metaphorical relation. Take "哑巴吃黄连 – 有苦难言 (*Yaba chi huanglian – you ku nan yan*)" as an example: what the whole intends to mean is the latter part "有苦难言 (*you ku nan yan*, 'it is hard to tell (the bitterness of coptis)')", whereas a metaphor is used in the former part: "哑巴吃黄连 (*yaba chi huanglian*, 'a mute eats coptis (an extremely bitter Chinese herb)')". When the two parts are put together, not only the meaning is strengthened, but also a deep impression is made upon people with a vivid image. In other two-part allegorical sayings, in addition to semantic extensions and metaphors, homophonic puns are employed so that a subtle and humourous style is achieved apart from the vivid image expressed by the sayings. A case in point is "电线杆上绑鸡毛 – 好大的胆(掸)子 (*dianxiangan shang bang jimao – hao da dedan (dan)zi*)": the metaphor in the former part is to denote "掸子 (*danzi*, 'a duster')", yet "掸 (*dan*, 'duster')" and "胆 (*dan*, 'gall/courage')" are homophonic, thus a homophonic pun is used to mean so big a gall (courage). Two-part allegorical sayings made up through so smart an approach are profound in implied meaning with a lingering potency and impressive rhetoric effects.

Chinese abounds in two-part allegorical sayings with comparatively flexible usage. In practice, sometimes the two parts may turn up at the same time, for example: "老鼠过街 – 人人喊打 (*Laoshu guo jie – renren han da*, 'Rats running across the street – Everyone shouting: kill them.')" and "肉包子打狗 – 有去无回

(*Rou baozi da gou – you qu wu hui*, 'A meat bun thrown at a dog – by no means retrievable.')". Sometimes only the latter part appears, for example, "癞蛤蟆想吃天鹅肉 (*Lai hama xiang chi tian'e rou*, 'A toad lusts after swan's flesh.')" and "黄鼠狼给鸡拜年 (*Huangshulang gei ji bai nian*, 'The weasel goes to pay his respects to the hen.')", etc. Because two-part allegorical sayings are comparatively plain and accessible, one can understand the meaning of the latter even if only the former is expressed.

Although two-part allegorical sayings are special linguistic forms with two parts, they function as one word in application as a fixed construction. They can be used as constituents in sentences, as independent sentences or as clauses in complex sentences.

5 Proper nouns

Proper nouns are fixed phrases specifically denoting certain things and meanings. They come into being with social communicative needs and many proper nouns co-exist with their short forms, from which people choose a proper one at their command in accordance with different communicative purposes. For example,

山东大学 (*Shandong Daxue*, "Shandong University")
人民警察 (*renmin jingcha*, "people's police")
支部书记 (*zhibu shuji*, "branch secretary")
大众日报 (*Dazhong Ribao*, "Dazhong Daily")
四个现代化 (*Sige Xiandaihua*, "Four Modernizations")
居民委员会 (*jumin weiyuanhui*, "residents' committee")
少年先锋队 (*Shaonian Xianfengdui*, "Young Pioneers")
人民代表大会 (*Renmin Daibiao Daihui*, "People's Congress")
政治协商会议 (*Zhengzhi Xieshang Huiyi*, "Political Consultative Conference")
上海电影制片厂 (*Shanghai Dianying Zhipianchang*, "Shanghai Film Studio")
北京语言大学 (*Beijing Yuyan Daxue*, "Beijing Language and Culture University")
北京航空航天大学 (*Beijing Hangkong Hangtian Daxue*, "Beijing University of Aeronautics and Astronautics")

6 Formulaic speech

Formulaic speeches are socially conventionalized ready-made words and expressions. They are fixed phrases or sentences conventionalized after long-time service in the community. Having the same properties as all the other fixed structures equivalent to words in function, they are building blocks of language; therefore, they are also supposed to be members of vocabulary. For example, "您好 (*Nin hao*, 'How are you')", "再见 (*Zaijian*, 'Good-bye')", "请进 (*Qing jin*, 'Come in, please')", "请坐 (*Qing zuo*, 'sit down, please')" and "对不起 (*Duibuqi*, 'sorry')", etc. are all formulaic speeches. Nevertheless, formulaic speeches used in the Chinese community are various and multifarious. Such conventional greetings as 吃饭了吗？(*Chi fan le ma*, 'Have you eaten' literally, an expression functioning like 'Good morning!', 'Good Afternoon' or 'Hi' for general people) and 上班去啊？ (*Shang ban qu a*, 'Are you going for work' literally, an expression functioning as a greeting to people who have a job) should not be included in vocabulary since they are seldom used as building blocks for sentences.

Words and fixed structures equivalent to words in function constitute vocabulary as a whole. The following diagram gives a glimpse of the content of vocabulary system with words and fixed structures equivalent to words in function as basic units:

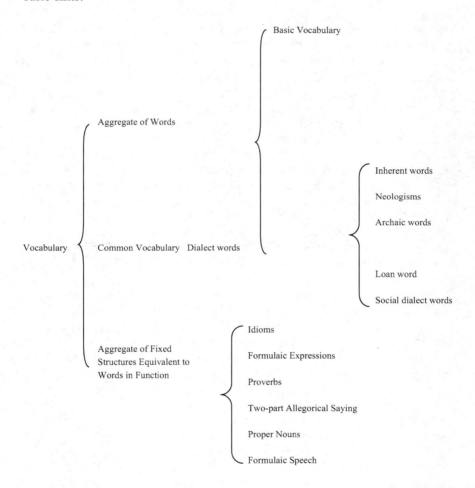

Section 2 Status and function of vocabulary in language

I On language elements

What are language elements? For such a hard question, its answer depends on the point of view and scope for the discussion. We find in our previous studies that the matter of linguistic elements is basically approached from the ingredients of language and that the ingredients of language are regarded as parts of instrument for communication with the function of forming words or sentences as immediate constituents. Therefore hereinafter we still approach the topic with such constituents of language.

Linguists disagree on language elements. Before 1980s far more people agree with Joseph Stalin in that speech sound, vocabulary and grammar are three major elements of language. But after that, people come to think differently on this matter. More and more people suspect the status of vocabulary as one of the elements of language in that vocabulary is interwined with speech sound, and they propose that the three elements of language are speech sound, meaning and grammar. Such a proposal is reasonable indeed because the three elements are independent from each other and there is no repetition and intersection anymore within it. Is this suggestion a final settlement on earth? It is my opinion that there is much more for reconsideration. The above-mentioned three elements are independent from each other, though the property of being used alone are in no sense the same from the point of view of language use: for speech sounds, their being used alone mainly lies in that phonemes can constitute syllables, yet syllables alone cannot be used to make words or sentences; by the same token, the self-sufficiency of meaning is also problematic: meaning in itself cannot be an independent direct reality and it cannot exist without attaching itself to speech sounds. Therefore, we conclude from this point of view and scope that speech sound, meaning and grammar should not constitute the language elements on the same level. Of course our conclusion is based on the above-mentioned precondition; hence we do not deny the independencies of speech sound and meaning on other occasions.

The reason for such a common saying "making words into sentences" is comprehensible from the actual situation of language. In everyday life, when people carry out communication, the most straightforward way is to organize words into sentences with grammatical rules to communicate with each other. So it is word and grammar that are directly involved in communicative processes. Nevertheless, by so saying is not meant to exclude speech sound and meaning from communication. Speech sound and meaning are undeniably directly involved in communicative processes. This is because that a word per se is a combination of sound and meaning and without sound or meaning there will be no word at all. However, once sound and meaning are combined into words, words will become the direct participants in communication whereas speech sound and meaning can only be ingredients of words instead of independent units participating in communication. Just think that if there are only sounds which do not express any meaning at all, such sounds are in no sense can be used to constitute sentences to carry out communication. As for the case that there is only meaning, this is even more inconceivable. Based on such linguistic facts, one ought to conclude that speech sound and meaning firstly form vocabulary and that only vocabulary and grammar are direct elements of language.

II. On the status and function of vocabulary in language

According to the above analysis, vocabulary is among elements of language and it is an undeniable fact that the function of vocabulary is to supply sentence-making materials for language. Just out of this, vocabulary is the most sensitive in reflecting society: it is in constant changing otherwise its capacity will be at odds with its function so as to make self-adjustments from various aspects.

Is it that all for the status and function of vocabulary in language? This is simply not the case. So long as we keep our eyes open, we will find that vocabulary is in various connections with all the aspects of language. The reason lies in that a word is a combination of sound and meaning, that words are the most direct and the most really subsistent unit involved in communication and that words are the concrete carriers of various elements of language.

Due to the fact that a word is the combination of sound and meaning, one cannot ignore their sounds and meanings when learning and using words. Words are bearers of speech sounds and linguistic meanings therefore neither speech sound nor meaning can realize without words as far as language, the instrument for communication, is concerned. Of course no word will there be without speech sound and meaning. Speech sound and linguistic meaning are unified harmoniously in words. Consequently people naturally get hold of speech sounds and linguistic meanings while touching upon words in language application.

Since words are building blocks for sentences, every sentence is produced through the manipulation of words under the government of grammatical rules. As a matter of fact, the grammatical rules of a language can only appear in the utterances composed of sentences and appear in the combination of words. It is in this sense that we say that words are the most real elements of language and that the combinations of words make the abstract grammatical rules concrete and make them generalized as a subsistent reality of grammatical rules.

As for the writing system, it is a written sign system to record language; therefore, this function requires that it should firstly record words, much more is this the case with Chinese characters.

There is no denying that there exists a close relation between language application and vocabulary. Various phenomena in language application can be reflected only through the concrete application of words, because words become speech only after they are combined to each other under the government of grammatical rules and communications between people become possible only after speech comes into being. In the concrete verbal communications, not only vocabulary per se changes, speech sounds and linguistic meanings are changing together more or less with it. Through the application of words, vocabulary, grammar and context are interconnected and interacted with each other, resulting in certain extremely vivid or even extraordinary collocations. Consequently, numerous, rich and colourful pragmatic patterns and rhetoric modes can be generalized through concrete verbal communications. It thus follows that the application of vocabulary is not only closely related with pragmatics, but also makes verbal communication an integral whole in motion to propel the development of the entire language system.

All this leads to the conclusion that a word is a combination of speech sound and linguistic meaning, that a word is a carrier of speech sound and linguistic meaning and that speech sound and linguistic meaning do not exist for real without words. Therefore, words are the bearers of speech sound and linguistic meaning. From the point of view of communication, sentences are composed of words and members of society cannot make sentences without words. Therefore, although language per se is always a combination of speech sound, linguistic meaning, vocabulary and grammar, etc. and no single one of these elements can be dispensed with, yet all other elements will become impossible without words. Thus, we can conclude that a word is a linguistic entity among a good many elements of language.

Our focus is on the status and function of vocabulary in language when we say that a word is a linguistic entity; in the meanwhile, it must be stressed that words are indivisibly connected with other elements of language. Therefore, when we learn or study vocabulary, we must put vocabulary in an extensive connection with speech sound, linguistic meaning, grammar and pragmatics, etc., instead of isolating vocabulary from others, and only in this way can we observe vocabulary holistically and analyze and understand vocabulary in depth. It is also natural to combine vocabulary with other aspects of language while dealing with vocabulary in vocabulary learning and teaching activities in society, for it will be of great significance to both vocabulary learning and vocabulary investigation if particular notice is put upon this point.

One point must be made clear here is that: although an emphasis is put on the matter of the status and function of vocabulary in language in the above discussion, we do not in any sense mean to put down such sub-disciplines of linguistics as phonetics and semantics etc. ; instead, we hold that phonetics, semantics, grammar, rhetoric, philology and pragmatics, etc. are always independent sub-disciplines of linguistics and that the researches and achievements of these regions will always have indisputable important significance and function to the linguistic inquiry as a whole.

Notes

1 Joseph Stalin (1971: P17), *Marxism and Problems of Linguistics*, Beijing: People's Publishing House.
2 The pronunciation of such words needs to be further conventionalized and standardized.

2 Words and semantic morphemes

Section 1 Words

Since vocabulary is an aggregate of words and words are individual elements in vocabulary, we must define words in the first place. Language is the most important instrument for human communication. It is with this instrument that people combine words into sentences to carry out communication in everyday life. For example, we can use such five words as "你 (*ni*, 'you')", "去 (*qu*, 'go')", "黄山 (*Huangshan*, 'Mount Huangshan')", "旅游 (*Lüyou*, 'travel')" and "吗 (*ma*, 'a particle indicating a question')" to produce a sentence "你去黄山旅游吗？" (Will you go on a trip to Mount Huangshan?). We can also tell that the sentence "我到学校去。 (I go to school)" is made up by four words "我 (*wo*, 'I')", "到 (*dao*, 'to')", "学校 (*xuexiao*, 'school')" and "去 (*qu*, 'go')". All these are basically clear for the Han people who speak Chinese. However, answers for such questions as the following are not so consistent: How many words are there in "大家能在一起过个春节不容易，应该好好地热闹热闹。" (*Daja neng zai yiqi guo ge Chunjie bu rongyi, yinggai haohao re'nao re'nao*, 'It is really not easy for us all to get together for Spring Festival and it deserves a good celebration.')? Why do we say that the small elements are words? How can one separate out these small elements within an utterance? As a matter of fact, we must first define what a word is in order to find answers for these questions.

I What is a word

Words are the bottom-most objects of lexicology because they are the individual elements in vocabulary and the units of linguistic sign. There exist various relations including superposition vs. non-superposition etc. between words and syntactic constituents in sentences because words are always put into sentences as syntactic constituents. Since words are often employed in information processing, words in Chinese may or may not correspond to the module-fashioned linguistic units (so-called engineering words) of high frequency in information processing. Furthermore, unlike Indo-European languages, words in Chinese fall short of morphological changes. All these lead to the difficulty of providing a comprehensive

28 *Words and semantic morphemes*

and clear-cut definition on words. What we are going to do here is just to probe into the question "what is a word" from the perspective of lexicology.

As is well-known, a word is a unit of linguistic sign and a combination of sound and meaning to represent meaning with sound, and its primary function in communication is to make up sentences to express ideas; therefore words are building blocks for sentences. It thus can be concluded that a word is a conventionalized sound-meaning paired construction and the smallest independent sentence-making unit. Based upon this understanding, six characteristics of words can be established as follows:

(I) A word must have phonetic form

Speech sound is the material crust of language, thus a word can only come into being and exist on the basis of phonetic form and without phonetic form there will be no word; therefore, every word must have its own phonetic form. For example, though they are different in meanings and in parts of speech, the words "老师 (*laoshi*, 'teacher')", "和 (*he*, 'and')", "同学 (*tongxue*, 'classmate')", "都 (*dou*, 'all')", "来 (*lai*, 'come')" and "了 (*le*, a modal particle signifying the change of situation)" all have their own phonetic forms, i. e., "*laoshi*", "*he*", "*tongxue*", "*dou*", "*lai*" and "*le*". Therefore, phonetic form is one of the indispensable elements of a word.

(II) A word must represent a certain meaning

A word is a combination of sound and meaning, so every word must have the meaning content of its own. For example, the lexical meaning of "麦苗 (*maimiao*)" is "wheat seedling" and its grammatical meaning is "noun, can be used as a subject or an object" with a "neutral" flavour. The lexical meaning of "坚强 (*jianqiang*)" is "strong; firm; staunch" and its grammatical meaning is "adjective, can be used as attributive, predicate" with a "commendatory" flavour. The lexical meaning of "奉承 (*fengcheng*)" is "to flatter; to fawn upon" and its grammatical meaning is "verb, can be used as predicate, attributive" with a "derogatory" flavour. The lexical meaning of "和 (*he*)" is "and" and its grammatical meaning is "connective for co-ordination" with a "neutral" flavour.

(III) A word is a fixed construction

The so-called "fixed" means that once the sound and meaning of a word is combined and is conventionalized by the language community, it will become relatively fixed in form, and the sound-meaning relation is an integral one and is fixed and cannot be altered at will in general. The so-called "construction" means that a word is also made up of many other elements. From the point of view of phonetic form, a word is not only composed of syllables that in turn are made up of phones representing phonemes; it is but also an integrated whole constituted by syllables various in number. From the point of view of meaning, a word is made up of semantic morphemes representing meanings within a certain frame of grammatical construction. Therefore, a word is an integrated whole with internal structures in the make-up of phonetic form, the composition of semantic morphemes and the combination of sound and meaning. All these lead to the conclusion that a word is a fixed construction.

(IV) A word can be used independently

As a unit of linguistic sign, a word is a self-existent individual independent of other conditions. In sentence-making, people can make up various sentences out of proper words in accordance with the meanings to be expressed according to grammatical rules. In this process, a word is an independent building block for sentence-making. For example, "天气 (*tianqi*)" is a word and also an independent individual in language, which can be used to make up "多好的天气啊！" (*Duo hao de tianqi a*! 'What a pleasant weather!') (a one-phrase sentence with "天气" as the head). It can also be used to made up "今天的天气真好！" (*Jintian de tianqi zhen hao*! 'It is a fine day today!') (a subject-predicate sentence with "天气" as the head of the subject). What is more, it can also be used to make up "天气的好坏不能影响工作的进度。" (*Tianqi de haohuai bu neng yingxiang gongzuo de jindu*. 'The weather will not have impact on the progress of the work') (a subject-predicate sentence with "天气" as the attributive in the subject). Another example is "钢笔" (*gangbi*, "pen"). It can be used as the subject of a sentence, e. g., "钢笔是写字的工具 (*Gangbi shi xiezi de gongju*. 'A pen is a tool for writing.')" It can also be used as the object of a sentence, e. g., "我买了钢笔。(*Wo mai le gangbi*, 'I bought a pen.')" and "他送给我钢笔。(*Ta song gei wo gangbi*, 'He sent me a pen.')", etc.

Certain words in Chinese language cannot make up a sentence alone, e. g., adverbs "很" (*hen*, "very") and "再" (*zai*, "again"), and classifiers such as "群" (*qun*, "flock"), "双" (*shuang*, "pair") and "只" (*zhi*, "for one of certain paired things"), etc. However, one point must be made clear: that a word cannot make a sentence alone does not mean that it cannot be used independently. The above words cannot make up sentences alone, though they still can be used independently in sentence-making and they are used as indispensable elements in relevant sentences. For example, "很 (*hen*, 'very')", "再 (*zai*, 'again')", "群 (*qun*, 'group')", "双 (*shuang*, 'pair')" and "只 (*zhi*, 'for one of certain paired things')" are used as independent units woven into the sentences "他很勇敢。(*Ta hen yonggan*, 'He is very brave.')", "你再去一趟吧。(*Ni zai qu yi tang ba*. 'Go there once more.')", "那里有一群人。(*Nali you yi qun ren*. 'There are a group of people over there.')" and "这双袜子只剩一只了。(*Zhe shuang wazi zhi sheng yi zhi le*. 'There is only one left for this pair of stocks.')" respectively, and they are indispensable for both the meaning and structure of each relevant sentence.

It will be seen from this that words can all be used independently. Just because of this property, people can use words to form different sentences.

(V) A word is a minimal unit

There are various minimal units in language, each of which has the scope and condition of its own. For example, a phone is the minimal unit from the point of view of timbre and a syllable is the minimal unit for phonetic structure. A word is also a minimal unit and it is a minimal unit for sentence making: as far as sentence-making materials are concerned, a word is the minimal and indivisible unit.

As a minimal indivisible whole, a word must have an independent and integral meaning. The meaning is specific in denoting a specific object or phenomenon, so in general situation it is not suitable to treat it as a simple addition of the meanings of the components of the word concerned. Consequently, a word is indivisible, otherwise it will no longer be in existence with its original meaning extinct, or it will turn into another word with its original meaning changed. For example, "地图 (*ditu*)" is "a drawing that shows the distribution of things and phenomena on the earth". Such a meaning is specific and is closely related with the objects ad hoc. Therefore, in no sense does it generally refer to any drawing on the earth, nor can it be divided into "地 (*di*)" and "图 (*tu*)", and if it is thus divided, it will become two words, "地 (*di*)" and "图 (*tu*)", instead of one word "地图 (*ditu*)", and what they denote cannot be otherwise than the meanings of the two words "地 (*di*, 'earth')" and "图 (*tu*, 'chart')" instead of the meaning of the word "地图 (*didu*, 'map')". Thus it can be seen that as one word, "地图 (*ditu*)" is a minimal unit and an indivisible whole. Other examples are: "铁路 (*tielu*, 'iron road' literally)" means "a road with steel rails on which trains travel" and "戏言 (*xiyan*, 'play saying' literally)" means "joking remarks that cannot be taken for real". Both of them have specific meanings connected with the specific things they denote. Therefore, neither "a road made only with iron sheet or iron plate" can be referred to as a "铁路 (*tielu*)", nor "what is said in a play" can be called "戏言 (*xiyan*)". As words in language, "铁路 (*tielu*)" and "戏言 (*xiyan*)" are both indivisible fixed sound-meaning paired constructions and the minimal independent unit for sentence-making. Please note that when we say that a word is indivisible in meaning, we do not mean that it is not divisible in structure: because a word is a construction, it is justified in being analyzable.

(VI) A word is a unit for sentence-making

There are various units in language, so we cannot say in general that a word is a linguistic unit. From the perspective of function, it is comparatively appropriate to say that a word is a sentence-making unit. Without doubt, a word can be used to make up a phrase etc. in addition to making up a sentence, yet the fundamental function of a word is to make up a sentence. The process of linguistic communication is basically a process to express ideas for mutual understanding by stringing words into sentences. Therefore, a word is a unit of linguistic sign and also a unit for sentence-making.

We discuss separately the six properties of words in the above. These six properties are unified, inseparable, interconnected and interactive and one cannot get a whole picture of words with any one of them omitted.

II How to identify words in the contemporary Chinese language

(I) Identification and division of words

On the basis of the above understanding, we can make an observation of the practical situation of words in Chinese and decide which elements in Chinese to be words.

Due to the fact that language is changing, one and the same element will be in different cases in contemporary Chinese and ancient Chinese. Therefore, our analyses in the following are made on the situations in contemporary Chinese from a synchronic point of view.

In the contemporary Chinese language, linguistic elements in the following cases should be classified as words:

1. A monosyllabic element with meaning that can be used independently in sentence-making is a word. For example,

   山 (*shan*, "mountain") 水 (*shui*, "water") 土 (*tu*, "earth") 泥 (*ni*, "mud") 树 (*shu*, "tree") 花 (*hua*, "flower") 草 (*cao*, "grass")
   人 (*ren*, "people") 马 (*ma*, "horse") 鸟 (*niao*, "bird") 牛 (*niu*, "cattle") 鱼 (*yu*, "fish") 鸡 (*ji*, "chicken") 蛇 (*she*, "snake")
   砖 (*zhuan*, "brick") 瓦 (*wa*, "tile") 车 (*che*, "car") 船 (*chuan*, "ship") 书 (*shu*, "book") 纸 (*zhi*, "paper") 布 (*bu*, "cloth")
   头 (*tou*, "head") 手 (*shou*, "hand") 嘴 (*zui*, "mouth") 脚 (*jiao*, "foot") 心 (*xin*, "heart") 肝 (*gan*, "liver") 胃 (*wei*, "stomach")
   飞 (*fei*, "fly") 走 (*zou*, "go") 跑 (*pao*, "run") 看 (*kan*, "see") 摔 (*shuai*, "fall") 碰 (*peng*, "touch") 丢 (*diu*, "lose")
   红 (*hong*, "red") 黄 (*huang*, "yellow") 深 (*shen*, "deep") 高 (*gao*, "high") 大 (*da*, "large") 甜 (*tian*, "sweet") 美 (*mei*, "beautiful")
   我 (*wo*, "I") 你 (*ni*, "you") 您 (*nin*, "you") 谁 (*shui*, "who") 这 (*zhe*, "this") 那 (*na*, "that") 哪 (*na*, "where")
   再 (*zai*, "again") 很 (*hen*, "very") 都 (*dou*, "all") 不 (*bu*, "no") 从 (*cong*, "from") 向 (*xiang*, "to") 被 (*bei*, "by")
   一 (*yi*, "one") 二 (*er*, "two") 千 (*qian*, "thousand") 百 (*bai*, "hundred") 个 (*ge*, "one") 趟 (*tang*, "trip") 次 (*ci*, "times")
   而 (*er*, "but") 或 (*huo*, "or") 与 (*yu*, "and") 啊 (*a*, "particle") 呀 (*ya*, "particle") 吗 (*ma*, "particle")

2. A construction with a specific meaning made up of two or more than two meaningless syllables that can be used independently in sentence-making is a word. For example,

   蜘蛛 (*zhizhu*, "spider") 参差 (*cenci*, "uneven") 踌躇 (*chouchu*, "hesitate") 吩咐 (*fenfu*, "tell") 忸怩 (*niuni*, "bashful")
   玲珑 (*linglong*, "exquisite") 忐忑 (*tante*, "disturbed") 仿佛 (*fangfo*, "as if") 含糊 (*hanhu*, "vague") 蹊跷 (*qiqiao*, "strange")

32 *Words and semantic morphemes*

犹豫 (*youyu*, "hesitate") 玻璃 (*boli*, "glass") 蟋蟀 (*xishuai*, "cricket") 蚯蚓 (*qiuyin*, "earthworm") 葡萄 (*putao*, "grape")
婆娑 (*posuo*, "whirling") 玫瑰 (*meigui*, "rose") 徘徊 (*paihuai*, "wandering") 傀儡 (*kuilei*, "puppet") 蜻蜓 (*qingting*, "dragonfly")
轱辘 (*gulu*, "wheels") 霹雳 (*pili*, "thunderbolt") 唠叨 (*laodao*, "nagging") 蹉跎 (*cuotuo*, "waste") 逍遥 (*xiaoyao*, "happy")
吧嗒 (*bada*, "click") 嘎吱 (*gazhi*, "creak") 扑通 (*putong*, "bump") 当啷 (*danglang*, "clang") 哗啦 (*huala*, "crash")
尼龙 (*nilong*, "nylon") 咖啡 (*kafei*, "coffee") 沙发 (*shafa*, "sofa") 吉普 (*jipu*, "jeep") 拷贝 (*kaobei*, "copy")
喀秋莎 (*Kaqiusha*, "Katyusha") 托拉斯 (*tuolasi*, "trust") 莫斯科 (*Mosike*, "Moscow") 加拿大 (*Jianada*, "Canada")

All the elements making up the above words are meaningless syllables. Syllables such as "忐 (*tan*)", "忑 (*te*)", "玻 (*bo*)", "雳 (*li*)", and "葡 (*pu*)", etc. are always meaningless. Whereas each of such elements as "婆 (*po*)", "通 (*tong*)", "龙 (*long*)", "沙 (*sha*)", "发 (*fa*)", "秋 (*qiu*)" and "加 (*jia*)", etc. has respective meaning when used in isolation, though it is a meaningless syllable only indicating sound in the above words because the meaning indicated by each element per se has nothing to do with the formation and the meaning of the respective construction: it is only their phonetic form is used in the above words.

3   A construction, made up of one or more meaningless syllable plus one syllable representing meaning, which has a specific meaning and can be used independently in sentence-making is a word. For example,

啤酒 (*pijiu*, "beer") 卡车 (*kache*, "truck") 酒吧 (*jiuba*, "bar") 沙皇 (*Shahuang*, "Czar") 卡片 (*kapian*, "card")
卡介苗 (*kajie miao*, "BCG vaccine") 法兰绒 (*falan rong*, "flannel") 霓虹灯 (*nihong deng*, "neon lights") 卡宾枪 (*kabin qiang*, "carbine")
太妃糖 (*taifei tang*, "toffee") 布鲁氏菌 (*bulushi jun*, "Brucella") 爱克司光 (*aikesi guang*, "X light") 高尔夫球 (*gao'erfu qiu*, "golf")

The characteristic of this type of words lies in that the part that does not indicate meaning at all is an imitation of sounds: some imitate the pronunciation of foreign words and a very few others imitate the natural sounds. In whichever case, the part not indicating meaning can neither be in existence nor be used independently, and the sound-imitating element can only have a certain meaning-indicating function after it is combined with a certain meaning-indicating element and a modifier-modified or restricting-restricted relation is formed. For example, "酒 (*jiu*, 'liquor')" in "啤酒 (*pijiu*, 'beer')" originally refers to "any liquor in general", and when it is combined with "啤 (*pi*, a sound imitation of a foreign word 'beer')" and "啤" is a modifier of "酒", so that "啤酒" can be used to refer to a kind of alcoholic drinks. Another example is "吧 (*ba*)" in "酒吧 (*jiuba*)". "吧", imitating the sound of a foreign word "bar", which originally means "a public house", is an element can neither indicate any meaning nor

Words and semantic morphemes 33

stand alone. The meaning of "吧" can be brought out only after it is combined with "酒 (*jiu*, 'liquor')", thus "酒" modifying "吧". A new construction "酒吧" is formed by "酒" and "吧" together and thus an independent element indicating a specific meaning is formed. All constructions like these in Chinese should be treated as words.

4   A construction composed of an element indicating meaning with a grammaticalized element, which has a specific meaning and can be used independently in sentence-making is a word. For example,

   阿姨 (*ayi*, "aunt") 老虎 (*laohu*, "tiger") 老鹰 (*laoying*, "eagle") 第二 (*di'er*, "second") 初五 (*chuwu*, "the fifth day of a lunar month")
   石头 (*shitou*, "stone") 想头 (*xiangtou*, "hope") 甜头 (*tiantou*, "benefit") 房子 (*fangzi*, "house") 扣子 (*kouzi*, "button")
   聋子 (*longzi*, "deaf person") 泥巴 (*niba*, "mud") 哑巴 (*yaba*, "mute") 忽然 (*huran*, "suddenly") 突然 (*turan*, "suddenly")
   合乎 (*hehu*, "conform to") 出乎 (*chuhu*, "be beyond") 摔搭 (*shuaida*, "drop") 扭搭 (*niuda*, "walk with a swing")
   电器化 (*dianqihua*, "electrification") 自动化 (*zidonghua*, "automation") 黑乎乎 (*heihuhu*, "black") 酸溜溜 (*suanliuliu*, "sour") 甜丝丝 (*tiansisi*, "pleasantly sweet")

The so-called grammaticalized elements in these constructions are voided in their lexical meaning, i. e., these elements have no overt function in indicating the lexical meaning. For example, "子 (*zi*)" in "帘子 (*lianzi*, 'curtain')" is different from that in "鱼子 (*yuzi*, 'fish roe')", and "头 (*tou*)" in "木头(*mutou*, 'wood')" is different from that in "地头 (*ditou*, 'head land')": the former are both immaterialized elements while the latter have substantive lexical meanings. Nevertheless, these grammaticalized elements have gained the function of overtly indicating grammatical meanings while losing lexical meanings. For example, in the above-mentioned examples, "阿 (*a*)" and "头 (*tou*)", etc. label a noun, "化 (*hua*)" labels a verb and "乎乎 (*huhu*)" and "溜溜 (*liuliu*)", etc. label an adjective.

5   If an element indicating meaning, which cannot be used independently in sentence-making, can be used in sentence-making independently after being reduplicated, the reduplicated new construction is a word. For example,

   伯伯 (*bobo*, "uncle") 孙孙 (*sunsun*, "grandson") 怏怏 (*yangyang*, "disgruntled") 嶙嶙 (*linlin*, "jagged") 绵绵 (*mianmian*, "continuous")
   纷纷 (*fenfen*, "in succession") 茫茫 (*mangmang*, "vast") 悄悄 (*qiaoqiao*, "quietly") 渐渐 (*jianjian*, "gradually") 巍巍 (*weiwei*, "towering")
   郁郁 (*yuyu*, "grief") 勃勃 (*bobo*, "vigorously") 默默 (*momo*, "silently") 朗朗 (*langlang*, "brightly") 奄奄 (*yanyan*, "feebly")
   凛凛 (*linlin*, "cold") 恰恰 (*qiaqia*, "precisely") 荧荧 (*yingying*, "gleaming") 蠢蠢 (*chunchun*, "wriggling") 匆匆 (*congcong*, "hurriedly")

Some words have two forms in the contemporary Chinese language: a simplex form and a reduplicated one. Most of such words are kinship terms, such as "妈 (*ma*, 'mom') – 妈妈 (*mama*, 'mom'), 姑 (*gu*, "father's sister") – 姑姑 (*gugu*, "father's sister"), 叔 (*shu*, 'father's brother') – 叔叔 (*shushu*, 'father's brother'), 舅 (*jiu*, 'mother's brother') – 舅舅 (*jiujiu*, 'mother's brother')"; others are words for general things, such as "星 (*xing*, 'star') – 星星 (*xingxing*, 'star'), 棒 (*bang*, 'bar') – 棒棒 (*bangbang*, 'bar'), 道 (*dao*, 'streak') – 道道 (*daodao*, 'streak'), 棱 (*leng*, 'ridge') – 棱棱 (*lengleng*, 'ridge')", etc. The two forms of these words represent the same meanings. It is a phenomenon that the two forms of words co-exist in the development and alternation of vocabulary. In some cases, these two forms can appear in the same context without any difference, e. g., "妈妈, 我回来啦(*Mama, wo huilai le*, 'Mom, I'm home.')". In other cases, a choice should be made in accordance with context. For example, in "我的妈妈是一个很坚强的人。(*Wo de mama shi yige hen jianqiang de ren*, 'My mother is a very strong person.')", it is unsuitable to use "妈" instead of "妈妈". This is determined by a multitude of factors such as context, intuition and pragmatic conditions, etc.

The formation of the above reduplication structure is an outcome of the disyllabification process of Chinese vocabulary and at the same time the imitation of child language also has a certain influence.

There is another type of reduplication structure in Chinese, which is a reduplicated form of an element indicating meaning that can be used in sentence-making independently. The reduplicated form attains some grammatical meaning and function with the basic meaning unaltered. Such reduplication structures are all forms of inflectional morphology, which should be treated as one word. The reduplication structures in Chinese are as follows.

The reduplication structure of this kind is completely different from "弟弟 (*didi*, 'younger brother')" and "纷纷 (*fenfen*, 'one after another')" in nature. Such forms as "弟弟" and "纷纷" are coined new forms because "弟 (*di*)" and "纷 (*fen*)" cannot be used indipendently as words, while "人人 (*renren*, 'every one, every people')" is an inflected form of the word "人 (*ren*, 'people')", i. e., it is a morphological change of the one and the same word to represent different grammatical meanings (a more detailed description is given in the section of inflectional morphology). Just because such reduplication form is the different inflection form of one and the same word, "人人 (*renren*, 'everyone')", "趟趟 (*tangtang*, 'every time')", "想想 (*xiangxiang*, 'reconsider')" and "狠狠 (*henhen*, 'severely')", etc. are all still one word. When identifying words, in no way can we treat "人人" etc. as two words.

6 A different new meaning is added if an element indicating meaning is reduplicated and the reduplication form can be used in sentence-making independently, such a reduplication structure is a word. For example,

落落 (*luoluo*, "natural and graceful") 斤斤 (*jinjin*, "fuss about") 区区 (*ququ*, "trivial") 熊熊 (*xiongxiong*, "raging") 统统 (*tongtong*, "all")

Words and semantic morphemes 35

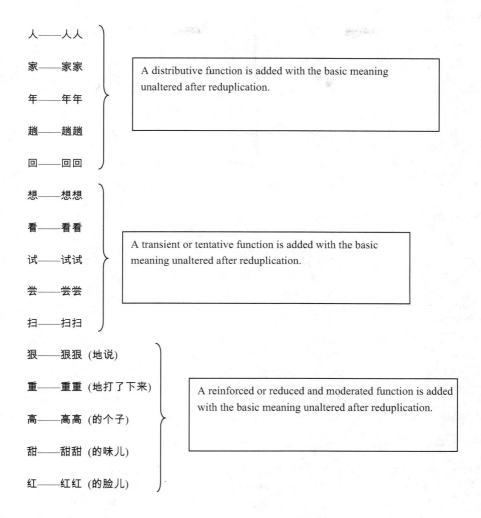

鼎鼎 (*dingding*, "great") 源源 (*yuanyuan*, "continuously") 翼翼 (*yiyi*, "cautiously") 断断 (*duanduan*, "definitely") 涓涓 (*juanjuan*, "trickling luggishly")
奕奕 (*yiyi*, "energetic") 济济 (*jiji*, "numerous") 津津 (*jinjin*, "delicious") 昂昂 (*ang'ang*, "high-spirited") 堂堂 (*tangtang*, "dignified or impressive")
万万 (*wanwan*, "absolutely") 通通 (*tongtong*, "all") 往往 (*wangwang*, "often") 奶奶 (*nainai*, "grandma") 太太 (*taitai*, "madame")

The above words fall into two categories: one includes "落", "斤", "区", "万", "通", and "断", etc., which can be words by themselves, the other includes "翼",

36 *Words and semantic morphemes*

"奕", "济", "涓" and "津", etc., only the reduplicated form of which can be words in the contemporary Chinese language. They are different in some aspects, though the two categories share a common characteristic: the original elements have meanings of their own and the meanings of the reduplicated forms are different from the original ones from the synchronic perspective. Nevertheless there is no denying that the meaning evolution of some words can be traced from the diachronic perspective.

7   If two elements indicating meaning, neither of which can be used independently in sentence-making, can be used in sentence-making independently with a new meaning after being conjoined, the conjoined new construction is a word. For example,

牺牲 (*xisheng*, "sacrifice") 丰茂 (*fengmao*, "luxuriant") 监督 (*jiandu*, "supervise") 参观 (*canguan*, "visit") 茅庐 (*maolu*, "thatched cottage")
融洽 (*rongqia*, "harmonious") 梭镖 (*suobiao*, "spear") 坦率 (*tanshuai*, "frank") 韬略 (*taolüe*, "military strategy") 颓靡 (*tuimi*, "dejected")
委婉 (*weiwan*, "euphemistic") 纨绔 (*wanku*, "sons of the rich") 咆哮 (*paoxiao*, "roar") 承袭 (*chengxi*, "inherited") 诬蔑 (*wumie*, "slander")
瞻仰 (*zhanyang*, "look at with reverence") 酝酿 (*yunniang*, "brew") 义愤 (*yifen*, "indignation") 哀悼 (*aidao*, "mourning") 昂首 (*angshou*, "raise one's head")
赞颂 (*zansong*, "praise") 苍翠 (*cangcui*, "green") 怜悯 (*lianmin*, "pity") 态势 (*taishi*, "situation") 迅捷 (*xunjie*, "fast")
疏忽 (*shuhu*, "negligence") 枢纽 (*shuniu*, "hinge") 羡慕 (*xianmu*, "envy") 晓畅 (*xiaochang*, "clear and smooth") 业绩 (*yeji*, "achievement")
习尚 (*xishang*, "customs") 危惧 (*weiju*, "worry and fear") 业务 (*yewu*, "business") 袭击 (*xiji*, "a surprise attack") 勘察 (*kancha*, "survey")
萧索 (*xiaosuo*, "desolate") 康复 (*kangfu*, "recovery") 蕴含 (*yunhan*, "contain") 遵循 (*zunxun*, "follow") 模拟 (*moni*, "simulation")

8   An element indicating meaning, which can be used independently in sentence-making, is conjoined with an element indicating meaning, which cannot be used independently in sentence-making. If the conjoined new construction can be used in sentence-making independently with a new meaning, such a new construction is a word. For example,

学习 (*xuexi*, "study") 人民 (*renmin*, "people") 简短 (*jianduan*, "brief") 借鉴 (*jiejian*, "draw lessons from") 宁静 (*ningjing*, "quiet")
取材 (*qucai*, "draw materials") 深奥 (*shen'ao*, "profound") 浓郁 (*nongyu*, "rich") 朴厚 (*puhou*, "simple and loyal") 鬼祟 (*guisui*, "sneaky")
崇高 (*chonggao*, "lofty") 肤浅 (*fuqian*, "superficial") 华美 (*huamei*, "gorgeous") 幽香 (*youxiang*, "delicate fragrance") 蔚蓝 (*weilan*, "sky blue")
透彻 (*touche*, "thorough") 思路 (*silu*, "thinking") 冷饮 (*lengyin*, "cold drink") 人杰 (*renjie*, "an outstanding personality") 幼苗 (*youmiao*, "seedling")

对偶 (*dui'ou*, "dual") 颂歌 (*songge*, "carol") 借故 (*jiegu*, "excuse") 解剖 (*jiepou*, "anatomy") 逃遁 (*taodun*, "escape")
杀戮 (*shalu*, "slaughter") 冲锋 (*chongfeng*, "charge") 抽搐 (*chouchu*, "twitch") 独创 (*duchuang*, "original") 反击 (*fanji*, "counter attack")
蒲绒 (*purong*, "cattail wool") 藏匿 (*cangni*, "hide") 旧历 (*jiuli*, "the lunar calendar") 碧空 (*bikong*, "blue sky") 卫兵 (*weibing*, "guard")
菊花 (*juhua*, "chrysanthemum") 鲤鱼 (*liyu*, "carp") 茅草 (*maocao*, "thatch") 芹菜 (*qincai*, "celery") 松树 (*songshu*, "pine")

Although all the constituents of the above words have meanings, they fall into different cases. For such elements as "学 (*xue*)" in "学习 (*xuexi*)" and "人 (*ren*)" in "人民 (*remmin*)", etc., not only do they bear meanings of their own, but also they can be words themselves in the contemporary Chinese language. Whereas for such elements as "习 (*xi*)" and "民 (*min*)", etc., they are on longer words nowadays, although they also bear meanings. All such new constructions, composed of the two constituents of this type, which both have the new meanings and can be used in sentence-making independently should be treated as words.

9 If an element indicating meaning but not being used independently in sentence-making originally is used in sentence-making independently in a concrete context, it should be treated as a word. For example, people usually say "人民 (*renmin*, 'people')" instead of "民 (*min*)" and "孩子 (*haizi*, 'child')" or "儿子 (*erzi*)" instead of "子 (*zi*)" in the contemporary Chinese language. But in a concrete context, one may well say "爱民如子 (*ai min ru zi*, 'love the subjects as if they were his own children')" in which both "民 (*min*)" and "子 (*zi*)" are used independently. For another example, people say "摄影 (*sheying*, 'take a photograph')" or "拍摄 (*paishe*, 'take a photograph')" instead of "摄 (*she*)", but they also say "本报记者摄 (*Benbao jizhe she*, 'Taken by a staff correspondent')"; people say "头发 (*toufa*, 'hair')" instead of "发 (*fa*)", but they also say "理了理发 (*li le li fa*, 'to have one's hair cut')" or "理了个发 (*li le ge fa*, 'to have one's hair cut')" and so on and so forth. In all the above contexts, we cannot deny that these elements are used independently in sentence-making, that they possess all the six conditions for words and that they have the function of words. Consequently all these elements should be treated as words in their respective concrete contexts.

10 A new construction composed of two or more meaningful elements that can be used independently in sentence-making with a new meaning derived and being used independently in sentence-making is a word. For example,

白菜 (*baicai*, "Chinese cabbage") 马车 (*mache*, "carriage") 道路 (*daolu*, "road") 剪纸 (*jianzhi*, "paper-cut") 信心 (*xinxin*, "confidence")
电灯 (*diandeng*, "electric light") 草药 (*caoyao*, "herbal medicine") 地球 (*diqiu*, "earth") 小说 (*xiaoshuo*, "novel") 祝词 (*zhuci*, "congratulations")
快车 (*kuaiche*, "express") 绿茶 (*lücha*, "green tea") 冷淡 (*lengdan*, "cold") 弱小 (*ruoxiao*, "small and weak") 笨重 (*benzhong*, "heavy")

38 *Words and semantic morphemes*

发动 (*fadong*, "launch") 带头 (*daitou*, "take the lead") 打捞 (*dalao*, "salvage") 出借 (*chujie*, "lend") 想象 (*xiangxiang*, "imagine")

印染 (*yinran*, "printing and dyeing") 光滑 (*guanghua*, "smooth") 空前 (*kongqian*, "unprecedented") 向往 (*xiangwang*, "yearning") 到来 (*daolai*, "arrival")

书本 (*shuben*, "book") 船只 (*chuanzhi*, "ships") 车辆 (*cheliang*, "vehicle") 人口 (*renkou*, "population") 布匹 (*bupi*, "cloth")

毛玻璃 (*maoboli*, "ground glass") 螺丝刀 (*luosidao*, "screw driver") 山水画 (*shanshuihua*, "landscape picture") 皮凉鞋 (*piliangxie*, "leather sandals")

走读班 (*zouduban*, "day class") 说明书 (*shuomingshu*, "instructions") 双眼皮 (*shuangyanpi*, "double-fold eyelids") 落花生 (*luohuasheng*, "groundnut")

The characteristics of this type of words include that all their components are meaningful and are words themselves. For example, "白 (*bai*, 'white')" and "菜 (*cai*, 'vagetable')" in "白菜 (*baicai*, 'Chinese cabbage')", "毛 (*mao*, 'gross, rude')" and "玻璃 (*boli*, 'glass')" in "毛玻璃 (*maoboli*, 'ground glass')", "山 (*shan*, 'mountain')", "水 (*shui*, 'water')" and "画 (*hua*, 'picture')" or "山水 (*shanshui*, 'landscape')" and "画 (*hua*, 'picture')" in "山水画 (*shanshuihua*, 'landscape picture')", "皮 (*pi*, 'leather')", "凉 (*liang*, 'cool')" and "鞋 (*xie*, 'shoe')" or "皮 (*pi*, 'leather')" and "凉鞋 (*liangxie*, 'sandals')" in "皮凉鞋 (*piliangxie*, 'leather sandals')", all these elements are meaningful and can be words themselves. Therefore, it is comparatively hard to identify the words like these. These words belong to the cases where words are confused with phrases.

When identifying these words, what we should pay attention to is still the characteristic that "a word is a fixed sound-meaning paired construction". Once a word is formed, it is an indivisible whole with a specific meaning and an independent sentence-making unit, so neither does the meaning of a word in any sense equal an addition of the meanings of its components under general situations, nor can it be extended into any larger constructions even according to the syntactic relations between its components. Take "白菜 (*baicai*)" as an example: as a fixed sound-meaning paired construction with the meaning of "in many varieties, herbaceous biennial, common vegetable with large leaves and pale-yellow flowers; also 大白菜 (*dabaicai*, 'Chinese cabbage')". It is obvious that it is a name of vegetable instead of "白的菜 (*bai de cai*, 'white vegetable')". The meaning of "白菜 (*baicai*)" is completely different from that of "白的菜 (*bai de cai*)". As a word with a fixed construction and a specific meaning, "白菜" can in no way be extended. By the same token, "马车 (*mache*, 'carriage')" cannot be extended into "马的车 (*madeche*, 'a car of horse's')" or "马拉的车 (*ma la de che*, 'a car pulled by a horse')", "道路 (*daolu*, 'road')" not into "道和路 (*dao he lu*, 'a way and a road')", "剪纸 (*jianzhi*, 'paper-cut')" not into "剪着纸 (*jian zhe zhi*, 'cutting the paper')" or "剪了纸 (*jian le zhi*, 'to have cut the paper')" and "毛玻璃 (*maoboli*, 'ground glass')" not into "毛的玻璃 (*mao de boli*, 'rude glass')". Thus it can be seen that such a fixed sound-meaning paired construction cannot in any sense be

Words and semantic morphemes 39

extended. We can pick out most of the words of this type in accordance with this property.

Among the above-mentioned ten types of words, one can discern quite easily those in the first nine types and most of the tenth type. The hard cases are among a small number of words in the tenth type because the semantic morphemes making up the words of this type are also words themselves. We will discuss this case in the following.

(II) the problem of distinguishing words from certain phrases

Words on the whole are so distinctively distinguished from phrases in Chinese that no confusion arises in general. A few in the tenth type of the above-mentioned words may be confused with phrases. They fall into four types according to our tentative investigations into the phenomena concerned:

1. There are indeed certain combinations with two different properties in Chinese vocabulary. For example, "江湖 (*jianghu*)" is a word because it is a sentence-making unit with indivisible specific meanings when it denotes "all places in the country; every corner" or "people living in a vagrant life as fortune-teller, quack doctor, entertainers, etc." However sometimes it really denotes "rivers" and "lakes". For example, "江湖" in "祖国的江湖多美啊！(*Zuguo de jiang hu duo mei a*, 'The rivers and lakes of the motherland are so beautiful')" can be separated into two words, "江 (*jiang*)" and "湖 (*hu*)", denoting two different things "rivers" and "lakes" respectively. It is a phrase in this case because "江湖" is only a temporary combination of the two words of "江" and "湖" and it has no qualification of a word. The following cases all fall into this type:

   笔墨 (*bi mo*): It is a word when denoting "writing or articles" and it is a phrase when signifying the two things of "pen" and "ink".
   山水 (*shan shui*): It is a word when denoting "water running down a mountain", "scenery with mountains and waters", or "landscape painting"; it is a phrase when simply meaning "mountain" and "water".
   妻子 (*qi zi*): It is a word when denoting "the spouse of a man, opposite to 'husband'"; it is a phrase when meaning "wife and son".
   红花 (*hong hua*): It is a word when denoting "annual herbal plant with alternate lanceolate thorny leaves and yellowish-red tubular flowers" or "a sort of traditional Chinese medicine"; it is a phrase when meaning "red flowers".

2. A few combinations in Chinese vocabulary indeed can be extended and the meaning of the extended construction is basically the same as that of the original one. For example, "象牙 (*xiangya*, 'ivory') – 象的牙 (*xiang de ya*, 'elephant teeth')", "牛奶 (*niunai*, 'milk') – 牛的奶 (*niu de nai*, 'milk from cow')", "羊肉 (*yangrou*, 'mutton') – 羊的肉 (*yang de rou*, 'meat of the

ram')", "猪肝 (zhugan, 'pork liver') – 猪的肝 (zhu de gan, 'pig liver')", "牛角 (niujiao, 'ox horn') – 牛的角 (niu de jiao, 'horn of ox')" and so on. However, we still regard "象牙", "牛奶", "羊肉", "猪肝" and "牛角", etc. as words and "象的牙", "牛的奶", "羊的肉", "猪的肝" and "牛的角", etc. as phrases. Because we observe that we cannot use "象的牙" and "牛的奶" instead of "象牙" and "牛奶" in one and the same context. For instance, we cannot say "这是象的牙雕刻。 (Zhe shi xiang de ya diaoke)" instead of "这是象牙雕刻。 (Zhe shi xiang ya diaoke, 'This is an ivory carving')" and we can neither say "我买了两盒牛的奶糖。 (Wo mai le lianghe niu de nai tang)" instead of "我买了两盒牛奶糖。 (Wo mai le liang he niunaitang, 'I bought two boxes of milk sugar')" respectively. It can be seen that this type of words cannot be extended in general in actual language use. It can also be seen that the combination of the components in these words is to some degree indivisible. Furthermore, these words as a whole have a considerably high frequency of use from the perspective of their application in the linguistic community of Chinese. All these facts lead to the conclusion that "象牙" and "牛奶", etc. are fixed constructions with specific meanings; therefore, they are words instead of phrases. Of course such forms as "象的牙" and "牛的奶", etc. are all phrases with constructions and properties completely different from those of "象牙" and "牛奶", etc.

3   The identification of such words as "抓紧(zhuajin, 'grasp')" and "打垮 (dakua, 'defeat')" is fairly hard because their components can be used independently as words and they themselves can be extended, e. g., "抓紧" can be extended into "抓得紧 (zhua de jin, 'can be grasped')" and "抓不紧 (zhua bu jin, 'cannot be grasped')", even into "抓得紧不紧 (zhua de jin bu jin, 'can it be grasped or not')", and "打垮" can also be extended into "打得垮 (da de kua, 'can be defeated')" and "打不垮 (da bu kua, 'cannot be defeated')". For this type of words, we can approach them from two ways: on the one hand, we should notice that although these words can be extended, not only can they be inextensible in many concrete contexts, but also their components are considerably tightly combined together. For example, neither "抓紧" in "我们必须抓紧时间学习 (Women bixu zhuajin shijian xuexi, 'We must make the best use of our time to study')" and nor "打垮" in "坚决打垮反动派 (Jianjue dakua fandongpai, 'Resolutely defeat the reactionaries')" can be extended at all. In accordance with such a situation of their actual application that they are fixed constructions as an integrated whole and they cannot be replaced with the extended counterpart in concrete contexts, it should be concluded that these combinations are words. On the other, after analysis and comparison we can see that the meanings of such constructions as "抓紧" and "打垮" show globality and generality to a certain degree in that their meanings are somewhat integrated on the basis of the meanings of their components. For example, "抓 ('to grasp' literally) 紧 ('tight' literally)" has been integrated to mean "pay close attention to", "打 ('to hit' literally) 垮 ('broken down' literally)" has been integrated to mean

"overturn"; therefore the meanings of the components making up the whole are more or less weakened in substantiality and concreteness. Of course the situations of the development processes of each words are various and different: the meaning-integration degree of "分清 (*fenqing*, 'distinguish')" and "搞好 (*gaohao*, 'do well')" are comparatively low. Yet it is certain that as one type in Chinese vocabulary, the meanings of these words will develop along the line from separation to integration and from being abstract to being generalized.

4 Segregatory words. Segregatory words refer to those words that are often separated in actual use. Segregatory words fall into two types. The first one includes those whose components can be used as words independently. For example,

起床: "起了床" "起不了床"
帮忙: "帮个忙" "帮了忙" "帮不了忙"
握手: "握着手" "握过手" "握了一次手"
伤心: "伤了心" "伤什么心"

The other includes the cases in which some of their components can only be used as an element indicating meaning instead of being used as an independent word. For example,

鞠躬: "鞠了个躬" "鞠一个躬"
革命: "革谁的命" "革反动派的命"
敬礼: "敬了个礼" "敬一个礼"
洗澡: "洗了澡" "洗个澡" "洗了个澡"

None of the elements such as "鞠", "躬", "革", "礼" and "澡" in the above examples can be used as a word independently.

The above two cases are somewhat different from each other, though they share a common property that they can be used either jointly or separately. For this type of constructions, we treat the un-extended ones as words and the extended as phrases, but we do not regard the un-extended ones as phrases. The reason lies in that the meanings of the segregatory words are different before and after being extended. For example, such words as "起床 (*qichuang*, 'get up')" and "鞠躬 (*jugong*, 'bow')" indicate an action respectively, whereas the extended forms "起了床 (*qi le chuang*, 'have gotten up')" and "鞠了个躬 (*ju le ge gong*, 'have made a bow')" signify the relevant situation concerning respective actions and different extended forms signify different meanings. This shows that before being extended these constructions are all words, i. e., indivisible integral sentence-making unit signifying specific meanings. After being extended, the components making up the constructions possess the characteristics of words and participate in the formation of the phrases with the status of words, that is to say, such elements as "鞠" and "躬" in "鞠躬" that have lost the status of words, are again used as independent words in the concrete contexts (please refer to No. 9 in Section 1 Identification and Division of Words).

It is considerably sophisticated to distinguish words from phrase in Chinese. In addition to the above four cases, the number of syllables and the characteristics in pronunciation and morphology can also be used for reference in practice.

We have discussed the identification of words in Chinese in two perspectives in the above discussion. On the basis of this understanding, we will segment words in the following two passages.

Words are marked by "一" and the number under "一" indicates one of the above-mentioned ten cases of the word.

The first passage: 有的人 (*Someone*) by Zang Kejia.

有 的 人 活着
1 1 1   1
他 已经 死了;
1 10   1
有 的 人 死了
1 1 1 1
他 还 活着。
1 1 1

有 的 人
1 1 1
骑 在 人民 头 上: "呵, 我 多 伟大!"
1 1 8 1 8   1 1 1 8
有 的 人
1 1 1
俯下 身子 给 人民 当 牛马。
 8   4 1 8 1 10

有 的 人
1 1 1
把 名字 刻 入 石头, 想 "不朽";
1 10 1 4   8   1   8
有 的 人
1 1 1
情愿 作 野草, 等着 地下 的 火 烧。
 10 1 10   1   1 1 1 1

有 的 人
1 1 1
他 活着 别人 就 不 能 活;
1 1 10 1 1 1 1
有 的 人
1 1 1
他 活着 为了 多数 人 更 好 地 活。
1 1 10 10 1 1 1 1 1

Words and semantic morphemes 43

骑 在 人民 头 上 的
1 1 8 1 1 1
人民 把 他 摔 垮;
8   1 1 1
给 人民 作 牛马 的
1 8   1 10 1
人民 永远 记住 他!
8   10   10 1

把 名字 刻 入 石头 的
1 10   1 1 4   1
名字 比 尸首 烂 得 更 早;
10   1 7   1 1 1 1
只要 春风 吹 到 的 地方
10   10   1 1 1 10
到处 是 青青 的 野草。
10   1 1   1 10
他 活着 别人 就 不 能 活 的 人,
1 1   10   1 1 1 1 1 1
他 的 下场 可以 看 到;
1 1 10   10   1 1
他 活着 为了 多数 人 更 好 地 活着 的 人,
1 1   10   10   1 1 1 1 1 1   1 1
群众 把 他 抬举 得 很 高, 很 高。
8   1 1 10   1 1 1   1 1

The second passage: a paragraph from 白杨礼赞 (*Tribute to White Poplar*) by Mao Dun.

它 没有 婆娑 的 姿态, 没有 屈曲 盘旋 的 虬枝。 也许 你 要 说 它
1 10   2   1 7   10   10   8   1 8   10   1 1 1 1
不 美。
1 1
如果 美 是 专指 "婆娑" 或 "旁 逸 斜 出" 之类 而 言, 那么,
10   1 1 1 1 2   1 1 9 1 1 1   1 9 1   9 1 4
白杨树 算 不 得 树 中 的 好 女子。 但是 它 伟岸, 正直, 朴质, 严肃,
10   1 1 1 1 1 1 1 8   10   1 8   10   7   8
也 不 缺乏 温和, 更 不 用 提 它 的 坚强 不 屈 与 挺拔, 它 是 树 中
1 1 10   10   1 1 1 1 1 1 1 1 1 1 1 1 8   10 1 10 1 1 1 1
的 伟 丈夫。
1 9 8

For the sign "—" in the first passage, the short dash refers to a word and the long one refers to the inflectional form of the word concerned. Some treat "着 (*zhe*)" and "了 (*le*)" in "活着 (*huo-zhe*)", "等着 (*deng-zhe*)" and "死了 (*si-le*)" as auxiliary words, however, as a matter of fact, they are attached after the main verb functioning as progressive and perfective. Therefore we treat them as inflectional endings. By the same token, "青青 (*qingqing*)" is also an inflectional form of "青" with a strengthening effect.

Section 2 Semantic morphemes

I What is a semantic morpheme?

A word is made up of its components, i. e., semantic morphemes. A semantic morpheme is also a fixed sound-meaning paired construction and it is the minimal independent structural unit of words. The so-called structural units of words refer to various units forming words and these structural units fall into three cases as a whole. The first one is the unit for word coinage. Word coinage is the most important function of semantic morphemes and all words are composed by semantic morphemes. The second one is the unit for word-formation. As a matter of fact, the units for word-formation coincide with and are as important as the units for word coinage. The third one is the inflectional unit, the structural unit of words operational in inflection. All the structural units existing within the words are structural components of words; therefore, they are all semantic morphemes.

Compared with the definition of word in Section 1, it can be seen that semantic morphemes and words are all the same in properties except that they are different units in language. This is not strange at all but helps us to understand further the distinctions between them and their properties. As far as the units in language are concerned, a word is a sentence-making unit while a semantic morpheme is a structural unit of words within the words, mainly the word coinage and word-formation unit. These completely different properties and functions illustrate the essential differences between words and semantic morphemes. Therefore a word can in no way be confused with a semantic morpheme. All the other properties of words and semantic morphemes are the same except for differences in properties and functions of the units they serve; what is more, a word and a semantic morpheme can co-exist in one and the same outer form. This illustrates from another aspect the mutual connection and relation between words and semantic morphemes. Both words and semantic morphemes are fixed combinations of sound and meaning and both of them are minimal units that can be used independently; but due to the differences in properties and functions, the scopes and conditions of their properties are different and their functions are accordingly constrained by the properties of their own. For words, such properties as "being minimal" and "can be used independently" manifest in sentence-making, e. g., "青山 (*qingshan*, 'green mountain')" and "绿水 (*lüshui*, 'green water')" are two words, so one can use them to make a sentence with other words such as "我爱祖国的青山绿水。(*Wo ai zuguo de qingshan lüshui*, 'I love the green mountains and rivers of my motherland')". Their functions are restricted in sentence-making but cannot step into the scope of word-making. As for semantic morphemes, these properties can only be reflected in word-making. For example, "参观 (*canguan*, 'visit')" is composed of two semantic morpheme: "参 (*can*, 'look')" and "观 (*guan*, 'look')". Both "参" and "观" are fixed combinations of sound and meaning and minimal word-making units that can be used independently. Not only can they be combined to make "参观", but also "参" can be combined to make "参加 (*canjia*, 'join')", "参阅 (*canyue*, 'consult')", "参考 (*cankao*, 'consult')", "参谋 (*canmou*, 'adviser')", "参照 (*canzhao*, 'refer')", "参赛 (*cansai*, 'take part in match')", "参与 (*canyu*, 'participate in')" and "参看 (*cankan*, 'see')", etc. with other semantic morphemes, and "观" can be combined to make "观察 (*guancha*, 'observation')", "观点 (*guandian*, 'viewpoint')", "观望 (*guanwang*, 'wait and see')", "观赏 (*guanshang*, 'view and admire')", "观众 (*guangzhong*, 'audience')", "主观 (*zhuguan*, 'subjective')", "乐观 (*leguan*, 'optimism')" and "可观 (*keguan*, 'considerable')", etc. with other semantic morphemes. Numerous words are composed by them, though all of them fall in the scope of word-making, because they can no longer be used to make sentences in the contemporary Chinese language. Of course some elements may have both properties, and one of them may be highlighted under certain conditions because certain words can be made up with free semantic morphemes. For example, as a word made up of a free semantic morpheme, "山 (*shan*)" can be used to make up sentences and at the same time, it can be a free semantic morpheme to not only make up the word "山", but also make up other words as a semantic morpheme. These two properties co-exist in the outer form of "山", but the specific realization of the relevant properties depends upon the practical situation of its application. Some elements may be words made up by free semantic morphemes in both ancient Chinese and contemporary Chinese; therefore they can be words as well as semantic morphemes in the historical development of Chinese. The above-mentioned "山" is a case in point. Another situation is that, an element was a word made up by a free semantic morpheme in ancient Chinese but it has turned into a bound semantic morpheme from a free one in the contemporary Chinese language. The above-mentioned "参" and "观" fall into this category. They were both words composed of a free semantic morpheme and were used to make up sentences as words, but with the losing of sentence-making function of "参" and "观", they have turned into bound semantic morphemes which can only be used to make up words instead of being able to make up sentences. It is observed thereof that the change of semantic morpheme typology and the change from word to non-word may happen at the same time (semantic morpheme typology will be discussed later on).

II Compounding semantic morphemes

(I) What is a compounding semantic morpheme?

A compounding semantic morpheme is a semantic morpheme resulted from the development and evolution of a compound word. For example, "孩子 (*haizi*, 'children')" in "孩子头 (*haizitou*, 'chief of children')", "老虎 (*laohu*, 'tiger')" in "纸老虎 (*zhilaohu*, 'paper tiger')", "教师 (*jiaoshi*, 'teacher')" in "教师节 (*jiaoshijie*, 'Teachers' Day')", and "豆腐 (*doufu*, 'bean curd')" in "豆腐皮 (*doufupi*, 'thin sheets of bean curd')", etc. They are termed as compounding semantic morphemes because these elements possess the properties of semantic morphemes and perform the function of semantic morphemes as a whole after compounding. For example, when the new word "孩子头" is coined, it is not in the least that the three elements "孩 (*hai*, 'child')", "子 (*zi*, 'son')" and "头 (*tou*, 'head')" are picked out separately at the same time to make up the word "孩子头" but that the form "孩子" has already existed in the lexicon as a whole and the two parts "孩子" and "头" are picked out to make up the new word "孩子头". Therefore "孩子" is used as a whole in the process of word coinage and thus acquires the properties and functions of a semantic morpheme. The elements like these are called "compounding semantic morphemes".

It has to be noted that we should not confuse compounding semantic morphemes with elements like compounding semantic morphemes in understanding compounding semantic morphemes. For example, "电热 (*dianre*, 'electric heating')" in "电热毯 (*dianretan*, 'electric blanket')", "高射 (*gaoshe*, 'high shoot')" in "高射炮 (*gaoshebao*, 'archibald')", "三字 (*sanzi*, 'three characters')" in "三字词 (*sanzici*, 'trisyllabic word')", "蘸水 (*zhanshui*, 'dip in water')" and in "蘸水笔 (*zhanshuibi*, 'dip pen')", etc., none of them is a compounding semantic morpheme. Because these elements are not a conventionalized whole before they are used to compose the words concerned, although such elements as "三字" and "蘸水" can signify a certain meaning, they are only free phrases and as for "电热" and "高射", they are not integral elements at all. Therefore, as far as the above-mentioned words are concerned, three semantic morphemes are picked out at the same time and are combined into new words out of the expressive demand thus they are all composed of three parts.

(II) The properties and characteristics of compounding semantic morphemes

As semantic morphemes, compounding semantic morphemes share the same properties and characteristics with other semantic morphemes, and word-making function is surely included so compounding semantic morphemes are units that can be used in word-making; therefore compounding semantic morphemes should not be excluded from semantic morphemes. Whether a compounding element can be a compounding semantic morpheme or not mainly lies in that whether it meets the prerequisites of a semantic morpheme and whether it has the properties and functions of a semantic morpheme. All the compounding elements possessing the prerequisites, properties and functions of a semantic morpheme should be recognized as semantic morphemes. Although these elements are compounding, as far as meaning is concerned, they are minimal indivisible word-making units that can be used independently as semantic morphemes; therefore the structural analyzability of the compounding elements cannot negate the indivisible integrity in meaning. Consequently compounding semantic morphemes are building blocks for word-making as well as simple semantic morphemes. Compounding semantic morpheme were termed as morpheme groups in some articles in the past. As a matter of fact, such a designation is inaccurate because there are various morpheme groups in word coinage, for example, "洗衣 (*xi yi*, 'wash clothes')",

"喝水 (*he shui*, 'drink water')" and "削发 (*xue fa*, 'shave hair')", even "高射 (*gao she*, 'high shoot')" can all be taken as morpheme groups. They can indeed be used to make up words, e. g., "洗衣机 (*xiyiji*, 'washing machine')", "喝水杯 (*heshuibei*, 'water cup')", "削发器 (*xuefaqi*, 'hair-shaving device')" and "高射炮 (*gaoshepao*, 'archibald')", but they are not compounding semantic morphemes at all. To be broader, can such a form as "洗衣机" be regarded as a morpheme group? From the perspective of grammar, a phrase per se with a proper intonation can become a sentence; therefore, can such morpheme groups as "喝水", "高射" and "洗衣机" per se become words directly? If the answer is yes, then what are the conditions for them to be words? Thus it can be seen that it will not be advisable that we should adopt the designation of morpheme group, because it will mix up many different questions with no immediate and clear-cut answer.

(III) The formation of compounding semantic morphemes

The formation of compounding semantic morphemes is an inevitable outcome of the development of vocabulary. From the point of view of linguistic application, the process in which a compound word turns into a compounding semantic morpheme through evolution is not only absolutely necessary but also entirely possible. In social communications, one can not only use a compound word denoting certain things to make up sentences, but can also use it to describe and illustrate certain characteristics of the concrete objects concerned. For example, to illustrate a "鹿 (*lu*, 'deer')" whose hide is spotted with figures resembling "梅花 (*meihua*, 'Chinese plum blossoms')", one can designate it as "梅花鹿 (*meihualu*, 'Chinese plum blossom deer' literally, 'spotted deer')" and to illustrate a "报纸 (*baozhi*, 'newspaper')" published by "国家机关 (*guojia jiguan*, 'state organs')" one can designate it as "机关报 (*jiguanbao*, 'organ newspaper')". On the other hand, one can also illustrate the things indicated by a compound word with other elements, e. g., "大合唱 (*dahechang*, 'chorus')", "垂杨柳 (*chuiyangliu*, 'weeping willow')", "皮上衣 (*pishangyi*, 'pelisse')", and "微电影 (*weidianying*, 'micro film')", etc. The application in this way may lead to that a compound word turns into a compounding semantic morpheme. From the point of view of the relation between words and semantic morphemes, it is also entirely possible for a compound word to turn into a compounding semantic morpheme in the application. This is due to that words and semantic morphemes share common properties: all the other properties of words and semantic morphemes are the same except for differences in properties and functions of the units they serve. This furnishes turning a compound word into a compounding semantic morpheme with a theoretical basis and possibility. It is therefore a certainty of the historical development of vocabulary for compound words to turn into compounding semantic morphemes. At the same time it has been proved that the appearance of a compounding semantic morpheme does not affect the state that the relevant construction keeps on being a compound word. Such a phenomenon cannot be otherwise than indicating that the relevant language element has possessed the properties and functions of a semantic morpheme in addition to those of a word.

48 *Words and semantic morphemes*

A compounding semantic morpheme is different from a simple semantic morpheme though both are semantic morphemes. The major difference lies in that: a simple semantic morpheme co-exists in general with the simple word made up by it, thus many simple semantic morphemes are free semantic morphemes, e. g., "人 (*ren*, 'person')", "天 (*tian*, 'sky')", "葡萄 (*putao*, 'grape')" and "仿佛 (*fangfo*, 'as if')", etc. ; whereas a compounding semantic morpheme is evolved from a compound word through development as a result of the long-time usage of a compound word in linguistic community, thus many compound words turning into compounding semantic morphemes are those with a considerably high frequency of use. Therefore, the compound words with high frequency are firmly fixed and in turn develop into compounding semantic morphemes. Accordingly, the high frequency of use in the linguistic community should be an extremely primary condition for the forming of a compounding semantic morpheme. Just because compounding semantic morphemes originate from compound words and at the very beginning they are combinations of simple semantic morphemes or combinations of simple semantic morphemes and compounding semantic morphemes, they are compounding wholes and words that can be used independently. All compounding semantic morphemes are non-word morphemes. After a compound word turning into a semantic morpheme, it always combines with other semantic morphemes as a non-word semantic morpheme to create a neologism, being just a part in the newly coined word with an integral form.

Because compounding semantic morphemes are evolved out of compound words, the initial forms of compounding semantic morphemes are made up of simple semantic morphemes. What must be made clear is that what the simple semantic morphemes make up are compound words instead of compounding semantic morpheme. In no stage of language growth does there exist the situation in which simple semantic morphemes constitute immediately compounding semantic morphemes, and what they make up are only compound words. Compounding semantic morphemes are evolved from compound words after long time usage and there must be a process of the evolution of compound words. Therefore compounding semantic morphemes are a sort of semantic morphemes resulted from the development and transformation of compound words.

(IV) The function of compounding semantic morphemes

The existence of compounding semantic morphemes is a necessary phenomenon in the continuous development of vocabulary. Compounding semantic morphemes have word-making function just like all other semantic morphemes. In the contemporary Chinese language compound words made up of compounding semantic morphemes with three syllables and more are increasing now in number and some compounding semantic morphemes are fairly productive. For example,

自然 (*ziran*, "natural"):
自然村 (*zirancun*, "natural village") 自然界 (*ziranjie*, "natural world") 自然力 (*ziranli*, "natural force") 自然美 (*ziranmei*, "natural beauty") 自然

法 (*ziranfa*, "natural law") 自然光 (*ziranguang*, "natural light") 自然物 (*ziranwu*, "natural objects") 大自然 (*daziran*, "nature") 自然主义 (*ziranzhuyi*, "naturalism") 自然规律 (*ziranguilü*, "natural law")

旅游 (*lüyou*, "travel; tour"):

旅游团 (*lüyoutuan*, "tourist group") 旅游图 (*lüyoutu*, "tourist map") 旅游者 (*lüyouzhe*, "tourist") 旅游热 (*lüyoure*, "tourist fever") 旅游袋 (*lüyoudai*, "tourist bag") 旅游鞋 (*lüyouxie*, "travel shoes") 旅游车 (*lüyouche*, "tourist bus") 旅游点 (*lüyoudian*, "tourist spots") 旅游帽 (*lüyoumao*, "tourist cap") 旅游装 (*lüyouzhuang*, "tourist outfit")

教育 (*jiaoyu*, "education"):

教育部 (*Jiaoyubu*, "Ministry of Education") 教育家 (*jiaoyujia*, "educator") 教育界 (*jiaoyujie*, "educational circles") 教育司 (*Jiaoyusi*, "Department of Education") 教育厅 (*Jiaoyuting*, "Education Department") 教育局 (*Jiaoyuju*, "Bureau of Education") 教育处 (*Jiaoyuchu*, "Education Section") 教育系 (*jiaoyuxi*, "department of education") 教育学 (*jiaoyuxue*, "pedagogy") 教育网 (*jiaoyuwang*, "education network")

交通 (*jiaotong*, "traffic"):

交通部 (*Jiaotongbu*, "Ministry of Communications") 交通局 (*Jiaotongju*, "Department of Transportation") 交通站 (*jiaotongzhan*, "traffic station") 交通线 (*jiaotongxian*, "traffic line") 交通车 (*jiaotongche*, "traffic vehicle") 交通岛 (*jiaotongdao*, "traffic island") 交通壕 (*jiaotonghao*, "traffic trench") 交通沟 (*jiaotonggou*, "traffic gap") 交通员 (*jiaotongyuan*, "underground messenger") 交通量 (*jiaotongliang*, "taffic volume")

工作 (*gongzuo*, "work"):

工作日 (*gongzuori*, "working day") 工作服 (*gongzuofu*, "work clothes") 工作者 (*gongzuozhe*, "worker") 工作证 (*gongzuozheng*, "employee's card") 工作组 (*gongzuozu*, "working group") 工作团 (*gongzuotuan*, "work team") 工作台 (*gongzuotai*, "workbench") 工作间 (*gongzuojian*, "workshop") 工作面 (*gongzuomian*, "working face") 工作餐 (*gongzuocan*, "working meal")

塑料 (*suliao*, "plastic"):

塑料袋 (*suliaodai*, "plastic bags") 塑料鞋 (*suliaoxie*, "plastic shoes") 塑料盒 (*suliaohe*, "plastic case") 塑料桶 (*suliaotong*, "plastic bucket") 塑料管 (*suliaoguan*, "plastic pipe") 塑料布 (*suliaobu*, "plastic cloth") 塑料板 (*suliaoban*, "plastic sheet") 塑料碗 (*suliaowan*, "plastic bowl") 塑料椅 (*suliaoyi*, "plastic chair") 泡沫塑料 (*paomosuliao*, "plastic foam")

The above compounding semantic morphemes are comparatively strong in productivity. Other compounding semantic morphemes can be used in making up a comparatively small number of compound words, e. g., "土豆 (*tudou*, 'potato')" can be used to make "土豆泥 (*tudouni*, 'mashed potatoe')", "土豆丝 (*tudousi*, 'potato shred')" and "土豆片 (*tudoupian*, 'potato flake')", "前提 (*qianti*, 'premise')" can be used to make "大前提 (*daqianti*, 'major premise')" and "小前提 (*xiaoqianti*, 'minor premise')", "细胞 (*xibao*, 'cell')" can be used to make "白细胞 (*baixibao*, 'white cell')" and "红细胞 (*hongxibao*, 'red cell')"; "包装

(*baozhuang*, 'package')" can be used to make "软包装 (*ruanbaozhuang*, 'soft package')"; "学生 (*xuesheng*, 'student')" can be used to make "学生会 (*xueshenghui*, 'student union')"; "研究 (*yanjiu*, 'research')" can be used to make "研究室 (*yanjiushi*, 'research office')", etc. Such compounding semantic morphemes prevail in contemporary Chinese.

From the above, we can see not only the word-making function of compounding semantic morphemes but also their characteristics of being rapid in reflecting and accurate in expressing social realities and human thoughts in the process of word-making. Thus it can be seen that the forming and existence of compounding semantic morphemes in vocabulary are not only completely inevitable but also entirely necessary.

III Classifications of semantic morphemes

Just like other language elements, the classifications of semantic morphemes can be made from different perspectives. We just make classifications of semantic morphemes on the synchronic plane in accordance with the different scenarios in which semantic morphemes making up words.

(I) The point of view of phonetic form

Semantic morphemes can be classified into monosyllabic semantic morphemes and polysyllabic semantic morphemes from the point of view of phonetic form. Monosyllabic semantic morphemes refer to those having only one syllable, e. g., 人 (*ren*, "people"), 天 (*tian*, "day"), 水 (*shui*, "water"), 山 (*shan*, "mountain"), 手 (*shou*, "hand"), 心 (*xin*, "heart"), 树 (*shu*, "tree"), 草 (*cao*, "grass"), 红 (*hong*, "red"), 光 (*guang*, "light"), 房 (*fang*, "room"), 物 (*wu*, "thing"), 兴 (*xing*, "rise"), 彩 (*cai*, "colour"), 平 (*ping*, "flat"), 面 (*mian*, "face"), 万 (*wan*, "ten thousand"), 千 (*qian*, "thousand"), 十 (*shi*, "ten"), 一 (*yi*, "one") and 二 (*er*, "two"), etc. Polysyllabic semantic morphemes refer to those with two syllables and more, e. g., 葡萄 (*putao*, "grape"), 蟋蟀 (*xishuai*, "cricket"), 蹉跎 (*cuotuo*, "wasted"), 朦胧 (*menglong*, "obscure"), 仿佛 (*fangfo*, "as if"), 忐忑 (*tante*, "disturbed"), 工作 (*gongzuo*, "work"), 旅游 (*lüyou*, "tourism"), 法兰西 (*falanxi*, "France"), 莫斯科 (*Mosike*, "Moscow"), 歇斯底里 (*xiesidili*, "hysteria") and so on.

(II) The point of view of internal structure

Semantic morphemes can be classified into simple semantic morphemes and compounding semantic morphemes from their internal structures. Simple semantic morphemes refer to those having one constituent, e. g., "书 (*shu*, 'book'), 纸 (*zhi*, 'paper'), 证 (*zheng*, 'certificate'), 官 (*guan*, 'officer'), 南 (*nan*, 'south'), 非 (*fei*, 'wrong'), 极 (*ji*, 'extremely'), 逍遥 (*xiaoyao*, 'happy'), 玻璃 (*boli*, 'glass')" and "拷贝 (*kaobei*, 'copy')", etc. Compounding semantic morphemes are those having two constituents and more, e. g., "参谋 (*canmou*, 'adviser'), 催眠 (*cuimian*, 'hypnosis'), 黄牛 (*huangniu*, 'cattle'), 美术 (*meishu*, 'fine arts'), 矛盾 (*maodun*, 'contradiction'), 科学 (*kexue*, 'science')" and so on.

(III) The point of view of linguistic function

From the point of view of linguistic function, semantic morphemes fall into two types: free semantic morphemes and bound semantic morphemes. Free semantic morphemes refer to those that can not only make up new words with other semantic morphemes, but also can form new words alone, i. e., they can occur as separate words per se, e. g., "花 (*hua*, 'flower'), 好 (*hao*, 'good'), 多 (*duo*, 'many'), 玫瑰 (*meigui*, 'rose') and 柠檬 (*ningmeng*, 'lemon')", etc. Bound semantic morphemes are those which are bound to other semantic morphemes to form new words instead of forming separate words per se, e. g., "策 (*ce*, 'policy'), 希 (*xi*, 'hope'), 访 (*fang*, 'interview'), 昌 (*chang*, 'flourishing'), 朴 (*pu*, 'simple'), 毕 (*bi*, 'finish'), 研 (*yan*, 'study'), 幽 (*you*, 'quiet'), 迫 (*po*, 'forced'), 恰 (*qia*, 'just'), 首 (*shou*, 'first'), 咨 (*zi*, 'consult')" and so on. The typology of semantic morphemes may change in the process of the development of language; therefore the typology of a semantic morpheme must be determined from a synchronic perspective. As far as Chinese is concerned, many free semantic morphemes in ancient Chinese turn into bound ones in contemporary Chinese. The following elements are all like this. In ancient Chinese,

民 (*min*): One can say "利于民而不利于君" (*The 13th Year of Duke Wen, Zuo Zhuan* (*The Zuo's Commentary*)), the word "民" means "common people".

兴 (*xing*): One can say "汉兴, 至孝文四十有余载" (*Annals of the Xiaowen Emperor, Records of the Grand Historian*), the word "兴" means "to rise; to establish".

习 (*xi*): One can say "民习以力攻难, 故轻死" (*Zhan Fa, Shangjun Shu*), the word "习" means "to get used to".

敏 (*min*): One can say "敏于事而慎于言" (*Xue Er, Analects of Confucius*), the word "敏" means "fast", "prompt".

务 (*wu*): One can say "务耕织" (*On the Fault of Qin*), the word "务" means "to dedicate on", "to undertake".

It can be seen that these elements appeared as separate words in the past and that the semantic morphemes that constitute these words were all free semantic morphemes. In contemporary Chinese, however, they cannot be otherwise than bound semantic morphemes to be used to form words with others.

In contemporary Chinese, as far as free semantic morphemes and bound semantic morphemes are concerned, in addition to the above cases, we should pay due attention to the matter that loan semantic morphemes come to be recognized by the community of Chinese.

With the continuous borrowing of loan elements, not only loan words appear in Chinese, but also loan semantic morphemes gradually come into being. For the present, loan semantic morphemes fall into two categories. The first type is transliterated elements turning into semantic morphemes. Some of the transliterated elements appear as free semantic morphemes at the same time as they are borrowed as loan words into Chinese. Currently they can be used to form new words with other semantic morphemes after years of development.

For example, "咖啡 (*kafei*, 'coffee')" can not only appear as a separate word, but can also be used to make up such words as "咖啡茶 (*kafeicha*, 'coffee tea')" and "咖啡糖 (*kafeitang*, 'coffee candy')". Others of the transliterated elements were only part in a loan word, but can now be used to make up new words together with other semantic morphemes. For example, "啤 (*pi*)" in "啤酒 (*pijiu*, 'beer')" can now be used as an element to constitute such words as "青啤 (*qingpi*, 'Qingdao beer')" and "扎啤 (*zhapi*, 'draught beer')", etc. and "的 (*di*)" in "的士 (*dishi*, 'taxi')" can now be used as an element to compose such words as "打的 (*dadi*, 'take taxi')", "面的 (*miandi*, 'van taxi')" and "轿的 (*jiaodi*, 'saloon taxi')", etc. Such semantic morphemes are all bound semantic morphemes for the time being. The second type is letters directly introduced from foreign languages, e. g., "B" in "B超 (B *chao*, 'B-ultrasound')" and "O" in "O型环 (O *xinghuan*, 'O-ring')". Of course all of these types of semantic morphemes are bound semantic morphemes because they cannot appear as separate words per se.

(IV) The point of view of properties and meaning expression

From the point of view of the properties and meaning expression, semantic morphemes can be divided into root semantic morphemes and affixes. Root semantic morphemes are usually called roots, which possess concrete lexical meanings and are the major parts in the stems of new words and also the main carriers of the lexical meanings of the new words. For example, "人 (*ren*, 'man')", "心 (*xin*, 'heart')", "小 (*xiao*, 'small')", " 水 (*shui*, 'water')", "核 (*he*, 'core')", "心 (*xin*, 'heart')", "光 (*guang*, 'light')", "明 (*ming*, 'bright')", "实 (*shi*, 'actual')", "力 (*li*, 'strength')", "人 (*ren*, 'man')", "造 (*zao*, 'make')", "革 (*ge*, 'leather')", "日 (*ri*, 'day')", "计 (*ji*, 'schedule')", "表 (*biao*, 'table')", "录像 (*luxiang*, 'videotape')", "带 (*dai*, 'belt')", "冷 (*leng*, 'cold')" and "处理 (*chuli*, 'treatment')" in such words as "人 (*ren*, 'man')", "心 (*xin*, 'heart')", "小 (*xiao*, 'small')", "水 (*shui*, 'water')", 核心 (*hexin*, 'core'), "光明 (*guangming*, 'light')", "实力 (*shili*, 'actual strength')", "人造革 (*renzaoge*, 'artificial leather')", "日计表 (*rijibiao*, 'daily schedule')", "录像带 (*luxiangdai*, 'videotape')" and "冷处理 (*lengchuli*, 'cold treament')" are all root semantic morphemes. It is quite obvious at the same time that the root semantic morphemes constitute the stems of the above words respectively and carry the lexical meanings of the new words. Hence it follows that root semantic morphemes are the fundamental components of the semantic morphemes and their status and functions in semantic morphemes are extremely important. Chinese abounds in root semantic morphemes. Free semantic morphemes and most bound semantic morphemes can be used as root semantic morphemes. It is on such a basis that a multitude of enormous neologisms in Chinese are created unceasingly.

Affixes are semantic morphemes indicating grammatical meanings and certain additional lexical meanings attached to root semantic morphemes. Affixes can be further divided into derivational affixes and endings. These semantic morphemes are all structural components of words and belong to semantic morphemes. They are all bound semantic morphemes of course because they are attached to root semantic morphemes.

Derivational affixes are usually referred to as affixes that can be attached to roots to form stems; therefore affixes are also semantic morphemes constituting stems. Derivational affixes can be divided into prefixes, infixes and suffixes. Prefixes come before the root semantic morphemes, e. g., "老 (*lao*), 阿 (*a*), 第 (*di*), 初 (*chu*)" in "老虎 (*laohu*, 'tiger'), 阿姨 (*ayi*, 'aunt'), 第一 (*diyi*, 'first'), 初五 (*chuwu*, 'the fifth day of a lunar month')" respectively. Infixes come between root semantic morphemes and are scarce in Chinese. Suffixes are attached to the end of each root semantic morpheme. For example, "头 (*tou*), 子 (*zi*), 儿 (*er*), 巴 (*ba*), 家 (*jia*), 乎乎 (*huhu*), 溜溜 (*liuliu*)" in "石头 (*shitou*, 'stone'), 甜头 (*tiantou*, 'benefit'), 桌子 (*zhuozi*, 'table'), 担子 (*danzi*, 'burden'), 鸟儿 (*niao'er*, 'bird'), 泥巴 (*niba*, 'mud'), 尾巴 (*weiba*, 'tail'), 姑娘家 (*guniangjia*, 'lassie'), 孩子家 (*haizijia*, 'kid') and 黄乎乎 (*huanghuhu*, 'yellowish'), 滑溜溜 (*hualiuliu*, 'slippery')" are all suffixes.

Inflectional suffixes are those attached to the end of stems to indicate grammatical meanings, which are usually referred to as endings. That a word has an ending can only indicate that the word has got a morphological change for a grammatical meaning, but not means that a new word is coined, because an ending is only an inflectional morpheme for morphological change of a word with no function to form another word, when it is attached to a word as a structural component, no new word will be coined.

Affixes are grammaticalized from roots in general. After long-time application, the lexical meaning of a root may be vacated and weakened due to the interaction of application habit and application conditions, and turned into an affix indicating a certain grammatical meaning. For example, such suffixes as "头 (*tou*)" and "子 (*zi*)" indicating grammatical meanings of noun are like this, whose meanings here are never their original lexical meanings at all. Such elements as "性 (*xing*)" and "化 (*hua*)" in contemporary Chinese have experienced a quite long process of grammaticalization and it is well established that they can be used as suffixes, but there are still obvious reminiscences of their lexical meanings. Because such so-called semi-affixes as "师 (*shi*)", "员 (*yuan*)", "手 (*shou*)" and "热 (*re*)" have evident lexical meanings and appear as roots in real application, it is suitable not to treat them as affixes.

What should be pointed out here is that when some roots become derivational affixes, it does not mean that the properties of the root have already vanished. As a matter of fact, a new and completely independent affix has been grown out of the original root due to the process of grammaticalization in linguistic application. Therefore, the root semantic morphemes and affixes co-exist in these morphemes and perform actively functions of their own. For example, "子 (*zi*)" in "棋子 (*qizi*, 'chess piece')" is a root while it is an affix in "桌子 (*zhuozi*, 'table')": they co-exist with obvious distinctions.

54 *Words and semantic morphemes*

Based on the above classifications, we can sum up the types of morphemes in the following diagram:

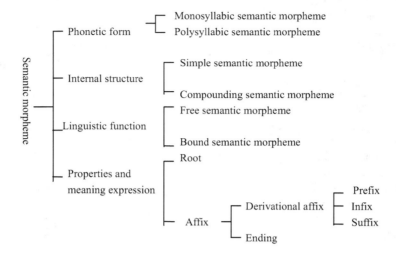

3 The emergence and structural forms of words

Section 1 The emergence of words

I *The ways through which words coming into being*

Language is a sign systems in which words are fundamental units: either language or speech is unthinkable without words because words are basic elements in utterance.

What is obvious to all is that vocabulary is the most active part of language and new words and expressions are generated with the development of society and the appearance of novelties so as to meet the needs of social communications. How on earth do words come into being?

In three perspectives can one probe into the ways in which words come into being following the trace of words. They are, first, neologisms are created by word coinage (see the next section please for the detailed explanation); second, phrases are conventionalized into words. "国家 (*guojia*, 'country')", "妻子 (*qizi*, 'wife')" and "朋友 (*pengyou*, 'friend')" are cases in point: they were all coordinative phrases in ancient Chinese and later on they turned into subordination compounds; third, forms of inflectional morphology of words evolve into independent words, such as "我们 (*women*, 'we')", "你们 (*nimen*, 'you')", "冷清清 (*lengqingqing*, 'cold and cheerless')" and "慢悠悠 (*manyouyou*, 'unhurriedly')", which were all forms of inflectional morphology of such words as "我 (*wo*, 'I')", 你 (*ni*, 'you')", "冷清 (*lengqing*, 'desolate')" and "慢悠 (*manyou*, 'slowly')" respectively, are now conventionalized into words. Therefore the above-mentioned three perspectives can be regarded as three ways through which words come into being.

II *Conditions for words coming into being*

No word comes into being from nothing; therefore, the prerequisite conditions for words coming into being are to be discussed before turning into the emergence of words. As a matter of fact, there exist two preconditions for any word to come into being: the cognition of human beings on objective things and the relevant thinking activities on the one side and the linguistic elements with the linguistic sign system of one's own ethnic groups as their substance on the other.

(I) The cognition and thinking activities of people

It is safe to say that the emergence of any word is an outcome of people's cognition and thinking on objective things. The cognition and thinking activities of people can not only bring about the birth of a word but also determine whether it can be socially conventionalized because it is only a component in parole of temporary nature after a word comes into being and only after being socially conventionalized can it turn into an element in language.

The issue of emergence of words is inevitably connected with how words come into being, i. e., the origin of language. The community of scholars has expressed various views on the origin of language and no consensus has been reached yet; therefore it will not be discussed here. We just offer our own opinions on the emergence of words. Because the cognition and thinking activities are prerequisites for the emergence of words, the first words are generated like this: on the basis of the cognition of the objective world, the outcome of cognition is combined with a certain materialized sound and the outcome of cognition turns into the meaning of a word and the materialized sound turns into its pronunciation thus a word comes into being. The meaning of a word is always the reflection of the objective things in people's mind, whether it is true or not; without the objective things or people's cognition and thinking activities on them, there will be no meaning formed forever; without meaning, which is combined with sound and expressed by sound, there will be no word; therefore, the birth of words is based upon the cognition and thinking of people in the very beginning. Of course, when the first words come into being, imaginal thinking is the principal part in the thinking activities of people, but one must admit that imaginal thinking undoubtedly belongs to thinking activities and it is an active part in the thinking activities of people even in modern times. Therefore, one cannot deny the significance of imaginal thinking in the forming of words. Without any credible records, we can only reach the conclusion on the basis of linguistic theory that the first words are brought into existence with the arbitrary combination of sound and meaning by imaginal thinking of people.

With the progressive development of society, the cognitive and mental capacities of people are also developed and enriched unceasingly; therefore, the function of cognition and thinking activities in the word emergence during the course of language development is all the more evident. All members of a linguistic community can participate in word coinage with their own cognitive and mental capacities: they can not only coin onomatopoeic words with their cognition on sound, but also produce many different kinds of words with different cognitions of things from different points of view. It is even more obvious to all that people can apprehend the objective world, create novelties and discover new phenomena so as to make neologisms in order to flourish social communicative activities and promote the progressive development of society. Consequently, there will be no word to be brought into existence without the cognition and thinking activities of people and the cognition and thinking activities of people are always one of the prerequisites for word formation.

(II) Language elements as the foundation of word formation

Another prerequisite for word formation is language elements. In the very beginning, when words are brought into existence, language elements are born at the same time; but after that, various materials in language elements are becoming more and more important as the basic conditions for word formation. Various words are made based on the original materials with such means as derivation and combination, etc.

Language elements used in word coinage are manifold: not only those in speech sound, vocabulary and grammar, but also those in writing and rhetoric are employed.

Speech sound: the timbre phonemes and non-timbre phonemes in the mother tongue and the combination laws and variations of phonemes can all be used in word coinage. All these language materials are in objective existence of language used by the members of society and are mastered consciously or unconsciously by people; therefore, whether people have scientific cognition of these elements or not, they can use them in accordance with the language habit of the linguistic community. For example, the word "喳喳" for bird croaking with the phonetic form of "*zhazha*" is created with onomatopoeia according to the combination law of initials, finals and tones of Chinese speech sound.

Vocabulary: various semantic morphemes in vocabulary supply rich and colourful materials for word formation. After language is in existence, the vast majority of new words are produced with the combinations of the original semantic morphemes; therefore, the situation of the combination of sound and meaning of the semantic morphemes already in existence has a direct influence on the appearance of the words to be coined. For example, "转椅 (*zhuanyi*, 'revolving chair')" is a chair that revolves, so the two component semantic morphemes "转, *zhuan*, 'revolving'" in "转动 (*zhuandong*, 'revolving')" and '椅 (*yi*, 'chair')" in "椅子 (*yizi*, 'chair')" are picked out to combine into the new word "转椅" with both the phonetic form and meaning content of the two original semantic morphemes brought into the new word and a new conventionalized construction with sound and meaning is thus formed. Numerous neologisms are thus created one after another in the development of vocabulary.

Grammar: the combination of semantic morphemes in word formation follows the relevant grammatical rules which are all conventionalized just like other language materials as part of the consensus of the linguistic community. For example, in accordance with the grammatical rule of "modifier-the modified", when referring to a red Chinese date, one must use the order of "红枣 (*hongzao*, red date, 'a red date')", whereas when referring to the colour of a date, one must reverse the order into "枣红 (*zaohong*, date red, 'as red as a date')". The language materials such as these are all conventionalized in language use and naturally act as the language foundation in the process of word formation.

Writing: various characteristics and contents of Chinese writing system are employed in word formation by those who have a certain command of written ability. For example, "丘八 (*qiuba*, 'soldier')" is coined in accordance with the combination characteristics of Chinese characters in shape. The definition for 丘八 in *The Contemporary Chinese Dictionary* is "(old, derog.) soldier, whose Chinese character, 兵 (*bing*) is composed of 丘 (*qiu*) and 八 (*ba*), hence the term 丘八". Such a way of using disassembly of Chinese character as semantic morphemes in word coinage is comparatively frequent: e. g., "弓长 (*gong chang*)" in "弓长张 (*gong chang zhang*)" and "立早 (*li zao*)" in "立早章 (*li zao zhang*)" are both cases in point. Characteristics of Chinese character pattern are more often than not used as semantic morphemes in word coinage. For instance, "丁 (*ding*)" in "丁字尺 (*dingzichi*, 'T-shaped ruler')", "一 (*yi*)" in "一字领 (*yiziling*, 'horizontal collar')", "八 (*ba*)" in "八字眉 (*bazimei*, 'slant eyebrows')" and "十" in "十字架 (*shizijia*, 'cross')" are all fair examples. It is obvious that the meanings of these new words are derived under the participation of the shape of the relevant Chinese characters. Nowadays, with the continuous introduction of loan morphemes, the forms of foreign letters are often used as semantic morphemes in word coinage: e. g., the O and V in "O形环 (*O-xinghuan*, 'O-ring')" and "V字领 (*V-ziling*, 'V-collar')" are both cases in point.

Rhetoric: rhetoric is the method and means of employing language and rhetoric devices are often used in word coinage. For example, a nail like "螺丝 (*luosi*, 'screw')" in shape is called "螺丝钉 (*luosiding*, 'screw spike')"; a toy like a "马 (*ma*, 'horse')" made of "木头 (*mutou*, 'wood')" is called "木马 (*muma*, 'wooden horse')"; even the jettison valve on the pressure water pipe is called "龙头 (*longtou*, 'dragon head' literally, 'faucet')" or "水龙头 (*shuilongtou*, 'water dragon head' literally, 'faucet')" because the way in which the water coming out of it. All these are the outcomes of the word coinage on the basis of rhetoric devices.

Language is an integrated whole and the elements of all perspectives of language are involved simultaneously in word coinage. Meanwhile, because the sound-meaning combination is relatively stable even though there is no inevitable connection between sound and meaning of the linguistic sign, one cannot change the combination once it is conventionalized by the linguistic community. For instance, when creating the words like "汽车 (*qiche*, 'automobile')", "火车 (*huoche*, 'train')" and "自行车 (*zixingche*, 'bicycle')", one can neither substitute "车 (*che*, 'car')" for "船 (*chuan*, 'ship')", nor can he change the phonetic form of "车", let alone reverse the order of the relevant syllables at will. It thus can be seen from this that the elements of every respect of language are not only the foundation for creating new words, but also have a certain constraining function to various aspects of word coinage as an integrated unity of language elements.

It is quite natural and inevitable that one uses language elements as the foundation for word coinage: now that one acquires language and gets familiar with language rules, one will inevitably use the language materials and rules to coin new words and it is impossible not to do so for the nature of inheritance and conventionalization of language.

The above is a brief account of the two conditions for word formation, which are interactive with each other in the process of word formation. With the development of society and the gradual abundance of language materials and the step-by-step enhance of people's ability in language use, the functions of these conditions are becoming more and more prominent and evident. It is well-known that one basic nature of language is its arbitrariness, yet a certain motivation can be found in the process of word formation as the foundation and condition for a word to be brought into existence, i. e., word formation comes to possess a certain motivation. Take "三角尺 (*sanjiaochi*, 'triangular ruler')" as an example: because the word is composed of three semantic morphemes "三 (*san*, 'three')", "角 (*jiao*, 'angle')" and "尺 (*chi*, 'ruler')", it is natural for one to take the meaning of the word "三角尺" as "a ruler with three angles". As for "唉 (*ai*, 'alas')", because it is an imitation of people's sigh, it is also natural for one to take it as an onomatopoeic word expressing "the sound of sigh", which is just what is expressed by the word itself. The motivation for word coinage and comprehension lies exactly in that the two prerequisites go together in word formation: the motivation and comprehensibility in word formation come from the intercommunity of people's cognition and thinking and the consensus on the language materials involved in word coinage.

One must be clear that when we talk about the motivation in word formation, without doubt, the recognition of the motivation of word formation does not equal the denial of the arbitrariness of sound-meaning combination because the motivation and arbitrariness stands in unity of opposites instead of contradiction: the motivation is one under the arbitrariness and the arbitrariness is one based on the motivation. For instance, "卷心菜 (*juanxincai*, 'headed cabbage')" and "大头菜 (*datoucai*, 'headed cabbage')" are both words with a certain motivation created from the shape of the vegetable; whereas the arbitrariness lies in the fact that one and the same objective thing can be called either "卷心菜" or "大头菜". It can be seen from this that any word formed on the motivation can be arbitrarily picked up under the constraint of arbitrariness.

III The base form of a word

The base form of a word refers to a language form based on which a word is created. In the very beginning of the language, the foundation of words is the thinking of people and the concrete and objective things in existence: a word is created when a certain sound form is combined with the meaning content of a certain thing through the cognition and thinking activities of people. Thus the meanings of the first words are usually in good correspondence with the contents of the objective things they refer to. After the appearance of language, a base language form usually comes first on the foundation of the objective existence through the cognition and thinking activities of people in word formation because language materials are involved in this process. In general, the base form of a word appears in the form of a word or a phrase. It can be assumed that the base form of this type is the rudiment of the relevant word in general, because the form and meaning of that word derives from the base form: a word is formed on the foundation of the base form. Every word is refined and condensed from its base form and every word has the base form upon which it is generated. Consequently, the form, the meaning and the structure of a word can be well explained and illustrated from its base form.

60 *The emergence and structural forms of words*

It is of great necessity to learn about the base form of a word. The formation and development of a word must be traced back to the base form upon which it is generated. Take the common word "夏至 (*Xiazhi*)" as an example: two different understandings of its meaning prevail, i. e., "Summer Solstice ('the climax of summer' literally)" vs. "the Beginning of Summer ('the establishment of summer' literally)". The issue can be settled by investigating its base form: in ancient China, 'the Beginning of Summer' was expressed by "立夏 (*Lixia*, 'the Establishment of Summer')" with "夏季到了 (*xiajidaole*, 'summer comes')" as its base form, whereas "夏至" was thought of as "夏季的极点 (*xiajidejidian*, 'the climax of summer')"; therefore the base form of "夏至" is "the climax of summer". Thus, only after one learns about the base form of the word formation can he grasp and interpret the meaning of a word and can he make a correct investigation and analysis of the etymology of a word.

The base form of a word is an outcome of the cognition and thinking activities of people, thus there exist different base forms due to different methods and ways for the base forms to come about because the points of view for people to investigate and observe the things are different. From the point of view of the forms of expression, the base forms of a word can be classified into the following three different types considering the three ways of word formation:

(I) A word as the base form

To use a word as the base form refers to the case in which a new word is derived on the basis of an original word. Under the interaction of subjective and/or objective conditions, a new element is derived on the basis of an old word through association, semantic extension, transformation and even the alteration and adjustment of the language elements in themselves and a new word is formed after the conventionalization of the members of society. The neologisms thus formed undoubtedly take the original words as the base form; the sound, meaning, appearance and structure of the newly combined word can all be traced back to the original old word.

New words derived from the word base form can be classified into the following types:

1   A new word is formed out of the sound change of the original one, e. g. :

  盖 (*gai*, "to cover") – 盖儿 (*gair*, "a cover")
  扣 (*kou*, "to button") – 扣儿 (*kour*, "a button")
  传 (*chuan*, "impart and inherit") – 传 (*zhuan*, "biography")

2   A new word is formed out of the semantic extension from the original one, e. g. :

  刻 (*ke*, "to carve") – 刻 (*ke*, "a quarter of an hour")

3   A disyllabic word derived from a monosyllabic word, e. g. :

  姑 (*gu*, "aunt") – 姑姑 (*gugu*, "aunt")
  弟 (*di*, "younger brother") – 弟弟 (*didi*, "younger brother")

4   A loan word derived from an alien word with the alien word as the base form, e. g. :

sofa – 沙发 (*shafa*, "sofa")
Coca-Cola – 可口可乐 (*Kekou Kele*, "Coca-Cola")

5   A word is derived from an inflectional form of the word with the original word before being inflected as the base form, e. g. :

慢悠 (*manyou*, "slow") – 慢悠悠 (*manyouyou*, "unhurriedly")
空荡 (*kongdang*, "empty") – 空荡荡 (*kongdangdang*, "empty")

Whether a word can be used as a base form to derive new words depends upon the conditions for word generation and the conditions of conventionalization and it is not that all words can be used as the base forms of the foundation for neologism-creation. Take inflectional morphology as an example: "我们 (*women*, 'we')", an inflectional form of "我 (*wo*, 'I')", has been conventionalized as a word, whereas "学生们 (*xueshengmen*, 'students')" and "朋友们 (*pengyoumen*, 'friends')", which are inflections of "学生 (*xuesheng*, 'student')" and "朋友 (*pengyou*, 'friend')" respectively, are still inflections; they have not been accepted as independent words yet.

(II) A phrase as the base form

To use a phrase as the base form of a word means that a new word is derived on the foundation of the linguistic form of a phrase. The case of this category is comparatively complicated and they fall into the following types:

1   The foundation of the new word is a phrase expressing a concept, e. g. :

洗衣服用的机器 ("a machine for washing clothes") – 洗衣机 ("washing machine")
挂在窗户上的帘子 ("a curtain hung on the window") – 窗帘 ("window curtain")
需要蘸着墨水写字的钢笔 ("a pen to write after dipping ink") – 蘸水笔 ("dip pen")

The base form of this type is often utilized by people and it is comparatively complicated to discriminate and analyze. Owing to the differences in ways of thinking of different people, some concepts are simple while others are complicated. Under such circumstances, then, how do we determine the base form of a word? As has been pointed out, the conditions for semantic morphemes to come into being should be taken into account first in determining the base form of a word: first, in creating a new word based on the phrase expressing the relevant concept, simplicity is of the primary priority, i. e., the meaning of the phrase must be clear; second, semantic morphemes can be drawn from the phrase directly or indirectly; third, choose the structural form of the phrase as simple as possible if they express the similar meanings. Consequently, the phrase acting as the base form of a word can reflect all or part of the characteristics of people's understanding, and so long as semantic morphemes can be drawn and the content of people's understanding can be explicitly reflected, the simplest phrase form will be the base form of the new word. Take "活捉 (*huozhuo*, 'capture alive')" as an example: both the phrases "用手或工具把人或动物活活地捉住 (*yong shou huo gongju ba ren huo dongwu huohuo de zhuozhu*, 'to capture alive a man or an animal with a hand or a tool')" and "活活地捉住 (*huohuo de zhuozhu*, 'to capture alive')" can express the meaning of the word, the latter, however, is simpler and more concise; therefore one takes it as the base form of the word "活捉". Another example is "活水 (*huoshui*, 'flowing water')": it may be derived from two phrase forms, i. e., "有源头而常流动的水 (*you yuantou er chang liudong de shui*, 'running water flowing from a source')" and "常流动的水 (*chang liudong de shui*, 'running water')", while the latter cannot explicitly express the meaning of the word; therefore, the former is the simplest and most concise form, thus it is the base form of the word under the requirement of definitely and truthfully expressing the meaning.

Of course, the simple and concise phrase form and the complex one are always connected in meaning and even exactly the same sometimes because they share the same cognitive content. Consequently, one can trace back to the situation of its complex phrase after having an understanding of the base form of a word in order to have a still further understanding of the word formation in more detail. If a word has a simple and concise phrase as base form, its semantic morphemes, the immediate constituents of the word, are extracted in a direct or indirect way out of the base form. For example, the two component semantic morphemes "活" and "捉" in the word "活捉" are both extracted directly and for the two component semantic morphemes "活" and "水" in the word "活水", "水" is extracted directly while "活" is extracted indirectly.

Such phrases being the base form of a word are basically of illustration in nature. For example, one uses phrases of this kind to illustrate an object, an action or a phenomenon, etc. When coining new words with the rhetorical method of personification, one also uses phrases of this kind as the base form, because the words are formed on the understanding of the similarities between things and expressed by a certain utterance where such rhetorical devices as metaphor etc. are employed: for example, "虎口 (*hukou*)" is illustrated as "part of the hand between the thumb and the index finger", "佛手 (*foshou*)" is illustrated as "an evergreen shrub with bright-yellow fruits that give the shape of a half-open hand". Metaphorical contents are included in such phrases and the metaphors of illustrative nature are the base form for the relevant words to come into being and these are also the foundation of the forms and contents of the new words.

It is quite natural for people to use a phrase of illustrative nature as the base form of a new word, because a phrase expressing a concept is first created in the cognitive process before a word expressing the same concept is coined.

2. A fixed phrase or high-frequency phrase abbreviated into a word with the original phrase as the base form of the abbreviate. For example,

外交部长 (*Waijiao Buchang*, "Foreign Minister") – 外长 (*Waizhang*)
山东大学 (*Shandong Daxue*, "Shandong University") – 山大 (*Shanda*)

科学技术 (*kexue jishu*, "science and technology") – 科技 (*keji*)
文化教育 (*wenhua jiaoyu*, "culture and education") – 文教 (*wenjiao*)
人民代表大会 (*Renmin Daibiao Dahui*, "People's Congress") – 人代会 (*Rendaihui*)
政治协商会议 (*Zhengzhi Xieshang Huiyi*, "Political Consultative Conference") – 政协 (*Zhengxie*)

3   A conventional phrase conventionalized into a word with the original phrase as the base form of the new word. For example,

国家 (*guojia*, "country")
窗户 (*chuanghu*, "window")
妻子 (*qizi*, "wife")
朋友 (*pengyou*, "friend")

(III) The sound in nature as the base form

Natural sound can also be the base form for a new word and onomatopoeic words are thus formed. This type of base form is comparatively special: it is the sound in nature, so it is an objective existence and onomatopoeic words take form out of the speech imitation of the sounds in nature. For example, the word "砰 (*peng*, 'ping')" in "砰的一声木板倒了 (*peng de yisheng muban dao le*, 'the wood block falls in a ping')" is an onomatopoeic word after the sound in nature and it takes the natural sound as its base form.

All onomatopoeic words in language are created after processing based on the imitation of the sounds in nature. The so-called processing refers to the process of reconstructing the sounds with speech sounds of human language. Sounds in nature are varied: some are simple, such as the above-mentioned "砰"; others are comparatively complex, such as the snores of human beings are "呼噜呼噜 (*hulu hulu*)", one after another instead of only once, but the grunts in Chinese is just one "呼噜 (*hulu*)", as a result of clipping just one segment of a succession of snores. In Chinese, the form "呼噜" can serve as two words: one stands for an onomatopoeic word of snoring, the other a noun indicating the phenomenon of snoring. This fact reflects evidently the situation of the processing of people's thinking. In whichever case, natural sounds are the base for these words coming into being.

Transliterations, in addition, come from imitating sounds of some kind and it is the sounds of alien words that are imitated, so the sounds of alien words are the base forms of transliterations.

Section 2 Word coinage and word formation

I An overview of word coinage

(I) What is word coinage?

Word coinage entails the creation of neologisms. It refers to the process of the birth of a new word. The purpose of word coinage is to meet the needs of social

64 *The emergence and structural forms of words*

communications: the development of objective things and people's understanding, the appearance of novelties and new phenomena and the development and adjustment of language per se will all put forward requirements for word coinage. Words in language are created to meet such requirements. People from generation to generation create various neologisms to meet the needs of social communications in the process of language development. Therefore, to investigate the formation of a neologism, one must investigate the condition and process of its formation, and most neologisms are created through various word formation, so word coinage is of first importance for the problem of word appearance.

As with the formation of all words, word coinage must meet the two prerequisites for word emergence: the cognition and thinking activities of people and the available language materials. As this has been discussed earlier, I will not repeat it here.

(II) Word coinage activities

Word coinage activities are carried out to meet the demands of social communications, and every social member can coin words in accordance with the need of communication; therefore word coinage activities are extensive ones in which all members of a society can take part. In word coinage activities, the cognition and thinking activities of people are of great importance: they are decisive, because neologisms are all created with the external actualization of linguistic materials through people's cognition and association in accordance with specific environments and conditions with the continuous springing up of novelties and new phenomena. As a matter of fact, such a word coinage activity is people's designation process of novelties and new phenomena. For example,

> The coinage of "落星湾 (*Luoxing Wan*)" and "落星石 (*Luoxing Shi*)":
>
> > There is an arm of lake named "落星湾" with a derrick stone in it called "落星石" within the northern lake of Poyang Lake on the southern foot of Lushan Mountain. The name of "落星湾 (*Luoxing Wan*, 'Falling Star Bay')" is named after the derrick stone named "落星石 (*Luoxing Shi*, 'Falling Star Stone')" within it. The name "落星石" originates from the legend that the stone was a meteor falling into the lake from the sky. Consequently it is held by the people in the lake region that "the stone in the lake today was the star from the sky".[1]
>
> The coinage of "响沙湾 (*Xiangsh Wan*)" and "落笔洞 (*Luobi Dong*)":
>
> > Sounding Sand Bay (响沙湾, *Xiangsha Wan*) of Dalad Banner in the east end of Hobq Desert is a sand hill with 50 meters in width and 40 meters in height. When one glides down from the dune crest or moves the sand with hand, whoops like airplanes or automobiles will come out from the sands; thus people call the bay "Sounding Sand Bay".[2]

Falling Pen Cave (落笔洞, *Luobi Dong*) is located at the northern suburbs of Sanya Town, Ya County of Hainan Island. It is a karst cave beside an isolated limestone peak with 3 *li* in circumference and several hundred meters in height. It is named after the beetling stalactites in the cave.[3]

Another example is the origin of "eight officers" (eight words with the semantic morpheme "员, *yuan*, 'officer'"). According to Lai Yuming, the former Director of Health Station of the 129 Division of the Eighth Route Army[4]:

> One day after the beginning of Great Campaign with One Hundred Regiments in 1940, the Feeder Department send us some canned food captured from the Japanese armies and the Chief decided to share the food with the support staff. I went to the courtyard and shouted: "伙夫 (*huofu*, "cooks")! 马夫 (*mafu*, "stablemen")! 卫兵 (*weibing*, "guardsmen")! 号兵 (*haobing*, "trumpeters")! All come on and here are the delicious!" . . . . . . The next day, Comrade Liu Bocheng summoned me to his office and asked me: "Our 伙夫, 马夫 and other staff men should have a better title and this is serious: it is a great matter for our revolutionary household and officers and men in our army are all equal and we are all members of the revolutionary family. From now on, 伙夫(*huofu*) is called 炊事员 (*chuishiyuan*, 'cooking officer'), 马夫(*mafu*) is called 饲养员 (*siyangyuan*, 'breeding officer'), 挑夫 (*tiaofu*) is called 运输员 (*yunshuyuan*, 'transporting officer'), 卫兵 (*weibing*) is called 警卫员(*jingweiyuan*, 'guarding officer'), 号兵 (*haobing*) is called 司号员(*sihaoyuan*, 'signalling officer'), 勤务兵 (*qinwubing*) is called 公务员(*gongwuyuan*, 'serving officer'), 卫生兵(*weishengbing*) is called 卫生员 (*weishengyuan*, 'medical officer') and 理发师傅 (*lifa shifu*) is called 理发员 (*lifayuan*, 'barbering officer') . . . We the people's armies are courtesy and civilized armies and the titles also should be civilized." . . . There was no people therefrom in the organ of the 129 Division who yelled such title as "伙夫 (*huofu*)" or "马夫 (*mafu*)", etc. Soon the titles of "eight officers" spread over the liberated area.

It can be seen from this that the word coinage activity is a designation activity based on the people's cognition. In word coinage, one and the same object may sometimes have different names due to different points of view of people's cognition and consideration. For example, "西湖 (*Xi Hu*, 'West Lake')" and "西子湖 (*Xizi Hu*, 'Xizi Lake')" are two different names for one and the same lake: "西湖" is named out of the fact that it is located in the west of Hangzhou and "西子湖" is out of that the beautifulness of the lake can be compared to that of Xi Shi, one of the four famous beauties in ancient China. Another example is the story of "国庆桃 (*Guoqing Tao*, 'the National Day peach')" in the article the *National Day Peach in the Summer Palace* on *Beijing Evening Newspaper*:

> Is there any relation between the National Day and peach? The answer is "yes".
> A late ripening peach was nurtured by the Summer Palace and it ripens in

September of the solar calendar and can be picked up during the National Day every year.

The peach is named "秋红 (*Qiuhong*, 'Red in autumn')" and is also called "颐红 (*Yihong*, 'Red in the Summer Palace')". It is as red as cinnabar with light green and the red passed through the whole flesh of the peach. . . .[5]

From the above quotation one can not only have a further understanding of the word coinage process from the birth of such words as "国庆桃", "秋红桃" and "颐红桃", but also have a clear awareness that the appearance of the neologisms will be directly influenced by the points of view of people's cognition. One and the same peach can be called "国庆桃" from the point of view of the picking-up time, "秋红桃" from the fact that it ripens in autumn and has a red colour, and "颐红桃" from the fact that it is produced in the Summer Palace and has a red colour.

Such word coinage activities and word formation prevail in the whole history of the development of vocabulary and the neologisms created with such means in modern social life are extremely common. For example, "晨练 (*chenlian*, 'morning exercises')" for "早晨起来进行身体锻炼的活动 (exercises done in morning)", "肉鸡 (*rouji*, 'table hen')" for "专门饲养以食其肉为目的的鸡 (the chicken specially bred for eating)", "网虫 (*wangchong*, 'web worms; netter')" for "迷于在电脑网上玩游戏或聊天的人 (people addicted to playing games or chatting on the computer)", "防盗门 (*fangdaomen*, 'anti-theft door; security door')" for "有防盗功能的门 (door with anti-theft function)", "教师节 (*Jiaoshijie*, 'Teachers' Day')" for "为教师确定的节日 (a holiday for teachers)", "大棚菜 (*dapengcai*, 'greenhouse vegetable')" for "在大棚里培植生长的菜 (vegetables grown in greenhouses)" and "双职工 (*shuangzhigong*, 'double workers; working couples')" for "夫妻两人都有工作的情况 (a situation in which both husband and wife are employed)", etc.

It is evident from the above that word coinage activities have a close relation with people's cognition and the specific environments and that the base forms are created from the concepts which are formed through thinking by people in accordance with specific environments and conditions and then words are coined on the basis of the base forms thereof. It is also evident from the above that in word coinage what is considered mainly is the proper term in designation instead of the internal structure of the relevant words, such as subordinate construction and subject-predicate construction.

II Word formation

(I) What is word formation?

Word formation refers to the ways in which neologisms are coined. Designation is a matter of word coinage and the ways utilized in designation a matter of word formation. In the process of word coinage, one can create various neologisms with language materials on hand in accordance with the language habits of his own. In the creation of such neologisms one utilizes a great variety of methods to designate the objects concerned and such methods are called word formation.

(II) Word formation in Chinese

Word formations in Chinese are multifarious and are preliminarily listed as follows:

1   Sound-meaning Arbitrary Combination

Sound-meaning arbitrary combination is a way of designating objects with a certain sound or sound combination. There is no necessary connection between the sound and meaning for the neologisms created in such a way. As is known that a word is a linguistic sign of which the sound-meaning combination is arbitrary in the very beginning: when a certain phonetic form is used to refer to a certain object, the phonetic form is assigned a certain meaning from the object concerned and a word is thus formed by the combination of sound and meaning. The first words in language come into being in such a way. For example,

人 (*ren*, "people") 手 (*shou*, "hand") 足 (*zu*, "foot") 头 (*tou*, "head") 口 (*kou*, "mouth") 日 (*ri*, "day; sun") 月 (*yue*, "month; moon")
树 (*shu*, "tree") 山 (*shan*, "mountain") 石 (*shi*, "stone") 风 (*feng*, "wind") 雨 (*yu*, "rain") 鸟 (*niao*, "bird") 兽 (*shou*, "beast")
牛 (*niu*, "cattle") 羊 (*yang*, "sheep") 刀 (*dao*, "knife") 车 (*che*, "vehicle") 弓 (*gong*, "bow") 桑 (*sang*, "mulberry") 蚕 (*can*, "silkworm")
粱 (*liang*, "fine grain") 稻 (*dao*, "rice") 阴 (*yin*, "yin") 阳 (*yang*, "yang") 大 (*da*, "large") 小 (*xiao*, "small") 高 (*gao*, "high")
深 (*shen*, "deep") 一 (*yi*, "one") 二 (*er*, "two") 十 (*shi*, "ten") 百 (*bai*, "hundred") 千 (*qian*, "thousand") 万 (*wan*, "ten thousand")
窈窕 (*yaotiao*, "gentle and graceful") 崔嵬 (*cuiwei*, "towering") 逍遥 (*xiaoyao*, "leisurely") 婆娑 (*posuo*, "whirling") 参差 (*cenci*, "uneven")
玲珑 (*linglong*, "exquisite") 蜻蜓 (*qingting*, "dragonfly") 蟋蟀 (*xishuai*, "cricket") 喇叭 (*laba*, "horn") 霹雳 (*pili*, "thunderbolt")
含糊 (*hanhu*, "vague") 徘徊 (*paihuai*, "linger") 慷慨 (*kangkai*, "generous") 蚯蚓 (*qiuyin*, "earthworm") 从容 (*congrong*, "calm")

There is no necessary connection between the sound and meaning for the above words: it is inexplicable why such a phonetic form is used to indicate a certain object.

Arbitrary combination of sound and meaning is used less and less as language elements abound in so much as raw materials for word coinage appear with the development of society and language per se. However, it is undeniable that such word formation is utilized at times nowadays. For example, the names of such chemical elements as "镍 (*nie*, 'nickel')" and "钠 (*na*, 'sodium')" are out of this way: there may be a certain base form for each of the names of these elements, though there is no reason for the combination between their sound and meaning.

2 Onomatopoeia

Onomatopoeia is a word formation by which neologisms are created by imitating and reforming of certain sounds with the phonetic forms of human language. As a matter of fact, it is the verbalization of certain sounds that makes them the words in language.

There are two cases for words coinage with onomatopoeia in Chinese:

The first is to coin words by imitating sounds of objects in nature. Cases of designating objects by the sounds thereof:

> 猫 (*mao* "cat") 鸦 (*ya*, "crow") 蛙 (*wa*, "frog") 蛐蛐 (*ququ*, "cricket") 蝈蝈 (*guoguo*, "long-horned grasshopper") 呼噜 (*hulu*, "snoring")
> The cases of depicting the properties of the objects by the sound thereof:
> 哪 (*na*, "ah") 嗯 (*ng*, "well") 唉 (*ai*, "alas") 呸 (*pei*, "bah") 哎呀 (*aiya*, "oh dear") 哼哼 (*hengheng*, "hum") 哈哈 (*haha*, "ha-ha")
> 当 (*dang*, "clank") 咚 (*dong*, "rub-a-dub") 吱 (*zhi*, "squeak") 呼 (*hu*, "whir") 咚咚 (*dongdong*, "thump-thump-thump") 当当 (*dangdang*, "rub-a-dub") 吱吱 (*zhizhi*, "squeak")
> 呼呼 (*huhu*, "whir") 哗哗 (*huahua*, "gurgle") 嗡嗡 (*wengweng*, "hum") 喳喳 (*zhazha*, "whisper") 汪汪 (*wangwang*, "woof woof")
> 吧嗒 (*bada*, "click") 嘎吱 (*gazhi*, "creak") 嘎巴 (*gaba*, "crack") 丁冬 (*dingdong*, "tinkle; dingdong") 丁当 (*dingdang*, "clatter")
> 哗啦 (*huala*, "crash") 轰隆 (*honglong*, "rumble") 当啷 (*danglang*, "clang") 噗嗤 (*puchi*, "snigger") 丁零 (*dingling*, "tinkle")
> 轰隆隆 (*honglonglong*, "tumble") 哗啦啦 (*hualala*, "gurgle") 噼里啪啦 (*pilipala*, "crackling") 丁丁当当 (*dingdingdangdang*, "clatter")

The second is to coin words by imitating sounds of those in foreign languages. Words of this type are often referred to as phonemic loans. In fact, phonemic loans belong to onomatopoeia, except that what is imitated is the sound of a foreign word. For example,

> 咖啡 (*kafei*, "coffee") 沙发 (*shafa*, "sofa")
> 夹克 (*jiake*, "jacket") 吉普 (*jipu*, "jeep")
> 巴黎 (*Bali*, "Paris") 马拉松 (*malasong*, "marathon")

The targets are different for the above two cases, though they share one point in common, i. e., the sounds imitated are reformed in one way or another with the phonetic forms of the Chinese language in order to conform to the characteristics

The emergence and structural forms of words 69

of Chinese speech sound. This process of imitation and reformation is the concrete process of the word coinage with onomatopoeia.

3   Phonetic Change

Phonetic change means to coin neologisms by changing the sound of relevant linguistic elements. Rhotacized final word formation in Chinese is such a way of phonetic change in word coinage. For example,

盖 (*gai*, verb, "to cover") – 盖儿 (*gair*, noun, "a cover")
扣 (*kou*, verb, "to buckle") – 扣儿 (*kour*, noun, "a button")
铲 (*chan*, verb, "to shovel") – 铲儿 (*chanr*, noun, "a spade")
黄 (*huang*, adjective, "yellow") – 黄儿 (*huangr*, noun, "yolk")
尖 (*jian*, adjective, "pointed") – 尖儿 (*jianr*, noun, "a point")
个 (*ge*, classifier, as in "一个人 (*yigeren*, 'one person')" – 个儿 (*ger*, noun, "stature")
本 (*ben*, noun, "stem or root of plants", as in "根本 (*genben*, 'base')"; classifier, as in "一本书 (*yibenshu*, 'one book')" – 本儿 (*benr*, noun, "a small book")

In addition, the following are also cases of phonetic change word formation:

好 (*hao3*, "好" in "好坏 (*hao3huai4*, 'good or bad')") – 好 (*hao2*, "好" in "爱好 (*aihao*, 'hobby')")
传 (*chuan*, "传" in "传递 (*chuandi*, 'to transmit')") – 传 (*zhuan*, "传" in "传记 (*aihao*, 'biography')")
见 (*jian*, "见" in "看见 (*kanjian*, 'to see')") – 见 (*xian*, the same as "现 (*xian*, 'to appear')")

This is common in the cases that a sense item of polysemes becomes an independent word through sound change.

It should be pointed out that the rhotacization is to put an "*er*" after another final to make it a apico-postalveolar final and it is a process of sound change within a syllable (i. e., the rhotacization influences the pronunciation of the inner part of the syllable) as far as *Putonghua* is concerned. Therefore, the neologisms thus brought into existence belong to word coinage with phonetic change. At present it is generally accepted by the scholars in Chinese language studies that the rhotacized part in rhotacized final is an independent suffix, which, according to my view, is open to discussion. A semantic morpheme is an independent word formation unit with an independent syllable as the phonetic form of its own, whereas "rhotacization" can only happen in other syllables and forms an apico-postalveolar final together with another final instead of forming an independent syllable by itself after the final concerned; therefore "*er*" should not be treated as an independent suffix because "rhotacization" is only a sound change within a syllable.

70 *The emergence and structural forms of words*

Of course, if "*er*" becomes an independent syllable put after another syllable like the "儿 (*er*)" in "鸟儿 (*niao'er*, 'bird')" and "风儿 (*feng'er*, 'wind')" in the children's song "风儿吹，鸟儿叫，小宝宝，睡醒了 (*Feng'erchui, niao'erjiao, xiaobaobao, shuixingliao*, 'The wind blows, the birds cry, and the baby wakes up')", it can be treated as a suffix, because it is not a rhotacized final.

Phonetic change word formation is a way in which neologisms are created by changing the phonetic form. Even though the new word is coined by a combination of a new phonetic form and a certain meaning, it is, nonetheless, totally different from the sound-meaning arbitrary combination. In phonetic change word formation, a new phonetic form is generated with some change made to the old sound to an extent on the basis of the original word indicating a meaning both related to and distinct from the meaning of the original one. Consequently the neologisms coined with phonetic change are always related to the original word base in meaning to some extent. It is not the case with the neologisms by arbitrary combination of sound and meaning, so the two word formations should be differentiated from each other.

4   Illustration

Illustration indicates a way of word formation by which neologisms are created through the illustration of the objects concerned. In designating objects, one makes certain illustrations to them with the available language materials in order to make others have an understanding of the objects concerned, thus a new term is determined as well as a neologism is created. The meaning of the neologism thus formed is comparatively clear and definite and easy-to-understand in general; therefore illustration is a common way of word formation.

There are different cases for words coined by illustration out of the different points of view of illustrating, which are listed as follows:

Illustration from the state of affairs. For example,

国营 (*guoying*, "state-run") 年轻 (*nianqing*, "young") 自动 (*zidong*, "automatic") 地震 (*dizhen*, "earthquake") 口红 (*kouhong*, "lipstick")

起草 (*qicao*, "draft") 知己 (*zhiji*, "confidant") 庆功 (*qinggong*, "celebrate success") 签名 (*qianming*, "autograph") 争气 (*zhengqi*, "try to make a good showing")

举重 (*juzhong*, "weightlifting") 删改 (*shangai*, "delete") 简练 (*jianlian*, "concise") 赞扬 (*zanyang*, "praise") 胆怯 (*danqie*, "timid")

抓紧 (*zhuajin*, "grasp") 洗刷 (*xishua*, "wash") 看见 (*kanjian*, "see") 提高 (*tigao*, "increase") 放大 (*fangda*, "enlarge")

脑溢血 (*naoyixue*, "cerebral hemorrhage") 胃溃疡 (*weikuiyang*, "gastric ulcer") 肝硬化 (*ganyinghua*, "cirrhosis") 肺结核 (*feijiehe*, "pulmonary tuberculosis")

落花生 (*luohuasheng*, "groundnut") 超声波 (*chaoshengbo*, "ultrasonic wave") 二人转 (*errenzhuan*, "song and dance duet") 婴儿安 (*yingeran*, "baby in safety")

Illustration from the properties and characteristics. For example,

方桌 (*fangzhuo*, "square table") 优点 (*youdian*, "advantage") 弹簧 (*tanhuang*, "spring") 硬席 (*yingxi*, "hard seat") 石碑 (*shibei*, "stone tablet")

理想 (*lixiang*, "ideal") 午睡 (*wushui*, "noontime snooze") 晚会 (*wanhui*, "evening party") 甜瓜 (*tiangua*, "melon") 谜语 (*miyu*, "riddle")

函授 (*hanshou*, "instruction by correspondence") 铅笔 (*qianbi*, "pencil") 绿茶 (*lücha*, "green tea") 热爱 (*re'ai*, "ardently love") 笔直 (*bizhi*, "perfectly straight")

前进 (*qianjin*, "go forward") 重视 (*zhongshi*, "attach importance to") 高级 (*gaoji*, "senior") 国旗 (*guoqi*, "national flag") 钢板 (*gangban*, "steel plate")

木偶戏 (*mu'ouxi*, "puppet show") 胶合板 (*jiaoheban*, "plywood") 丁字尺 (*dingzichi*, "T-square") 武昌鱼 (*Wuchangyu*, "Wuchang fish")

大理石 (*dalishi*, "marble") 电动机 (*diandongji*, "motor") 回形针 (*huixingzhen*, "paper clip") 石棉瓦 (*shimianwa*, "asbestos tile")

Illustration from the usage. For example,

雨衣 (*yuyi*, "raincoat") 燃料 (*ranliao*, "fuel") 烤炉 (*kaolu*, "oven") 书桌 (*shuzhuo*, "desk") 护膝 (*huxi*, "kneepad")

围脖 (*weibo*, "collar") 顶针 (*dingzhen*, "thimble") 裹腿 (*guotui*, "leggings") 餐具 (*canju*, "tableware") 耕地 (*gengdi*, "cultivated land")

医院 (*yiyuan*, "hospital") 牙刷 (*yashua*, "toothbrush") 枕巾 (*zhenjin*, "pillow towel") 浴盆 (*yupen*, "bathtub") 陪嫁 (*peijia*, "dowry")

保温瓶 (*baowenping*, "thermos flask") 消毒水 (*xiaodushui*, "disinfecting water") 织布机 (*zhibuji*, "loom") 托儿所 (*tuo'ersuo*, "nursery")

洗衣粉 (*xiyifen*, "washing powder") 抽水机 (*choushuiji*, "water pump") 吸铁石 (*xitieshi*, "lodestone") 扩音器 (*kuoyinqi*, "megaphone")

收割机 (*shougeji*, "harvester") 避雷针 (*bileizhen*, "lightning arrester") 消炎片 (*xiaoyanpian*, "anti-inflammatory tablets") 漱口水 (*shukoushui*, "mouth wash")

Illustration from the possession. For example,

豆芽 (*douya*, "bean sprouts") 鱼鳞 (*yulin*, "scale") 牛角 (*niujiao*, "ox horn") 树叶 (*shuye*, "leaf") 日光 (*riguang*, "sunlight")

羊毛 (*yangmao*, "wool") 虎皮 (*hupi*, "tiger") 盒盖 (*hegai*, "box lid") 瓶口 (*pingkou*, "nottle mouth") 笔尖 (*bijian*, "penpoint")

床头 (*chuangtou*, "head of a bed") 刀把 (*daoba*, "handle of a knife") 瓜子 (*guazi*, "melon seed") 衣领 (*yiling*, "collar") 灯口 (*dengkou*, "lamp socket")

屋顶 (*wuding*, "roof") 猪肝 (*zhugan*, "pig liver") 象牙 (*xiangya*, "ivory") 鞋带 (*xiedai*, "shoelace") 刀刃 (*daoren*, "blade")

火车头 (*huochetou*, "locomotive") 细胞核 (*xibaohe*, "nucleus") 桂圆肉 (*guiyuanrou*, "longan meat") 棉花种 (*mianhuazhong*, "cotton seed")

72 *The emergence and structural forms of words*

白菜心 (*baicaixin*, "cabbage heart") 橘子皮 (*juzipi*, "orange peel") 鸡蛋黄 (*jidanhuang*, "egg yolk") 丝瓜瓤 (*siguarang*, "luffa sponge")

Illustration from the colour. For example,

红旗 (*hongqi*, "red flag") 绿豆 (*lüdou*, "green gram") 紫竹 (*zizhu*, "black bamboo") 黄铜 (*huangtong*, "brass") 白面 (*baimian*, "flour")
白云 (*baiyun*, "white clouds") 蓝天 (*lantian*, "blue sky") 紫菜 (*zicai*, "laver") 白酒 (*baijiu*, "white spirit") 黄土 (*huangtu*, "loess")
青红丝 (*qinghongsi*, "green and red silk") 黑猩猩 (*heixingxing*, "chimpanzee") 红领巾 (*honglingjin*, "red scarf") 红绿灯 (*honglüdeng*, "traffic lights")
红药水 (*hongyaoshui*, "red potion") 黄花菜 (*huanghuacai*, "day lily") 白眼珠 (*baiyanzhu*, "the white of the eye") 紫丁香 (*zidingxiang*, "lilac")
黑穗病 (*heisuibing*, "smut") 黄刺玫 (*huangcimei*, "yellow rose") 黑板报 (*heibanbao*, "blackboard newspaper") 红蜘蛛 (*hongzhizhu*, "red spider")

Illustration from the number. For example,

二伏 (*erfu*, "the second of the three ten-day periods of the hot season") 两岸 (*liang'an*, "cross straits") 两可 (*liangke*, "ambiguous") 三角 (*sanjiao*, "triangle") 三秋 (*sanqiu*, "the three autumn jobs (harvesting, ploughing and sowing)")
四时 (*sishi*, "the four seasons") 五代 (*wudai*, "the Five Dynasties") 五律 (*wulü*, "five-character eight-line poem") 六书 (*liushu*, "the six categories of Chinese characters") 七绝 (*qijue*, "seven-character four-line poem")
八卦 (*Bagua*, "Eight Diagrams") 九泉 (*jiuquan*, "the nether world") 十分 (*shifen*, "very") 十足 (*shizu*, "full") 百般 (*baiban*, "all")
百姓 (*baixing*, "common people") 千金 (*qianjin*, "daughter") 千秋 (*qianqiu*, "a thousand years") 万物 (*wanwu*, "all things on earth") 万能 (*wanneng*, "omnipotent")
一言堂 (*yiyantang*, "one person alone has the say") 二重奏 (*erzhongzou*, "duet") 三合土 (*sanhetu*, "tabia") 四边形 (*sibianxing*, "quadrilateral")
五角星 (*wujiaoxing*, "five-pointed star") 六弦琴 (*liuxianqin*, "guitar") 七言诗 (*qiyanshi*, "seven-character poem") 八宝饭 (*babaofan*, "eight treasures rice")
九重霄 (*jiuzhongxiao*, "the highest heavens") 十三经 (*Shisanjing*, "the Thirteen Classic Works") 百日咳 (*bairike*, "pertussis") 千里马 (*qianlima*, "a horse that covers a thousand *li* a day")

Illustration with specification. Specification with the category of the specified. For example,

菊花 (*juhua*, "chrysanthemum") 芹菜 (*qincai*, "celery") 茅草 (*maocao*, "thatch") 淮河 (*Huai He*, "the Huaihe River") 蝗虫 (*huangchong*, "grasshopper")

The emergence and structural forms of words 73

鹞鹰 (*yaoying*, "sparrow hawk") 松树 (*songshu*, "pine") 父亲 (*fuqin*, "father") 心脏 (*xinzang*, "heart") 糯米 (*nuomi*, "glutinous rice")
牡丹花 (*mudanhua*, "peony flower") 白杨树 (*baiyangshu*, "poplar tree") 水晶石 (*shuijingshi*, "crystal stone") 乌贼鱼 (*wuzeiyu*, "cuttlefish")
吉普车 (*jipuche*, "jeep") 芭蕾舞 (*baleiwu*, "ballet") 桑拿浴 (*sangnayu*, "sauna") 比萨饼 (*bisabing*, "pizza")

Specification with the name of the unit. For example,

人口 (*renkou*, "population") 纸张 (*zhizhang*, "paper") 房间 (*fangjian*, "room") 马匹 (*mapi*, "horse") 船只 (*chuanzhi*, "ship")
车辆 (*cheliang*, "vehicle") 枪支 (*qiangzhi*, "firearms") 案件 (*anjian*, "case") 花朵 (*huaduo*, "flower") 信件 (*xinjian*, "letter")
钢锭 (*gangding*, "steel ingot") 书本 (*shuben*, "book") 花束 (*huashu*, "bouquet") 米粒 (*mili*, "rice") 石块 (*shikuai*, "stone")

Specification with the state of affairs of the specified. For example,

静悄悄 (*jingqiaoqiao*, "very quiet; soundless") 白茫茫 (*baimangmang*, "vast expanse of whiteness") 恶狠狠 (*ehenhen*, "fierce") 亮晶晶 (*liangjingjing*, "sparkling")
光秃秃 (*guangtutu*, "bald") 呆愣愣 (*dailengleng*, "stupefied") 笑嘻嘻 (*xiaoxixi*, "grinning") 雾蒙蒙 (*wumengmeng*, "misty")
喘吁吁 (*chuanxuxu*, "panting") 泪汪汪 (*leiwangwang*, "tearful") 冷冰冰 (*lengbingbing*, "frosty") 颤悠悠 (*chanyouyou*, "shaky")
赤裸裸 (*chiluoluo*, "naked") 响当当 (*xiangdangdang*, "resounding") 好端端 (*haoduanduan*, "in perfectly good condition") 明晃晃 (*minghuanghuang*, "gleaming")
沉甸甸 (*chendiandian*, "heavy") 矮墩墩 (*aidundun*, "stumpy") 娇滴滴 (*jiaodidi*, "delicately") 黑沉沉 (*heichenchen*, "gloomy")

Illustration with the addition of functional elements in language to change the meaning of the original words. For example,

聋子 (*longzi*, "deaf person") 乱子 (*luanzi*, "trouble") 日子 (*rizi*, "date") 腰子 (*yaozi*, "kidney") 推子 (*tuizi*, "hairclippers")
想头 (*xiangtou*, "hope") 看头 (*kantou*, "sth. worth seeing or reading") 甜头 (*tiantou*, "benefit") 劲头 (*jintou*, "strength") 盼头 (*pantou*, "hope")
哑巴 (*yaba*, "mute") 岸然 (*anran*, "in a solemn manner") 油然 (*youran*, "spontaneously") 几乎 (*jihu*, "almost") 在乎 (*zaihu*, "care about")
黑乎乎 (*heihuhu*, "blackened; rather dark") 红乎乎 (*honghuhu*, "red") 酸溜溜 (*suanliuliu*, "sour") 灰溜溜 (*huiliuliu*, "gloomy")

Such words like "黑乎乎 (*heihuhu*, 'blackened; rather dark')" are similar in form to "静悄悄 (*qingqiaoqiao*, 'very quiet; soundless')" in the above, but they belong to a totally different case. The reduplication forms in the latter part of "静悄悄" and "白茫茫" are all semantic morphemes with concrete lexical meaning, which depict the major semantic morphemes of the former part of the relevant words, such as "汪汪" and "晶晶", etc. Some of these lexical morphemes can be used as independent words, such as "悄悄地走了 (*qiaoqiaode zou le*, 'quietly left')" and "茫茫的大海 (*mangmang de dahai*, 'the boundless sea')", etc. The reduplication forms in the latter part of "黑乎乎" are of a quite different type: they belong to the conventional functional elements in language.

In addition to the above examples, illustration can be used in many other different situations to coin new words and it is a flexible way of word formation with a great productivity.

5 Rhetorical Comparison

Rhetorical comparison means to create neologisms with the rhetorical devices such as analogy and/or metaphor with the available language materials. Sometimes the whole neologism created in such a way is a metaphor. For example,

龙头 (*longtou*, "faucet") 龙眼 (*longyan*, "longan") 佛手 (*foshou*, "fingered citron") 螺丝 (*luosi*, "screw") 下海 (*xiahai*, "go to sea")
鸡胸 (*jixiong*, "chicken breast") 银耳 (*yin'er*, "tremella") 猴头 (*houtou*, "hedgehog hydnum") 鸡眼 (*jiyan*, "clavus") 虎口 (*hukou*, "tiger's mouth; part of the hand between the thumb and the index finger")
蚕食 (*canshi*, "nibble") 骑墙 (*qiqiang*, "sitting on the fence") 贴金 (*tiejin*, "gild") 琢磨 (*zhuomo*, "pondering") 鸟巢 (*niaochao*, "the bird's nest")
仙人掌 (*xianrenzhang*, "cactus") 纸老虎 (*zhilaohu*, "paper tiger") 拴马桩 (*shuanmazhuang*, "hitching post")

Sometimes a part of the neologism is a metaphorical element. For example,

木耳 (*mu'er*, "wood ear") 雪花 (*xuehua*, "snowflake") 木马 (*muma*, "trojan") 天河 (*Tianhe*, "the Milky Way") 虾米 (*xiami*, "small shrimp")
板油 (*banyou*, "leaf lard") 云梯 (*yunti*, "scaling ladder") 瓜分 (*guafen*, "carve up") 林立 (*linli*, "stand in great numbers") 冰冷 (*bingleng*, "icy")
火热 (*huore*, "fiery") 笔直 (*bizhi*, "perfectly straight") 雪白 (*xuebai*, "snow-white") 墨黑 (*mohei*, "inkiness") 杏黄 (*xinghuang*, "apricot yellow")
蜂窝煤 (*fengwomei*, "honeycomb briquette") 狮子狗 (*shizigou*, "pug dog") 鸭舌帽 (*yashemao*, "peaked cap") 喇叭花 (*labahua*, "morning glory")
金丝猴 (*jinsihou*, "golden monkey") 牛皮纸 (*niupizhi*, "kraft paper") 鸡冠花 (*jiguanhua*, "cockscomb") 笑面虎 (*xiaomianhu*, "a smiling tiger – an outwardly kind but inwardly cruel person")

6 Semantic Extension

Semantic extension entails creating neologisms with the semantic extension of meaning with the available language materials. For example, from the action of "打开 (*dakai*, 'open; turn on')" and "关上 (*guanshang* 'close; turn off')", one can designate "操纵打开和关上的物件 (*caozong dakai he guanshang de wujian*, 'the thing through which one opens and closes other things')" as "开关 (*kaiguan*, 'switch; disjunctor')" through association and semantic extension. This is a case of word formation of semantic extension. Other examples are as follows:

收发 (*shoufa*, "receive and dispatch") 领袖 (*lingxiu*, "leader") 口舌 (*koushe*, "quarrel") 骨肉 (*gurou*, "flesh and blood") 山水 (*shanshui*, "landscape")
裁缝 (*caifeng*, "tailor") 组织 (*zuzhi*, "organization") 出纳 (*chu'na*, "cashier") 是非 (*shifei*, "right and wrong") 左右 (*zuoyou*, "entourage")
锻炼 (*duanlian*, "physical exercise") 针线 (*zhenxian*, "needle") 规矩 (*guiju*, "rules") 爪牙 (*zhaoya*, "lackeys") 见闻 (*jianwen*, "experiences.")
手足 (*shouzu*, "brothers") 唇舌 (*chunshe*, "words") 江湖 (*jianghu*, "rivers and lakes") 江山 (*jiangshan*, "country") 岁月 (*suiyue*, "years")
网罗 (*wangluo*, "trap") 身手 (*shenshou*, "skill") 矛盾 (*maodun*, "contradiction") 天地 (*tiandi*, "world") 笔墨 (*bimo*, "pen and ink")

A neologism formed through the differentiation by semantic extension of the meaning of a word also belongs to semantic extension. For example, the word "年(*nian*)" means "ripens (of millet)" in origin, and "年 (*nian*)" indicating "the time period of 365 days" is differentiated by semantic extension in accordance with the interlude in which millet ripens: two homophones of "年 (*nian*)" are thus formed so that a neologism comes into being. The following examples are all case in point. For example,

岁 (*sui*, "Jupiter") – 岁 (*sui*, "years")
月 (*yue*, "moon") – 月 (*yue*, "month")
日 (*ri*, "sun") – 日 (*ri*, "day")
刻 (*ke*, "carve") – 刻 (*ke*, "a quarter")
钟 (*zhong*, "bell") – 钟 (*zhong*, "clock")

7 Disyllabification

Disyllabification means to coin neologisms through disyllabificating a monosyllabic word. This is a word formation in company with the disyllabification of Chinese vocabulary and the disyllabificated new words are also coined on the basis of the available language materials. The common cases of disyllabifications in the contemporary Chinese language are as follows:

(1) A disyllabificated word is created by repetition on the basis of a monosyllabic word and the meaning of the neologism is identical to or basically the same as that of the original monosyllabic word. For example,

妈妈 (*mama*, "mom") 爸爸 (*baba*, "dad") 伯伯 (*bobo*, "father's elder brother") 姑姑 (*gugu*, "aunt") 叔叔 (*shushu*, "father's younger brother")

嫂嫂 (*saosao*, "sister in law") 哥哥 (*gege*, "elder brother") 姐姐 (*jiejie*, "elder sister") 弟弟 (*didi*, "younger brother") 妹妹 (*meimei*, "younger sister")

星星 (*xingxing*, "star") 炯炯 (*jiongjiong*, "shining") 恰恰 (*qiaqia*, "just") 渐渐 (*jianjian*, "gradually") 悄悄 (*qiaoqiao*, "quietly")

茫茫 (*mangmang*, "vast") 耿耿 (*genggeng*, "devoted") 草草 (*caocao*, "hastily") 纷纷 (*fenfen*, "one after another") 忿忿 (*fenfen*, "indignant")

蠢蠢 (*chunchun*, "stirring") 活活 (*huohuo*, "alive") 匆匆 (*congcong*, "hurriedly") 常常 (*changchang*, "often") 汩汩 (*gugu*, "gurgle")

(2) A disyllabificated word is created by repetition on the basis of a monosyllabic word and the meaning of the neologism is basically different from the original monosyllabic word. For example,

爷爷 (*yeye*, "grandpa") 奶奶 (*nainai*, "grandma") 宝宝 (*baobao*, "baby") 万万 (*wanwan*, "absolutely") 通通 (*tongtong*, "all")

断断 (*duanduan*, "definitely") 往往 (*wangwang*, "often") 在在 (*zaizai*, "everywhere") 落落 (*luoluo*, "natural and graceful") 区区 (*ququ*, "trivial")

历历 (*lili*, "distinctly") 斤斤 (*jinjin*, "fuss about") 源源 (*yuanyuan*, "continuously") 翼翼 (*yiyi*, "cautiously") 涓涓 (*juanjuan*, "trickling sluggishly")

津津 (*jinjin*, "delicious") 济济 (*jiji*, "numerous") 昂昂 (*angang*, "high-spirited") 堂堂 (*tangtang*, "dignified or impressive") 熊熊 (*xiongxiong*, "flaming")

(3) A disyllabificated word is created by combining two monosyllabic words which are the same, close or relevant in meaning and the meaning of the neologism is the same as or close to that of the original monosyllabic word. For example,

道路 (*daolu*, "road") 朋友 (*pengyou*, "friend") 语言 (*yuyan*, "language") 旗帜 (*qizhi*, "flag") 人民 (*renmin*, "the people")

英雄 (*yingxiong*, "hero") 年岁 (*niansui*, "age") 睡眠 (*shuimian*, "sleep") 包裹 (*baoguo*, "package") 世代 (*shidai*, "generation")

脸面 (*lianmian*, "face") 坟墓 (*fenmu*, "grave") 购买 (*goumai*, "purchase") 增加 (*zengjia*, "increase") 依靠 (*yikao*, "rely on")

更改 (*genggai*, "change") 生产 (*shengchan*, "production") 解放 (*jiefang*, "liberate") 爱好 (*aihao*, "hobby") 斥责 (*chize*, "rebuke")

斟酌 (*zhenzhuo*, "consider") 书写 (*shuxie*, "write") 帮助 (*bangzhu*, "help") 学习 (*xuexi*, "study") 批改 (*pigai*, "correct")

答复 (*dafu*, "reply") 把持 (*bachi*, "control") 集聚 (*jiju*, "gather") 洗刷 (*xishua*, "wash") 喜悦 (*xiyue*, "joy")

寒冷 (*hanleng*, "cold") 弯曲 (*wanqu*, "bend") 美丽 (*meili*, "beautiful") 繁多 (*fanduo*, "various") 宽阔 (*kuankuo*, "wide")

The emergence and structural forms of words 77

孤独 (*gudu*, "lonely") 伟大 (*weida*, "great") 艰难 (*jiannan*, "difficult") 富裕 (*fuyu*, "affluent") 寂静 (*jijing*, "silent")

(4) A disyllabificated word is formed by affixing a conventional functional element to a monosyllabic word and the meaning of the neologism is identical to that of the original monosyllabic word. For example,

石头 (*shitou*, "stone") 木头 (*mutou*, "wood") 砖头 (*zhuantou*, "brick") 舌头 (*shetou*, "tongue") 指头 (*zhitou*, "finger")
桌子 (*zhuozi*, "table") 椅子 (*yizi*, "chair") 帽子 (*maozi*, "hat") 裙子 (*qunzi*, "skirt") 碟子 (*diezi*, "plate")
尾巴 (*weiba*, "tail") 盐巴 (*yanba*, "salt") 泥巴 (*niba*, "mud") 忽然 (*huran*, "suddenly") 竟然 (*jingran*, "unexpectedly")
突然 (*turan*, "suddenly") 老师 (*laoshi*, "teacher") 老虎 (*laohu*, "tiger") 老鹰 (*laoying*, "eagle") 老鼠 (*laoshu*, "mouse")
阿姨 (*ayi*, "aunt") 阿婆 (*apo*, "grandma") 第一 (*diyi*, "first") 第三 (*disan*, "third") 初五 (*chuwu*, "fifth day of a lunar month")

From the above four cases, we can see that all disyllabificated words are neologisms created on the basis of a monosyllabic word with disyllabification. With the development of language, some of the monosyllabic words which serve as the base form of the neologisms can still be used as words independently, while others can only be used as semantic morphemes instead of independent words. However, when disyllables were formed on the basis of these elements, these monosyllabic words were independent words existing in language at that time.

8 Abbreviation

Abbreviation is a way of word formation through which a word is formed from a phrase by contraction. Some objects are designated with a phrase in the Chinese language and to contract a phrase to a word is also a way by which neologisms are formed. For example, "山大 (*Shanda*)" is contracted from "山东大学 (*Shandong Daxue*, 'Shandong University')" with the first semantic morpheme of each of the two words extracted. "扫盲 (*saomang*)" is contracted from "扫除文盲 (*saochu wenmang*, 'eliminate illiteracy')" with the first semantic morpheme of the first word and the second semantic morpheme of the second one extracted. Abbreviations in the Chinese language are diverse. For example,

土地改革 (*tudi gaige*, "land reform") – 土改 (*tugai*)
文化教育 (*wenhua jiaoyu*, "cultural education") – 文教 (*wenjiao*)
旅行游览 (*lüxing youlan*, "tour") – 旅游 (*lüyou*)
支部书记 (*zhibu shuji*, "branch secretary") – 支书 (*zhishu*)
人民警察 (*renmin jingcha*, "people's police") – 民警 (*minjing*)
外交部长 (*Waijiao Buzhang*, "Foreign Minister") – 外长 (*Waizhang*)
整顿作风 (*zhengdun zuofeng*, "rectify the style of work") – 整风 (*zhengfeng*)

历史、地理 (*lishi, dili*, "history and geography") – 史地 (*shidi*)
青年、少年 (*qingnian, shaonian*, "youth") – 青少年 (*qingshaonian*)
指挥员、战斗员 (*zhihuiyuan, zhandouyuan*, "commander and combatant") – 指战员 (*zhizhanyuan*)
支部委员会 (*zhibu weiyuanhui*, "branch committee") – 支委会 (*zhiweihui*)
少年先锋队 (*ShaonianXianfengdui*, "Young Pioneers") – 少先队 (*Shaoxiandui*)
人民代表大会 (*Renmin Daibiao Dahui*, "People's Congress") – 人代会 (*Rendaihui*)
政治协商会议 (*Zhengzhi Xieshang Huiyi*, "Political Consultative Conference") – 政协 (*Zhengxie*)
北京电影制片厂 (*Beijing Dianying Zhipianchang*, "Beijing Film Studio") – 北影 (*Beiying*)
供销合作社 (*gongxiao hezuoshe*, "supply and marketing cooperative") – 供销社 (*gongxiaoshe*)
新华通讯社 (*Xinhua Tongxunshe*, "Xinhua News Agency") – 新华社 (*Xinhuashe*)
父亲、母亲 (*fuqin, muqin*, "father and mother") – 双亲 (*Shuangqin*)
百花齐放、百家争鸣 (*baihua qifang, baijia zhengming*, "Let a hundred flowers bloom and a hundred schools of thought contend") – 双百 (*shuangbai*, "Two Hundred Guidelines")
身体好、工作好、学习好 (*shentihao, gongzuohao, xuexihao*, "being healthy, work hard and study hard") – 三好 (*Sanhao*)
阴平声、阳平声、上声、去声 (*yinpingsheng, yangpingsheng, shangsheng, qusheng*, "level tone, rising tone, falling-rising tone, falling tone") – 四声 (*sisheng*)
农业现代化、工业现代化、国防现代化、科学技术现代化 (*Nongye-Xiandaihua, GongyeXiandaihua, GuofangXiandaihua, KexueJishuXiandaihua*, "Modernization of Agriculture, Industry, National defense and Science and Technology") – 四化 (*Sihua*)

The meaning of a neologism created by abbreviation is identical to that of the original phrase because it is contracted from the original one. Owing to different means of contraction, it is sometimes easy to guess the meaning of some abbreviates just from the surface form, for example, "文化教育" is abbreviated to "文教" and "彩色电视" to "彩电", it is still quite obvious that the abbreviate is identical in meaning with the original phrase. However, for some other abbreviates, their meanings are not so clear and definite because of the complexity of their surface forms out of the differences in the contraction methods used. The abbreviates containing numbers such as "三好 (*sanhao*, 'three-goodness')" and "四声 (*sisheng*, 'four tones')" are cases in point: it is quite difficult to understand that "三好" refers to "身体好 (*shentihao*, 'being healthy'), 工作好 (*gongzuohao*, 'work hard') and 学习好 (*xuexihao*, 'study hard')" and "四声" to "阴平 (*yinping*, 'level'), 阳平 (*yangping*, 'rising'), 上声 (*shangshegn*, 'falling-rising') and 去声 (*qusheng*, 'falling')" just from the surface forms of the abbreviates concerned.

Consequently it is necessary to make some interpretations on the basis of the meanings of the base forms of the original phrases for the understanding of the meanings of this type of abbreviates.

It should be pointed out that this section mainly concerns word formation with abbreviation, though not all abbreviated elements are words: some are still phrases after contraction, e. g., "四个现代化 (*SigeXiandaihua*, 'Four Modernizations')" is a phrase abbreviated from "农业现代化 (*Nongye Xiandaihua*, 'Modernization of Agriculture'), 工业现代化 (*Gongye Xiandaihua*, 'Modernization of Industry'), 国防现代化 (*Guofang Xiandaihua*, 'Modernization of National Defense') and 科学技术现代化 (*Kexue Jishu Xiandaihua*, 'Modernization of Science and Technology')", and "四化 (*Sihua*, 'Four-Izations')" is a word further abbreviated from "四个现代化". In fact, the meaning of "四个现代化" is not self-evident just from the surface form of its own. In order to have a clear and accurate understanding of such abbreviated words as "四化", one should trace all the way back to the original phrase form of "农业现代化, 工业现代化, 国防现代化, 科学技术现代化".

Ways of word formation are rich and colourful in the Chinese language and what are listed above are just a few common ones. To make a thorough and detailed analysis of the word formations in the Chinese language is an important mission in the lexical research from now on.

Word coinage activities are of comprehensive community nature and all members in a linguistic community can coin neologisms and this is a good illustration of the national nature of language. A neologism created by a member of a linguistic community can be preserved as a language element so long as it is conventionalized by the community concerned and the language itself is thus unceasingly enriched and developed.

Section 3 Word structure and lexical morphology

I An overview of word structure

Word structure is the internal structure of a word. It studies the words already in existence. The studies of word structure involve observing and analyzing the internal structure of words and summarizing the rules of the internal structure of words.

Word structure is different from word coinage. Word coinage is one carried out by people catering for the needs of social communications and every member of a linguistic community can take part in it and as far as the neologisms thus coined, every member of a linguistic community must get in touch with and employ them and participate in the conventionalization of them. It is not the case as far as word structure is concerned, however, because what people concerned in social life is the fact that they need, create and employ a certain word instead of the internal structure of the word. Therefore the investigation of word structure, whose domain is narrower than that of word coinage, falls into the range of scientific research of a certain people. Of course the findings of these investigations can be accepted by people because these findings can not only make people understand

80 *The emergence and structural forms of words*

and analyze words more clearly but also provide scientific rules and foundation for their word coinage activities. With the popularization of the scientific knowledge and the enhance of people's cultural literacy, these scientific findings will play a more and more important role.

II Lexical morphology

Lexical morphology indicates the rules governing the internal structure of words, i. e., the ways in which semantic morphemes are combined with each other. All words in language are the objects of study of lexical morphology and all their internal structures can be analyzed from the point of view of word structure. For example, "插秧机 (*chayangji*, 'transplanting machine')" can be analyzed from the point of view of word structure: it is a subordinate compound with "插秧 (*chayang*, 'transplant rice seedlings')" as the modifier and "机 (*ji*, 'machine')" as the head being modified by "插秧". The internal structure of the modifier "插秧 (*chayang*)" can be further analyzed: it is of V-O type with "插 (*cha*, 'transplant')" as the verb and "秧 (*yang*, 'rice seedling')" as the object.

Lexical morphology of the Chinese language includes the following aspects:

(I) The aspect of phonetic form

1 Monosyllabic Words vs. Polysyllabic Words

A monosyllabic word consists of only one syllable. For example,

> 天(*tian*, "sky") 地 (*di*, "earth") 人 (*ren*, "people") 手 (*shou*, "hand") 树 (*shu*, "tree") 鸟 (*niao*, "bird") 车 (*che*, "vehicle") 船 (*chuan*, "ship") 红 (*hong*, "red") 绿 (*lü*, "green") 高 (*gao*, "high") 长 (*chang*, "long") 一 (*yi*, "one") 二 (*er*, "two") 千 (*qian*, "thousand") 百 (*bai*, "hundred")

A disyllabic or polysyllabic word consists of more than one syllable. A disyllable consists of two syllables, for example:

> 人民(*renmin*, "the people") 哲学 (*zhexue*, "philosophy") 宇宙 (*yuzhou*, "universe") 客观 (*keguan*, "objective") 生活 (*shenghuo*, "life") 趣味 (*quwei*, "interest") 风景 (*fengjing*, "scenery") 建筑 (*jianzhu*, "architecture") 鸳鸯 (*yuanyang*, "mandarin duck") 麒麟 (*qilin*, "kylin") 凤凰 (*fenghuang*, "phoenix") 栩栩 (*xuxu*, "vivid") 炯炯 (*jiongjiong*, "shining") 坦克 (*tanke*, "tank") 纽约 (*niuyue*, "New York") 卡片 (*kapian*, "card")

A polysyllabic word consists of three or more than three syllables, for example:

> 世界观(*shijieguan*, "world outlook") 修辞学 (*xiucixue*, "rhetoric") 交响乐 (*jiaoxiangyue*, "symphony") 电视机 (*dianshiji*, "television") 圆珠

The emergence and structural forms of words 81

笔 (*yuanzhubi*, "ball pen") 霓虹灯 (*nihongdeng*, "neon lights") 摩托车 (*motuoche*, "motorcycle") 布谷鸟 (*bugu'niao*, "cuckoo") 资本主义 (*zibenzhuyi*, "capitalism") 南斯拉夫 (*Nansilafu*, "Yugoslavia") 奥林匹克 (*Aolinpike*, "Olympics") 布尔什维克(*Bu'ershiweike*, "Bolshevik")

A word with three syllables can also be referred to as trisyllabic word in general.

2   Reduplication Word vs. Non-reduplication Word

A reduplication word refers to one containing reduplicated syllables. A whole-reduplication word refers to one in which every syllable is reduplicated. Some are ones with reduplicated monosyllables, for example:

弟弟(*didi*, "younger brother") 妹妹 (*meimei*, "younger sister") 星星 (*xingxing*, "star") 往往 (*wangwang*, "often") 哗哗 (*huahua*, "gurgling") 喋喋 (*diedie*, "talkative") 侃侃 (*kankan*, "openly and without sense of guilt") 冉冉 (*ranran*, "slowly") 巍巍 (*weiwei*, "towering") 孜孜 (*zizi*, "diligently") 翩翩 (*pianpian*, "dance lightly") 渐渐 (*jianjian*, "gradually") 耿耿 (*genggeng*, "devoted") 茫茫 (*mangmang*, "vast") 悄悄 (*qiaoqiao*, "quietly") 源源 (*yuanyuan*, "continuously") 草草 (*caocao*, "hastily") 区区 (*ququ*, "trivial") 娓娓 (*weiwei*, "tirelessly") 谆谆 (*zhunzhun*, "earnestly and tirelessly") 迢迢 (*tiaotiao*, "far away")

Others are ones with each syllable of a disyllable reduplicated separately, for example:

花花绿绿(*huahua lülü*, "brightly coloured") 星星点点 (*xingxing diandian*, "tiny spots") 战战兢兢 (*zhanzhan jingjing*, "trembling with fear") 唯唯诺诺 (*weiwei nuonuo*, "say 'yes, yes' repeatedly") 婆婆妈妈 (*popo mama*, "womanishly fussy") 病病歪歪 (*bingbingwaiwai*, "sick") 密密麻麻 (*mimimama*, "as thick as huckleberries") 满满登登 (*manman dengdeng*, "full to the brim") 兢兢业业 (*jingjingyeye*, "be conscientious and do one's best") 影影绰绰 (*yingyingchuochuo*, "shadowy") 浑浑噩噩 (*hunhun'e'e*, "muddle along without any)

A partial-reduplicated word is one with part of syllables reduplicated, for example:

绿油油(*lüyouyou*, "bright green") 喘吁吁 (*chuanxuxu*, "panting") 雾蒙蒙 (*wumengmeng*, "misty") 凉飕飕 (*liangsousou*, "chilly") 冷丝丝 (*lengsisi*, "a bit chilly") 黑糊糊 (*heihuhu*, "rather dark") 活生生 (*huoshengsheng*, "living") 泪汪汪 (*leiwangwang*, "tearful") 美滋滋 (*meizizi*, "very pleased") 假惺惺 (*jiaxingxing*, "hypocritically") 毛毛雨 (*maomaoyu*, "drizzle") 哈哈镜 (*hahajing*, "magic mirror") 麻麻亮 (*mamaliang*, "dawning") 甜兮兮 (*tianxixi*, "unpleasantly sweet") 红乎乎 (*honghuhu*, "red") 酸唧唧 (*suanjiji*, "rather sour") 滑溜溜 (*hualiuliu*, "slippery")

82 *The emergence and structural forms of words*

A non-reduplication word refers to one consists of different syllables. For example,

> 论题(*lunti*, "thesis") 偶像 (*ouxiang*, "idol") 品质 (*pinzhi*, "quality") 人格 (*renge*, "personality") 精神 (*jingshen*, "spirit") 物质 (*wuzhi*, "material") 希望 (*xiwang*, "hope") 鼓动 (*gudong*, "agitate") 爽快 (*shuangkuai*, "frank") 充沛 (*chongpei*, "abundant") 辽阔 (*liaokuo*, "vast") 刊物 (*kanwu*, "periodical") 图书馆 (*tushuguan*, "library") 打印机 (*dayinji*, "printer") 天文台 (*tianwentai*, "observatory") 日光灯 (*riguangdeng*, "fluorescent lamp") 向日葵 (*xiangrikui*, "sunflower") 拖拉机 (*tuolaji*, "tractor") 吉普车 (*jipuche*, "jeep")

Some of non-reduplication words are words with alliterated disyllables or rhymed disallybles.

An alliterated disyllable word means a disyllable with the same initial in the two syllables forming the word. For example,

> 伶俐(*lingli*, "clever") 蜘蛛 (*zhizhu*, "spider") 参差 (*cenci*, "uneven") 踌躇 (*chouchu*, "hesitate") 澎湃 (*pengpai*, "surging") 坎坷 (*kanke*, "rough") 仿佛 (*fangfo*, "as if") 玲珑 (*linglong*, "exquisite") 忐忑 (*tante*, "disturbed") 含糊 (*hanhu*, "vague") 蹊跷 (*qiqiao*, "strange") 忸怩 (*niuni*, "bashful")

A rhymed disallyble word means a disyllable with the same final in the two syllables forming the word. For example,

> 逍遥(*xiaoyao*, "leisurely") 混沌 (*hundun*, "chaos") 嘟噜 (*dulu*, "bunch") 吧嗒 (*bada*, "click") 朦胧 (*menglong*, "obscure") 苗条 (*miaotiao*, "slim") 徘徊 (*paihuai*, "linger") 霹雳 (*pili*, "thunderbolt") 蹉跎 (*cuotuo*, "idle away") 轱辘 (*gulu*, "wheel") 葫芦 (*hulu*, "gourd") 迷离 (*mili*, "blurred")

In traditional Chinese philology, alliterated disyllables and rhymed disyllables are only confined to the disyllables containing only one semantic morpheme and for those containing two semantic morphemes, however, no alliterated disyllabic and/or rhymed disyllabic analysis is applicable to them.

(II) The aspect of the number of semantic morpheme

As words are composed of semantic morphemes, they can be classified into simple words and compound words from the point of view of the number of semantic morpheme.

A simple word consists of only one semantic morpheme. For example,

> 笔(*bi*, "pen") 书 (*shu*, "book") 纸 (*zhi*, "paper") 画 (*hua*, "painting") 看 (*kan*, "look") 热 (*re*, "heat") 琵琶 (*pipa*, "pipa") 孑孓 (*jiejue*, "wriggler") 萝卜 (*luobo*, "radish") 糊涂 (*hutu*, "confused") 咖啡 (*kafei*, "coffee") 夹克 (*jiake*, "jacket") 意大利 (*Yidali*, "Italy") 喀秋莎 (*Kaqiusha*, "Katyusha") 孟什维克 (*Mengshiweike*, "Menshevik") 奥林匹克 (*Aolinpike*, "Olympics")

The emergence and structural forms of words 83

A compound word consists of more than one semantic morpheme. For example,

木头 (*mutou*, "wood") 房子 (*fangzi*, "house") 老虎 (*laohu*, "tiger") 阿姨 (*ayi*, "aunt") 映衬 (*yingchen*, "set off") 贯通 (*guantong*, "link up") 成因 (*chengyin*, "cause of formation") 欢迎 (*huanying*, "welcome") 春分 (*Chunfen*, "the Spring Equinox") 槐树 (*huaishu*, "pagoda tree") 文化宫 (*wenhuagong*, "cultural palace") 研究生 (*yanjiusheng*, "graduate student") 世界观 (*shijieguan*, "world outlook") 日光灯 (*riguangdeng*, "fluorescent lamp") 红彤彤 (*hongtongtong*, "bright red") 亮晶晶 (*liangjingjing*, "sparkling")

(III) The nature and composite relations of semantic morphemes

As words are composed of semantic morphemes, there exist different ways of word formation due to differences in nature or composite relations of semantic morphemes.

For a simple word consisting of only one semantic morpheme, the semantic morpheme is always a root semantic morpheme and there is no composite relation for it.

For complex words containing more than one semantic morpheme, the situation is much more complicated. The ways of word formation of complex words in the Chinese language are as follows:

1   Root semantic morpheme + affix. Such complex words are usually referred to as derivatives. For example,

    Prefix + root:

    老鹰 (*laoying*, "eagle") 老虎 (*laohu*, "tiger") 老师 (*laoshi*, "teacher") 阿姨 (*ayi*, "aunt") 第一 (*diyi*, "first") 第三 (*disan*, "third") 初五 (*chuwu*, "the fifth day of a lunar month") 初十 (*chushi*, "the tenth day of a lunar month")

    Root + suffix:

    帽子 (*maozi*, "hat") 房子 (*fangzi*, "house") 石头 (*shitou*, "stone") 锄头 (*chutou*, "hoe") 猛然 (*mengran*, "abruptly") 忽然 (*huran*, "suddenly") 泥巴 (*niba*, "mud") 盐巴 (*yanba*, "salt") 合乎 (*hehu*, "conform to") 似乎 (*sihu*, "It seems that")

    敢于 (*ganyu*, "dare to") 属于 (*zhuyu*, "belong to") 扭搭 (*niuda*, "walk with a swing") 甩搭 (*shuaida*, "throw") 敲搭 (*qiaoda*, "knock")

    姑娘家 (*guniangjia*, "girl") 孩子家 (*haizijia*, "kid") 红乎乎 (*honghuhu*, "rather red") 酸溜溜 (*suanliuliu*, "sour")

2   Root semantic morpheme + root semantic morpheme. Such complex words are usually referred to as compounds. The roots in these words are combined to each other in accordance with syntactical rules. They can be further classified into the following types:

    (1) Coordinate compounds: the relation between the two component semantic morphemes in such compounds are equal and coordinate.

84 *The emergence and structural forms of words*

Coordinate compounds with synonymous semantic morphemes, for example:

语言 (*yuyan*, "anguage") 泥土 (*nitu*, "earth") 声音 (*shengyin*, "voice") 包裹 (*baoguo*, "package") 坟墓 (*fenmu*, "grave")

离别 (*libie*, "farewell") 制造 (*zhizao*, "manufacture") 行走 (*xingzou*, "walk") 倒退 (*daotui*, "go backwards") 积累 (*jilei*, "accumulation")

打击 (*daji*, "strike") 爱好 (*aihao*, "hobby") 依靠 (*yikao*, "rely on") 把持 (*bachi*, "control") 斟酌 (*zhenzhuo*, "consider")

明亮 (*mingliang*, "bright") 艰难 (*jiannan*, "difficult") 富裕 (*fuyu*, "affluent") 美丽 (*meili*, "beautiful") 宽阔 (*kuankuo*, "wide")

Coordinate compounds with antonymous semantic morphemes, for example:

来往 (*laiwang*, "contact") 始终 (*shizhong*, "from beginning to end") 天地 (*tiandi*, "world") 收发 (*shoufa*, "receive and dispatch") 出纳 (*chuna*, "cashier")

是非 (*shifei*, "right and wrong") 反正 (*fanzheng*, "anyway") 伸缩 (*shensuo*, "stretch out and draw back") 褒贬 (*baobian*, "pass judgement on") 贵贱 (*guijian*, "cheap or expensive")

得失 (*deshi*, "gain and loss") 长短 (*changduan*, "length") 开关 (*kaiguan*, "switch") 深浅 (*shenqian*, "depth") 高低 (*gaodi*, "height")

今昔 (*jinxi*, "present and past") 安危 (*anwei*, "safety") 好歹 (*haodai*, "anyhow") 利害 (*lihai*, "interest") 买卖 (*maimai*, "business")

上下 (*shangxia*, "up and down") 多寡 (*duogua*, "amount") 轻重 (*qingzhong*, "weight") 冷热 (*lengre*, "hot and cold") 左右 (*zuoyou*, "the left and right sides")

Coordinate compounds with related semantic morphemes, for example:

豺狼 (*chailang*, "jackals and wolves") 领袖 (*lingxiu*, "leader") 骨肉 (*gurou*, "flesh and blood") 禽兽 (*qinshou*, "beast") 江湖 (*jianghu*, "rivers and lakes")

眉目 (*meimu*, "looks") 岁月 (*suiyue*, "years") 皮毛 (*pimao*, "superficial knowledge") 心血 (*xinxue*, "blood") 山水 (*shanshui*, "landscape")

人物 (*renwu*, "character") 窗户 (*chuanghu*, "window") 干净 (*ganjing*, "clean") 热闹 (*renao*, "lively") 妻子 (*qizi*, "wife")

描写 (*miaoxie*, "describe") 琢磨 (*zhuomo*, "pondering") 记载 (*jizai*, "record") 保管 (*baoguan*, "safekeeping") 爱惜 (*aixi*, "cherish")

安乐 (*anle*, "comfort") 清凉 (*qingliang*, "cool and refreshing") 柔软 (*rouruan*, "soft") 简明 (*jianming*, "concise") 笨重 (*benzhong*, "heavy")

(2) Subordinate compounds: the relation between the two component semantic morphemes in such compounds are modifier-modified. For example,

汉语 (*Hanyu*, "Chinese") 红旗 (*hongqi*, "red flag") 同学 (*tongxue*, "classmate") 特写 (*texie*, "feature") 奇迹 (*qiji*, "miracle")

The emergence and structural forms of words 85

飞机 (*feiji*, "aircraft") 公路 (*gonglu*, "highway") 电车 (*dianche*, "tram") 开水 (*kaishui*, "boiling water") 收条 (*shoutiao*, "receipt")
导师 (*daoshi*, "tutor") 宋词 (*songci*, "cí poetry of the Song dynasty") 西医 (*xiyi*, "western medicine") 防线 (*fangxian*, "defense") 跑鞋 (*paoxie*, "running shoes")
重视 (*zhongshi*, "attach importance to") 沉思 (*chensi*, "meditation") 狂欢 (*kuanghuan*, "carnival") 欢fl (*huanying*, "welcome") 长跑 (*changpao*, "long-distance run")
热情 (*reqing*, "enthusiasm") 绝妙 (*juemiao*, "excellent") 美观 (*meiguan*, "beautiful") 雪白 (*xuebai*, "snow-white") 笔直 (*bizhi*, "perfectly straight")
生产力 (*shengchanli*, "productivity") 人造丝 (*renzaosi*, "rayon") 中山服 (*zhongshanfu*, "Chinese tunic suit") 梅花鹿 (*meihualu*, "spotted deer")
木偶戏 (*mu'ouxi*, "puppet show") 计算机 (*jisuanji*, "computer") 纪念碑 (*jinianbei*, "monument") 羽毛画 (*yumaohua*, "feather painting")
玻璃窗 (*bolichuang*, "casement window") 葡萄干 (*putaogan*, "raisin") 哈哈镜 (*hahajing*, "magic mirror") 毛毛雨 (*maomaoyu*, "drizzle")

(3) Complement compounds: the relation between the two component semantic morphemes of such compounds are complement-complemented or specifying-specified. These can be further classified into specifying compounds and verb-complement compounds.

A   The specifying compounds fall into the following types:

Specifying with the category of the specified, for example:

松树 (*songshu*, "pine") 柳树 (*liushu*, "willow") 韭菜 (*jiucai*, "leek") 芹菜 (*qincai*, "celery") 蝗虫 (*huangchong*, "grasshopper")
梅花 (*meihua*, "plum") 菊花 (*juhua*, "chrysanthemum") 淮河 (*Huai He*, "the Huaihe River") 汾河 (*Fen He*, "the Fen He River") 玉石 (*yushi*, "jade")
鲤鱼 (*liyu*, "carp") 鲫鱼 (*jiyu*, "crucian") 茅草 (*maocao*, "thatch") 鹞鹰 (*yaoying*, "sparrow hawk") 糯米 (*nuomi*, "glutinous rice")
月季花 (*yuejihua*, "Chinese rose") 水晶石 (*shuijingshi*, "crystal stone") 茅台酒 (*Maotaijiu*, "Maotai wine") 水仙花 (*shuixianhua*, "narcissus")

Specifying with the unit of the specified, for example:

船只 (*chuanzhi*, "ships") 枪支 (*qiangzhi*, "firearms") 钢锭 (*gangding*, "steel ingot") 书本 (*shuben*, "book") 纸张 (*zhizhang*, "paper")
车辆 (*cheliang*, "vehicle") 人口 (*renkou*, "population") 房间 (*fangjian*, "room") 花朵 (*huaduo*, "flower") 花束 (*huashu*, "bouquet")
马匹 (*mapi*, "horse") 布匹 (*bupi*, "cloth") 米粒 (*mili*, "rice") 钟点 (*zhongdian*, "hour") 银两 (*yinliang*, "silver")
灯盏 (*dengzhan*, "oil lamp") 地亩 (*dimu*, "field") 事件 (*shijian*, "event") 稿件 (*gaojian*, "manuscript") 信件 (*xinjian*, "letter")

86 *The emergence and structural forms of words*

> Supplementarily specifying with the state of affairs of the object, for example:
>
> 白茫茫 (*baimangmang*, "a vast expanse of whiteness") 静悄悄 (*jingqiaoqiao*, "quietly") 凉飕飕 (*liangsousou*, "chilly") 恶狠狠 (*ehenhen*, "fierce")
>
> 笑嘻嘻 (*xiaoxixi*, "grinning") 笑哈哈 (*xiaohaha*, "laughingly") 喘吁吁 (*chuanxuxu*, "panting") 呆愣愣 (*dailengleng*, "stupefied")
>
> 雾蒙蒙 (*wumengmeng*, "misty") 冷冰冰 (*lengbingbing*, "frosty") 泪汪汪 (*leiwangwang*, "tearful") 乐悠悠 (*leyouyou*, "cheerful")
>
> 水淋淋 (*shuilinlin*, "dripping wet") 灰蒙蒙 (*huimengmeng*, "dusky") 亮晶晶 (*liangjingjing*, "sparkling") 直挺挺 (*zhitingting*, "bolt upright")

B Verb-complement compounds, for example:

> 提高 (*tigao*, "increase") 改进 (*gaijin*, "improve") 离开 (*likai*, "leave") 撕毁 (*sihui*, "tear up") 降低 (*jiangdi*, "reduce")
>
> 削弱 (*xueruo*, "weaken") 隔绝 (*gejue*, "isolate") 揭露 (*jielu*, "expose") 放大 (*fangda*, "enlarge") 缩小 (*suoxiao*, "narrow")
>
> 分清 (*fenqing*, "distinguish") 说明 (*shuoming*, "explain") 推动 (*tuidong*, "promote") 改正 (*gaizheng*, "correct") 冲淡 (*chongdan*, "dilute")
>
> 促成 (*cucheng*, "facilitate") 记住 (*jizhu*, "remember") 打倒 (*dadao*, "overthrow") 保全 (*baoquan*, "preserve") 延长 (*yanchang*, "extend")
>
> 推翻 (*tuifan*, "overthrow") 推进 (*tuijin*, "advance") 克服 (*kefu*, "overcome") 说服 (*shuofu*, "persuade") 抓紧 (*zhuajin*, "grasp")
>
> 遇见 (*yujian*, "meet") 改良 (*gailiang*, "improve") 立正 (*lizheng*, "stand at attention") 革新 (*gexin*, "innovate") 扩大 (*kuoda*, "expand")

(4) Verb-object compounds: the relation between the two component semantic morphemes of such compounds is that of governer-governed. For example,

> 知己 (*zhiji*, "confidant") 顶针 (*dingzhen*, "thimble") 董事 (*dongshi*, "director") 司机 (*siji*, "driver") 理事 (*lishi*, "director")
>
> 描红 (*miaohong*, "trace in black ink over characters printed in red") 裹腿 (*guotui*, "leggings") 围脖 (*weibo*, "collar") 护膝 (*huxi*, "kneepad") 迎春 (*yingchun*, "winter jasmine")
>
> 隔壁 (*gebi*, "next door") 贴心 (*tiexin*, "intimate") 立夏 (*Lixia*, "the Beginning of Summer") 管家 (*guanjia*, "housekeeper") 连襟 (*lianjin*, "husbands of wife's sisters; brother-in-law")
>
> 埋头 (*maitou*, "immerse oneself in") 起草 (*qicao*, "draft") 整风 (*zhengfeng*, "rectify the style of thinking and work") 动员 (*dongyuan*, "mobilize") 担心 (*danxin*, "worry")
>
> 负责 (*fuze*, "be responsible for") 留意 (*liuyi*, "pay attention to") 出版 (*chuban*, "publish") 失踪 (*shizong*, "disappear") 避难 (*bi//nan*, "take refuge")
>
> 剪彩 (*jiancai*, "ribbon-cutting") 出气 (*chuqi*, "give vent to one's anger") 接力 (*jieli*, "relay") 失眠 (*shimian*, "lose sleep") 毕业 (*biye*, "graduation")

怀疑 (*huaiyi*, "doubt") 冒险 (*maoxian*, "adventure") 抱歉 (*baoqian*, "regret") 观光 (*guanguang*, "sightseeing") 吹牛 (*chuiniu*, "brag")
露骨 (*lugu*, "barefaced") 耐烦 (*naifan*, "impatient") 得意 (*deyi*, "proud") 安心 (*anxin*, "peace of mind") 吃力 (*chili*, "laborious")

(5) Subject-predicate compounds: the relation between the two component semantic morphemes of such compounds are that of subject-predicate. For example,

秋分 (*Qiufen*, "the Autumnal Equinox") 霜降 (*Shuangjiang*, "First Frost") 地震 (*dizhen*, "earthquake") 山崩 (*shanbeng*, "landslide") 海啸 (*haixiao*, "tsunami")
日食 (*rishi*, "solar eclipse") 蝉蜕 (*chantui*, "cicada slough") 口红 (*kouhong*, "lipstick") 事变 (*shibian*, "incident") 心得 (*xinde*, "experience")
自觉 (*zijue*, "conscious") 胆怯 (*danqie*, "timid") 面熟 (*mianshu*, "familiar") 眼红 (*yanhong*, "jealous") 性急 (*xingji*, "impatient")
心寒 (*xinhan*, "chilling") 气馁 (*qinei*, "discouraged") 人为 (*renwei*, "artificial") 风凉 (*fengliang*, "cool") 发指 (*fazhi*, "bristle with anger")
神往 (*shenwang*, "be carried away") 锋利 (*fengli*, "sharp") 声张 (*shengzhang*, "disclose") 肉麻 (*rouma*, "nauseating") 手软 (*shouruan*, "be soft-hearted")
肩负 (*jianfu*, "shoulder") 自动 (*zidong*, "automatic") 目击 (*muji*, "witness") 耳鸣 (*erming*, "tinnitus") 自杀 (*zisha*, "suicide")
心绞痛 (*xinjiaotong*, "angina") 肾结石 (*shenjieshi*, "kidney stone") 肝硬化 (*ganyinghua*, "cirrhosis") 脑溢血 (*naoyixue*, "cerebral hemorrhage")
肺结核 (*feijiehe*, "pulmonary tuberculosis") 胃下垂 (*weixiachui*, "gastroptosis") 炎得平 (*yandeping*, "anti-inflammation") 痛可宁 (*tongkening*, "dicentrine")

(6) Reduplication compounds: the relation between the two semantic morphemes of such words is that of superposition. The Chinese language abounds in words of reduplication in form and the characteristics of reduplication compounds lie in that they are reduplicated out of the root semantic morphemes and that most reduplication compounds are related with the constituent root semantic morphemes in meaning in one way or another. For example,

妈妈 (*mama*, "mom") 姑姑 (*gugu*, "aunt") 星星 (*xingxing*, "star") 杠杠 (*ganggang*, "certain limits and stipulations") 点点 (*diandian*, "little")
渐渐 (*jianjian*, "gradually") 悄悄 (*qiaoqiao*, "quietly") 茫茫 (*mangmang*, "vast") 沉沉 (*chenchen*, "heavy") 重重 (*chongchong*, "layer upon layer")
婆婆妈妈 (*popomama*, "womanishly fussy") 星星点点 (*xingxingdiandian*, "tiny spots") 满满登登 (*manmandengdeng*, "full to the brim")
颤颤巍巍 (*chanchanweiwei*, "trembling tottering") 战战兢兢 (*zhanzhanjingjing*, "trembling with fear") 病病歪歪 (*bingbingwaiwai*, "be in extremely delicate and fragile health")

III Word formation and word morphology: a joint analysis

Now that word coinage is different from word structure and word formation is different from word morphology, one can carry out analysis and investigation of words from much more aspects. For whichever word, one can not only probe into the reasons and approaches of its emergence from the point of view of word coinage and word formation, but also explore its form and internal structure from the point of view of word structure and word morphology.

Some words are analyzed from these two aspects as follows:

Words	Word Formation	Word Morphology
人	Arbitrary combination of sound and meaning	Monosyllabic, simple word
扣儿 (kour)	Phonetic change	Monosyllabic, simple word
沙沙	Onomatopoeia	Disyllable, simple, reduplicated word
参差	Arbitrary combination of sound and meaning	Disyllable, simple, alliterated word
腼腆	Arbitrary combination of sound and meaning	Disyllable, simple, rhymed word
劲头	Illustration	Disyllable, complex, root+ suffix derivative
阿姨	Disyllabification	Disyllable, complex, root+ prefix derivative
石头	Disyllabification	Disyllable, complex, root+ suffix derivative
摇篮	Illustration	Disyllable, complex, subordinate compound
龙眼	Rhetorical comparison	Disyllable, complex, subordinate compound
三好	Abbreviation	Disyllable, complex, subordinate compound
扫盲	Abbreviation	Disyllable, complex, verb-object compound
失望	Illustration	Disyllable, complex, verb-object compound
神往	Illustration	Disyllable, complex, subject-predicate compound
建筑	Disyllabification	Disyllable, complex, synonymous coordinate compound
成败	Semantic extension	Disyllable, complex, antonymous coordinate compound
骨肉	Semantic extension	Disyllable, complex, meaning-correlated coordinate compound
柳树	Illustration	Disyllable, complex, specifying compound
改正	Illustration	Disyllable, complex, verb-complement compound
眼睁睁	Illustration	Polysyllabic, complex, partial-reduplicated, supplementary specification compound
红乎乎	Illustration	Polysyllabic, complex, root + reduplicated suffix derivative

The above analysis indicates that the word with the same word formation may be different in word morphology and vice versa. Therefore to carry out the analysis of word formation and that of word morphology separately is quite necessary.

It is much more complicated as far as word formation and word morphology are concerned in the reality of the Chinese language. A joint utilization of a variety of word formations or that of word morphologies are often involved in one word.

Here are some examples of the joint use of word formations. The word "万年青 (*wannianqing*, 'evergreen')" illustrates the state in which a plant is evergreen; therefore, one can say that it is a case of illustration and it is metaphorical to use "万年 (*wannian*, 'ten thousand years')" to illustrate the situation of being evergreen: for the coinage of "万年青" it is a joint use of illustration and rhetorical comparison as far as the ways of word formation is concerned. Another example is "乒乓球 (*pingpangqiu*, 'ping-pong ball')": it indicates a ball with "乒乓 (*pingpang*, 'ping-pong')" illustrating "球 (*qiu*, 'ball')", so it belongs to illustration. What is more, the specification part of "乒乓" is an onomatopoeia; therefore, the coinage of the word "乒乓球" is a joint use of illustration and onomatopoeia.

The word "脑溢血 (*naoyixue*, 'cerebral hemorrhage')" is a case for the joint use of word morphology: it is composed of three semantic morphemes – "脑 (*nao*, 'cerebrum')" and "溢血 (*yixue*, 'hemorrhage')" is in subject-predicate relation whereas "溢 (*yi*, 'overflow')" and "血 (*xue*, 'blood')" is in verb-object relation, i.e., it has two structures of subject-predicate and verb-object at the same time but according to the tradition of Chinese syntactic analysis the subject-predicate one is taken as the primary relation in this word.

In addition, different word formation and word morphology can also be found from the aspect of hierarchical analysis of the structure of words. Take the word "三好生 (*sanhaosheng*, 'three good student')" as an example: as far as word formation is concerned, the combination at the first layer of "三好 (*sanhao*, 'three-good')" and "生 (*sheng*, 'student')" is an illustration and the combination at the second layer of "三 (*san*, 'three')" and "好 (*hao*, 'good')" is an abbreviation. As far as word morphology is concerned, the combination at the first layer "三好" and "生" is a subordinate compound and the combination of "三" and "好" is also a subordinate compound. Take the word "朝阳花 (*chaoyanghua*, 'sunflower')" as another example: as far as word formation is concerned, the combination at the first layer of "朝阳 (*chaoyang*, 'face the sun')" and "花 (*hua*, 'flower')" is an illustration and the combination at the second layer of "朝 (*chao*, 'face')" and "阳 (*yang*, 'the sun')" is also an illustration. As far as word morphology is concerned, the combination at the first layer "朝阳" and "花" is a subordinate compound whereas the combination of at the second "朝" and "阳" is a verb-object compound. It can be seen from the above that the analysis of word formation and word morphology is a rather painstaking matter.

Section 4 Logical foundation of word coinage and word structure

I The common logical foundation of word coinage and word structure

Word coinage activities are all carried out on the basis of people's cognition and the available language elements and the cognition and thinking of people determine the basic appearance of the coined words. Language and thought are so closely connected that people's cognition and laws of thinking are more often than not reflected through the form of language. Different ways of word formation discussed in the above illustrate fully the cognition activities in word formation. The neologisms coined through all the ways of word formation also indicate completely the new concepts formed through all kinds of cognition activities in word coinage. Meanwhile the laws of thinking are naturally represented through the internal structures of words by a great variety of grammatical rules. Therefore the comprehensibility of the laws of thinking in word coinage ensures the analyzability of the rules of word structure because the thinking activities and thinking outcomes in word coinage are consistent with those reflected in word structure: this leads to a logical conclusion that word coinage and word structure share the same logical foundation and that word formation and word morphology share the common logical law. For example, both the first element of "地震 (*dizhen*, 'earthquake')" and "电动 (*diandong*, 'power-driven')" are nominal and both the second are verby, and both of them are coined through illustration. In the analysis of their word structure, however, "地震" is grouped into subject-predicate compounds while "电动" subordinate compounds. What is the reason for this situation? The reason lies in that when "地震" is coined, the logic behind it is to illustrate that "地震动了 (*di zhendong le*, 'the earth is in motion')", so a logic form of judgement is required to express it and the grammatical structure of the word is one of subject-predicate, while the case for the word "电动" is quite different: when this word is coined, it does not in any sense illustrate that "电震动了 (*dian zhendong le*, 'power is in motion')", what this word really illustrates is one of the situations of "动 (motion)" and the cause of "动" is "电 (power)", consequently the logic relation between "电" and "动" is that of modifier-modified and the grammatical structure of this word is that of a subordinate structure. It is evident from this that the thinking activities in word coinage and the base form thus formed are closely connected with the structural rules of the word structure.

II A concrete analysis of the logical foundation of word coinage and word structure

Language is different from thought, so linguistic rules differ from logical ones. The word structure rules and logical relationships between semantic morphemes are complicated instead of a one-to-one correspondence.

The logical foundation of word coinage and word structure in the Chinese language is also quite sophisticated. We make a tentative analysis on the disyllables in the contemporary Chinese language as follows.

(I) Identical relation

Identical relation indicates that the extension of two concepts is identical or identical for the most part. All words coined on the basis of identical relation in Chinese are coordinate compounds as far as word structure is concerned. For example,

美丽 (*meili*, "beautiful") 增加 (*zengjia*, "increase") 积累 (*jilei*, "accumulate") 帮助 (*bangzhu*, "help") 丢失 (*diushi*, "lose")

制造 (*zhizao*, "manufacture") 道路 (*daolu*, "road") 依靠 (*yikao*, "rely on") 购买 (*goumai*, "purchase") 寒冷 (*hanleng*, "cold")

The extensions of the concepts denoted by the two component semantic morphemes of this type of words are basically identical, for example: the two component semantic morphemes "美 (*mei*)" and "丽 (*li*)" of the word "美丽" both denote the concept of "beautiful, good-looking" and the extensions of them are identical for the most part so that the two semantic morphemes are compounded into one word. The conceptual identical relation is the logical foundation for this type of compounds.

The meanings of the neologisms based on the conceptual identical relation are in general the result of the complementation and integration of the meanings of the semantic morphemes and the meaning of a neologism thus coined is synonymous with that of its semantic morphemes.

(II) Appositive relation

Appositive relation indicates that the two different but relevant concepts are concepts of species under the same concept of genus and the two concepts are in appositive relation. All words coined on the basis of appositive relation of concepts in Chinese are coordinate compounds related in meaning as far as word structure is concerned. For example,

豺狼 (*chailang*, "beast of prey") 书报 (*shubao*, "book and the press") 笔墨 (*bimo*, "writings") 学习 (*xuexi*, "study") 批改 (*pigai*, "correct")
钢铁 (*gangtie*, "steel") 粮草 (*liangcao*, "forage") 禽兽 (*qinshou*, "beast") 针线 (*zhenxian*, "needle") 花草 (*huacao*, "flowers")

The word "豺狼" is composed of "豺 (*chai*, 'jackal')" and "狼 (*lang*, 'wolf')" and "豺" and "狼" denote two different concepts but they are in appositive relation with respect to such a concept of genus as "beast of prey". The appositive relation of concepts in the law of thinking is the logical foundation of the combination of these semantic morphemes.

The meaning of a neologism formed on the basis of appositive relation is in general integration, complementation and deepening of the meanings of the two component semantic morphemes, but the situations are various. In some cases, the meaning of the neologism is identical or related to the concept of genus to which the appositive concepts of species belong. For example, the meaning of "豺狼" is "flagitious beast of prey", which is identical to that of "beast of prey". The meaning of "书报" is identical to "book and the press", which is related to the concept of genus, "reading material", to which "书 (*shu*, 'book')" and "报 (*bao*, 'newspaper')" belong. In other cases, the meaning of the neologism is a new development in the process of integration and deepening because it is constrained in one way or another by some aspects within language or of application in society. For example, the word "笔墨" does no longer refer to "pen and ink" but "writings" instead. Such words as "领袖 (*lingxiu*, 'leader')", "爪牙 (*zhaoya*, 'jackal')", "口舌 (*koushe*, 'quarrel')", "人物 (*renwu*, 'personality')", "窗户 (*chuanghu*, 'window')" and "干净 (*ganjing*, 'clean')" are all the same cases. All of them are compounds based on the appositive relation of the semantic morphemes; the only difference lies in that for words like "领袖", "爪牙" and "口舌", a completely new concept different from the original semantic morphemes is denoted by the new compound through semantic extension and metaphor based on the original elements, while cases are different for words like "人物", "窗户" and "干净": due to the difference in ways of word formation, they have all evolved into subordination compound words in which the meaning of the neologism is equivalent to one of the two component semantic morphemes and the meaning of the other component semantic morpheme vanishes. Nonetheless, there is no denying that the logical foundation for compounding these semantic morphemes is still the conceptual appositive relation between them.

(III) Opposite relation

Opposite relation indicates the contradictory relation and opposite relation between the concepts.

Contradictory relation means that two concepts are included in one and the same concept of genus with their extensions mutually exclusive and that the sum total of their extension equals the extension of the concept of genus to which they belong. Take, for example, the semantic morpheme "生 (*sheng*, 'living')" and "死 (*si*, 'death')" in "生死 (*shengsi*, 'life and death')"; the extensions of the two component semantic morphemes are mutually exclusive and both of them are included within the extension of the concept of genus "living and death".

Opposite relation means that two concepts are within one and the same concept of genus with their extensions mutually exclusive but that the sum total of their extensions is less than the extension of the concept of genus to which they belong. The semantic morphemes "甘 (*gan*, 'sweetness')" and "苦 (*ku*, 'bitterness')" in "甘苦 (*ganku*, 'sweetness and bitterness; hardships and difficulties')" are a case in point: "甘" and "苦" are mutually exclusive in extension but are included within the extension of one and the same concept of genus "味 (*wei*, 'flavour')" whereas the sum total of the extensions of "甘" and "苦" are less than the extension of "味".

For either contradictory concepts or opposite concepts, because their extensions are mutually exclusive, their intensions are opposite, i. e., in opposite relation. All words coined on the basis of opposite relation in Chinese are antonymous coordinate compounds related in meaning as far as word structure is concerned. For example,

多少 (*duoshao*, "how much/many") 呼吸 (*huxi*, "breathe") 来往 (*laiwang*, "contact") 开关 (*kaiguan*, "switch") 出纳 (*chuna*, "cashier")

长短 (*changduan*, "length; accidents; right and wrong; merits and demerits") 深浅 (*shenqian*, "depth") 收发 (*shoufa*, "receive and dispatch") 始终 (*shizhong*, "from beginning to end") 左右 (*zuoyou*, "the left and right sides")

The emergence and structural forms of words 93

The semantic morphemes in this type of words all denote a pair of concepts in opposition to each other. For example, the two concepts denoted by "多 (*duo*, 'many; much')" and "少 (*shao*, 'few')" are opposite in both extension and intension but they are included in the extension of the concept of genus "quantity".

The situation of the meanings of the compound neologisms based on opposite relation is much complicated. For some words, their word meanings reflect the concept of genus to which the two concepts denoted by the two component semantic morphemes belong. For example, "呼吸 (*huxi*, 'breathing')" is the concept of genus to which "呼 (*hu*, 'breathing out')" and "吸 (*xi*, 'breathing in')" belong. For others, in addition to their concept of genus, certain objects or situations can be denoted by the word meanings because of the new development of meaning on this basis. Take "长短 (*changduan*)" for example: it can denote "accidents" and "right and wrong; merits and demerits" in addition to "length". For still other words, they denote the objects relevant to the concepts denoted by their semantic morphemes instead of the concept of genus to which their semantic morphemes belong. For example, "开关 (*kaiguan*, 'switch')" only denotes the designation of the object relevant to the actions of "开 (*kai*, 'to switch on')" and "关 (*guan*, 'to switch off')".

(IV) Subordination relation

Subordination relation means the case in which the concept of species with a smaller extension is included in the concept of genus with a larger extension and the concept of species is subordinated to the concept of genus, thus the two concepts are in a subordination relation. In Chinese, all words coined on the basis of the subordination relation are the type of specification with the category of the specified of the complementation compounds as far as word structure is concerned. For example,

> 鲤鱼 (*liyu*, "carp") 柳树 (*liushu*, "willow") 梅花 (*meihua*, "plum") 芹菜 (*qincai*, "celery") 淮河 (*Huai He*, "The Huaihe River")
> 茅草 (*maocao*, "thatch") 玉石 (*yushi*, "jade") 蝗虫 (*huangchong*, "grasshopper") 鹞鹰 (*yaoying*, "sparrow hawk") 菊花 (*juhua*, "chrysanthemum")

The concepts denoted by the two component semantic morphemes of this type of words are of subordination relation between the concept of species and the concept of genus. For example, "梅 (*mei*, 'Chinese plum')" was originally a designation of a flower and it is a concept of species of "花 (*hua*, 'flower')" and "花" is its concept of genus, thus "梅" and "花" are in subordinate relation.

The meanings of the neologisms compounded through subordination relation are always identical to the meanings of the semantic morpheme denoting the concept of species concepts of species. From the point of view of word structure, the semantic morpheme denoting the concept of genus specifies and supplements the semantic morpheme denoting the concept of species in meaning.

(V) Attributive relation

Attributive relation means that among the two concepts A and B, concept A is the principal one and concept B restricts and illustrates concept A; thus the restricted concept A transits into a concept with a smaller extension from a concept with a largger extension with an increase in intension. Consequently the compounds coined through attributive relation will make the concept of genus with a broad extension turn into a concept of species with a narrow extension. From the point of view of words, the concept denoted by all the neologisms compounded on the basis of attributive relation is a concept of species of the concept denoted by the principal semantic morpheme of the compounds. For example, "汉语 (*Hanyu*, 'Chinese; the language spoken by the Han people')" is a compound of attributive relation between "汉 (*Han*, 'Han people')" and "语 (*yu*, 'language')": "汉" restricts and modifies "语", thus the concept denoted by "汉语" is a concept of species of the concept denoted by "语" and the relation between "汉语" and "语" is that between the concept of species and the concept of genus. All words coined on the basis of attributive relation in Chinese are subordinates as far as word structure is concerned. For example,

> 电扇 (*dianshan*, "electric fan") 胶鞋 (*jiaoxie*, "rubber overshoes") 公路 (*gonglu*, "highway") 飞机 (*feiji*, "aircraft") 红旗 (*hongqi*, "red flag")
> 台灯 (*taideng*, "table lamp") 主观 (*zhuguan*, "subjective") 奇迹 (*qiji*, "miracle") 狂欢 (*kuanghuan*, "carnival") 雪白 (*xuebai*, "snow-white")

Compounds based on attributive relation abound in Chinese vocabulary. Take "桌 (*zhuo*, 'table; desk')" as an example: "方 (*fang*, 'square')" and "圆 (*yuan*, 'round')" are used in "方桌 (*fangzhuo*, 'square table')" and "圆桌 (*yuanzhuo*, 'round table')" to restrict "桌" from the aspect of shape whereas "饭 (*fan*, 'dinner')" and "书 (*shu*, 'book')" are used in "饭桌 (*fanzhuo*, 'dining table')" and "书桌 (*shuzhuo*, 'writing desk')" to restrict "桌" from the aspect of usage respectively. People can restrict different objects from various angles, thereby coining neologisms by compounding semantic morphemes with different meanings.

Nevertheless, language is different from logic; therefore new changes and development can be found in their meanings during the course of use and conventionalization of some words after their formation. Take "红旗 (*hongqi*)" and "白旗 (*baiqi*)" for example: after their formation, their meanings do not only denote "red flag" and "white flag", but become even more abstract and bear a richer and more profound new content of "a symbol of revolution" and "a signal of surrender in wartime" respectively.

It should be pointed out that for some subordinate compounds in Chinese, although they are formed based on the conceptual attributive relation between the constituent semantic morphemes, they are quite different from what has been discussed in the above. Such words as "雪白 (*xuebai*, 'snow-white')", "冰凉 (*bingliang*, 'ice cold')", "墨黑 (*mohei*, 'inkiness')" and "火热 (*huore*, 'fervent')", etc. are all cases in point: a figurative attributive relation exists between the concepts denoted by the two component semantic morphemes in these words – the concept denoted by the vehicle restricting the concept denoted by the tenor – for example, "as white as snow" in "雪白" or "as cold as ice" in "冰凉". The concepts denoted by the compound neologisms are more reinforced than those indicated by the original semantic morphemes (modification by "很 (*hen*, 'very')" is not permitted for these words in general), but no relation of the concept of species and the concept of genus are formed here.

In addition to subordinate compounds, specification with the unit of the specified in complementation compounds can also be found in the word coinage based on the conceptual attributive relation. For example,

> 布匹 (*bupi*, "cloth") 纸张 (*zhizhang*, "paper") 房间 (*fangjian*, "room") 人口 (*renkou*, "population") 船只 (*chuanzhi*, "ship")
> 车辆 (*cheliang*, "vehicle") 事件 (*shijian*, "event") 花朵 (*huaduo*, "flower") 枪支 (*qiangzhi*, "firearms") 书本 (*shuben*, "book")

The semantic morphemes denote two different concepts in the above examples, of which the latter denoting the concept of the unit restricts the former denoting the object and specifies and supplements the restricted concept. The words thus formed often refer to the collective concept of the restricted objects.

(VI) Government relation

Government relation means that the first concept denotes an action while the second concept denotes the object and/or situation that the action involves, thus the former governs the latter. Many Chinese compounds are based on government relation. For example,

> 埋头 (*maitou*, "immerse oneself in") 起草 (*qicao*, "draft") 庆功 (*qinggong*, "celebrate success") 动员 (*dongyuan*, "mobilize") 整风 (*zhengfeng*, "rectify the style of thinking and work")
> 担心 (*danxin*, "worry") 知己 (*zhiji*, "confidant") 顶针 (*dingzhen*, "thimble") 裹腿 (*guotui*, "leggings") 分红 (*fenhong*, "share out bonus")

The words above are compounds on the basis of the government relation between the concepts and they are verb-object in structure. The semantic morphemes of verb-object compounds are of the relation between an action and the object the action involves.

The meanings of the compounds based on government relation are integrated by semantic extension by the meanings of the two component semantic morphemes with the meaning of the predicative semantic morpheme playing a major role.

In addition, there are also verb-complement compounds in Chinese vocabulary, for example:

> 提高 (*tigao*, "improve") 削弱 (*xueruo*, "weaken") 离开 (*likai*, "leave") 改进 (*gaijin*, "improve") 降低 (*jiangdi*, "reduce")

撕毁 (*sihui*, "tear up") 击破 (*jipo*, "break") 放大 (*fangda*, "enlarge") 隔离 (*geli*, "insulate") 促成 (*cucheng*, "facilitate")

The logical foundation for these compounds is also government relation between the concepts. Verb-complement compounds are, without doubt, different from verb-object compounds. The relation between the concepts denoted by the two component semantic morphemes of a verb-complement compound more often than not is that of the action and the situation brought about by the action itself. For example, "提高 (*tigao*, 'improve')" indicates the situation in which "提 (*ti*, 'raise')" brings about "高 (*gao*, 'high')" and "撕毁 (*sihui*, 'tear up')" the situation in which "撕 (*si*, 'tear')" brings about "毁 (*hui*, 'destroyed, damaged')". Therefore, even though what the predicative semantic morpheme in verb-complement compounds involves is not the object that it governs, it involves the situation it brings about: there will be no situation thus brought about without the action, so it is from this sense that one may conclude that the concept denoted by the latter semantic morpheme is governed by that denoted by the former one. The logical foundation for verb-complement compounds are also government relation between the concepts.

The characteristics of the meaning of the verb-complement compounds based on government relation are the same as those of the verb-object compounds. The meanings of the compounds are also integrated by semantic extension from the meanings of the two component semantic morphemes with the meaning of the predicative semantic morpheme playing a major role.

(VII) Predication relation

Predication relation means that the concepts are united together to constitute a judgement with the former concept as the subject and the latter the predicate of the judgement. All words coined on the basis of predication relation in Chinese are subject-predicate compounds as far as word structure is concerned. For example,

性急 (*xingji*, "impatient") 自觉 (*zijue*, "conscious") 国营 (*guoying*, "state-run") 民办 (*minban*, "civilian-run") 年轻 (*nianqing*, "young")
地震 (*dizhen*, "earthquake") 胆怯 (*danqie*, "timid") 心虚 (*xinxu*, "lacking in self-confidence") 眼馋 (*yanchan*, "be envious") 口吃 (*kouchi*, "stutter")

The concepts denoted by the two component semantic morphemes of such compounds can be the subject and predicate of a judgement in logic, thus they form a judgement. For example, "性急 (*xingji*)" means that "性子是急的 (*xingzi shi jide*, 'the temper is impatient')", which is a judgement.

(VIII) Coincidence relation

Coincidence relation, which is simple, means the repetition relation between concepts by repeating one and the same concept. Words of coincidence relation are reduplication compounds in word structure. It should be pointed out that in word formation for some neologisms by reduplicating root semantic morphemes, their meanings are identical to those of the root semantic morphemes, but for others, their meanings are an integration and development of the meanings of the root semantic morphemes.

It can be seen from the above analysis that word coinage and word structures in Chinese is closely related to logic: although it is not that all elements that have logical relationship can be compounded into words and although a number of words are coined in accordance with the characteristics of Chinese per se (for example, the characteristics of Chinese morphology), the semantic morphemes of all words constituted out of syntactic relations are composed on a certain logical foundation. The law of cognition and thinking at the time when the words are coined is the foundation for the semantic morphemes to combine with each other and the ways of combination do not only reflect the various logic relations between the compounded semantic morphemes, but also ensure the explicability of the relevant combinations.

It is of practical significance in understanding and analyzing the formation of words after having learned about the logical foundation of word coinage and word structure. Take "鲫鱼 (*jiyu*, 'crucian')" and "带鱼 (*daiyu*, 'ribbon fish')" for example: both of them designate fish and they are similar in form, but their ways of word formation are quite different because the logical relationships between the semantic morphemes of each word are different. The "鲫 (*ji*, 'crucian')" in "鲫鱼" designates a fish in itself and the relation between "鲫" and "鱼" is of concept of species and concept of genus; therefore the logical foundation of word coinage and word structure for this word is the subordinate relation between concepts, so "鱼" just complements and specifies "鲫", and consequently "鲫鱼" is a specification with the category of the specified. The case for "带鱼" is quite different: "带 (*dai*, 'ribbon')" by itself does not designate fish at all and it designates fish only when it is combined with "鱼 (*yu*, 'fish')" to form a compound "带鱼". Therefore, the relation between "带" and "鱼" is an attributive relation between concepts with "鱼" as the major semantic morpheme while "带" restricting "鱼" from shape, so "带鱼" is a subordinate in word structure.

It is easy to analyze word structure based on the logical relationship between semantic morphemes. For example, people differ on the word structure of "河流 (*heliu*, 'river')". Some scholars propose that "河流" is a subject-predicate compound, which is open to question. [6] We can solve this problem from logical relationship: "河流" is composed of two component semantic morphemes "河 (*he*, 'river')" and "流 (*liu*, 'flow')", and if "河流" is treated as a subject-predicate construction, it amounts to say that "河流" is a judgement in logic, thus the word will mean "the river flows", which is illogical: because it is only "水 (*shui*, 'water')" that flows instead of the whole "河"; therefore the logical foundation for "河" and "流" to combine into a word is in no sense the predication relation and the word "河流" is not a subject-predicate compound at all. As a matter of fact, "河" and "流" are combined to form "河流" on the conceptual identity relation: what "流" designates in "河流" is "current" instead of the concept of "flow" (the sixth sense of "流" in the *Dictionary of Contemporary Chinese, Revised Edition*), so "河" is a "current" and "流" also designates "current", consequently "河" and "流" are in identical relation in the compound "河流" and as far as the word structure is concerned, "河流" is a synonymous coordinate of coordinate compounds. As far as the word structure is concerned, the differences in opinion are not rare: for example, are "自动 (*zidong*, 'automatic; voluntarily; of one's own accord')" and "主动 (*zhudong*, 'active; initiative')" the same in word structure? Are 电流 (*dianliu*, 'current')" and "饼干 (*binggan*, 'biscuit')" subject-predicate compounds or subordinate compounds? Are "摇篮 (*yaolan*, 'cradle')", "拉锁 (*lasuo*, 'zipper')" and "跳棋 (*tiaoqi*, 'Chinese draughts')" verb-object compounds or subordinate compounds? It is not difficult to furnish the right answer for these questions after an analysis based on the logical foundation of word coinage and word structure.

Recognition of the explicability of constituent semantic morphemes, nevertheless, does not mean that the meanings of all the neologisms formed in this way are only simple reflections of the concepts denoted by their relevant constituent semantic morphemes and the logical relationship between the concepts. It can also be seen from the relevant analysis in the above that the meanings of the neologisms may have new and further development on the basis of the original meanings of the constituent semantic morphemes through figurative semantic extension or due to the development of the objective things and the conventionalization in linguistic community. Therefore it is not suitable to grasp the meanings of complex words only based the meanings of the semantic morphemes and their relations. Despite all this, we must keep in mind that there exist logical laws in the combination of semantic morphemes in accordance with the cognition and thinking of people when the complex words are coined and this constitutes the logical foundation of word coinage and word structure, which can never be neglected in the analysis of word coinage and word structure.

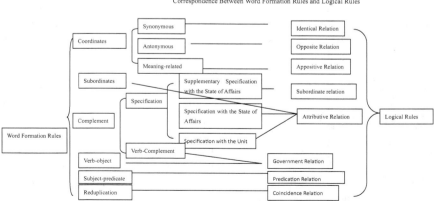

Correspondence Between Word Formation Rules and Logical Rules

The emergence and structural forms of words 99

Section 5 Inflectional morphology in Chinese

I Inflection and inflectional morphology

Inflection is indicative of the inflectional changes: different grammatical meanings are indicated by different inflections. The way in which a word inflects is its inflectional morphology. The situations and functions of inflectional morphology are different in different languages: in such inflectional languages as Russian and English, the function of inflection is quite obvious while its function in a non-inflectional language is comparatively weak.

II Inflectional morphology in Chinese

There is no inflection for many words in such a non-inflectional language as Chinese. Certain inflections are available in Chinese for a few words such as some of nouns, pronouns, verbs, adjectives and classifiers. Cases are quite different for such words alone: inflections are only available for nouns designating "people" or nouns with classifier properties and for personal pronouns. Of course this does not include active usages in parole.

Types of inflectional morphology in Chinese are comparatively few and the following are familiar ones:

(I) Affixation

Affixation means to affix an inflectional ending after a stem. For example,

我 (*wo*, "I") – 我们 (*women*, "we")
你 (*ni*, "you") – 你们 (*nimen*, "you")
老师 (*laosi*, "teacher") – 老师们 (*laoshimen*, "teachers")
朋友 (*pengyou*, "friend") – 朋友们 (*pengyoumen*, "friends")

The above examples belong to the situation in which the ending "们 (*men*)" is affixed after pronouns or the nouns denoting human beings: after the affixation of "们" a grammatical meaning of "plural" is added.

Other examples are as follows:

看 (*kan*, "look") – 看着 (*kanzhe*, "looking")
看 (*kan*, "look") – 看了 (*kanle*, "looked")
看 (*kan*, "look") – 看过 (*kanguo*, "have looked")
商量 (*shangliang*, "discuss") – 商量着 (*shangliangzhe*, "discussing")
商量 (*shangliang*, "discuss") – 商量了 (*shangliangle*, "discussed")
商量 (*shangliang*, "discuss") – 商量过 (*shangliangguo*, "have discussed")

In the above, the endings of "着 (*le*)", "了 (*zhe*)" and "过 (*guo*)" are affixed to verbs respectively and a grammatical meaning of "aspect" is added after the affixation: "着" denotes the grammatical meaning of "progressive", "了" denotes the grammatical meaning of "perfect" and "了" denotes the grammatical meaning of "pluperfect".

(II) Superposition

Superposition means an inflectional change by superposing the whole word, or by superposing every constituent semantic morpheme of a word respectively, or by superposing some of the constituent semantic morphemes of a word.

Superposition of the whole word:

AA Type:

人 (*ren*, "person") – 人人 (*renren*, "every person")
天 (*tian*, "day") – 天天 (*tiantian*, "every day")
家 (*jia*, "family") – 家家 (*jiajia*, "every family")
件 (*jian*, "case") – 件件 (*jianjian*, "every case")
个 (*ge*, "individual") – 个个 (*gege*, "every individual")
趟 (*tang*, "time") – 趟趟 (*tangtang*, "every time")
走 (*zou*, "walk") – 走走 (*zouzou*, "take a walk for a short period of time")
扫 (*sao*, "sweep") – 扫扫 (*saosao*, "sweep for a short period of time")
洗 (*xi*, "wash") – 洗洗 (*xixi*, "try to wash")
高 (*gao*, "high") – 高高 (*gaogao*, "much higher")
红 (*hong*, "red") – 红红 (*honghong*, "much redder")
长 (*chang*, "long") – 长长 (*changchang*, "much longer")

ABAB Type:

研究 (*yanjiu*, "research") – 研究研究 (*yanjiu yanjiu*, "research with care")
调查 (*diaocha*, "investigate") – 调查调查 (*diaocha diaocha*, "have an investigation")
考虑 (*kaolü*, "consider") – 考虑考虑 (*kaolü kaolü*, "think about")
整理 (*zhengli*, "reorganize") – 整理整理 (*zhenglizhengli*, "tidy up")
雪白 (*xuebai*, "snow-white") – 雪白雪白 (*xuebaixuebai*, "as white as snow")
笔直 (*bizhi*, "perfectly straight") – 笔直笔直 (*bizhibizhi*, "upright")

Superposition respectively of every constituent semantic morpheme:

AABB Type:

大方 (*dafang*, "generous") – 大大方方 (*dadafangfang*, "much more generous")
利索 (*lisuo*, "agile") – 利利索索 (*lilisuosuo*, "quick and efficient")
安静 (*anjing*, "quiet") – 安安静静 (*ananjingjing*, "peaceful and serene")
快乐 (*kuaile*, "happy") – 快快乐乐 (*kuaikuailele*, "full of joy")
勤恳 (*qinken*, "diligent") – 勤勤恳恳 (*qinqinkenken*, "diligently and conscientiously")
轻快 (*qingkuai*, "brist") – 轻轻快快 (*qingqingkuaikuai*, "lightly")

Superposition of some of the constituent semantic morpheme:

AAB Type:

跑步 (*paobu*, "run") – 跑跑步 (*paopaobu*, "have a run")
把关 (*baguan*, "check on") – 把把关 (*babaguan*, "have a check")
抓紧 (*zhuajin*, "grasp") – 抓抓紧 (*zhuazhua jin*, "try to grasp")
喷香 (*penxiang*, "delicious") – 喷喷香 (*pen pen xiang*, "extremely delicious")
梆硬 (*bangying*, "hard") – 梆梆硬 (*bangbangying*, "extremely hard")
滚热 (*gunre* "burning hot") – 滚滚热 (*gungunre*, "extremely hot")

ABB Type:

冷清 (*lengqing*, "desolate") – 冷清清 (*lengqingqing*, "cold and cheerless")
亮堂 (*liangtang*, "bright") – 亮堂堂 (*liangtangtang*, "brilliant")
干巴 (*ganba*, "wizened") – 干巴巴 (*ganbaba*, "dry as dust")
慢腾 (*manteng*, "slowly") – 慢腾腾 (*mantengteng*, "sluggishly")
干净 (*ganjing*, "clean") – 干净净 (*ganjingjing*, "neat and tidy")
暖和 (*nuanhe*, "warm") – 暖和和 (*nuanhehe*, "nice and warm")

A li AB Type:

模糊 (*mohu*, "vague") – 模里模糊 (*molimohu*, "vague")
马虎 (*mahu*, "casual") – 马里马虎 (*malimahu*, "careless")
糊涂 (*hutu*, "confused") – 糊里糊涂 (*hulihutu*, "muddle-headed")
肮脏 (*anzang*, "dirty") – 肮里肮脏 (*angliangzang*, "filthy")
啰唆 (*luosuo*, "wordy") – 啰里啰唆 (*luoliluosuo*, "verbose")
慌张 (*huangzhang*, "flustered") – 慌里慌张 (*huanglihuangzhang*, "all in a fluster")

The above are the ways of inflectional morphology available at present in Chinese. It is observed from the above that for different parts of speech, some of the ways of inflectional morphology are the same while others are different with various grammatical meanings.

As far as "AA type" is concerned, a grammatical meaning of "distributive referring" is added after superposition for nouns and classifiers, i. e., a meaning of "each" is added for the superposed forms. The grammatical meanings of superposition of verbs are that of "transient aspect" and/or "tentative aspect": a meaning of "for a short period of time; just for a try" is added in addition to the original lexical meaning after superposition: "看看 (*kankan*, 'have a look at')" and "试试 (*shishi*, 'have a try')" are cases in point. In addition to adding a flavour of "emphasis", the superposition of adjectives indicates a grammatical meaning of "in some degree, temperate" in most cases. In the meanwhile, an emotional colour of "favour" and "praise" is assigned to the word, for example, "甜甜的 (*tiantiande*, 'a little bit sweet')" and "辣辣的 (*lalade*, 'a little bit hot; spicy')" are quite different from "很甜 (*hentian*, 'very sweet')" and "很辣 (*henla*, 'very hot')" in flavour, although their basic meanings are "sweet" and "hot" respectively.

102 *The emergence and structural forms of words*

As far as "AAB type" is concerned, after inflectional change, a flavour of "transientness" and "emphasis" are added for verbs while a grammatical meaning of "emphatic aspect" with an obvious flavour of "emphasis" is added for adjectives.

As far as "ABB type" is concerned, most words involved in this inflectional morphology are adjectives and a grammatical meaning of "emphatic aspect" is added while the lexical meaning of the word concerned is reinforced.

As far as "ABAB type" is concerned, this is an inflection in which the whole word is superposed and both verb and adjectives are involved. The grammatical meanings of "transientness" and "tentativeness" are added for verbs while the grammatical meaning of "emphatic aspect" with the flavour of "extreme emphasis" is added for adjectives after inflection.

As far as "AABB type" is concerned, what are involved are mainly adjectives and a grammatical meaning of "emphatic aspect" is added after inflection. A flavour of "praise and positiveness" is also added besides the reinforcement of meaning.

As far as "A li AB type" is concerned, this is also an inflection for adjectives, but it is used for the words with derogatory sense in general and in addition to a grammatical meaning of "reinforcement", an emotive flavour of "disgust" is also added after inflection.

It is observed from the above analysis that superposition is a major way of inflectional morphology in Chinese and adjectives are the major part of speech involved. Because Chinese is a non-inflection language, there are no inflectional changes for many words in Chinese. For example, "天空 (*tiankong*, 'sky')", "客观 (*keguan*, 'objective')", "显微镜 (*xianweijing*, 'microscope')" and "超声波 (*chaoshengbo*, 'ultrasonic wave')", etc. Others may have inflectional changes. The inflectional paradigm for each word is on the whole relatively fixed. If the inflectional paradigm of a word is changed into another under a certain condition, the part of speech of the word is consequently changed and its lexical meaning will also be changed accordingly. For example, "热闹 (*renao*)" is an adjective with AABB as its inflectional paradigm and a grammatical meaning of "reinforcement" is added to the superposition "热热闹闹 (*rerenaonao*, 'buzzing with excitement; lively')". However, "热闹" can sometimes be superposed with ABAB into "热闹热闹 (*renaorenao*, 'to have a blast; to enliven')" as in "同学们准备在新年晚会上热闹热闹。(*Tongxuemen zhunbei zai xinnian wanhui shang renao renao*, 'The students are going to have a blast at the new year's party')". The original part of speech of "热闹" is an adjective, because the reduplication form has changed, it turns into a verb while its lexical meaning turns from "lively" into "enliven".

III Differentiation of word formation and inflection

Word structure and inflection are two completely different concepts so word formation and inflectional morphology are also completely different. Word formation studies individual words: to enquire the structural rules of a word and the lexical meaning closely associated with such rules through the analysis of its stem.

Inflectional morphology studies different forms of the paradigm of a word which are attached to an individual word: to enquire the different grammatical meanings and lexical meanings and meanings with special flavour attached to different forms of the word through the analysis of the different forms of the paradigm. It is obvious that the object of study and scope of word formation and inflectional morphology are quite different.

Although word formation and inflectional morphology are distinct from each other in Chinese vocabulary, they sometimes share the same devices and forms; therefore, it is necessary to differentiate word formation from inflectional morphology.

We can differentiate word formation from inflectional morphology in the following two aspects in general:

(I) The meaning aspects

Word formation studies the formation of stems and lexical meanings; therefore, all those lexical meanings do not change at all or change completely after the forms of the word changed belong to word formation. Inflectional morphology deals with the grammatical meanings and the attached lexical meanings and meanings with special flavour by different forms of a word; therefore, all those the lexical meanings do not change basically or only the grammatical meanings or the attached lexical meanings and meanings with special flavour changed belong to inflection.

The following examples belong to word formation:

妈 (*ma*, "mum") – 妈妈 (*mama*, "mum")
姑 (*gu*, "aunt") – 姑姑 (*gugu*, "aunt")
星 (*xing*, "star") – 星星 (*xingxing*, "star")
舅 (*jiu*, "uncle") – 舅舅 (*jiujiu*, "uncle")

The disyllabic forms in the above are all reduplicated by the monosyllabic forms and the two forms before and after reduplication are the same in lexical meanings, grammatical meanings and meanings with special flavour; consequently the monosyllabic forms and the disyllabic forms in the above are all words. All the disyllabic forms are words coined by disyllabification accommodating the disyllabification trend of Chinese and are reduplicated words in word structure.

Another case of word formation is that the meanings of the reduplicated forms are completely different from the original and neologisms with new meanings are coined. For example,

断 (*duan*, "cut; judge") – 断断 (*duanduan*, "absolutely")
通 (*tong*, "open; clear up") – 通通 (*tongtong*, "all")
宝 (*bao*, "treasure") – 宝宝 (*baobao*, "endearment for young child")

斤 (*jin*, "unit of weight") – 斤斤 (*jinjin*, "be particular about small matters")
祖辈 (*zubei*, "ancestor") – 祖祖辈辈 (*zuzubeibei*, "from generation to generation")
缝补 (*fengbu*, "sew and mend") – 缝缝补补 (*fengfeng bubu*, "sew up")
旮旯 (*gala*, "corner") – 旮旮旯旯 (*gagalala*, "all corners")

Some of the above are reduplicated by monosyllabic words; others are reduplicated by disyllables and they are common in that the lexical meanings before reduplication are different from those after reduplication. Consequently, they are all individual words by themselves instead of inflections of words.

Inflections are distinct from this. For example,

同志 (*tongzhi*, "comrade") – 同志们 (*tongzhimen*, "comrades")
同学 (*tongxue*, "classmate") – 同学们 (*tongxuemen*, "classmates")
我 (*wo*, "I") – 我们 (*women*, "we")
他 (*ta*, "he") – 他们 (*tamen*, "they")

Only the grammatical meaning of "plurality" is added, while both the stems and lexical meanings of each word do not change at all after the ending "们" is attached to the original words.

看 (*kan*, "look") – 看着 (*kanzhe*, "looking"), 看了 (*kan le*, "looked"), 看过 (*kanguo*, "have looked")
想 (*xiang*, "think") – 想着 (*xiangzhe*, "thinking"), 想了 (*xiangle*, "thought"), 想过 (*xiangguo*, "have thought")
写 (*xie*, "write") – 写着 (*xiezhe*, "writing"), 写了 (*xiele*, "wrote"), 写过 (*xieguo*, "have written")
说 (*shuo*, "speak") – 说着 (*shuozhe*, "speaking"), 说了 (*shuole*, "spoke"), 说过 (*shuo guo*, "have spoken")

Only a grammatical meaning of "aspect" is added after endings "着 (*zhe*)", "了 (*le*)" and "过 (*guo*)" are attached to the original words in the above. No lexical meanings change in the above examples whatever aspectual grammatical meanings are expressed.

人 (*ren*, "person") – 人人 (*renren*, "every person")
年 (*nian*, "year") – 年年 (*niannian*, "every year")
天 (*tian*, "day") – 天天 (*tiantian*, "every day")
家 (*jia*, "family") – 家家 (*jiajia*, "every family")
趟 (*tang*, "times") – 趟趟 (*tangtang*, "every time")
件 (*jian*, "piece") – 件件 (*jianjian*, "every piece")

The above examples are inflections of classifiers: the monosyllabic classifiers are reduplicated in AA form and only a grammatical meaning of distributive "each" is added while the lexical meanings do not change for the words such as "人" and "年", etc.

Other Examples:

AA Type:

走 (*zou*, "walk") – 走走 (*zouzou*, "take a walk")
找 (*zhao*, "look for") – 找找 (*zhaozhao*, "try to find")
读 (*du*, "read") – 读读 (*dudu*, "try to read")
玩 (*wan*, "play") – 玩玩 (*wanwan*, "play for a little while")
猜 (*cai*, "guess") – 猜猜 (*caicai*, "try to guess")
瞧 (*qiao*, "look") – 瞧瞧 (*qiaoqiao*, "take a look")

AAB Type:

鼓掌 (*guzhang*, "applause") – 鼓鼓掌 (*guguzhang*, "applause")
把关 (*baguan*, "check on") – 把把关 (*babaguan*, "have a check")
跑步 (*paobu*, "run") – 跑跑步 (*paopaobu*, "have a run")
留心 (*liuxin*, "be careful of") – 留留心 (*liuliuxin*, "take care of")
讲情 (*jiangqing*, "plead for sb") – 讲讲情 (*jiangjiang qing*, "try to plead for sb")
受罪 (*shouzui*, "suffer") – 受受罪 (*shoushou zui*, "suffer for a little while")

ABAB Type

研究 (*yanjiu*, "research") – 研究研究 (*yanjiuyanjiu*, "have a research")
调查 (*diaocha*, "investigate") – 调查调查 (*diaochadiaocha*, "have an investigation")
考虑 (*kaolü*, "consider") – 考虑考虑 (*kaolü kaolü*, "try to consider")
商量 (*shangliang*, "discuss") – 商量商量 (*shangliangshangliang*, "have a discussion")
学习 (*xuexi*, "study") – 学习学习 (*xuexi xuexi*, "have a study")
讨论 (*taolun*, "discuss") – 讨论讨论 (*taolun taolun*, "have a discussion")

The above examples are inflections of verbs: monosyllabic verbs are reduplicated in AA type and disyllabic verbs are reduplicated in AAB type or ABAB type. The grammatical meanings of "transientness" and "tentativeness" are added after the inflectional change. For a few disyllabic verbs, such as "打巴 (*daba*, 'hit')" and "甩搭 (*shuaida*, 'throw')", they become "打巴打巴 (*dabadaba*, 'hit repeatedly')" and "甩搭甩搭 (*shuaidashuaida*, 'throw repeatedly')" respectively after reduplication and a grammatical meaning of "iterative aspect" is added. In whichever case, the lexical meanings of the verbs do not change at all.

Still other examples:

AA Type:

高 (*gao*, "high") – 高高 (*gaogao*, "much higher")
红 (*hong*, "red") – 红红 (*honghong*, "much redder")
白 (*bai*, "white") – 白白 (*baibai*, "much whiter")

大 (*da*, "large") – 大大 (*dada*, "much larger")
深 (*shen*, "deep") – 深深 (*shenshen*, "much deeper")
胖 (*pang*, "fat") – 胖胖 (*pangpang*, "much fatter")

AAB Type:

喷香 (*penxiang*, "delicious") – 喷喷香 (*penpenxiang*, "very delicious")
冰凉 (*bingliang*, "icy cold") – 冰冰凉 (*bingbingliang*, "ice cold")
梆硬 (*bangying*, "hard") – 梆梆硬 (*bangbangying*, "much harder")
滚热 (*gunre*, "boiling hot") – 滚滚热 (*gungunre*, "boiling hot")
冷清 (*lengqing*, "deserted") – 冷清清 (*lengqingqing*, "desolate")
乱腾 (*luanteng*, "disorder") – 乱腾腾 (*luantengteng*, "in great disorder")
亮堂 (*liangtang*, "bright") – 亮堂堂 (*liangtangtang*, "much brighter")
干巴 (*ganba*, "wizened") – 干巴巴 (*ganbaba*, "dry as dust")

AABB Type:

冷清 (*lengqing*, "deserted") – 冷冷清清 (*lenglengqingqing*, "desolate")
大方 (*dafang*, "generous") – 大大方方 (*dadafangfang*, "much more generous")
简单 (*jiandan*, "simple") – 简简单单 (*jianjiandandan*, "uncomplicated")
清楚 (*qingchu*, "clear") – 清清楚楚 (*qingqingchuchu*, "much clearer")
快乐 (*kuaile*, "happy") – 快快乐乐 (*kuaikuailele*, "full of joy")
利索 (*lisuo*, "agile") – 利利索索 (*lilisuosuo*, "quick and efficient")
勤恳 (*qinken*, "diligent") – 勤勤恳恳 (*qinqinkenken*, "diligent and conscientious")
马虎 (*mahu*, "careless") – 马马虎虎 (*mamahuhu*, "careless")

ABAB Type:

梆硬 (*bangying*, "hard") – 梆硬梆硬 (*bangyingbangying*, "much harder")
雪白 (*xuebai*, "snow-white") – 雪白雪白 (*xuebaixuebai*, "snowy white")
笔直 (*bizhi*, "perfectly straight") – 笔直笔直 (*bizhibizhi*, "upright")
喷香 (*penxiang*, "delicious") – 喷香喷香 (*penxiangpenxiang*, "much more delicious")
彤红 (*tonghong*, "red") – 彤红彤红 (*tonghongtonghong*, "much redder")
墨黑 (*mohei*, "black") – 墨黑墨黑 (*moheimohei*, "inky black")

A li AB Type:

马虎 (*mahu*, "careless") – 马里马虎 (*malimahu*, "careless")
慌张 (*huangzhang*, "panic") – 慌里慌张 (*huanglihuangzhang*, "in a hurried and confused manner ")
糊涂 (*hutu*, "confused") – 糊里糊涂 (*hulihutu*, "in disorderly fashion")
肮脏 (*angzang*, "dirty") – 肮里肮脏 (*angliangzang*, "filthy")
啰唆 (*luosuo*, "wordy") – 啰里啰唆 (*luoliluosuo*, "garrulous")
邋遢 (*lata*, "slovenly") – 邋里邋遢 (*lalilata*, "unkempt")

The above examples are inflections of adjectives: monosyllabic adjectives are reduplicated in AA type and disyllabic adjectives have five forms of reduplication,

The emergence and structural forms of words 107

i. e., AAB type, ABB type, AABB type, ABAB type and AliAB type. Some adjectives have two reduplicated forms of inflectional morphology: for example, "冷清 (*lengqing*)" can be reduplicated either into "冷清清 (*lengqingqing*)" or "冷冷清清 (*lenglengqingqing*)", "梆硬 (*bangying*)" either into "梆梆硬 (*bangbangying*)" or "梆硬梆硬 (*bangyingbangying*)", "慌张" either into "慌里慌张 (*huanglihuangzhang*)" or "慌慌张张 (*huanghuangzhangzhang*)", etc. In whichever inflection, only the grammatical meanings of "reinforcement", "lightness" or "repugnance" are added after the reduplication of the adjectives while all their lexical meanings remain unchanged.

(II) The form aspects

Because inflection concerns the inflectional changes of one and the same word, all the forms before inflectional change are words. Word formation, nevertheless, is totally different from this: because a word is composed of semantic morpheme(s), the form before the change may be a free semantic morpheme identical to the form of a word or a bound semantic morpheme with which a word is to be formed and what is the most important is that all the new forms after the change are neologisms combined by the semantic morphemes in accordance with the ways of word formation and all the new forms are independent forms with their own lexical meanings: the new forms are not forms of inflectional morphology at all. One should pay much attention to differentiate the reduplicated forms. Let's take some synchronic cases, for example:

津 (*jin*) – 津津 (*jinjin*, "delicious")
冉 (*ran*) – 冉冉 (*ranran*, "slowly")
翩 (*pian*) – 翩翩 (*pianpian*, "dancing")
萋 (*qi*) – 萋萋 (*qiqi*, "luxuriant")
妈 (*ma*, "mum") – 妈妈 (*mama*, "mum")
舅 (*jiu*, "uncle") – 舅舅 (*jiujiu*, "uncle")
断 (*duan*, "break") – 断断 (*duanduan*, "definitely")
落 (*luo*, "fall") – 落落 (*luoluo*, "yo")
祖辈 (*zubei*, "ancestor") – 祖祖辈辈 (*zuzubeibei*, "from generation to generation")
缝补 (*fengbu*, "sew and mend") – 缝缝补补 (*fengfengbubu*, "sew up")
走 (*zou*, "go") – 走走 (*zouzou*, "take a walk")
尝 (*chang*, "taste") – 尝尝 (*changchang*, "have a taste")
大 (*da*, "large") – 大大 (*dada*, "greatly")
圆 (*yuan*, "circle") – 圆圆 (*yuanyuan*, "round")

In the above examples, such elements as "津", "冉", "翩" and "萋" are non-word semantic morphemes because they cannot be used as words independently; therefore, the reduplicated forms of these elements are all words; such elements as "妈", "舅", "祖辈" and "缝补" are all semantic morphemes making up words and the reduplicated forms such as "妈妈", etc. are all words. What should be pointed

108 *The emergence and structural forms of words*

out that they are semantic morphemes instead of words when these elements are reduplicated and they are reduplicated according to the rules of word formation; consequently, this is quite distinct from inflection as far as the lexical meaning is concerned: the lexical meanings of "妈" and "舅" do not change at all after reduplication while the lexical meanings of "祖辈" and "缝补" changed totally after reduplication, and for all the examples in the above, the neologisms are formed with reduplication. Cases are totally different for "走", "尝", "大" and "圆": their lexical meanings do not change at all after reduplication, while their grammatical meanings change totally: they all belong to the inflectional changes of one and the same word and therefore are cases of inflection instead of word formation.

More examples:

1. (1):

    呱呱叫 (*guaguajiao*, "tiptop") – 呱叫 (*gua jiao*)
    芨芨草 (*jijicao*, "splendid achnatherum") – 芨草 (*ji cao*)
    毛毛雨 (*maomaoyu*, "drizzle") – 毛雨 (*mao yu*)
    婆婆丁 (*popoding*, "dandelion") – 婆丁 (*po ding*)
    哈哈镜 (*hahajing*, "magic mirror") – 哈镜 (*ha jing*)
    猩猩草 (*xingxingcao*, "euphorbia heterophylla") – 猩草 (*xing cao*)

(2):

    鼓鼓掌 (*guguzhang*, "applause") – 鼓掌 (*guzhang*, "applause")
    讲讲情 (*jiangjiangqing*, "plead for sb") – 讲情 (*jiangqing*, "try to plead for sb")
    冰冰凉 (*bingbingliang*, "ice cold") – 冰凉 (*bingliang*, "icy cold")

2. (1):

    眼巴巴 (*yanbaba*, "eagerly") – 眼巴 (*yan ba*)
    美滋滋 (*meizizi*, "very pleased with oneself") – 美滋 (*mei zi*)
    绿油油 (*lüyouyou*, "bright green") – 绿油 (*lü you*)
    甜丝丝 (*tiansisi*, "pleasant sweet") – 甜丝 (*tian si*)
    雄赳赳 (*xiongjiujiu*, "valiant") – 雄赳 (*xiong jiu*)
    明晃晃 (*minghuanghuang*, "gleaming") – 明晃 (*ming huang*)

(2):

    慢悠悠 (*manyouyou*, "unhurriedly") – 慢悠 (*manyou*, "leisurely")
    暖和和 (*nuanhehe*, "warm") – 暖和 (*nuanhe*, "warm")
    昏沉沉 (*hunchenchen*, "drowsy") – 昏沉 (*hunchen*, "drowsy")

3. (1):

    星星点点 (*xingxingdiandian*, "tiny spots") – 星点 (*xing dian*)
    兢兢业业 (*jingjingyeye*, "be conscientious and do one's best") – 兢业 (*jing ye*)
    满满登登 (*manmandengdeng*, "full to the brim") – 满登 (*man deng*)
    唯唯诺诺 (*weiwei uonuo*, "obsequious") – 唯诺 (*wei nuo*)

婆婆妈妈 (*popo mama*, "womanishly fussy") – 婆妈 (*po ma*)
病病歪歪 (*bingbingwaiwai*, "sick") – 病歪 (*bing wai*)

(2):

蹦蹦跶跶 (*bengbengdada*, "skip") – 蹦跶 (*bengda*, "jumping around")
磨磨蹭蹭 (*momocengceng*, "dawdle") – 磨蹭 (*moceng*, "dawdle")
爽爽快快 (*shuangshuangkuaikuai*, "unhesitatingly") – 爽快 (*shuangkuai*, "frank")
明明白白 (*mingmingbaibai*, "as clear as noonday") – 明白 (*mingbai*, "clear")

The words in class (1) have the same reduplication forms superficiality as those in class (2) in each of the three groups and they share one common point: the words before the dash in each pair of class (1) are reduplicated forms of those after the dash which are two separate non-word semantic morphemes, i. e., the former are reduplicated words made up of the latter in accordance with word formation rules so the reduplication forms are a matter of word formation while for those in (2), the forms after the dash are individual words and those before the dash are the forms of inflectional morphology of the former, i. e., the inflectional changes of the word; consequently, the reduplication forms are a matter of inflection. Thus one can see that word formation can also be distinguish from inflection through the analysis of the forms before reduplication.

It is extremely necessary to distinguish word formation from inflection because it has a great impact on our understanding of word and word segmentation. Take "大家讨论讨论 (*Dajia taolun taolun*, 'We shall discuss it over')" and "一个个 (*yigege*, 'one after another')" for example: how many words are there in each of the above phrases? The right answer is, of course, there are two words in each of the phrase, because "讨论讨论" and "个个" are inflections of "讨论" and "个" respectively, and it is incorrect to take each of them as two words.

Notes

1 Wu Shengyang: The Riddle of Falling Star,*Wenhui Newpaper*, December 14, 1983.
2 Mysterious Sounding Sand Bay,*Wenhui Newpaper*, February 28, 1984.
3 A New Discovery in Hainan Island,*Wenhui Newpaper*, February 28, 1984.
4 Zhang Jinbiao: The Origin of "Eight Officers", *Party and Government Tribune*, 1999, (7): 24.
5 The National Day Peach in the Summer Palace by Kang Chengzong, *Beijing Evening Newspaper*, October 9, 1983.
6 See Cui Fuyuan (1957: 32), *Examples of Word Formation in Contemporary Chinese*, Shandong: Shandong People's Publishing House. In addition, some textbooks also agree with this opinion.

4 Word meaning

Section 1 An overview of word meaning

Because a word is a combination of sound and meaning, every word in language has its own sound and meaning: sound is its form and meaning its content. The meaning content is, so to speak, hereinafter referred to as the word meaning. However, it is insufficient to grasp word meaning only in this way. Thus further discussion is necessary.

I The contents of word meaning

Now that word meaning is the meaning content a word designates, first we should investigate what kind of meanings a word can designate before discussing word meaning. For example, "书 (*shu*)" designates "a set of printed pages that are held together in a cover so that one can read them", "杰出 (*jiechu*)" means " (of talent and achievement) outstanding; remarkable; prominent" and "奉承 (*fengcheng*)" indicates "to flatter, to fawn upon; to ingratiate oneself". These are, of course, undeniably the contents included in word meaning. With further consideration, however, one may find that, in addition to the meanings listed above, "书" also designates "noun, can be a subject and an object", can be used in oral or written context with a neutral flavour; "杰出" also designates "adjective, can be an attributive" with a commendatory flavour and "奉承" also designates "verb, can be a predicate or an attributive" with a derogatory sense, etc. All the above are meanings designated by the words respectively, well then, are these meanings the contents of word meaning? It should be admitted that all these are the contents of word meaning and can be called word meaning. Thus it can be concluded that all meanings designated by a word belong to the range of word meaning and that what is included in word meaning is quite rich.

Word meaning in general includes three parts, i. e., lexical meaning, grammatical meaning and meaning with special flavour.

(I) Lexical meaning

The lexical meaning of a word indicates the meaning of the objects, phenomena and relations in the objective world denoted by it. For example, the lexical meaning of "书 (*shu*)" is "a set of printed pages that are held together in a cover so that one can read them", that of "杰出 (*jiechu*)" is "(of talent and achievement) outstanding; remarkable; prominent", and that of "奉承 (*fengcheng*)" is "to flatter, to fawn upon; to ingratiate oneself". All words in language are intended to denote the object, phenomena and relations in the objective world; consequently every word has a lexical meaning of its own. It is the case with both content words and function words. There exist different opinions on the issue whether a function word has lexical meanings and designates concepts or not in the present academic community of linguistics: some scholars hold the view that a function word does not designate any concept and that it has only grammatical meanings with no lexical meaning at all. This issue should be illustrated first of all, in fact, from the fundamental function of a word. It is undeniable that a word is a combination of sound and meaning and that it is a sign designating the realities existing in the objective world, including the abstract realities apprehended by people and it is also undeniable that a word designates the meaning content of the realities. This is the case for all words with no exception. Function words are among the components of vocabulary and their lexical meanings are mostly reflections of the relations existing in the objective world; for example, the lexical meaning of "并且 (*bingqie*)" is "increased degree", that of "以至 (*yizhi*)" is "the extension of time, number, degree, scope, etc." and that of "和 (*he*)" is "and; together with". There are also function words designating a certain sentiment and attitude of humans in objective existence; for example, "to indicate the sentiment and attitude of surprise" is the lexical meaning of "啊 (*a3*), "to express the sentiment and attitude of agreement and realization" is the lexical meaning of "啊 (*a4*)" and "to designate response or sighing" is the lexical meaning of "唉 (*ai*)". It is beyond any doubt that the sentiment and attitude these function words designate are also an objective existence and the cognition of such sentiment and attitude can also result in corresponding concept; for example, the lexical meanings designated by the above words are all concepts, and consequently we can come up with the conclusion that function words all have lexical meanings.

(II) Grammatical meaning

The grammatical meaning of a word indicates the meaning of the grammatical function designated by it. The grammatical meanings of a word are manifested by the grammar functions through the clusters of words; therefore it is more abstract and generalized. For example, "noun" is a grammatical generalization of the words representing objective things and "subject" is a generalization of the grammar function of such a word class as noun. Every word in language belongs to the cluster and generalization of a certain syntactic relation; thus all of them possess a certain grammatical meaning. For example, the grammatical meaning of "书" is "noun, can be a subject and an object", that of "杰出" is "adjective, can be an attributive", that of "奉承" is "verb, can be a predicate or an attributive", that of "并且" is "conjunction, used to combine co-ordinated verbs, adjectives, adverbs and clauses", and that of "以至" is "conjunction, used to combine two or more words, phrases and clauses".

(III) Meaning with special flavour

The meaning with special flavour of a word indicates the meaning of a certain tendency or sentiment designated by a word, which is also conventionalized by the relevant linguistic community. For example, what "股骨 (*gugu*, 'thigh bone')" and "大腿骨 (*datuigu*, 'thigh')" and "祖母 (*zumu*, 'grandmother')" and "奶奶 (*nainai*, 'grandma; grannie')" designate are both the same things and share the same lexical meanings and grammatical meanings respectively; however their meanings with special flavour are different: "股骨" and "祖母" have a flavour of written language while "大腿骨" and "奶奶" one of colloquialism. By the same token, "效果 (*xiaoguo*, 'effect')", "结果 (*jieguo*, 'result')" and "后果 (*houguo*, 'consequence')" are also different as far as meaning with special flavour is concerned: in addition to a neutral flavour, "效果" possesses an ameliorative flavour more often than not, while "后果" has a derogatory flavour and "结果" only has a neutral flavour. Every word has the meaning with special flavour of its own. Some words possess an image flavour, e. g., "佛手 (*foshou*, 'finger citron')", "龙眼 (*longyan*, 'longan; dragon's eye')" and "鸡冠花 (*jiaguanhua*, 'cockscomb')", etc. ; others have an amiable flavour, e. g., "同志 (*tongzhi*, 'comrade')", "乡亲 (*xiangqin*, 'villager')" and "妈妈 (*mama*, 'mom')", etc. ; others bear a solemn and serious flavour, e. g., "瞻仰 (*zhanyang*, 'look with reverence')", "诞辰 (*danchen*, ' (for old and venerable people) birthday')" and "会晤 (*huiwu*, 'meet with')", etc. ; still others take on an abominating and disgusting flavour, e. g., "叛徒 (*pantu*, 'traitor; apostate')", "流氓 (*liumang*, 'rascal; hooligan')" and "走狗 (*zougou*, 'lackey; running dog')", etc. ; further more words have a neutral flavour, e. g., "人 (*ren*, 'people; human being')", "树 (*shu*, 'tree')", "钢笔 (*gangbi*, 'pen')", "粮食 (*liangshi*, 'foodstuff')", "所以 (*suoyi*, 'therefore')", "并且 (*bingqie*, 'and; also')", "以至 (*yizhi*, 'so . . . that. . . . ')", "但是 (*danshi*, 'however; but')" and so on. A word may has only one or more than one meaning with special flavour, for example, "母亲 (*muqin*, 'mother')" has several meanings with special flavour: amiable, solemn and serious and more often used in written language.

The lexical meaning, grammatical meaning and meaning with special flavour of a word is interconnected and integrated and they serve as the content of word meaning as a whole. An all-around understanding of the word meaning can only be reached through a comprehensive analysis from the above three aspects.

It is undeniable, of course, that lexical meaning is the most important among the three facets. The reason lies in that only if a word has lexical meaning, can it be a sign designating objective existence and thus a word in language and can the grammatical meaning and meaning with special flavour be acquired on this foundation; therefore, the term "word meaning" is used more often than not to refer only to lexical meaning per se.

II The characteristics of word meaning

Characteristics of word meaning are manifold and they are discussed as follows:

(I) The objectivity of word meaning

Words are linguistic signs designating objective existence – lexical meaning, the main part of word meaning, expresses the objects, phenomena and relations in the objective world and grammatical meaning and meaning with special flavour are also reflections of objective existence – all this leads to the conclusion that word meaning designates objective existence and that objective existence and people's cognition of objective existence are the foundation of word meaning. Without objective existence, no word meaning is generated, and without people's cognitive activities on objective existence, no word meaning is generated either. For example, just because the objective thing "树 (tree)" exists in the objective world, people can have cognition on it and the word "树 (*shu*, 'tree')" is created and its word meaning also comes into being.

Even though objective existence is the foundation of the emergence of word meaning, it is not justified that to consider that word meaning is completely conform or identical to objective existence and it is even more erroneous to think that word meaning is objective existence per se, because when expressing objective existence, word meaning is constrained by people's cognition. Due to differences in people's cognition, situations of word meaning expressing objective existence are also distinct. For example, the meanings of some words are based on the correct and thorough cognition of the objective entities thus their word meanings are comparatively compliant to the reality of the objective entities: e.g., the word meaning of "农具 (*nongju*)" is "farm implements; farm tools" and that of "画像 (*huaxiang*)" is "portrait", etc. The meanings of other words are based on partial cognition of the objective entities, so even though they express certain characteristics of the objective entities, they cannot manifest the total situations of the objective entities; a case in point was the past cognition on "水 (*shui*, 'water')": "a colourless liquid necessary for daily life". The meanings of a small number of words are based on the wrong cognition of objective existence: "鬼 (*gui*, 'ghost')", "神 (*shen*, 'spirit; god')", "幽灵 (*youling*, 'specter; ghost')" and "魂魄 (*hunpo*, 'soul')" are all cases in point. The meanings of still a small number of words are based on the cognition of objective existence and subjective imaginary elements: the word meaning of "天堂 (*tiantang*, 'heaven')", "仙女 (*xiannü*, 'female celestial; fairy maiden')", "天神 (*tianshen*, 'god')" and "阎王 (*Yanwang*, 'King of Hell')" are cases in point. That is to say, people's fantasies are also generated on the basis of objective existence.

The above examples illustrate that word meaning is not identical to objective existence at all, while the emergence of word meaning is closely connected with objective existence: whether it is based on the correct or wrong cognition of objective existence, word meaning is based on the objective existence and objective existence is always an indispensable foundation of word meaning.

(II) The generality of word meaning

Word meaning designates a class of objective entities; therefore it is a generalization of the objective entities falling into one and the same class. Word meaning generalizes the common characteristics shared by all the members of a class of objective entities and discards some concrete characteristics possessed only by some members, so it obtains the qualification of designating the whole class of objective entities. For example, the meaning of the word "人 *(ren*, 'human being')" is a generalization of the objective thing of "human being": it generalizes all the common characteristics of human beings and discards the concrete characteristics only possessed by some human beings; therefore the meaning of "人" is a generic term for the class of the objective things of "human beings" instead of designating any specific human being.

Not only the meanings of common words are generalized, the meanings of proper words are also generalized, e. g., the meaning of the word "鲁迅 (*Lu Xun*)" generalizes all the characteristics of the person Lu Xun and it generalizes the situations of Lu Xun in different periods; i. e., it can be used to designate both Lu Xun in his youth and Lu Xun in his old age.

(III) The communal nature of word meaning

As the content of a word, word meaning is also conventionalized by the linguistic community as other linguistic elements. Because a word is a combination of sound and meaning and it is conventionalized by the members of a linguistic community, only when all members of a linguistic community have a common understanding of the lexical meaning, grammatical meaning and meaning with special flavour of a word, can communication be carried out between them. The communal nature of word meaning is determined by the communal nature of language.

(IV) The subjectivity of word meaning

Although it is of communal nature, word meaning is also of subjectivity in the concrete use. The subjectivity of word meaning indicates that the cognition and understanding of word meaning is influenced by differences in age, living conditions, levels of education and cognition ability under the condition that people share basically the same understanding. For example, little children may not have completely the same understanding on the word meaning of "电 (*dian*, 'electricity')" with physicists and the average man are definitely different in the understanding of the word meaning of "海带 (*haidai*, 'sea tangle')" from ocean biologists. The subjectivity of word meaning shows up at any moment in language application; however, the differences caused by the subjectivity do not influence people's communication because the subjectivity does not and will never exceed the scope of communal nature and generality of word meaning.

(V) The developmental nature of word meaning

As with other linguistic elements, word meaning has its own relative stability once it is formed. It is not invariable, however: with the development of society, the change of objective things and people's cognition and the differences of language use will all influence the change and development of word meaning. The fact that differences in word meanings between ancient and present times are frequently encountered is a good example of the developmental nature of word meaning. Word meaning development is not only a diachronic phenomenon but also a synchronic one: e. g., the word "舌头 (shetou)" has acquired a new sense of "an enemy soldier captured alive for the purpose of extracting information" in addition to that of "an organ in the mouth used in the ingestion of food, the perception of taste and the articulation of speech sounds". This is a case in point of the synchronic development of word meaning in the stage of the contemporary Chinese language. The meanings of "硬件 (yingjian, 'hardware')", "菜单 (caidan, 'menu')", "窗口 (chuangkou, 'window')" and "包装 (baozhuang, 'package')" are also developed more or less. It is extremely necessary to apprehend the developmental nature of word meaning when employing words and expressions because only after being aware of this point can one understand and employ the word meaning in a correct way.

(VI) The ethnic nature of word meaning

Because word meaning belongs to the category of language and every ethnic group has its own language and word meaning is conventionalized by the community in which the ethnic group lives, the appearance of word meaning is usually constrained by the conditions in which the ethnic group employs the language during the process of formation and development of word meaning and literacy, psychology and living customs etc. will all have effects on word meaning. For example, the meanings of "龙 (long, 'dragon')" and "凤 (feng, 'phoenix')" have deep ethnic nature: both of them are animals in ancient myths of the Han nationality and the Han people usually take them as the symbols for dignity, solemnity, fineness and fortunate etc., and there are such expressions as "龙袍 (longpao, 'imperial robe')" and "凤冠 (fengguan, 'phoenix coronet')" and so on in Chinese. Another example: the meaning of "钢笔 (gangbi)" in Chinese is equivalent to that of "pen" in English, but originally "pen" meant "feather" whereas "钢笔" had no such a sense; this is also due to the influence of ethnic conditions: there existed a custom to write with "feather" in England so "pen" and "feather" could be connected in meaning. The ethnic nature of word meaning is more obvious as far as meaning with special flavour is concerned. For example, the Chinese word "小 (xiao, 'little; small')" has only a neutral flavour whereas of the two English words "little" and "small" equivalent to the lexical meaning of "小", the former has a diminutive flavour. For another example, "家伙 (jiahuo, 'fellow; guy')" is pejorative in denoting human beings in Chinese while "fellow" has a commendatory flavour and "guy" is derogatory in English.

(VII) Correspondence between word meaning and concept

Word meaning is generalized and in most cases it designates a class of objective things and consequently it designates the concept of a class of the objective things; therefore word meaning is correspondent to concept.

Word meaning is correspondent to concept in all cases. When a word is a member in vocabulary existing in a system of linguistic sign, word meaning can only designate a class of objective things and it inevitably designates the concept of the class of the objective things. Under such circumstances, word meaning is correspondent to concept.

When a word is used to make a concrete sentence in a specific linguistic environment, word meaning is still correspondent to its concept. For example, in the sentence of "鱼生活在水中 (*Yu shenghuo zai shui zhong*, 'Fish live in water')", the word "鱼 (*yu*, 'fish')" designates the objects in the class of "fish", so the word meaning of fish is correspondent to its concept. While in the sentence "这条鱼真大 (*Zhe tiao yu zhen da*, 'This fish is so big')", "鱼" denotes a specific "fish", though there is no denying that it still denotes the objective things of "fish" instead of any other class of objects; therefore, the word meaning "fish" here still designates the contents included in the concept of "fish" and is correspondent to its concept.

(VIII) Correspondence between word meaning concrete object

The correspondence between word meaning and concrete object means that although word meaning is generalized and correspondent to concept, it is used to denote a concrete and objective thing in actual linguistic communication, i. e., word meaning always corresponds to concrete object. Every word will be used in specific verbal communication; therefore word meaning is correspondent to concrete object.

The correspondence between word meaning and concrete object is based on the foundation of the correspondence between word meaning and concept: only when word meaning is correspondent to concept can it denote specific objective things in the actual context and thus correspondent to concrete objects. For example, in the above-mentioned "这条鱼真大 (*Zhe tiao yu zhen da*, 'This fish is so big')", the word meaning of "鱼" does not only designate the concept of "fish", but also denote "such a" specific "fish"; here the word meaning of "fish" is correspondent to the "big and specific fish" in addition to being correspondent to the concept of "fish", thus the word meaning of "fish" is not only correspondent to concept, but also correspondent to a concrete object. For another example, in "小王的书是新买的 (*Xiao Wang de shu shi xin mai de*, 'Xiao Wang's book is newly bought')", "书 (*shu*, 'book')" does not only designate the concept of book, but also denote the specific "book" that newly bought by Xiao Wang: thus the word meaning is not only correspondent to concept but also correspondent to a concrete object.

When word meaning is correspondent to concrete object, its extension will be narrowed down and its intension be enriched, so what it designates is much richer than when it only corresponds to concept.

The characteristics of word meaning are manifold and are interconnected at the same time. Only after having a thorough and proper understanding of the characteristics of word meaning can one have a thorough and proper mastery of word meaning and employ words in a comparatively right manner.

Section 2 Word meaning and concept

I. The relationship and difference between word and concept

The issue of the relationship and difference between word meaning and concept is different from that of the relationship and difference between word and concept, so it is necessary to discuss the relationship and difference between word and concept prior to discussing those between word meaning and concept.

As we know, a concept is a generalized reflection of a class of objective entities and it reflects the sum total of all the general and substantial characteristics of a class of objective entities and all the complex connections and relationships of these characteristics recognized by people at a certain stage of development in science. A concept is a thinking outcome on the objects, phenomena and relationship in the objective world by people, and it belongs to the domain of thinking.

Different from concepts, words are the external form designating concepts. Without the concepts reflecting objective entities, that is to say, without the thinking outcomes of people's cognition on the objective entities, there will be no words at all. Therefore, concepts are the foundation for words to come into being. Conversely, without words, no concept can be expressed; therefore, words are the external form for concepts. Thus we can say that concepts are the contents of words and words are the forms of concepts; therefore the relationship between them is that of contents and forms.

Words and concepts are connected and related in such a way, though there are essential differences between them.

First of all, the relationships between words, concepts and objective entities are different. There is no necessary connection between words and objective entities: it is arbitrary and conventionalized to designate a certain objective entities and concepts with certain words. Therefore, the same concept may be designated by words of different forms in different languages of different ethnic groups and may also be designated by words of different forms even in the language of one and the same ethnic group. For example, the concept of "book" can be designated by "书 (*shu*)" in Chinese and by "book" in English, which belongs to the first case; and the concept of "father" can be expressed by either "*fuqin* (父亲)" or "*baba* (爸爸)" in Chinese, which belongs to the second case. There exists an inevitable connection between concepts and objective entities: concepts are a corresponding product of the relevant objective entities. For example, the objective thing "bird" can fly; therefore, the property of "flying" must be included in the concept of "bird". Whereas the objective thing "human being" cannot fly, therefore, the property of "flying" cannot be included in the concept of "human being". It is just because there exists an inevitable connection between concepts and objective entities that people from different ethnic groups share the same understanding on the same concept.

Secondly, words are not completely equivalent to concepts. Although words in language are correspondent to concepts in logical thinking, the correspondence is not of the one-to-one equivalent relationship: a word may designate a concept, yet a concept is not necessarily expressed by the form of a word, for example, the concepts of "他的哥哥 (*ta de gege*, 'his elder brother')", "高等学校 (*gaodeng xuexiao*, 'institutions of higher learning')" and "自动铅笔 (*zidong qianbi*, 'propelling pencil')", etc. are all expressed by phrases. It is also complicated for words to designate concepts. For example, in the cases of "book" and "father" discussed above, both belong to that one and the same concept is designated by different forms of words. On the other hand, we can find that one and the same linguistic form can indicate different concepts. For example, the polysemous word "*baofu* (包袱, 'cloth-wrapper; load')" can designate either the concept of "cloth-wrapper" or that of "load". For another example, "*dujuan* (杜鹃, 'rhododendron; cuckoo')" can also indicate either the concept of "rhododendron" or that of "cuckoo". Thus one can see that we must make a specific analysis of the cases in which words designate concepts.

II The relationship between word meaning and concept

The relationship between word meaning and concept is completely different from the relationship between word and concept. The inseparability of language and thought leads to the inseparability of word meaning and concept. The relationship between word meaning and concept manifests mainly in two aspects: one is that concept is the foundation for word meaning to take shape; the other is that word meaning reflects concept and concept becomes direct reality by right of word meaning. People basically agree upon this issue; however, their opinions are different in the concrete understanding and explanation of this relationship. A common practice is that one only compares and analyzes lexical meaning in word meaning with concept and makes no mention of other aspects of word meaning. It is difficult, however, to reveal the complex relationship between word meaning and concept only confined to this understanding. Consequently we must analyze this issue from a far more extensive scope. We discuss this issue from the three aspects of word meaning as follows.

(I) Lexical meaning and concept

Lexical meaning indicates the meaning denoting the objective things and the reflection of people's rational knowledge of the objective things in word meaning. It is beyond the shadow of any doubt that such a meaning is directly connected with concept. It is common knowledge that concept is a generalized reflection of a class of objective entities, whereas lexical meaning designates the objects, phenomena and relationships in the objective world; therefore, both of them are the contents designated by the form of words, and thus the connection and relationship between lexical meaning and concept are determined: all lexical meanings are formed based upon the foundation of concepts and represent the content of concepts as the straightforward reality, so we can say that when a concept is designated by a word, the content of a concept is basically identical to the lexical meaning of a word. Therefore, the concept connected with the lexical meaning does not only determine the essential content of the lexical meaning of a word, but also assigns the denoting function of its lexical meaning, and consequently determines the value of its emergence and existence. Thus one can see that the lexical meaning of a word in language is correspondent to the concept in logical thinking. This is the case for not only content words but also function words.

(II) Grammatical meaning, meaning with special flavour and concept

The grammatical meaning of a word is that shown in the properties, characteristics and relational structures of language, and although it is not directly correspondent to the concept of the objective things designate by the word as is the case with the lexical meaning, there is no denying that it is connected in one way or another with the concept. As an instrument for communication, language is an objective existence per se, and various phenomena and elements within language are of course part of objective existence; therefore, people's cognition on this part of objective existence will by the same token become part of word meaning correspondent to concept. All concepts in language, including grammatical concepts, come into being in this way. It is just based upon this understanding that we put forward that the grammatical contents in word meaning belong to objective existence. Various typical grammatical concepts are abstracted and generalized gradually from different grammatical properties, characteristics and functions of various individual word meanings through people's cognition and are used in turn to illustrate the grammatical properties, characteristics and functions of word meaning and thereby constitute the grammatical meanings of words. Therefore, it can be seen that grammatical meaning in word meaning is also interconnected with concept.

The connection between grammatical meaning of a word and concept is, of course, different from that between lexical meaning and concept which is of specificity. The specificity illustrates that the concept reflecting the properties and characteristics of objective things assigns word meaning a function designating a certain specific objective things; therefore, there exists a substantial and inevitable connection between lexical meaning and concept, i. e., it is certain that what lexical meaning designates what concept. The connection between grammatical meaning and concept is quite different: the concept in grammatical meaning will always have a generic function to the grammatical meaning of a word through the word meaning designating the concept. The genericity of the connection between grammatical meaning and concept indicates that the categories of grammatical meanings of a word are illustrated through grammatical concepts, i. e., whether a word possesses the attributes of a noun or a verb. The grammatical meanings of a word have in general manifold attributes at the same time, for example, the grammatical meanings of the word "词典 (*cidian*, 'dictionary')" include both the attribute of "being a noun" and the function that "serving as a subject, an object or an attributive". In this case, certain grammatical concepts are employed to illustrate the grammatical attributes, syntactic categories and grammatical functions of the word "词典". Thus it can be seen that grammatical meaning is manifested through the form of word meaning by the concept in grammar; therefore, grammatical meaning is also connected with concept and even connected with the integration of several concepts.

The connection between meaning with special flavour and concept is basically the same as the case of grammatical meaning. The meaning with special flavour of a word is attached to the lexical meaning of this word and it also designates the people's cognition, attitude, inclination and sentiment except that what it designates is beyond the content of lexical meaning, but there is no denying that it also reflects an objective situation as far as the meaning with special flavour per se is concerned. A certain cognition, attitude, sentiment or inclination of people constitutes the content of a certain meaning with special flavour, e. g., affability flavour, solemnity flavour, image flavour, colloquialism flavour, etc., and the contents of these meanings with special flavour are all abstracted from many individual words through people's cognition and at the same time such a cognition also constitutes various corresponding concepts and these concepts are at the same time consolidated by the corresponding forms of words with "affability flavour", etc. : various clusters of meaning with special flavour in language are reflected through these concepts with the help of word meanings or meanings of expressions and they in turn have a generic referring function to the meanings with special flavour of each individual word. For example, the meaning with special flavour of "妈妈 (*mama*, 'mum')" is illustrated by the meaning of the words and expressions designating such concepts as "affability flavour" and "colloquialism flavour"; therefore, the connection between the meaning with special flavour and concept is one of genericity.

Owing to that one and the same word may usually possess two or more meanings with special flavour, the multiplicity of meaning with special flavour determines that it may be associated with several different concepts at the same time. Therefore, the meaning with special flavour is not only connected with concept but may also be connected with an integration of many concepts just as the case with grammatical meaning.

In conclusion, the relationship between word meaning and concept is far from that between lexical meaning and concept; concept is connected with all the three parts of word meaning, although the specific situations are different, there is no denying that they are all connected with concept. All word meaning has the content of the three parts and all parts are connected with concept; thus we say that word meaning is an integrated reflection of concept.

III The difference between word meaning and concept

After realizing the basic consistency and mutual correspondence between word meaning and concept, in particular that between lexical meaning and concept, we must be aware that word meaning and concept are not completely identical after all, because they belong to different domains; therefore they are different from each other in essence. So far as grammatical meaning and meaning with special flavour are concerned, they are easy to understand and grasp because they only have a genericity function to concept in language application. The situation of lexical meaning, however, is much more complicated; therefore, it is necessary to make more illustration in the following.

(I) The flexibility of the correspondence between lexical meaning and concept

The difference between lexical meaning and concept boils down to their different functions. Concepts belong to the domain of logical thinking and their functions consist in apprehending and reflecting the objective world; therefore, a prerequisite to a complete concept is that it must reflect the sum total of all the general and substantial characteristics of the objective entities and all the complex connections and relations between all these characteristics. Lexical meaning of a word belongs to the domain of language and its function consists in enabling people to communicate ideas with each other for mutual understanding; therefore, it is fairly sufficient for lexical meaning to designate the characteristics differentiating a class of objects from others although it also designates the objects, phenomena and relations in the objective world, and thus lexical meaning usually designates an incomplete concept in most cases. For example, the concept of "荧光灯 (*yingguangdeng*, 'fluorescent lamp')" should be "a type of lamp, fitted with electrodes at both ends, having a coating of fluorescent material on its inner surface and containing mercury vapour whose bombardment by electrons from the cathode provides ultraviolet light which causes the material to emit visible light, the light produced by the common type of such a lamp being akin to sunlight, also called "日光灯 (*riguangdeng*, 'daylight lamp')". The situation for the lexical meaning of "荧光灯", on the other hand, is not exactly the same: on the occasion of scientific researches and discussions, the word meaning of "荧光灯" must be in compliance with the content of the technical term; thus the content of the word meaning is all the same as the content of the above-mentioned concept and the lexical meaning is correspondent to a complete concept in this case. In everyday life, however, "荧光灯" may well be defined as "a kind of long tubular lamp with an ivory-white colour and pearl opal light will be produced under the function of fluorescent powder after the current is switched on" and it is sufficient to distinguish "荧光灯" from other objects by this definition; therefore, it is justified to use the word meaning thus defined in communication to fulfill the communicative functions of word meaning. It is fairly obvious that the lexical meaning thus employed is correspondent to an incomplete concept.

Furthermore, it should be pointed out that although different people may communicate with each other, the contents of the concepts and word meanings grasped vary among different people, because the degrees of the understanding of concepts and lexical meanings vary a lot due to the differences in age, literacy, profession and living condition between different people. For example, compared with youngsters, older people have a deeper and more thorough understanding on concepts and lexical meanings in general and professionals also have a deeper and more thorough understanding on the concepts and lexical meanings of the technical terms in their professions than other people.

Therefore, lexical meanings are flexible in their richness as far as the content and information transmitted in verbal communication are concerned.

(II) The uniformity between word meaning and concept manifested in people's cognition

The flexibility of lexical meaning is discussed from the mastery of word meaning by different members in a linguistic community, it will be, nevertheless, completely different if viewed from the situation of one and the same member per se. Therefore, it must be made clear that the degree in which different people understand and master the concept and lexical meaning may be different, though for one and the same person, in whichever stage of his growing, the extent to which he understands and masters concept and lexical meaning will always be the same. If one's cognition on the lexical meaning of "水 (*shui*, 'water')" is just "a colourless, odourless and drinkable liquid", his understanding on the concept of "水" can only reach such a degree instead of to that of "the chemical composition of water is H_2O", so we say that the concept of "水" he masters is just an incomplete concept. On the contrary, if he has a clear and comprehensive cognition on the concept of "水", his understanding on the lexical meaning of "水" will also be comprehensive and profound, and it is obvious that his understanding on the lexical meaning of "水" has already come to the profundity of concept.

The above-mentioned situations make us realize that although concept is the reflection of people's cognition on a class of objective entities at a certain stage of development of science, people do not and cannot grasp the content of every concept in a correct and comprehensive way; in more cases, however, what people grasp is an incomplete concept consistent with the lexical meaning they get to know. Everybody can acquire an incomplete concept first and then master the complete concept step by step. He can also gradually develop from a comparatively partial and superficial understanding of lexical meaning to a more comprehensive and profound understanding of it. As one and the same person, nevertheless, his understanding on the concept and corresponding lexical meaning and the extent to which his understanding develops are always the same.

The flexibility of lexical meaning and concept is interconnected with the uniformity of lexical meaning and concept, and being aware of this is vital to the practical application of language. For example, in compiling dictionaries, the definitions of the terms will be adjusted to meet different needs of readers, which is a concrete manifestation of this flexibility and uniformity. As a matter of fact, it will not do otherwise because it is the linguistic rules people learn and master that make it so. These rules may also frequently show up in other aspects of language application.

5 Word meaning clustering

Section 1 Criteria and principles of word meaning clustering

Words in a language are not isolated; they usually form various clusters by certain common characteristics per se, such as phonetic, lexical or grammatical characteristics and so on. For instance, such clusters as homophones, monosyllabic words, polyphonic words and so on can be formed based on phonetic forms; such clusters as dialect words, loan words, archaic words and so on can be formed based on the sources of words and such clusters as noun, verb, adjective and so on can be formed based on parts of speech. By the same token, various clusters of word meaning can be formed based on corresponding connections or relationships between word meanings.

Owing to the richness and colourfulness of Chinese vocabulary, word meaning in Chinese is also extremely splendid. In the face of this phenomenon of word meaning which is colourful and complicated, people should not only learn it, master it and employ it, but also strive to investigate it, collate it and try to reveal its laws of development and organization as far as possible. Based on the present research situation, we think it feasible to approach this issue from such two different points of view as the synchronic perspective and the diachronic perspective. To study and collate word meaning from the synchronic perspective, it is obvious that what is to be touched upon first is the clustering of word meaning because it is a synchronic phenomenon whose actual contents will be different in different synchronic stages. We will be concentrating on the clustering of word meaning from the synchronic perspective in this chapter. The investigation and collation of word meaning from the diachronic perspective, of course, will involve exploring and collating the laws of evolution and development of word meaning longitudinally in a tracing-to-the-source manner from the historical perspective. This issue will be dealt with in Chapter Six.

I On the current situation of studies on clustering of word meaning

It is already established that words cluster by their meanings. In general, in accordance with common characteristics of word meaning different clusters of word meanings can be derived through analyzing the contents of word meaning. Such clusters of word meaning as monosemy, polysemy, synonymy and antonymy etc. are thus derived and there is no disagreement on the establishment of these types in the academic community of linguistics for years.

However, there still exists much confusion on this issue in some cases. The division criteria for such clusters as monosemy and polysemy are quite easy to follow, while there are wide divergences on the division of such clusters as synonymy and near synonymy etc. For instance, we all agree that "好 (*hao*, 'good')" and "坏 (*huai*, 'bad')" are antonyms, but why do only a few people agree that "效果 (*xiaoguo*, 'effect')" which means "a good result" and "后果 (*houguo*, 'consequence')" which means "a bad result" should be treated as antonyms while most people think that they should be categorized as near-synonyms? For another example, some people classify "父亲 (*fuqin*, 'father')" and "爸爸 (*baba*, 'papa')" as synonyms while others group them as near-synonyms. For still another example, how should one treat and classify such words as "老师 (*laoshi*, 'teacher')" and "学生 (*xuesheng*, 'student')", "红 (*hong*, 'red')" and "白 (*bai*, 'white')", "红 (*hong*, 'red')" and "黑 (*hei*, 'black')", "红 (*hong*, 'red')" and "黄 (*huang*, 'yellow')" and "红 (*hong*, 'red')" and "绿 (*lü*, 'green')", etc. ? In my opinion, the fundamental cause for such problems lies in that people have different views on the classification criteria and there are even some divergences and deficiencies in theory. Therefore, further studies on the clustering of word meaning are quite necessary based on the existing research and the division criteria of the clustering of word meaning are of the first priority. So we start our discussion on this issue.

Since the division of clusters of word meaning is based on analyzing the contents of word meaning, if we want to solve this issue, I think we still should begin with analyzing the characteristics of word meaning, i. e., the characteristics of lexical meaning, grammatical meaning and meaning with special flavour which are involved in word meaning.

II Criteria and analysis principles of the division of word meaning clustering

Every word meaning contains three aspects, i. e., lexical meaning, grammatical meaning and meaning with special flavour. They are all indispensable to word meaning. Therefore, the complete word meaning of any word consists of these three parts, which jointly provide a comprehensive explanation to the word meaning by the particular contents and functions of each own. It is just because these three parts are all indispensable in word meaning that the peculiar contents and characteristics of all of them can find their way in the whole word meaning and all these peculiar contents and characteristics play different and irreplaceable distinctive roles in dividing word meaning clustering. Therefore, we can find a quite reliable foundation for division criteria of word meaning clustering by making a distinctive analysis on the contents and characteristics of lexical meaning, grammatical meaning and meaning with special flavour of words.

Of course, it is undeniable that the cases of lexical meaning, grammatical meaning and meaning with special flavour are different. Generally speaking, among these three parts of meaning, lexical meaning is always dominant and it is the core of word meaning; therefore when we divide clusters of word meaning, lexical meaning is always a decisive condition, while grammatical meaning is a necessary condition. As for meaning with special flavour, it is neither a decisive condition nor a necessary condition, but since it is one part of the contents of word meaning, it surely plays a certain role in dividing clusters of word meaning; therefore it is also an indispensable condition. We are making specific interpretations on this point of view.

(I) Lexical meaning

Lexical meaning is a decisive condition for dividing clusters of word meaning. As the rational meaning of a word, lexical meaning is the reflection of people's rational knowledge of things, phenomena and relationships in the objective world in word meaning; therefore, lexical meaning is correspondent to each concept it represents and makes word meaning possess the concept correspondence of its own. The reason that we put forward the concept correspondence of word meaning lies in that word meaning designates concept, concept is the foundation for word meaning and word meaning is intangible without concept.

The concept correspondence of word meaning is one of the characteristics of word meaning; it belongs to the category of linguistics. Part of the contents and characteristics of the concept can be highlighted by the concept correspondence of word meaning out of the needs of the cognition and communication of people, so although word meaning can be correspondent to the complete concept, on most of occasions, it is correspondent to various incomplete concepts of different levels resulted from the gap of people's cognition and understanding. These incomplete concepts, however, are naturally constrained by complete concepts, that is to say, incomplete concepts cannot overstep the boundaries of the extension and connotation of complete concepts in any case. Therefore, even if there are some differences in the quantity of the connotation of incomplete concepts which people can grasp, their commonality and uniformity is absolute. Not only such a case guarantees people to use and understand language in communication, but also people's practice of acquiring and employing lexical meaning of a word and its concept correspondence provides us with conditions and foundations for dividing clusters of word meaning based on the lexical meaning of a word and its concept correspondence.

It thus can be concluded from the above that the concept correspondence of word meaning is a property of word meaning. Because word meaning and concept are inevitably correspondent to each other, the concept correspondence of a word and lexical meaning of that word are uniform in content. Lexical meaning and its concept correspondence are the core of word meaning, so they naturally become the major foundation for dividing clusters of word meaning. We can roughly classify clusters of word meaning in accordance with the characteristics of lexical meaning and its concept correspondence.

What should be pointed out is that even though we have made it clear that lexical meaning and its concept correspondence are the major criterion for dividing clusters of word meaning and acknowledged that there is conformity between the two, we cannot completely mix them up. Therefore, when analyzing concept correspondence, we should start with the characteristics included within it and differentiate the essential characteristics and the general characteristics, i. e., the analysis on concept correspondence is connected with its characteristics. As for word meaning, what we should analyze is the major semantic components and minor semantic components included within it, and even conventionalized semantic components or implied semantic components etc. if necessary, i. e., the analysis on lexical meaning is connected with its semantic components. Although they have much in common, they are distinctive as far as the perspectives are concerned. For example, both the word meanings of "父亲 (*fuqin*, 'father')" and "爸爸 (*baba*, 'papa')" are "a man who has a child (or children)" while the essential characteristics of concept correspondence of the two word meanings are "a male elder who has bred children"; thus it is obvious that neither the perspective of analysis or the interpretation is the same. On the other hand, however, we can see that both the lexical meaning and the concept correspondence of these two words are completely the same and thus we can conclude that the contents designated by the two words are identical and it is thus certain that they belong to the cluster of synonyms.

(II) Grammatical meaning

Grammatical meaning is a necessary condition for defining word meaning clustering. Necessary condition indicates that the words in the same cluster must have the same grammatical meaning, i. e., they have both the same part of speech and grammatical functions. Only when they have the same grammatical meaning can words belong to one and the same logical domain and the word meanings or concepts which do not belong to one and the same logical domain cannot be grouped into the same cluster.

Therefore, the identity of grammatical meaning is a precondition for discussing and analyzing word meaning and it is an indispensable prerequisite, so it is said to be a necessary condition.

(III) Meaning with special flavour

As has been mentioned earlier, meaning with special flavour is neither a decisive condition nor a necessary condition in distinguishing word meaning clustering, but it is an indispensable condition. The reason lies in that the meanings with special flavour of words in one and the same cluster can be either the same or different and they can be of decisive differentiating function in analyzing the inside of word meaning clustering under a certain condition. For example, various sub-clusters can be classified within a synonymy cluster in accordance with the difference in meaning with special flavour, e. g., "眉毛 (*meimao*, 'eyebrow')" and "眼眉 (*yanmei*, 'eyebrow')" are a pair of complete synonyms which have the same lexical meaning, grammatical meaning and meaning with special flavour while "土豆 (*tudou*, 'potato')" and "马铃薯 (*malingshu*, ' (slang) potato; murphy')" are a couple of incomplete synonyms which have the same lexical meaning and grammatical meaning but different meanings with special flavour. In addition, while meanings with special flavour of antonyms are contained in their lexical meanings, the distinct commendatory and/or derogatory sense can be highlighted prominently upon comparison.

III Understanding word meaning clustering from static and dynamic perspectives

There are also static clusters and dynamic clusters in word meaning clustering. Static clusters are relatively stable ones conventionalized in language system while most dynamic clusters formed catering for the needs of expression with the help of the context exist in parole and are of obvious temporary nature. Therefore, some elements which cannot go into one and the same cluster in the static state may come into one and the same temporary cluster of word meaning in the dynamic application, for example, when we say "这颗菜真好 (*Zhe ke cai zhen hao*, 'How nice this vegetable is')" in front of a "白菜 (*baicai*, 'Chinese cabbage')", the word "菜 (*cai*, 'vegetable')" by now has a specific reference of "白菜" and the two terms have the same lexical meaning and concept correspondence as well as the grammatical meaning and meaning with special flavour; thus "菜" and "白菜" are temporary synonyms in this context.

With the increase in the frequency of the elements in various temporary clusters of word meaning, some may be conventionalized by the society as members of static clusters. Take antonymy as an example: "红 (*hong*, 'red')", "黄 (*huang*, 'yellow')", "蓝 (*lan*, 'blue')", "白 (*bai*, 'white')", "黑 (*hei*, 'black')" and "绿 (*lü*, 'green')", etc. were originally co-hyponyms; various antonymous relations, however, are formed by these elements as words or as morphemes in speech under the function of context. For example, "红军 (*hongjun*, 'red corps')" and "白军 (*baijun*, 'white corps')" can be used in the context of revolution and reaction while "红灯 (*hongdeng*, 'red light')" and "绿灯 (*lüdeng*, 'green light')" can be used in the context of traffic lights and in these two specific contexts, "红" and "白" and "红" and "绿" are antonymous semantic morphemes respectively; consequently the two pairs of words "红" vs. "白" and "红" vs. "绿" become antonymous words respectively. Although these two pairs of words have now been standardized as language elements, but we still cannot say that "红" vs. "白" and "红" vs. "绿" are already standardized antonymous words or antonymous semantic morphemes in the static state. Therefore, when determining the nature of a language element, we must make specific analyses according to specific circumstances.

We are illustrating word meaning clustering in Chinese in accordance with the criteria and principles of word meaning clustering as follows.

Section 2 Monosemes and polysemes

I Monosemes

A word with only one lexical meaning is called a monoseme. The lexical meaning of a monoseme only corresponds to one concept. For instance,

鹿 (*lu*, "deer") 鹤 (*he*, "crane") 藕 (*ou*, "lotus") 豹 (*bao*, "leopard") 氧 (*yang*, "oxygen") 氯 (*lü*, "chlorine") 汞 (*gong*, "mercury")

镭 (*lei*, "radium") 诗 (*shi*, "poetry") 搓 (*cuo*, "rub") 熄 (*xi*, "quench") 搀 (*chan*, "support with one's hand") 瘸 (*que*, "lame") 熨 (*yun*, "iron")

葡萄 (*putao*, "grape") 钢笔 (*gangbi*, "pen") 电子 (*dian*, "electron") 外语 (*waiyu*, "foreign languages") 元音 (*yuanyin*, "vowel")

词组 (*cizu*, "phrase") 淮河 (*Huai He*, "the Huaihe River") 长江 (*Changjiang*, "the Changjiang River") 杂货 (*zahuo*, "groceries") 南京 (*Nanjing*, "Nanjing")

电视机 (*dianshiji*, "television") 世界观 (*shijieguan*, "world outlook") 格律诗 (*gelüshi*, "metrical poem") 心电图 (*xindiantu*, "electrocardiogram")

高低杠 (*gaodigang*, "asymmetrical bars") 语言学 (*yuyanxue*, "linguistics") 管弦乐 (*guanxianle*, "orchestral music") 黄梅戏 (*Huangmeixi*, "Huangmei Opera")

Because a monoseme has only one meaning, the meaning is explicit with no confusion in any context. Most scientific terms are monosemes. In addition, names of some objects and brand-new neologisms are usually monosemous.

Monosemes are not absolute. In the process of language development, some monosemes may turn into polysemes while some polysemes may become monosemes due to the change or extinction of sense items.

II Polysemes

(I) The definition of polysemes

A word with two or more related but different lexical meanings is called a polyseme. For instance,[1]

剪影: (1) paper-cut silhouette; cut the silhouette of a human face, a human body or an object out of a paper.
(2) (fig.) outline; sketch.

Not only the word "剪影 (*jianying*)" has two different senses, but also the two senses are connected to some degree in "the outline of objects", so it is a polyseme. Here is another example:

彩排: (1) dress rehearsal (before a play, dance, etc. is to take place).
(2) dress rehearsal (before a large-scale event such as a festival parade or a gala party).

Word meaning clustering 129

The word "彩排 (*caipai*)" also has two different senses and the two senses also have a certain connection in "dress rehearsal"; therefore, it is also a polyseme. Here is still another example:

记录: (1) to record; to put down what is heard or happens.
(2) minute; notes.
(3) note-taker.
(4) record; best result recorded at a specific time on a specific occasion.

The word "记录 (*jilu*)" has four senses: the first is a verb for an action; the second is a noun for the result of the action; the third is also a noun for the agent of the action and the fourth is still a noun for a certain specific result of the action. Although these four senses are not identical as far as the parts of speech are concerned, they are all related to "putting down what is heard or what happens" to a certain degree, which means that the four senses of "记录" have a certain connection so it is also a polyseme.

A word is usually monosemous at its birth and in the process of language development some words may usually become polysemous gradually on the basis of monosemy. Therefore, the longer history a word has, the more possible it is polysemous. Polysemes abound in Chinese since it has a long history and it is particularly the case for some long-standing monosyllabic words in Chinese, most of which are polysemous. In the contemporary Chinese language, polysemes are still being produced, developing and playing an active role in the application of language.

(II) Polysemes and polysemous morphemes

So far as language is developing, words and word meanings in language are also constantly developing. Some monosemous words in ancient Chinese may become polysemous in the contemporary Chinese language. Some elements which were words in ancient Chinese may become only morphemes instead of independent words in the contemporary Chinese language. Therefore, such cases as word versus non-word and word meaning versus semantic morpheme meaning are comparatively complex, and it is particularly the case for monosyllabic words. Furthermore, whether a certain meaning is lexical meaning or semantic morpheme meaning is different in different historical periods. An analysis and differentiation on word meaning and semantic morpheme meaning in the contemporary Chinese language is made from the synchronic perspective as follows. For example,

习: (1) practice; review: 自习 (*zixi*, "study by oneself") | 实习 (*shixi*, "fieldwork").
(2) be accustomed to; be familiar with: 习见 (*xijian*, "commonly seen") | 习闻 (*xiwen*, "often hear").
(3) habit: 积习 (*jixi*, "old habit") | 恶习 (*exi*, "bad habit").

观: (1) see; look at: 观看 (*guangkan*, "watch; observe; visit") | 观礼 (*guangli*, "attend a ceremony").

130 *Word meaning clustering*

    (2) sight; view: 奇观 (*qiguan*, "marvellous spectacle") |改观 (*gaiguan*, "change the appearance or look of").

    (3) outlook; view; concept: 乐观 (*leguan*, "optimism") |悲观 (*beiguan*, "pessimism").

Both "习 (*xi*)" and "观 (*guan*)" have three sense items and both have three different senses with a certain connection, so they are both polysemous elements. However, in the contemporary Chinese language, neither "习" nor "观" is independent word; therefore both of them can only be polysemous semantic morphemes and their three sense items can only be semantic morpheme senses in the contemporary Chinese language. Here is another example:

欠: (1) owe; have not returned belongings, etc., borrowed from others: 欠了账 (*qian le zhang*, "have been in debt") |欠了情 (*qian le qing*, "owe somebody afavour")

(2) not enough; insufficient: 说话欠考虑 (*shuohua qian kaolü*, "be thoughtless in speech")

    冰: (1) ice; solid form of water at or below zero degree centigrade: 水已结成冰了 (*Shui yi jie cheng bing le*, "The water was frozen over")

    (2) feel cold from contact with cold things: 刚到中秋, 河水已经有些冰腿了 (*Gang dao zhongqiu, heshui yijing youxie bing tui le*. "It is only midautumn, yet the river is already a little iced over")

    (3) put something on the ice or in cold water to make it cool: 把汽水冰上 (*baqishui bing shang*, "put ice in soda water")

In contemporary Chinese, both "欠 (*qian*)" and "冰 (*bing*)" are words that can be used independently from the perspective of sentence-making. Both the two sense items of "欠" and all the three sense items of "冰" can be used as word meanings to act as sentence-making elements. Therefore, both "欠" and "冰" are polysemes and all the senses designated by all the sense items are word meanings. Of course, from the point of view of word formation, these elements are all free semantic morphemes and all the senses designated by their sense items can be used as semantic morphemes to participate in word formation independently. Therefore, they are all units of word formation and all their meanings are also semantic morpheme meanings, so these elements are also polysemous semantic morphemes. Here are still other examples:

宝: (1) treasure:粮食是宝中之宝 (*Liangshi shi bao zhong zhi bao*, "Grain is the treasure of all treasures")

(2) precious; treasured: 宝剑 (*baojian*, "a treasured sword") |宝石 (*baoshi*, "gemstone")

(3) (polite) [designating other party's wife and children or company etc.] : 宝眷 (*baojuan*, "your wife and children" |宝号 (*baohao*, "your firm")

    书: (1)   write: 书法 (*shufa*, "calligraphy")

    (2) style of calligraphy; script: 楷书 (*kaishu*, "regular script") |隶书(*lishu*, "official script")

(3) book: 一本书 (*yi ben shu*, "one book")
(4) letter: 家书 (*jiashu*, "letter to or from home") |书札 (*shuzha*, "letters")
(5) document: 证书 (*zhengshu*, "certificate") |申请书 (*shenqingshu*, "application")

In the above example, "宝 (*bao*)" has three sense items and "书 (*shu*)" has five. But in contemporary Chinese, only the first sense item of "宝" and the third of "书" can be used as word meaning independently, while others can only act as semantic morpheme meanings. From the perspective of contemporary Chinese, it should be considered that "宝" and "书" are monosemes and they are polysemous semantic morphemes meanwhile, because each of their respective sense items can be used in word formation. There is still another case:

飞: (1) fly; flit; (of birds or insects) move through the air by flapping wings: 鸟飞了 (*Niao fei le*, "The bird flew away")
(2) fly; aviate; move in the air by using mechanical equipment; 飞机在天上飞 (*Feiji zai tianshang fei*, "The plane is flying in the sky")
(3) hover or flutter in the air: 飞雪花了 (*Fei xuehua le*, "snow-flakes flew about")
(4) swift; fast: 飞奔 (*feiben*, "run at full speed") |飞跑 (*feipao*, "race")
(5) unexpected; look accidental; ungrounded; groundless: 飞灾 (*feizai*, 'unexpected disaster") |飞祸 (*feihuo*, "unexpected calamity")

走: (1) walk; go; person, bird or animal moves feet forward alternately: 人都走了 (*Ren dou zou le*, "All people have left")
(2) run; move: 奔走相告 (*ben zou xiang gao*, "run about spreading the news")
(3) move; drive: 钟不走了 (*Zhong bu zou le*, "The clock has stopped")
(4) leave; go away: 车刚走 (*Che gang zou*, "The car has just left")
(5) (of relatives and friends) visit; call on: 走娘家 (*zou niangjia*, "visit the bride's home") |走亲戚 (*zou qinqi*, "visit a relative")
(6) through; from: 请走这个门出去 (*Qing zou zhe ge men chuqu*, "Please go out through this door")
(7) leak; let out; escape: 走了气 (*Zou le qi*, "The gas is leaking") |走了风 (*zou le feng*, "disclose a secret")
(8) depart from the original; lose the original shape, flavour, etc.: 你把鞋穿走样了 (*Ni ba xie chuan zou yang le*, "You've worn your shoes out of shape")

In the above example, both "飞 (*fei*)" and "走 (*zou*)" are words with multifold sense items. Among the five sense items of "飞", the first, second and third ones are word meanings and among the eight sense items of "走", the first, third, fourth, fifth, sixth, seventh and eighth ones are word meanings. Therefore, "飞" and "走" are both polysemes, and at the same time, they are polysemous semantic morphemes.

It can be seen from the above analysis that it is extremely necessary to distinguish word meaning and semantic morpheme meaning from the synchronic perspective. While word meaning can be used to make a sentence independently, semantic morpheme meaning can only be used in word coinage and word formation. Because of the differentiation of word meaning and semantic morpheme meaning, an element with multiple meanings can be either a polyseme or a monoseme. However, since all these meanings can serve as semantic morphemes, they can also be used as semantic morpheme meanings in word coinage and word formation. Therefore, all polysemous elements, whether monosemes or polysemes, are polysemous semantic morphemes. On the contrary, a semantic morpheme meaning cannot serve independently as a word meaning in sentence-making, so such monosyllabic polysemous semantic morphemes as "习" and "观", etc. can no longer be considered as polysemes.

(III) *The causes and means of the emergence of the sense items of a polyseme*

Words are monosemous originally and they gradually developed into polysemes in the process of evolution due to the addition of sense items. Therefore, all the sense items of a polyseme have been developed on the basis of the existing sense of the word. The reasons for the development of the sense items are manifold, but it mainly depends on the development of people's cognition and mental capacity. As people live in society and continue to apprehend and contact with a variety of objective things, it is possible to find some connections between different objects or some common aspects of them, thus it is possible to use a word designating A to refer to B. This results in the addition and development of sense items. For example, the word "圈子 (*quanzi*)" originally referred to "a circle or a ring". Later on, people feel that "范围 (*fanwei*, 'scope')" also refers to a certain aspect of things, just as the circling of a "圈子", so people use the "圈子" to refer to "the scope of groups or activities" in such expressions as "小圈子 (*xiao quanzi*, 'clique')" and "生活圈子 (*shenghuo quanzi*, 'circle of life; living world')", etc. As a result, a new sense item is added to "圈子" and it turned into a polyseme. Therefore, people's cognition contributes to the development of polysemes and the development of polysemes also reflects the development of people's cognition and mental capacity to a certain extent.

The difference in people's cognition brings about a variety of methods and means for the emergence of the sense items of polysemes, which are listed as follows:

1 Semantic Extension

New senses can be created by semantic extension based on the original meaning. For example,

老: (1) (as opposed to young) old in age: 人老了 (*Ren lao le*, "The man is old")
(2) (as opposed to new) existed long ago: 老厂 (*laochang*, "old factory") | 老关系 (*lao guanxi*, "former association")

(3) dated; antiquated: 老毛病 (*lao maobi*ng, "chronic ailment")
(4) original; unchanged; same: 老地方 (*laodifang*, "the same old place")

The first one is the primary among the four sense items of "老 (*lao*)" and the second, the third and the fourth are all semantic extensions based on association with the characteristics of the original meaning of "old". "Old in age" means that the growth time is bound to be long, thus it must have "existed long ago" and since "old in age" means that the growth time is bound to be long, thus compared with the "new", it is bound to be "dated and antiquated" and "original and unchanged" and so on. The new sense items of "老" emerged based on associations and semantic extension in this way.

2 Metaphor

New senses can also be produced through metaphor based on the original meaning in accordance with the similarities between the things. For example,

酝酿: (1) ferment; brew
(2) (figurative) make preparations; deliberate on: 酝酿候选人名单 (*yunniang houxuanren mingdan*, 'consider and discuss the list of candidates')

Before the wine is 酒造 (*niangzao*, 'brewed'), there is a process of 发酵 (*fajiao*, 'fermentation') and there is also a process to prepare and consider before something being made; thus the two share some similarities. The new sense item of "酝酿" thus came into being on the basis of metaphor.

3 Metonymy

New senses can also be produced by metonymy: based on highlighting the function of the original meaning, a thing or concept is referred to by the name of something closely associated with that thing or concept, or a word designating parts is used to refer to the whole, thus new senses emerge. For example,

花: (1) flower; shoot of the sporophyte of a seed plant modified for reproduction, having leaves, calyces, thalami, and pistils, some featuring splendidcolours and emitting fragrance: 一朵花 (*yi duo hua*, "a flower")
(2) plant cultivated for ornamentation: 种花 (*zhong hua*, "grow flowers") |一盆花儿 (*yi pen huar*, "a pot of flowers")

    舌头: (1) tongue; organ attached to the floor of the mouth, used in the ingestion of food, the perception of taste, and the articulation of sounds: 用舌头舔了一下 (*yong shetou tian le yi xia*, "licked with the tongue")
    (2) enemy soldier captured for the purpose of extracting information: 捉到了一个舌头 (*zhuo dao le yi ge shetou*, "captured an enemy soldier for espionage purpose")

The first sense item of "花 (*hua*)" is the original meaning, referring to the name of a part of something. Later, on the basis of highlighting the original meaning, the term designating parts is used to the refer to the whole, thus the second sense of "花" came into being. This is a process of metonymy in which a part is used to refer to the whole. As far as "舌头 (*shetou*)" is concerned, its first sense item is the original meaning and the second sense item is also formed based on highlighting the meaning and function of "舌头": because the main feature of the enemy soldier known as the "舌头" lies in that we are going to extract information through his "舌头 (*tongue*)". For this "enemy soldier", "舌头" is also a part of his body, so the second sense item of "舌头" is also generated by the part-whole metonymy. Another case of metonymy is as follows:

翻译: (1) translate: 他翻译了许多文章 (*Ta fanyi le xuduo wenzhang*, "He has translated many articles")
(2) translator: 他是一位翻译 (*Ta shi yiwei fanyi*, "He is a translator")

The original meaning of "翻译 (*fanyi*)" was an action; later on a person who performs this action was also referred to as "翻译". In this process, on the basis of highlighting the function of the original meaning, a thing or concept was referred to by the name of something closely associated with that thing or concept and thus a new sense emerged.

4 Specific Reference

Specific reference means that on the basis of the original meaning, a word with a larger designating scope originally is used to refer to a certain specific thing within this scope and thus new senses emerge. For example,

喜事: (1) happy event; joyous occasion
(2) wedding

Obviously, "wedding" is included in the "happy event", so the former is a specific event within the scope of the latter and this is a case of specific reference and by this way the second sense item of "喜事 (*xishi*)" is produced.

Four methods of the emergence of sense items of a polyseme are discussed separately in the above. In fact, several different sense items of a polyseme can come into being by one method or by several different methods. For example,

负担: (1) bear; carry; shoulder: 负担任务 (*fudan renwu*, "carry out a task") | 负担 责任 (*fudanzeren*, "shoulder responsibility")
(2) stress; responsibility: 学生的负担太重 (*Xuesheng de fudan tai zhong*, "The stress of the students is too heavy")
(3) burden; strain: 思想负担 (*sixiang fudan*, "mental burden")

The first sense item of "负担 (*fudan*)" is the original meaning and the second one is derived by semantic extension while the third one by metaphor.

(IV) Various meanings of a polyseme and their relationship

All polysemes are developed from monosemes; therefore, the original meaning is differentiated from derived meanings. The original meaning is the meaning of a word at the very beginning and all the meanings generated on the basis of the existing meanings are derived meanings. Sometimes a new derived meaning may also be generated on the basis of an existing derived meaning.

From the derivational relationship of the sense items of a word, the one serving as the basis of the emergence of new meanings is called the primary meaning and all the derived new meanings are called non-primary meanings.

From the application of word meaning in society, the most commonly used and the most important meaning is called the generally used sense and all the others are called non-generally used senses.

The various meanings of a polyseme often show an intricate and complex situation as language constantly changes and develops.

When a word just appeared, its original meaning is its generally used sense and of course its primary meaning. With the development of language, there are two directions of evolution for the original meaning. The first is that the original meaning has been passed down and at any stage of the development of society it is both the generally used sense and the primary meaning. Such words as "人 (*ren*, 'person')", "山 (*shan*, 'mountain')", "水 (*shui*, 'water')", "树 (*shu*, 'tree')" and "手 (*shou*, 'hand')", etc. are all of this type. The second is that in the process of development, the original meaning was no longer a generally used sense in society, nor even could it be used as a word meaning independently yet, while one of its derived meanings became the generally used sense and gradually became the primary meaning as the source for other meanings to derive. For example, the original meaning of "兵 (*bing*)" in ancient Chinese was "weapon", while at present its generally used sense is "soldier"; the original meaning of "强 (*qiang*)" was "a powerful bow" while its generally used sense now is "powerful" and "strong". Obviously, in contemporary Chinese the original meaning and the generallyused sense of both "兵" and "强" are no longer identical. After the generallyused senses of these words were changed, the qualification as an independent word meaning of most of the original meanings would be lost and they could only be used as semantic morpheme meanings in certain cases, except that some of the original meanings were preserved in a number of conventional expressions. Thus, the original meaning, generally used sense and primary meaning of a word are not exactly identical and they can be changed and converted during the process of development.

The relationship between the generally used sense and the primary meaning of a word is comparatively close. In general, the generally used sense of a polyseme is often its primary meaning, which is the foundation for all new meanings to come into being and all the other sense items of the polyseme are directly or indirectly produced on the basis of this meaning. Take the above-mentioned "老 (*lao*)" as an example: all its derived meanings are directly derived from its primary meaning. Take "打 (*da*)" as another example, both its generally used sense and primary meaning are "beat; strike", e. g., "打鼓 (*da gu*, 'beat/play the drum')", "打人 (*da ren*, 'beat a man')", etc. Because there are striking actions when people make certain instruments, then a sense of "make" was derived from the primary meaning "beat; strike", e. g., "打一把刀 (*da yiba dao*, 'make a knife')" and "打一个橱子 (*da yige chuzi*, 'make a cupboard')", etc. Because "knitting/weaving" is also a making activity, then a sense of "knitting/weaving" was derived from "make", e. g., "打毛衣 (*da maoyi*, 'knit a woolen sweater')", "打帘子 (*da lianzi*, 'weave a curtain')", etc. As far as these senses are concerned, "make" was directly derived from "beat", and "knit/weave" was directly derived from "make"; therefore, "knit/weave" was indirectly derived from "beat". Without "beat", there is no "make" and it is impossible to derive "knit/weave". Therefore, "beat" is fundamental and it is the foundation for other new meanings to derive either directly or indirectly form it. The non-primary meaning plays an intermediary role in the process of indirect derivation. Take the "make" sense of "打" for example, although it has the property of the primary meaning, it cannot be called the primary meaning. This is because a polyseme can only have one primary meaning in a certain stage of development and only in this way can we clearly observe and analyze how the sense items of a polyseme are produced as well as how they are interconnected with each other. As far as "make" is concerned, it can be called "a non-primary meaning with the property of primary meaning". If there are more than one cases like this in a polyseme, we can call them "the first non-primary meaning with the property of primary meaning", "the second non-primary meaning with the property of primary meaning" and so on according to the order in which they came into being. If we can illustrate the emergence of all the sense items of each polyseme in such a way, it will be easy to understand how word meanings evolved and developed.

(V) Polysemy and multiple-category membership

Because a polyseme is a word with several inter-related but different meanings; therefore it belongs to polysemy.

There is a close relationship between polysemy and multiple-category membership in grammar. From the perspective of polysemy, some senses of a polyseme belong to multiple-category membership. For example,

落 (là) (1) missing; left out: 这里落了两个字 (*Zheli la le liang ge zi*, "Two words are missing here.")
(2) leave behind; forget to bring along: 把书落家里了 (*ba shu la jiali le*, "have left one's books behind at home")
(3) fall behind; trail: 他走得慢, 落下很远 (*Ta zou de hen man, la xia hen yuan*. "He walked slowly and fell far away")

The three senses of "落" (*la*) are different, but they all express an action with the same grammatical function and they all belong to verb. Of course this kind of polysemy is irrelevant to multiple-category membership.

Word meaning clustering 137

However, some polysemes are quite different from this. For example,

辣: (1) pungent; hot: 这菜又酸又辣 (*Zhe cai you suan you la*, "The dish is sour and spicy") (adj.)
(2) (of smell or taste) hot and stinging: 辣眼睛 (*la yanjing*, "make one's eye sting") (v.)
(3) vicious; ruthless: 心狠手辣 (*xin hen shou la*, "vicious and ruthless") (adj.)

　短: (1) short: 衣服太短 (*Yifu tai duan*, "The clothes are too short") (adj.)
　(2) lack; owe: 短他三元钱 (*duan ta san yuan qian*, "owe him three yuan") (v.)
　(3) shortcoming; deficiency: 不要当面揭短 (*Buyao dangmian jieduan*, "Don't rake up other's faults face to face.") (n.)

In the above two examples, the three senses of "辣 (*la*)" belong to adjective and verb respectively, while the three senses of "短 (*duan*)" belong to adjective, verb and noun respectively. Polysemy here is also multiple-category membership.

Not all polysemous words belong to multiple-category membership, but all words of multiple-category membership belong to polysemy in Chinese. Both polysemy and multiple-category membership are illustration of word meaning. Polysemy illustrates the content of word meaning emphasizing lexical meaning, while multiple-category membership illustrates the grammatical property and characteristics of word meaning focusing on grammatical meaning. Therefore, when analyzing and understanding a polyseme, we should not only clarify the content of lexical meaning that each sense item expresses, but also pay attention to the grammatical meaning of each sense item and make clear their grammatical property and grammatical category because only in this way can we fully understand a polyseme.

(VI) The monosemy of polysemes

When a polyseme exists in isolation, it is polysemous, but when it is put in concrete use, it is monosemous. This is the monosemy of polysemes. It is precisely because of the monosemy of polysemes in the concrete use that no confusion in communication can occur and that people can accurately express themselves and communicate clearly.

The monosemy of polysemes is determined by the concrete linguistic context. The concrete context can not only highlight and explicitly express a certain sense of a polyseme, but also make the sense get concrete correspondence with the concrete object. For example, the word "嗓子 (*sangzi*)", in the sentence "小红把嘴张开，请大夫看看嗓子 (*Xiaohong ba zui zhang kai, qing daifu kankan sangzi*, 'Xiaohong, open your mouth and let the doctor look at your throat')", means "throat" and its correspondence to the concrete object is Xiaohong's throat instead of the throat of any other person's. Whereas in "小王的嗓子好，就让他唱吧 (*Xiao Wang de sangzi hao, jiu rang ta chang ba*, 'Xiao Wang has a good voice and let him sing')", it is obvious that "嗓子" means "voice" and it can only be Xiao Wang's voice instead of anyone else's voice. All this depends upon concrete context.

Many contexts are conducive to the monosemy of polysemes. A word, an expression in one's eyes or a gesture, can all form a context that affects meaning. In general, there are two contexts: first, the context of the language itself, i. e., the context of the utterances; second, the context of social life, i. e., the concrete living environments of communication.

Many polysemes can show their monosemy with the help of linguistic contexts. For example, in the sentence "他太骄傲了, 听不进别人的批评意见 (*Ta tai jiao'ao le, ting bu jin bieren de piping yijian*, 'He is too proud to listen to other people's criticisms')", "骄傲 (*jiao'ao*)" means "arrogant, self-righteous". But in "作为一个中国人, 我感到无比骄傲 (*Zuo wei yi ge Zhongguoren, wo gandao wubi jiao'ao*, 'As a Chinese, I feel very proud')", obviously, "骄傲" means "proud". For another example, in the sentence "这个故事情节比较简单 (*Zhege gushi qingjie bijiao jiandan*, 'The plot of this story is quite simple')", "简单 (*jiandan*)" means "simple in structure; uncomplicated"; while in "这个人头脑太简单 (*Zhege ren tounao tai jiandan*, 'This man has too simple a mind')", it means "(of experience, ability, etc.) commonplace; ordinary"; but in "我们不能简单从事 (*Women buneng jiandan congshi*, 'We cannot take rash actions')", it designates "oversimplified; casual; rash".

There are also a small number of polysemes whose monosemy cannot be shown up only with the help of linguistic contexts. For example, in "你又扮演了一个很不光彩的角色 (*Ni you banyan le yige hen bu guangcai de juese*, 'You played an inglorious part again')", it is not easy to determine whether the meaning of "角色 (*juese*, 'role; part')" refers to "the character that the actor plays" or "the disreputable doings that a person does in a certain place" just by this sentence alone. In this case, we need to resort to the specific communicative environments. If the two are talking about the characters in the play, "角色" certainly means the former; if the two are talking about a matter or a situation in life, it obviously refers to the latter. Thus, although polysemes in Chinese are quite rich, they always appear with a monosemous nature in concrete use because of the function of contexts.

(VII) Polysemes and homophones

Homophones refer to the words which have the same phonetic form but completely different meanings. In Chinese, only those words identical in all the three aspects of initial, final and tone can be called homophones. For example,

米 (*mi*, "rice") – 米 (*mi*, "a meter")
汗 (*han*, "sweat") – 旱 (*han*, "drought")
杜鹃 (*dujuan*, "cuckoo") – 杜鹃 (*dujuan*, "rhododendron")
数目 (*shumu*, "number") – 树木 (*shumu*, "tree")

Homophones have the same phonetic form, and in particular, some homophones have the same written form; therefore, superficiality, homophones have

Word meaning clustering 139

the same form with multifold meanings just like polysemes and accordingly they are often confused with polysemes.

But in essence homophones and polysemes are two phenomena totally different from each other. The distinction between them lies in that homophones are separate and different words with no connection between the meanings of each word. Whereas a polyseme is just one word no matter how many sense items it has, because all the senses of the word are inter-related.

Homophones and polysemes are also very different from each other as far as their formation processes are concerned. Homophones appear as a result of word coinage in different historic stages of language development, different regions and different occasions. The formation of homophones is entirely a coincidence of two different words with the same phonetic form and it is a matter of chance. Polysemes are otherwise. From the general trend of the development of word meaning, polysemes emerge as an inevitable development of language; from the creation of each sense item of polysemes, all the sense items are motivated, so polysemes appear as a rational result. It cannot be excluded naturally that some particular sense items of certain polysemes are not interconnected with the other sense items of the same word any more due to the long-time diachronic development, and under such circumstances such sense items may well be differentiated from other sense items and become homophones of the original words.

In general, the distinction between homophones and polysemes is extremely obvious and clear. It is absolutely inadvisable that to take out the identical polysemous semantic morphemes from a homophone and on this basis to merge homophones into polysemes deliberately.

(VIII) Polysemes and homographs

A homograph is a word that shares the same written form with another word but has both a different meaning and a different phonetic form. For example,

行 (*xing*, "walk") – 行 (*hang*, "row")
长 (*zhang*, "grow") – 长 (*chang*, "long")
传 (*chuan*, "transmit") – 传 (*zhuan*, "biography")
好 (*hao3*, "good") – 好 (*hao4*, "like")

If only judged from the written form, homographs seem to indicate different meanings with the same forms. But it must be made clear that homographs are essentially different from polysemes. First, the various forms of homographs are not identical in pronunciation, which proves that they are two words. Second, their meanings are different. Although there exist certain traces of mutual evolution between these meanings, there is no relation of primary meaning and derived meaning between these meanings as those in polysemes. Homographs are not homophones, because their phonetic forms are quite different except that they have the same written form. Homographs are different words completely independent from each other with only the same written form. Therefore when we investigate the types of word meanings, we should distinguish homographs from polysemes and even from homonyms etc. in written language.

Section 3 Synonyms

I Synonyms and their characteristics

(I) The definition of synonym

It has been well established for years in Chinese linguistic community that synonyms are a group of words having the same or similar meanings. I myself have also been using this definition for a long time. But I always have a feel in applying the definition that the problem has not been thoroughly solved yet. First of all, this definition falls short of the reality: it is a definition for synonyms in name but it basically covers near-synonyms in reality while the essence of near-synonyms is that they are different in meaning and cannotsubstitute for each other. How can near-synonyms be treated as synonyms? The second problem is that when people study, discuss, and learn synonyms, true synonyms have always been overlooked because such a definition not only fails to guide people to seriously understand, learn, study and differentiate synonyms but on the contrary obliterates their existence intentionally or unintentionally, let alone acknowledging the significance and value of the existence of synonyms. Suffice it to say that the above two points are sufficient to prove that the current definition of synonyms in academia is inappropriate.

As a word meaning cluster, synonyms always exist in vocabulary as an undeniable fact active in the real speech of people. Therefore, we must face it, acknowledge it, study it and correctly assess the value of its existence and give it the position it deserves in vocabulary.

Synonyms are supposed to be defined as words with the same meaning in language. For example,

衣服 (*yifu*, "clothes") – 衣裳 (*yishang*, "clothes")
水平 (*shuiping*, "level") – 水准 (*shuizhun*, "level")
祖母 (*zumu*, "grandmother") – 奶奶 (*nainai*, "grandmother")
诞辰 (*danchen*, "birthday") – 生日 (*shengri*, "birthday")
丈夫 (*zhangfu*, "husband") – 老公 (*laogong*, "husband")
容貌 (*rongmao*, "appearance") – 长相 (*zhangxiang*, "appearance")

The vast majority of synonyms in Chinese are different in phonetic forms while only a very few of them have the same phonetic form with the same meaning, for example, "口形 (*kouxing*, 'mouth shape')" and "口型 (*kouxing*, 'mouth shape'). However, homophonic synonyms like these in a language are really very rare and they are resulted from the writing system rather than the spoken form.

(II) The defining criteria and characteristics of synonyms

Since synonyms are words with the same meaning, it is obvious that the essential characteristic of synonyms is that they have the same meaning. According to the criteria for dividing word meaning clustering previously discussed, this essential characteristic is mainly reflected on the identity of lexical meaning, grammatical meaning and concept correspondence. This is because only when lexical meaning and concept correspondence are exactly the same can the requirements of being synonymous be met and the essential characteristics of synonyms be reflected. Being identical in grammatical meaning is the prerequisite for dividing word meaning clustering and it also the case with synonyms: only words belonging to the same word class can belong to the same conceptual category in meaning and only on the basis of the same conceptual category can they be connected and related in meaning and thus whether they are synonyms or not can be determined in turn on this basis.

In determining the criteria for dividing word meaning clustering, although word meaning is broken down to several aspects as it is analyzed and interpreted, these aspects are an integrated and interconnected whole in practical application. As far as lexical meaning is concerned, it is naturally consistent with concept correspondence, but it must be combined with grammatical meaning when dealing with specific words. For example, so far as grammatical meaning is concerned, the three words "哥哥 (*gege*, 'elder brother')" and "兄长 (*xiongzhang*, 'elder brother')" and "弟弟 (*didi*, 'younger brother')" are all kinship terms and belong to the same conceptual category. It suffices for comparing them on this prerequisite, but their relationships cannot be determined just based on this and only after a differentiation and analysis combined with their lexical meaning can we determine that "哥哥" and "兄长" are synonyms, because they have the same lexical meaning and concept correspondence, while "弟弟" does not meet this requirement; therefore it cannot enter the cluster of synonymy of the former two words.

From the above we can see that only the words with exactly the same meaning are synonyms, being identical in meaning is their essential characteristic and the identity in lexical meaning, grammatical meaning and concept correspondence of word meaning is the fundamental basis for determining the cluster of synonyms.

II Types of synonyms

As discussed in the above, we can use these criteria to determine the scope of synonymy cluster. In addition, because there are such different forms of word meaning representation in language as monosemy, polysemy and multiple-category membership etc., in the analysis of lexical meaning, we should take one sense of a word (i. e., one sense item) as the analysis unit for accuracy and only in this way, can we discuss the issue in detail and in-depth.

Clustering of synonymy can be classified into the following four types.

142 *Word meaning clustering*

(I) Complete synonyms

Complete synonyms, also known as absolute synonyms, are words that have the same lexical meaning, grammatical meaning and meaning with special flavour. For example,

忌妒 (*jidu*, "envy") – 妒忌 (*duji*, "envy")
衣服 (*yifu*, "clothes") – 衣裳 (*yishang*, "clothes")
互相 (*huxiang*, "mutual") – 相互 (*xianghu*, "mutual")
床板 (*chuangban*, "bedplate") – 铺板 (*puban*, "bedplate")
眉毛 (*meimao*, "eyebrow") – 眼眉 (*yanmei*, "eyebrow")
手臂 (*shoubi*, "arm") – 胳膊 (*gebo*, "arm")
暖瓶 (*nuanping*, "thermos bottle") – 热水瓶 (*reshuiping*, "thermos bottle")
灯泡 (*dengpao*, "lamp bulb") – 电灯泡 (*diandengpao*, "lamp bulb")
卷心菜 (*juanxincai*, "cabbage") – 包心菜 (*baoxincai*, "cabbage")
山茶花 (*shanchahua*, "camellia") – 耐冬花 (*rendonghua*, "camellia")
和 (*he*, "and") – 同 (*tong*, "and")
路 (*lu*, "road; way") – 道 (*dao*, "road; way")
吞 (*tun*, "swallow") – 咽 (*yan*, "swallow")

Based on the criteria for determining synonyms, we analyze "眉毛" and "眼眉", "包心菜" and "卷心菜" as follows.

	眉毛 *(meimao)*	眼眉 *(yanmei)*
Lexical Meaning	hair on the upper rim of the eye	hair on the upper rim of the eye
Concept Correspondence	black, short hair on the upper rim of the eye	black, short hair on the upper rim of the eye
Grammatical Meaning	noun	noun
Meaning with Special Flavour	neutral	neutral

	包心菜 *(baoxincai)*	卷心菜 *(juanxincai)*
Lexical Meaning	headed cabbage	headed cabbage
Concept Correspondence	cabbage, leaves wrapped up in layers, shaped like balls	cabbage, leaves wrapped up in layers, shaped like balls
Grammatical Meaning	noun	noun
Meaning with Special Flavour	image flavour	image flavour

From the above analysis on the two groups of synonyms we can see that complete synonyms are identical in all aspects of the word meaning, which is the essential character of this type of synonyms.

The meanings of the complete synonyms (i. e., absolute synonyms) are identical, so they have exactly the same role in linguistic communication, thus, they can replace with each other in specific contexts. For example, there is no difference in saying "我买卷心菜 (*Wo mai juanxincai*, 'I want to by cabbage')" or "我买包心菜 (*Wo mai baoxincai*, 'I want to by cabbage')" and "他忌妒你 (*Ta jidu ni*, 'He is envious of you')" or "他妒忌你 (*Ta duji ni*, 'He is envious of you')". However, it is precisely because that complete synonyms have the same role in communication, their co-existence in language is unnecessary. Therefore, only one out of a group of complete synonyms can remain and the others have been filtered away in application and conventionalization in the linguistic community and there is no need for them to co-exist in language forever.

Complete synonymy always exists in language as a lexical phenomenon. From the perspective of historical development, the members of complete synonyms are always in a circulation of continuously disappearing and generating. Because these complete synonyms have the same functions, they are all faced with a normalization process and there are two different situations of development. One case is that one of a group of the synonyms will be retained and the other will be eliminated. This is the case of "向日葵 (*xiangrikui*, 'sunflower')" and "向阳花 (*xiangyanghua*, 'sunflower')": it is evident that the former has been used more frequently than the latter from the present condition of application. Another case of the development of complete synonymy is that some absolute synonyms, in the development process, gradually embarked on the road of differentiation in meaning and as a result, each of them has obtained their own meaning characteristics; therefore, they are all preserved by virtue of their own features and developed into a pair of incomplete synonyms from a pair of complete synonyms. For example, "魂灵 (*linghun*)" and "灵魂 (*hunling*)" were a pair of complete synonyms and they both referred to "魂 (*hun*, 'soul')". Later on, "灵魂" gradually developed into a polyseme meaning "soul; idea" and "personality; conscience", etc. ; thus, "魂灵" and "灵魂" have a division of labour and are differentiated. As a result, they are both preserved and continue to exist in the linguistic application of people because of their own characteristics and functions in meaning.

Complete synonyms exist in the language of any age and any ethnic group. It is only natural that there exist complete synonyms in language, because people's word coinage activities from different angles will constantly bring about a variety of complete synonyms in language. Take a coal sheet once used in households as an example: some people call it "蜂窝煤 (*fengwomei*, 'honeycomb coal')", finding its appearance like a honeycomb, while others call it "藕煤 (*oumei*, 'lotus root coal')", since it looks like lotus root. Different ways of word coinage make "蜂窝煤" and "藕煤" a pair of complete synonyms. Now through the application and conventionalization in society, it is obvious that "蜂窝煤" has been widely spread. In addition, the evolution and adjustment of the vocabulary system may also bring about complete synonyms due to the internal change of word meaning.

Complete synonyms are constantly produced and they will always exist in language. Complete synonyms will always be constantly standardized and normalized: some are preserved, others are eliminated, and still others are differentiated in application. This is the law of the development of complete synonyms.

144 *Word meaning clustering*

(II) Incomplete synonyms

By incomplete synonyms are meant a pair of words with the same lexical meaning, concept correspondence and grammatical meaning but different in meaning with special flavour. Because these words are completely equipped with the characteristics and basis of synonyms, they also fall in the scope of synonyms. Such words as "父亲 (*fuqin*, 'father')" vs. "爸爸 (*baba*, 'papa')" and "生日 (*shengri*, 'birthday')" vs. "诞辰 (*danchen*, 'birthday')", etc. are cases in point. Now we take two groups of words "会晤 (*huiwu*)" vs. "见面 (*jianmian*)" and "土豆 (*tudou*)" vs. "马铃薯 (*malingshu*)" as examples. We use the criteria for determining synonyms to analyze them as follows.

	会晤 (*huiwu*)	见面 (*jianmian*)
Lexical Meaning	meet each other face to face	meet each other face to face
Concept Correspondence	meet each other	meet each other
Grammatical Meaning	verb	verb
Meaning with Special Flavour	written and serious	oral

	土豆 (*tudou*)	马铃薯 (*malingshu*)
Lexical Meaning	edible oval shaped tuber	edible oval shaped tuber
Concept Correspondence	annual plant, oval, large tuber, edible	annual plant, oval, large tuber, edible
Grammatical Meaning	noun	noun
Meaning with Special Flavour	oral	scientific style

From the analysis of the above two groups of words, we can see that incomplete synonymy is also entirely based on the identity of lexical meaning, concept correspondence as well as grammatical meaning and it is thus safe to say that the identity in these three aspects is decisive for synonymy while differences in meaning with special flavour bring about incomplete synonymy.

Language abounds in meanings with special flavour and incomplete synonyms based on different meanings with special flavour are also diverse and varied. We make a specific analysis as follows.

1   Language style, for example:

   祖母 (*zumu*, "grandmother") – 奶奶 (*nainai*, "granny")
   会晤 (*huiwu*, "meet with") – 见面 (*jianmian*, "meet")
   吝啬 (*linse*, "stingy") – 小气 (*xiaoqi*, "niggardly")
   美丽 (*meili*, "beautiful") – 好看 (*haokan*, "good-looking")

Word meaning clustering 145

The former ones of these groups all have a written language or solemn and serious flavour, while the latter have a colloquial or amiable emotive flavour. For other examples:

买 (*mai*, "buy") – 购买 (*goumai*, "purchase")
看 (*kan*, "look") – 观看 (*guankan*, "watch")
飞 (*fei*, "fly") – 飞翔 (*feixiang*, "fly; hover")
坐 (*zuo*, "take") – 乘坐 (*chengzuo*, "take")

The former ones of these groups are commonly used in daily life with an obvious colloquial flavour while the latter are often used in written and literary works and are sometimes used in certain comparatively serious occasions, so they have a flavour of written language and literary style and a serious flavour to a certain degree. For still other examples:

水银 (*shuiyin*, "hydrargyrum") – 汞 (*gong*, "mercury")
土豆 (*tudou*, "murphy") – 马铃薯 (*malingshu*, "potato")
盐 (*yan*, "salt") – 氯化钠 (*lühuana*, "sodium chloride")
蚂蚱 (*mazha*, "locust") – 蝗虫 (*huangchong*, "grasshopper")

The above groups of words reflect the differences in colloquial style and the flavour of scientific terminology. Obviously, the former all have a colloquial flavour while the latter all possess a flavour of the scientific terminology.

2   Emotive flavour, for example:

孩子 (*haizi*, "child") – 宝宝 (*baobao*, "baby")
黄河 (*Huang He*, "the Huanghe River") – 母亲河 (*muqin he*, "the mother river")
松树 (*songshu*, "pine tree") – 青松 (*qingsong*, "verdant pine")
老头儿 (*laotour*, "old man") – 老头子 (*laotouzi*, "old fogey") – 老大爷 (*laodaye*, "uncle")

The above groups of words are incomplete synonyms formed by different emotive flavour. Obviously, "宝宝 (*baobao*, 'baby')" and "孩子 (*haizi*, 'child')" can both refer to kids of one's own in a certain context, but "宝宝" is much richer than "孩子" in the feeling of fondness. Compared with "黄河 (*Huang He*, 'the Huanghe River')", "母亲河 (*muqin he*, 'the mother river')" also clearly reflects the reverent, passionate and amiable feelings of Chinese people to the Yellow River. Compared with "松树 (*songshu*, 'pine')", "青松 (*qingsong*, 'verdant pine')" fully expresses the people's appreciation and praise on the evergreen, erect and strong characters of "pine". The three words in the group of "老头儿 (*laotour*, 'old man')" are all colloquial words with a colloquial flavour, and in general they also have a neutral colour. But their emotive flavours are different: "老大爷 (*laodaye*)" often has an emotive flavour of respect, "老头儿 (*laotour*)" has more affectionate colour, and "老头子 (*laotouzi*)" sometimes is used for derogatory occasions with

146 *Word meaning clustering*

a disgusting colour, so in the context of "那个老头子真讨厌 (*Na ge laotouzi zhen taoyan*, 'That old fogey is really disgusting')", one does not use "老头儿" or "老大爷" in general.

3   Exotic flavour, for example:

> 出租车 (*chuzuche*, "taxi") – 的士 (*dishi*, "taxi")
> 激光 (*jiguang*, "laser") – 镭射 (*leishe*, "laser")
> 维生素 (*weishengsu*, "vitamin") – 维他命 (*weitaming*, "vitamin")
> 超短裙 (*chaoduanqun*, "mini-skirt") – 迷你裙 (*miniqun*, "mini-skirt")

The above synonyms involve the differentiation between ethnic flavour and exotic flavour. Although they are all products of Chinese word formation, as compared with the former words in the group, which all have an ethnic flavour, the latter ones all have an exotic flavour due to the influence of foreign sounds in their base form. In general, words of this category are interchangeable because they all designate the same lexical meaning and grammatical meaning and correspond to the same concept. However, in the process of application, due to the language habits and the acceptability of thought patterns and other reasons, the words with ethnic flavour tend to be more and more popular while the words with exotic flavour will be gradually eliminated due to their diminishing frequency of use. The fact that the once used "瓦斯 (*wasi*, 'gas')" and "德律风 (*delüfeng*, 'telephone')" are later replaced by "煤气 (*meiqi*, 'gas')" and "电话 (*dianhua*, 'telephone')" respectively are cases in point for this law of vocabulary development. The word "镭射 (*leishe*)" listed in the above has gradually been replaced by "激光 (*jiguang*)" from the situation of its use in society, and the scope and frequency of "迷你裙 (*miniqun*)" have become evidently smaller and smaller.

However, this law of vocabulary development is just for general cases and things will be different for specific words. Take "维他命" as an example, although it is used less than "维生素", but it has a vigorous vitality and it will still continue to be used by the Chinese community based on the current application of the word. As for the word "的士 (*dishi*)", although it is a new word coined in recent years, it has been accepted by the community and included in *The Contemporary Chinese Dictionary*.

4   Image flavour, for example:

> 羡慕 (*xianmu*, "envy") – 眼馋 (*yanchan*, "covet")
> 桂圆 (*guiyuan*, "longan") – 龙眼 (*longyan*, "longan")
> 白 (*bai*, "white") – 雪白 (*xuebai*, "snow-white")
> 抽油机 (*chouyouji*, "oil pumping unit") – 磕头机 (*ketouji*, "kowtow machine")

The above groups of words are differentiated by neutral flavour and image flavour. Obviously, in the above examples, the former words of each group have a neutral flavour, while the latter an image flavour. In general, such synonyms can be replaced with each other in linguistic application with the latter being more vivid and vivacious.

5   Age flavour, for example:

    护士 (*hushi*, "nurse") – 看护 (*kanhu*, "nurse")
    知识分子 (*zhishifenzi*, "intellectual") – 臭老九 (*choulaojiu*, "stinking Number Nine")
    剧院 (*juyuan*, "theatre") – 剧场 (*juchang*, "theatre") – 戏院 (*xiyuan*, "theatre")
    保姆 (*baomu*, "house maid") – 佣人 (*yongren*, "servant") – 老妈子 (*laomazi*, "amah")

These groups of words are synonyms with different age flavour that can reflect the charm and the situation of language application of a certain age. As for the above words, the lexical meaning and grammatical meaning of the words in each group are the same while the ages in which they are coined and used are different, so each word has an intense age mark as far as the meaning with special flavour is concerned. The age flavour of a word does not necessarily display only in the long and different periods, some may be manifested within a very short period of time. The word "臭老九 (*choulaojiu*, 'stinking Number Nine')" in the above example reflects the age flavour of people's cognition in a specific period, although it designates the same thing with its counterpart in the same group.

Words with different age flavour designate the same objective things, so using different words can also reflect different characteristics of the same object in different periods and even can make people understand the historical circumstances of different social stages. For example, "酒店 (*jiudian*, 'restaurant')" and "饭店 (*fandian*, 'restaurant')" are a group of synonyms of this type; nowadays people generally begin to use the "酒店" instead of "饭店", so one can know that it has already existed in the past just from the name of "北京饭店 (*BeijingFandian*, 'Peking Restaurant')". By the same token, through the word "臭老九", one can immediately recall the situations in "Cultural Revolution (1966–1976)". Because they are different in age flavour, the synonyms of this type are not mutually interchangeable in general.

6   Local flavour, for example:

    口气 (*kouqi*, "tone") – 语口儿 (*yukour*, "tone")
    白薯 (*baishu*, "sweet potato") – 红薯 (*hongshu*, "sweet potato") – 地瓜 (*digua*, "sweet potato")
    玉米面 (*yumimian*, "corn flour") – 苞米面 (*baomimian*, "corn flour") – 棒子面 (*bangzimian*, "corn flour")
    聊天儿 (*liaotianr*, "chat") – 拉呱儿 (*laguar*, "chat") – 唠嗑 (*laoke*, "chat")

The words of the above groups differ mainly in local flavour. Local flavours of synonyms are various: some differ in a flavour of *Putonghua* and local flavour, for example, "聊天儿 (*liaotian*, 'chat')" and "唠嗑 (*laoke*, 'chat')"; others differ in the flavour of different application regions, for example "红薯 (*hongsu*, 'sweet potato')" and "地瓜 (*digua*, 'sweet potato')". Although they differ in local flavour, the words in each group are mutually interchangeable in general except in certain special contexts.

Although the above words have the same lexical meaning and grammatical meaning, they differ in concrete application due to their differences in meaning with special flavour, in spite of the fact that the meaning with special flavour of some words and their application scenarios are not absolute, for example, some words with written language flavour can be used in spoken language, while some words with colloquial flavour can sometimes be used in written language, which shows that certain synonyms with different flavour can be replaced for each other. Nonetheless, it is necessary to distinguish the words differ in meaning with special flavour in actual use; because they differ remarkably in meaning-expressing and even in a certain specific context, one cannot replace one of the words in a group of incomplete synonyms with another. For example, in "今天是小明的生日 (*Jintian shi Xiaoming de shengri*, 'Today is Xiaoming's birthday.')", "生日 (*shengri*, 'birthday')" cannot be replaced by "诞辰 (*danchen*, 'birthday')" and in "我买了两包盐 (*Wo maile liang bao yan*, 'I bought two packages of salt.')", neither "买 (*mai*, 'buy')" can be replaced by "购买 (*goumai*, 'purchase')", nor "盐 (*yan*, 'salt')" can be replaced by "氯化钠 (*lühuana*, 'sodium chloride')". One cannot even replace "火柴 (*huochai*, 'match')" and "汽油 (*qiyou*, 'gasoline')" by such words with a clear bygone age flavour as "洋火 (*yanghuo*, 'imported match')" and "洋油 (*yangyou*, 'imported oil')" respectively nowadays. Although the lexical meanings of incomplete synonyms are identical and the concept correspondence and expression of the concrete meaning will not be influenced even if exchanged in use, it does not conform to the social language habits and it is nonstandard in so doing.

Thus it is obvious that although incomplete synonyms have the same lexical meaning and concept correspondence, they are not redundant elements in language. On the contrary, just because they have different meanings with special flavour, their presence can enhance language expression so as to make people's communication life much richer and more colourful.

(III) Sense-corresponding synonyms

By sense-corresponding synonyms are meant two or more different words whose meanings are not the same on the whole but there is a correspondence in a certain sense so as to form synonyms. For example, "短" (*duan*) is a polyseme with three senses: 1. adjective, (as opposed to 'long') short, brief. 2. verb, lack, owe. 3. noun, shortcoming; deficiency; weak point. These three senses of "短" are all word meanings that can be used as sentence-making unit independently and may form synonyms with the sense of other words in both static and dynamic state. For example, the verbal "短" can constitute synonyms with "缺少 (*queshao*, 'lack')" and "欠 (*qian*, 'owe')" and the nominal "短" can constitute synonyms with "缺

点 (*quedian*, 'shortcoming')" and "短处 (weakness)". With the increase of neologisms and the polysemes, such sense-crossing synonyms will become more and more developed.

Since sense-corresponding synonyms in the static state of language have usually only an objective or even a potential connection and corresponding relationship, people generally do not regard them as synonyms. However, in dynamic application, especially in a concrete context, this synonymous relationship will emerge. We offer more examples as follows:

For example, the definitions for "愿望 (*yuanwang*)" and "希望 (*xiwang*) in *The Contemporary Chinese Dictionary* (*Revised Edition*) are:

> 愿望: desire; wish; aspiration; idea to achieve a certain goal in the future: 他参军的愿望终于实现了 (*Ta canjun de yuanwang zhongyu shixian le*, "His wish to join the army has finally come true.")
>
> 希望: 1   aspire; yearn; hanker; dream: 他从小就希望做一个医生 (*Ta congxiao jiu xiwang zuo yige yisheng*. "He has aspired to become a doctor since childhood.")
> 2   hope; wish; dream: 这个希望不难实现 (*Zhe ge xiwang bu nan shixian*. "It is easy to turn this hope into reality.")

From the definitions we can see that "愿望" is a noun while "希望" is a multi-category word. Its first sense item is a verb designating an action or behaviour and the second sense item is a noun, meaning the same as "愿望". In this case, "愿望" and the second sense item of "希望" share the same part of speech and the same lexical meaning and concept correspondence, so they are a pair of synonyms. For another example, the definitions of "工作(*gongzuo*)", "职业 (*zhiye*)", "业务 (*yewu*)" and "任务 (*renwu*)" in *The Contemporary Chinese Dictionary (Revised Edition)* are:

> 工作: 1   work, referring to manual or mental labour, and, in a broad sense, the productive role of a machine or tool operated by man: 铲土机正在工作 (*Chantuji zhengzai gongzuo*. "The spading machine is in operation")
> 2   job: 在资本主义国家，经常有成千上万的人找不到工作 (*Zai ziben zhuyi guojia, jingchang you chengqianshangwan de ren zhao bu daogongzuo*. "In capitalist countries, thousands of people are often unable to find jobs.")
> 3   work: 工会工作 (*gonghui gongzuo*, "trade union work") |科学研究工作 (*kexue yanjiu gongzuo*, "scientific research")
>
> 职业: job or principal activity as the means of livelihood
> 业务: vocational work; professional work; business: 业务范围 (*yewu fanwei*, "scope of business")
> 任务: task; assignment; quota: 政治任务 (*zhengzhi renwu*, "political work") |超额完成任务 (*chao'e wancheng renwu*, "over fulfill one's work")

From the above definitions of the words we can see that the first sense item of "工作" is a verb and the second and third sense item are the nouns. Such words as "职

业", "业务" and "任务" are nouns. Therefore, so far as the nominal part of speech is concerned, diagnosed from their lexical meaning and the concept correspondence of word meaning, the second sense item of "工作" is synonymous with "职业" and the third sense item of it is synonymous respectively with such words as "业务" and "任务", etc. It thus can be seen that the sense-corresponding synonyms are entirely caused by polysemy and multiple-category membership. It is also clear that the identity of part of speech is the necessary condition for synonymy.

The formation of sense-corresponding synonyms is an inevitable result of the monosemy of polysemes. Sense-corresponding synonyms can only be realized based on the use of language and context of this type.

Because the connections of the synonyms formed by the corresponding relationship between the sense items of polysemes are based on the basic identity of lexical meaning, grammatical meaning and meaning with special flavour of these words, synonyms of this type are sometimes interchangeable in a certain context. For example, "旧 (*jiu*)" means "陈旧 (*chenjiu*, 'out-of-date')", and one sense item of the polysemous "老 (*lao*)" is also "陈旧 ('out-of-date')", thus "旧" and "老" are synonyms in this sense and they can be used interchangeably in some contexts. It is completely possible that we say "这式样太老了 (*Zhe shiyang tai lao le*, 'This pattern is too out-of-date')" instead of "这式样太旧了 (*Zhe shiyang tai jiu le*, 'This pattern is too out-of-date')". It can be said only from this situation that these synonyms are equivalent in meaning. However, we cannot hence think that such synonyms are exactly the same because they cannot be used interchangeably in any context. For example, we cannot say "这双鞋太老了 (*Zhe shuang xie tai lao le*)" instead of "这双鞋太旧了 (*Zhe shuang xie tai jiu le*, 'This pair of shoes are too worn-out')". For another example, we can use "包裹 (*baoguo*, 'parcel; package')" to replace "包袱 (*baofu*, 'package')" in "我把包袱在你这里放一下 (*Wo ba baofu zai ni zheli fang yixia*, 'I will put the package here')", whereas we cannot use "包袱" to replace "包裹" in "我去邮局取包裹 (*Wo qu youju qu baoguo*, 'I will go to the post office to take the parcel')". There are a small number of words in these types of synonyms that are rarely exchangeable; for example, one sense item of "孩子 (*haizi*)" is synonymous with "儿童 (*ertong*)" meaning "children; kids", but these two words are not exchangeable in most cases except in such a context as "这些孩子真可爱 (*Zhe xie haizi zhen ke'ai*, 'These children are really lovely.')" and a few other contexts. For instance, one cannot use "孩子 (*haizi*)" instead of "儿童 (*ertong*)" in such contexts as "儿童医院 (*ertong yiyuan*, 'children's hospital')", "儿童公园 (*ertong gongyuan*, 'children's park')", "儿童玩具 (*ertong wanju*, 'children's playthings')" and "儿童福利 (*ertong fuli*, 'child welfare')", etc. In contrast, one cannot use "儿童 (*ertong*)" instead of "孩子 (*haizi*)" in such contexts as "这些事让孩子去做吧 (*Zhexie shi rang haizi qu zuo ba*, 'Let children do these things.')" and "我有三个孩子 (*Wo you sange haizi*, 'I have three children.')", etc. It can be seen that these words are context-conditioned in application. Therefore, we should strive to differentiate the similarities and differences between these synonyms.

So far as sense-corresponding synonyms are concerned, it can be the meaning of a monoseme corresponding to a certain sense item of a polyseme or it can be a certain sense item of two or more than two polysemes corresponding to each other. For example, "树 (*shu*)" can mean both "a single tree" and "many trees" while "树木 (*shumu*)" can only mean "many trees", thus the second sense item of "树" and the meaning of "树木" can only form synonyms in such a context as "这些树长得真茂盛 (*Zhe xie shu zhang de zhen maosheng*, 'These trees are really flourishing')" because it is through the words "这些 (*zhe xie* 'these')" in the preceding context that the second sense item of "树" can be highlighted. In this case, the monoseme "树木" corresponds to the latter sense item of the polyseme "树". For another example, "包袱", "包裹" and "负担" are three polysemes:

包袱 (*baofu*): 1. cloth-wrapper
2 bundle wrapped in a cloth
3 (*fig.*) millstones round one's neck; load; burden: 思想包袱 (*sixiang baofu*, "a load on one's mind")
4 humorous content in comic dialogue or quick-patter

包裹 (*baoguo*): 1. wrap up; bind up. 用布把伤口包裹起来 (*Yong bu ba shangkou baoguo qilai*, "Bandage up the wound")
2 bundle; package; parcel: 他肩上背着一个小包裹 (*Ta jianshang bei zhe yi ge xiao baoguo*, "He carried a small bundle on his shoulder.")

负担 (*fudan*): 1. bear; carry; shoulde: 负担责任 (*fudan zeren*, "to shoulder a responsibilty")
2 weight; strain; encumbrance: 学生的负担太重 (*Xuesheng de fudan tai zhong*, "The students' burden is too heavy.")
3 burden; load: 思想负担 (*sixiang fudan*, "mental burden")

From the comparison of the above three words, we will find that it is difficult to form a synonymous relationship between them for the whole meaning content of each word, but so far as the relationship and correspondence between their various sense items are concerned, the second sense of "包袱" and the second sense of "包裹" are synonymous; thus, "包袱" and "包裹" can be a pair of synonyms within the scope of this sense. Similarly, the third sense of "包袱" and the third sense of "负担" can also be related and correspond to each other, so "包袱" and "负担" can also become a pair of synonyms within the range of this sense.

(IV) Rhetoric synonyms

By rhetoric synonyms are meant the synonyms that are formed with the help of context in verbal communication. The words designating concepts of genus are in general not synonymous with the words indicating concepts of species, because the words representing concepts of genus have different word meaning content from the words indicating concepts of species, so the prerequisite for synonyms is not satisfied. But in a concrete context, a word denoting the concept of genus often possesses correspondence to a concrete object with the help of the communicative conditions; therefore, it may refer to the concept of species and becomes a rhetoric synonym with the word denoting the concept of species it temporarily refers to. For example, a man points to a bunch of chrysanthemum and says: "These flowers are very beautiful." Obviously, the flowers here refer to chrysanthemums, so in this context, "flower" and "chrysanthemum" can form a pair of rhetoric synonyms. In concrete contexts, the change in grammatical meaning may also result in rhetoric synonyms. For example, in the context of "他的聪明和才智也是他在科研上获得成功的原因之一 (*Ta de congming he caizhi ye shi ta zai keyan shang huode chenggong de yuanyin zhiyi*, 'His 聪明 (clever) and 才智 (wisdom) are also one of the reasons for his great success in scientific research')", the adjective "聪明" gains the grammatical nature of a noun; therefore "聪明 (clever)" and "才智 (wisdom)" can form a pair of rhetoric synonyms in this context.

Rhetoric synonyms can only come into being in verbal communication and exist dependent on the context, so their life is short and they have a strong temporality. However, this type of synonyms abound in verbal communication; in addition to their flexibility and diversity, they can timely change the correspondence to concrete objects of their own in accordance with the communicative needs so as to make verbal communication concise and lively with a full demonstration of their unique and distinctive expressive effect.

All the above-mentioned four types of synonyms belong to clustering of synonymy. But each of them possesses distinctive characteristics different from all the other ones. Firstly, from the point of view of complete synonymy versus incomplete synonymy, except for the second class which belongs to incomplete synonymy, all the first, the third and the fourth belong to complete synonymy, i. e., the words within each synonymous group are identical in meaning. The cases for existence, application and development, however, are not exactly the same among these three classes. For the first class, its existence per se determines that the members within a synonymous group cannot co-exist for a long time, so there is definitely a process in which one member in the group is preserved while the other(s) eliminated, or their functions are differentiated; for the third class, although they belong to complete synonymy, they can co-exist for a long time and even are enriched with the development of language, because they are sense items existing within the word meanings of different and distinct individual words. Moreover, some of the synonyms are not interchangeable in application and the situation is even more distinct for the fourth class because this type of synonyms is produced in speech and they cannot exist without the relevant context; nevertheless, this type of synonyms always exists in speech as a temporary phenomenon of word meaning clustering. Secondly, from the perspective of static and dynamic state of language existence, we can also see clearly that the first, second and third classes are language elements in a static existence form. Whether they are used or not, these clusters will objectively exist in the language system in an explicit or inexplicit form, while the fourth class is different because it is a speech element in a dynamic form of existence. Although some of them may well be conventionalized into language elements after being used for a long time, this requires a process of development and conversion. The emergence, existence, application and development of rhetoric synonyms are also a non-negligible content in our studies on the dynamic state of vocabulary.

Through the above analysis, first of all, we can clearly understand that clusters of synonyms have their own scope and rich contents and it is absolutely necessary to separate clusters of synonyms as a type of word meaning clustering to study and explore. Secondly, we also clearly recognize that the classification of word meaning clustering should also be based on a certain theoretical standard. In determining synonyms the basic characteristic of the identity of lexical meaning and concept correspondence of the relevant words must be emphasized. Of course, the identity of grammatical meaning is also the basis for the formation of synonyms; nonetheless, if there is no identity of lexical meaning, no synonyms can be formed even if the relevant words have the same part of speech. For example, "人 (*ren*, 'people')" and "树 (*shu*, 'tree')" are both nouns, "美丽 (*meili*, 'beautiful')" and "宁静 (*ningjing*, 'serenity')" are both adjectives, but because their lexical meanings are completely different, they cannot form synonyms respectively. The same is true for meaning with special flavour: in the formation of synonyms, meaning with special flavour also has a certain function. For example, if lexical meaning and grammatical meaning are the same, whether meaning with special flavour is the same or not, synonyms can be formed, but words with the same meaning with special flavour in addition to the identity in both lexical meaning and grammatical meaning are complete synonyms, and words with different meaning with special flavour in addition to the identity in both lexical meaning and grammatical meaning are incomplete synonyms. Nonetheless, if there is no basis of the identity in lexical meaning, even if meaning with special flavour is exactly the same, no synonyms can be formed. For example, both "太阳 (*taiyang*, 'sun')" and "月亮 (*yueliang*, 'moon')" are nouns, and they both have a neutral flavour; both "后果 (*houguo*, 'consequence')" and "叛徒 (*pantu*, 'traitor')" are nouns, and they both have a derogatory flavour, however, because neither of the two pairs are identical in their lexical meanings, they are not synonyms respectively.

III The reasons and ways for the emergence of synonyms

Synonyms are very active in vocabulary and the richness and abundance of synonyms not only indicate the development of vocabulary but also reflect the development of language and mental capacity of people to some extent.

The progressive development of human society, mental capacity of people and language itself can all contribute to the emergence and development of synonyms. Under the influence of the above-mentioned aspects, the ways in which synonyms are formed are manifold.

(I) Different perspectives of people on the same objective thing result in different words, thus synonyms are formed. Take "荧屏 (*yingping*, 'fluorescent screen')" and "屏幕 (*pingmu*, 'screen curtain')" for example: although they designate the same thing, i. e., the photographic part of a television set, but they are two different words: "荧屏" focus on the role of the fluorescent powder while "屏幕" focus on the picture of "幕 (*mu*, 'curtain')" and thus synonyms are formed. The following words are also of this type:

信封 (*xinfeng*, "envelope") – 信皮 (*xinpi*, "envelope")
合作 (*hezuo*, "cooperate") – 协作 (*xiezuo*, "cooperate")
争辩 (*zhengbian*, "debate") – 争论 (*zhenglun*, "debate")
发卡 (*faqia*, "hairpin") – 头卡 (*touqia*, "hairpin")
西湖 (*Xi Hu*, "West Lake") – 西子湖 (*Xizi Hu*, "Xizi Lake")
番茄 (*fanqie*, "tomato") – 西红柿 (*xihongshi*, "tomato")

(II) Different feelings and attitudes of people towards things result in different words, thus synonyms are formed. For example,

老头子 (*laotou·zi*, "old fogey") – 老头儿 (*laotour*, "old man")
孩子 (*haizi*, "child") – 宝宝 (*baobao*, "baby")
诞辰 (*danchen*, "birthday") – 生日 (*shengri*, "birthday")
助手 (*zhushou*, "assistant") – 帮凶 (*bangxiong*, "accomplice")
遗体 (*yiti*, "remains") – 尸体 (*shiti*, "corpse")
教导 (*jiaodao*, "teach") – 教唆 (*jiaosuo*, "abet")

(III) Evolution of word meaning results in synonyms. For example, "大夫 (*dafu/daifu*)" was originally a title of feudal official position and it was also used to refer to the medical officer resulting in a sense of "医生 (*yisheng*, 'medical doctor')"; thus it became a synonym of "医生". Other examples:

丈夫 (*zhangfu*, "husband") – 老公 (*laogong*, "husband")
丈人 (*zhangren*, "father-in-law") – 岳父 (*yuefu*, "father-in-law")
时髦 (*shimao*, "fashionable") – 摩登 (*modeng*, "modern")
岁 (*sui*, "year") – 年 (*nian*, "year")

(IV) The result of absorbing dialect words. Dialect word absorbed to *Putonghua* becomes a synonym of the original word therein. For example,

搞 (*gao*, "do") – 干 (*gan*, "make") /做 (*zuo*, "do")
把戏 (*baxi*, "trick") – 手段 (*shouduan*, "means")

(V) A word coined under the influence of the phonetic form of a foreign word becomes a synonym for the words that are not influenced by the foreign phonetic forms. For example,

镭射 (*leishe*, "laser") – 激光 (*jiguang*, "laser")
米 (*mi*, "meter") – 公尺 (*gongchi*, "meter")
拷贝 (*kaobei*, "copy") – 复制 (*fuzhi*, "copy")
维他命 (*weitaming*, "vitamin") – 维生素 (*weishengsu*, "vitamin")

(VI) A scientific term becomes a synonym of a word for daily use. For example,

汞 (*gong*, "mercury") – 水银 (*shuiyin*, "hydrargyrum")
昆虫 (*kunchong*, "insect") – 虫子 (*chongzi*, "worm")

氯化钠 (*lühuana*, "sodium chloride") – 食盐 (*shiyan*, "table salt")
齿龈 (*chiyin*, "gingiva") – 牙床 (*yachuang*, "teeth ridge") – 牙床子 (*yachuangzi*, "gum")

(VII) A word in written language becomes a synonym of a word for daily use. For example,

烟霭 (*wu'ai*, "haze") – 云雾 (*yunwu*, "mist")
部署 (*bushu*, "deploy") – 安排 (*anpai*, "arrange")
黎明 (*liming*, "dawn") – 早晨 (*zaochen*, "morning")
措施 (*cuoshi*, "measure") – 办法 (*banfa*, "method")

(VIII) The result of disyllabification of Chinese words leading to synonyms. For example,

眼 (*yan*, "eye") – 眼睛 (*yanjing*, "eye")
路 (*lu*, "road") – 道路 (*daolu*, "road")
丢 (*diu*, "lose") – 丢失 (*diushi*, "lose")
到 (*dao*, ""arrive") – 到达 (*daoda*, "arrive")

(IX) Different word orders result in synonyms. For example,

觉察 (*juecha*, "perceive") – 察觉 (*chajue*, "perceive")
情感 (*qinggan*, "emotion; feeling") – 感情 (*ganqing*, "emotion; feeling")
相互 (*huxiang*, "mutual") – 互相 (*huxiang*, "mutual")
忌妒 (*jidu*, "envy") – 妒忌 (*duji*, "envy")

Reasons and ways leading to synonyms are very diverse, for example, euphemism in language and certain terms in social dialects can also form synonyms of words for daily use. The formation and development of synonyms, consequently, is also a very important aspect in exploring the development of language and vocabulary.

Section 4 Near-synonyms

Near-synonyms are a class of words that the lexicological community has long been familiar with but very difficult to deal with, because the definition of and criteria for near-synonyms are quite difficult to agree on. In the past near-synonyms were treated as a sub-category of synonyms. However, "being identical" and "being near" are different after all. Because near-synonyms do not have the same essential characteristic of being identical in lexical meaning and concept correspondence as synonyms, it is not easy to clarify the problem to group the two into one and the same type. So now I differentiate near-synonyms from synonyms and try to make some exploration from the perspectives of lexical meaning and its concept correspondence.

I Near-synonyms and their characteristics

Near-synonyms are a group of words with the same grammatical meaning and similar lexical meaning. The same grammatical meaning, as mentioned above, indicates that the group of words must be in the same conceptual category; otherwise it is impossible to compare. Similar lexical meaning means that the semantic components of a group of near-synonyms can be classified into major and minor ones in the componential analysis of lexical meaning of these near-synonyms and their conceptual characteristics can also be classified into major and minor ones in the analysis of the characteristics of concept correspondence of these words. Because near-synonyms are the same in both major semantic components of their meaning and major essential characteristics of the concept, their basic contents are exactly the same, and that is why they can form near-synonyms. And because near-synonyms are different to a certain extent in minor semantic components and general characteristics, this difference determines that they cannot be regarded as synonyms. Thus, the criterion of near-synonyms also has their own characteristics. For example, as mentioned earlier, the major semantic component and essential characteristics of "效果" and "后果", both of which mean "result", are the same, while such semantic components as "good" and "bad" do not affect the expression of the basic meaning at all in practical use, so they belong to minor semantic components; therefore, "效果" and "后果" are a pair of near-synonyms. We now analyze "整理 (*zhengli*)" and "整顿 (*zhengdun*)" as follows:

	major semantic component and essential characteristic	*minor semantic component and general characteristic*
整理	to make the objects neat and in good order	physical
整顿	to make the objects neat and in good order	abstract

It is obvious that because their major semantic component and essential characteristics are the same, "整理" and "整顿" are near-synonyms and they can co-exist within the same concept of genus of "to make the objects neat and in good order". The reason we treat the distinction of "physical" and "abstract" as minor semantic components and general characteristics lies in that this distinction is resulted more often than not from the difference in collocation. This difference does not affect the essential characteristics of the concept. These minor components can distinguish word meanings so as to form near-synonyms. So far as the two concepts of "整理" and "整顿" are concerned, they are differentiated by the understanding of people through language practice, but these characteristics do not change the essential characteristics of the concepts and the expression of the basic content, so they are the general characteristics of the concept.

Just because the meaning content of near-synonyms can be classified into major and minor one, for a long time, in dealing with near-synonyms, people treated them as synonyms because they have the same major meaning content and at the same time, people had to pay special attention and emphasis to the so-called problem of "the discrimination of synonyms" while treating them as synonyms, because near-synonyms are different in their minor meaning content.

From the above analysis we can see that the fundamental condition for clustering of near-synonyms lies in that there exists a distinction between major and minor component in lexical meaning and concept correspondence in addition to that they have the same grammatical meaning, whatever the degree and scope of word meaning will be. The major components are fundamental while the minor ones are auxiliary but indispensable, because although near-synonyms reflect the same essential characteristics in word meaning and concept, they can co-exist with each other within a group of near-synonyms just because of the non-essential characteristics in their word meaning and if there is no such distinctive non-essential contents and characteristics, it is impossible for near-synonyms, and in turn, for clustering of near-synonyms, to exist. This is the clustering criterion and characteristic of near-synonyms.

The basic meanings expressed by near-synonyms are the same, thus misuse of near-synonyms will not affect the expression of the basic meanings in verbal communication, except that they are wrong application of language flouting linguistic collocation conventions. But it is not allowed not to distinguish the subtle differences in word meanings and not to follow linguistic conventions in actual use of language. With the continuous enrichment and development of people's mental capacity, the emergence of near-synonyms is inevitable. Moreover, in language application, a large number of near-synonyms not only enrich the means of language use, but also greatly enhance the expressiveness of language so as to make people's speech communication more meticulous and perfect. Therefore, we must not only correctly cognize and carefully treat near-synonyms, but also pay more attention to the discrimination of near-synonyms so as to use them more precisely.

II Type of near-synonyms

Near-synonyms can be classified into two types in first approximation.

(I) Near-synonyms with similar lexical meaning, the same grammatical meaning and different meaning with special flavour. For example,

鼓动 (*gudong*, "agitate") – 煽动 (*shandong*, "incite")
保护 (*baohu*, "protect") – 庇护 (*bihu*, "shelter")
爱好 (*aihao*, "hobby") – 嗜好 (*shihao*, "avocation")
效果 (*xiaoguo*, "effect") – 后果 (*houguo*, "consequence")

As can be seen from the above examples, both "鼓动 (*gudong*)" and "煽动 (*shandong*)" are verbs. Their major semantic component and essential characteristic are "make sb. into action", but "鼓动" means to "gird sb. into action with rhetoric; agitate" with a neutral and commendatory flavour while "煽动" refers to "instigate sb. to do sth. bad" with a derogatory flavour. It can be seen that their minor semantic component and general characteristic are still different. Take "保

护 (*baohu*)" and "庇护 (*pihu*)" as another example. Both of them are also verbs and mean "protect". But "保护" means "care and protect from harm; safeguard" while "庇护" means "to give unprincipled protection". Therefore, the former has a neutral flavour while the latter has a derogatory flavour.

For near-synonyms with similar lexical meaning, the same grammatical meaning and different meaning with special flavour, their meanings with special flavour are in conformity with their lexical meanings, because meanings with special flavour are often implied in lexical meanings. People can understand the general situation of meaning with special flavour from the interpretation of lexical meaning. Such near-synonyms are not interchangeable with each other in specific sentences.

(II) Near-synonyms with similar lexical meaning and the same grammatical meaning and meaning with special flavour. For example,

整理 (*zhengli*, "put in order") – 整顿 (*zhengdun*, "rectify")
优良 (*youliang*, "good") – 优秀 (*youxiu*, "excellent")
机灵 (*jiling*, "clever") – 机智 (*jizhi*, "witty")
抵偿 (*dichang*, "counter") – 赔偿 (*peichang*, "compensate for")
勇敢 (*yonggan*, "brave") – 英勇 (*yingyong*, "heroic")
指斥 (*zhichi*, "denounce") – 指责 (*zhize*, "accuse")

Near-synonyms of this type abound in language and to discriminate these words correctly and carefully is of great necessity to the research and use of language. The similarity of lexical meanings of this type of near-synonyms can be analyzed as follows now that both their grammatical meaning and meaning with special flavour are the same.

The scopes of reference of lexical meaning are different: it means that the meanings of the two words in a set of near-synonyms are different in scope of reference. For example, "家属 (*jiashu*)" and "家族 (*jiazu*)" are a set of near-synonyms. Their common major semantic component and essential characteristic both refer to "family members", but their minor semantic component and general characteristic are different. The word "家属" only refers to "family members of a certain person" and with a relatively small scope of reference, while "家族" refers to "family members including several branches and several generations of the blood lineage with the same family name" with a relatively large scope of reference. For another example, "过程 (*guocheng*)" and "历程 (*licheng*)" are also a set of near-synonyms. Their common content is "process" and their difference lies in that the scope of "过程" is relatively larger, referring to "the process of everything" while "历程" only refers to "a long and extraordinary process that people experience", which is small in scope of reference. Because of the difference in the scope of reference of their word meaning, such near-synonyms are not interchangeable in the same context.

The degree of lexical meaning is different: this means that in a set of near-synonyms, one is stronger in meaning and the other is weaker, or vice versa. For example, all the words of "优良 (*youliang*)", "优秀 (*youxiu*)" and "优异 (*youyi*)" mean "good", but "优良" means "very good", "优秀" means "extremely good", and "优异" means "especially good". As far as the degree of word meaning is concerned, "优良" is much lighter, "优秀" is heavier than "优良", and the meaning of "优异" is much heavier than the first two; therefore the degrees of meanings of the three words are different. For another example, both "爱惜 (*aixi*)" and "珍惜 (*zhenxi*)" mean "cherish; treasure" but compared with "爱惜", "珍惜" mean "pay special attention to" additionally, so the meaning of "珍惜" is heavier than that of "爱惜". Near-synonyms with different degrees of meaning can neither be used interchangeably in the concrete context.

The emphasis on lexical meaning is different: this refers to that different words in a set of near-synonyms differ in emphasis of word meaning. For example, both "证明 (*zhengming*)" and "证实 (*zhengshi*)" are verbs and they both mean "show or determine the authenticity of people or things with reliable materials". However, "证明" focuses on "telling what the things are" while "证实" focuses on "proving the authenticity". For another example, both "广博 (*guangbo*)" and "渊博 (*yuanbo*)" are adjectives and they both refer to "(of knowledge) wide and extensive". But the meaning of "广博" does not involve the depth of knowledge while the meaning of "渊博" means "profound and wide". Thus, these near-synonyms can accurately and delicately reflect subtle differences of things. Therefore, these near-synonyms are neither interchangeable with each other in specific utterances.

The subtle differences in word meaning of near-synonyms can sometimes affect the collocation of words. Take the above-mentioned "整理" and "整顿" for example, because the scopes of reference and objects involved are different for these two words, their collocations are also different: "整理" focuses on "to sort out and reorganize the scattered things" and it can only collocate with the words designating concrete objects, such as "整理东西 (*zhengli dongxi*, 'tidy up things')", "整理书籍 (*zhengli shuji*, 'organize books')" and "整理房间 (*zhengli fangjian*, 'clean up the room')", etc., while "整顿" focuses on "to rectify the disordered", so it often collocates with the words designating abstract things, such as "整顿纪律 (*zhengdun jilü*, 'rectify discipline')" "整顿作风 (*zhengdun zuofeng*, 'rectify the style of work')", "整顿组织 (*zhengdun zuzhi*, 'rectify the organization')" and so on. Misuse of the near-synonyms that cannot be used interchangeably may either affect the exact expression of meaning, e. g., "优良的成绩 (*youliang de chengji*, 'good performance')" vs. "优异的成绩 (*youyidechengji*, 'excellent performance')" or may cause confusion and error in language expression, e. g., "整顿作风 (*zhengdun zuofeng*, 'rectify the style of work')" vs. "*整理作风 (*zhengli zuofeng*, '*organize the style of work')". Therefore, it is extremely necessary to distinguish and employ these near-synonyms with great care.

Section 5 Antonyms

I Antonyms and their characteristics

Antonyms are words that have the same grammatical meaning but opposite lexical meanings. For example,

高 (*gao*, "high") – 低 (*di*, "low")
生 (*sheng*, "alive") – 死 (*si*, "dead")

恩 (*en*, "favour") – 仇 (*chou*, "enmity")
上 (*shang*, "up") – 下 (*xia*, "down")
成功 (*chenggong*, "success") – 失败 (*shibai*, "failure")
光明 (*guangming*, "light") – 黑暗 (*hei'an*, "dark")
安全 (*anquan*, "safe") – 危险 (*weixian*, "dangerous")
大方 (*dafang*, "generous") – 小气 (*xiaoqi*, "stingy")
热情 (*reqing*, "enthusiastic") – 冷漠 (*lengmo*, "indifferent")
积极 (*jiji*, "positive") – 消极 (*xiaoji*, "passive")

So far as grammatical meanings are concerned, since antonyms are words falling within the same conceptual category, their parts of speech must be identical and so are their grammatical meanings. Being opposite or contrary of antonyms is mainly reflected on lexical meanings and concept correspondence. The major characteristic of antonyms lies in that what are extracted from the semantic components of lexical meanings and the content of the conceptual features are major semantic components of the lexical meaning and the essential characteristics of the concept, while being identical, reverse and opposite among these major semantic component and essential characteristics constitute the fundamental contents of antonyms. We now analyze a pair of well-recognized antonyms "生 (*sheng*, 'living')" and "死 (*si*, 'dead')" as follows.

Primary semantic component of word meaning

活 creature have life
死 creature lose life

Essential characteristics of concept

活 alive living body the growth and metabolism of the cell of the organism is going on
死 dead living body the growth and metabolism of the cell of the organism has been stopped

For the above two words, two major semantic components and two essential characteristics are selected. The reason why these are important and essential lies in that these two parts constitute the lexical meanings and the corresponding concepts of the two words and both of them are indispensable.

As can be seen from the above analysis, antonyms are based on the identity, reverse and opposition of the primary semantic components and essential characteristics. Among all these primary semantic components and essential characteristics, the common parts reflect meaning contents and characteristics of their common superordinate concept which illustrate that they co-exist within one and the same conceptual category while the rest are the particular essential characteristics of each word which embody the characteristics and particularities only possessed by the word per se and it is just based upon the reverse and opposition of these characteristics that antonyms are formed. The lexical meaning of every word within a group of antonyms is constituted by the essential characteristics of these two parts, meanwhile reflecting the content of its corresponding concept. Thus it can be seen that the essential characteristic of antonyms lies in the fact that two or more words not only designate the essential characteristics of the superordinate concept but also indicate the essential characteristics being opposite with each other and the sum total of the two parts constitutes the reverse or opposite meaning content of the antonyms. Antonyms are clustered based on the commonality of essential characteristics of the superordinate concept and are opposing to each other based on the essential characteristics of each own, so both the two parts of the essential characteristics included in word meaning play a decisive role in the formation of antonyms. Such words are well-demarcated in meaning and are definitely not interchangeable in use.

Antonyms are a reflection of contradictory relations in objective reality in vocabulary, hence only words that reflect contradictory relations of objective things can form antonyms. Consequently, not all words have their antonyms, such words as "房子 (*fangzi*, 'house')", "书本 (*shuben*, 'book')", "玻璃 (*boli*, 'glass')" and "天空 (*tiankong*, 'sky')", etc., for example, have no antonyms in general.

Generally speaking, because verbs indicate different actions and behaviours and adjectives indicate different properties and states, and contradictory relations are easy to find in these fields, so there are comparatively more antonyms in verbs and adjectives. Antonyms in noun are also numerous. For example,

天 (*tian*, "sky") – 地 (*di*, "earth")
手 (*shou*, "hand") – 脚 (*jiao*, "foot")
左 (*zuo*, "left") – 右 (*you*, "right")
前 (*qian*, "front") – 后 (*hou*, "back")
城市 (*chengshi*, "city") – 乡村 (*xiangcun*, "countryside")
精神 (*jingshen* "spirit") – 物质 (*wuzhi*, "substance")
海洋 (*haiyang*, "ocean") – 陆地 (*ludi*, "land")
朋友 (*pengyou*, "friend") – 敌人 (*diren*, "enemy")

Contradictory relations in objective reality are rather complicated, so are the relations of antonyms in vocabulary. For instance, "失败 (*shibai*, 'failure')" and "成功 (*chenggong*, 'success')" are a pair of antonyms in the context of scientific experiment, whereas it forms a pair of antonyms with "胜利 (*shengli*, 'victory')" under the condition of war. For still a number of words, they do not form a distinctive opposite relation in objective existence but become antonyms in specific contexts. For instance, "钢 (*gang*, 'steel')" and "铁 (*tie*, 'iron')" indicate a name of metal respectively and they are not antonyms in isolation, while in "这里需要的是钢，而不是铁 (*Zheli xuyao de shi gang, er bu shi tie*, 'What we need here is steel instead of iron.')", "钢" and "铁" form a pair of antonyms. Therefore the conditions for forming antonyms must be analyzed case by case.

II Types of antonyms

As is noted above, antonyms are reflections of the contradictory relations of objective reality in vocabulary. Contradictory relations in objective reality are reflected as contradictory and opposite relations among concepts in logical thinking. Word meaning expresses concept; thus the reason why the meanings of antonyms are contradictory and opposite, as a matter of fact, lies in that antonyms designate a pair of concepts with a contradictory or opposite relation. From this point of view, we can say that the contradictory and opposite relations among concepts are the logical foundation of antonyms and this foundation is in turn based on the contradiction and opposition of objective things.

Based on different logical foundations of antonyms, they fall into two types.

(I) Absolute antonyms

Absolute antonyms are those formed based on the contradictory relation of concepts. The characteristic of this type of antonyms lies in that there exists no intermediate concept between the concepts designated by the two antonyms. They are completely mutually exclusive in term of meaning contents: the denial of one member implies the assertion of the other. Antonyms of this type can be used positively or negatively, i. e., both of them can be put before the other and both can be affirmed or negated firstly. Take "死 (*si*, 'dead')" and "活 (*huo*, 'living')" as an example: there is no intermediate concept between them, so both "死 – 活" and "活 – 死" can be used. Both the negative phrase "不死 (*busi*, 'not dead; alive')" and "不活 (*buhuo*, 'not alive; dead')" can be used when they are combined with such a negative word as "不 (*bu*, 'not')", etc. to form phrases. Both the affirmative and negative forms are contradictory in meaning. The following examples are also of this kind:

开 (*kai*, "open") – 关 (*guan*, "close")
动 (*dong*, "moving") – 静 (*jing*, "static")
精神 (*jingshen*, "spirit") – 物质 (*wuzhi*, "substance")
动物 (*dongwu*, "animal") – 植物 (*zhiwu*, "vegetable")

(II) Relative antonyms

Relative antonyms are formed based on the opposite relation between concepts. Its characteristic is that there is a third or more intermediate concepts between two concepts designated by the two antonyms; therefore, the two antonyms are not necessarily reverse to each other so far as their contents are concerned. Antonyms of this kind are only formed under a certain condition. Furthermore, the denial of one side of the pair does not imply the assertion of the other; therefore they must be used positively rather than negatively. For instance, "黑 (*hei*, 'black')" and "白 (*bai*, 'white')" are a pair of antonyms, meanwhile, there is a third or even more concepts between them, such as "灰 (*hui*, 'grey')", "深灰 (*shenhui*, 'dark grey')" and "浅灰 (*qianhui*, 'light grey')", etc. ; therefore we can only use the form of "黑 (*hei*, 'black')" – "白 (*bai*, 'white')" or "白 (*bai*, 'white')" – "黑 (*hei*, 'black')" and we cannot use their negative forms. The reason lies in that when we combine these words with such a negative word as "不 (*bu*, 'not')" to form phrases like "不黑 (*buhei*, 'not black')" and "不白 (*bubai*, 'not white')", the latter may not be antonymous and they are even synonymous for both may denote "灰 (*hui*, 'grey')". Therefore, for words like these, the denial of one does not mean the assertion of the other; the opposite of "不黑 (*buhei*, 'not black')" may not be "不白 (*bubai*, 'not white')" or "白 (*bai*, 'white')" and the opposite of "不白 (*bubai*, 'not white')" may not be "不黑 (*buhei*, 'not black')" or "黑 (*hei*, 'black')"; thus, this type of words cannot be used negatively. Special attention must be paid to the application of antonyms of this type and analyses should be carried out in accordance with specific contexts in which they are used.

Although the above two types of antonyms are different in terms of logical foundations, they are nevertheless exactly the same as far as their relations are based on the unity of opposites. Whether two antonyms are absolutely opposite or relatively opposite to each other, they are dependent on each other in meaning and are in a relation of the unity of opposites. Only when there is one side of a contradiction can there be the other side of the contradiction and if there is no part A of the contradiction there will be definitely no part B of the contradiction, just like that there will be no "生 (*sheng*, 'alive')" without "死 (*si*, 'dead')" and there will be no "福 (*fu*, 'fortune')" without "祸 (*huo*, 'misfortune')". Therefore, when observing, differentiating and analyzing antonyms, we should make it clear that only words that are within the same unity (i. e., the nearest concept of genus) designating a contradictory but interdependent relation are antonyms.

Some temporary antonyms can be formed in dynamic linguistic communication. They are formed catering for the needs of communication in specific contexts. Some of them may develop into language elements and others are just cases of temporary application.

Furthermore, synonymy is also connected with antonyms to a certain extent. Complex cross relationships may usually be found between antonyms and synonyms. For instance, "开 (*kai*, 'open')" and "关 (*guan*, 'close')" are a pair of antonyms, while "开 (*kai*, 'open')", "张开 (*zhangkai*, ' stretch')" and "启开 (*qikai*, 'unwrap')" are a group of synonyms, whereas "关 (*guan*, 'close')" and "闭 (*bi*, 'shut')" are also a pair of synonyms; therefore, in different contexts, "开 (*kai*, 'open')" may constitute antonyms with "闭 (*bi*, 'shut')" and "合 (*he*, 'close')", while "关 (*guan*, 'close')" may form antonyms with "张开 (*zhangkai*, 'stretch')" and "启开 (*qikai*, 'unwrap')".

Section 6 Co-hyponyms, generic words and kinship words

I Co-hyponyms

Co-hyponyms are words designating a series of coordinate concepts. For example,

金属 (metal) – 金、银、铜、铁、锡等等 (gold, silver, copper, iron, tin, etc.)
颜色 (colour) – 红、黄、蓝、白、黑等等 (red, yellow, blue, white, black, etc.)
四季 (four seasons –) – 春、夏、秋、冬 (spring, summer, autumn, winter)

四声 (four tones) – 阴平、阳平、上声、去声 (level tone, rising tone, falling-rising tone, falling tone)

方位 (directions) – 东、西、南、北、前、后、左、右等等 (east, west, south, north, front, back, left, right, etc.)

Coordinate concepts are a series of concepts of species that are in the equi-position under the same concept of genus. For instance, all words after the dash in the above examples are co-hyponyms designating coordinate concepts, and those before the dash such as "金属 (*jinshu*, 'metal')" are words that indicate the concepts of genus. A coordinate phenomenon can form a cluster and the words designating such a cluster are co-hyponyms. All co-hyponyms belong to the same concept of genus; therefore, each word of a cluster of co-hyponyms can reflect the same essential characteristics of the concept of genus that they belong to and it is because that they share the same essential characteristics that they can form a coordinate cluster. In addition, every word within a cluster of co-hyponyms has its own distinctive essential characteristics and it is based on these distinctive characteristics that the particular meaning content of each word is formed and that each word of a cluster of co-hypomyns can be differentiated clearly from each other and at the same time these co-hyponyms are in an equi-position under the same hypernym. Therefore, the concept and lexical meaning of each co-hyponym is a sum total of the essential characteristics of their concept of genus and that of their own. Co-hyponyms are almost the same as antonyms as far as this point is concerned. However, co-hyponymy is by no means the same as antonymy and their difference lies in that the distinctive characteristics of each word in antonymy are totally opposite to each other so the contents of every word within a pair of antonyms is contrary or opposite to each other, while the distinctive characteristics of every word in co-hyponymy are only related with each other; thus the meaning content of each word within a set of co-hyponyms is only related with each other: this is the fundamental basis to differentiate co-hyponymy from antonymy. For example, "春 (*chun*, 'spring')", "夏 (*xia*, 'summer')", "秋 (*qiu*, 'autumn')" and "冬 (*dong*, 'winter')" are a group of co-hyponyms, and we can make an analysis as follows:

Primary semantic components of word meaning

春 **(spring)**	season	The first season of a year	Three months from the beginning of spring to the beginning of summer
夏 **(summer)**	season	The second season of a year	Three months from the beginning of summer to the beginning of autumn
秋 **(autumn)**	season	The third season of a year	Three months from the beginning of autumn to the beginning of winter
冬 **(winter)**	season	The fourth season of a year	Three months from the beginning of winter to the beginning of spring

Essential characteristics of concept

春 **(spring)**	season	Three months from the beginning of spring to the beginning of summer	A period in which all things recover
夏 **(summer)**	season	Three months from the beginning of summer to the beginning of autumn	A period in which all things grow
秋 **(autumn)**	season	Three months from the beginning of autumn to the beginning of winter	A period in which crops are ripe
冬 **(winter)**	season	Three months from the beginning of winter to the beginning of spring	A period in which common plants and insects go into winter sleep

From the above analysis we can see that among the semantic components and conceptual characteristics of the words of "春 (*chun*, 'spring')", "夏 (*xia*, 'summer')", "秋 (*qiu*, 'autumn')" and "冬 (*dong*, 'winter')", the first item, i. e., "season", is common to all the four word meanings and it is also the characteristic by which the four words belong to the same semantic field and the same domain of the concept of genus and the other two items are different from each other, and it is by these different semantic components and characteristics that one can differentiate one word meaning from the others. The relation of word meanings of co-hyponyms is that of being equal and coordinate and one cannot be replaced by the other in actual use.

It thus can be said that the essential characteristic of co-hyponyms lies in that the common essential characteristics of the concept of genus of a group of co-hyponyms and the distinctive essential characteristics of each individual word within the group constitute the meaning contents of each individual word of the group and form an interdependent relation between the members of the group.

There is no denying that the relation between each member of a group of co-hyponyms is that one is related with the other. But we must make it clear that this is looked from the static point of language. The situations will be complicated and diverse, however, if co-hyponyms are observed in the process of the development of language.

Co-hyponyms may change radically under the requirements of context in dynamic speech. For instance, "金 (*jin*, 'gold')", "银 (*yin*, 'silver')", "铜 (*tong*, 'copper')", "铁 (*tie*, 'iron')" and "锡 (*xi*, 'tin')" are co-hyponyms, and each word is in a coordinate relation with each other in static existence. But the case will be different in dynamic application. They are still co-hyponyms when appear in the context of "金、银、铜、铁、锡都是金属 (*Jin, yin, tong, tie, xi doushi jinshu*, 'Gold, silver, copper, iron and tin are all metals')". But if two words among them are in the same context, the types of their relations may change. For example, if "金" and "银" appear in the context of "金银财宝 (*jin yin cai bao*, 'treasures and jewelry')", they will form a synonymous relation; if they appear in the context of "他们要求是用金做的, 而不是用银做的。(*Tamen yaoqiu shi yong jin zuo de, er bushi yong yin zuo de*, 'They require that this be made in gold instead of sliver.')", it is obvious that "金" and "银" are opposite to each other here and form an antonymous relation. This antonymous relation sometimes can even appear in a more extensive social context. For example, in "不能让社会的阅读领域存在黄色的东西。(*Buneng rang shehui de yuedu lingyu cunzai huangse de dongxi*, 'Vulgar and unhealthy things should not exist in readings in our society.')", "黄色 (*huangse*, 'yellow')" in this sentence means "低级的 (*diji de*, 'vulgar')" and "不健康的 (*bu jiankang de*, 'unhealthy')" and its meaning forms an antonymous relation with "红色的 (*hongse de*, 'red')" and "健康的 (*jiangkang de*, 'healthy')" in the ideological field of society. It is obvious that "红" and "黄", the two co-hyponymic semantic components, play a significant role in forming this opposite phenomenon in the above-mentioned extensive context.

It is ordinary that co-hyponyms change in dynamic application. People frequently encounter this phenomenon in verbal communication and they can understand and accept this semantic expression. What is more important is that since people usually make continuous use of this semantic change, these words are so frequently used that they are gradually conventionalized into various antonyms and antonymous semantic morphemes; thus they turn into language elements from speech elements and go into the system of linguistic sign. Examples of this type abound: "上 (*shang*, 'up')" vs. "下 (*xia*, 'down')", "高 (*gao*, 'high')" vs. "低 (*di*, 'short')", "太阳 (*taiyang*, 'sun')" vs. "月亮 (*yueliang*, 'moon')", "强大 (*qiangda*, 'strong')" vs. "弱小 (*ruoxiao*, 'weak')" are cases of antonyms and "红 (*hong*, 'red')" in "红灯 (*hongdeng*, 'red light')" vs. "绿 (*lü*, 'green')" in "绿灯 (*lüdeng*, 'green light')", "红 (*hong*, 'red')" in "红军 (*hongjun*, 'red corps')" vs. "白 (*bai*, 'white')" in "白军 (*baijun*, 'white corps')", "左 (*zuo*, 'left')" in "左倾 (*zuoqing*, 'left deviation')" vs. "右 (*you*, 'right')" in "右倾 (*youqing*, 'right deviation')", "海 (*hai*, 'sea')" in "海鱼 (*haiyu*, 'sea water fish')" vs. "河 (*he*, 'river')" in "河鱼 (*heyu*, 'fresh water fish')" are cases of antonymous semantic morphemes.

II Generic words

Generic words are words that indicate the generic relation of concept. For example,
There are many groups of generic words in the above two examples. For instance,

树 (tree) – 松树 (pine) – 红松 (red pine)
树 (tree) – 松树 (pine) – 马尾松 (Chinese red pine)
树 (tree) – 杨树 (poplar) – 银白杨 (populus alba)
树 (tree) – 杨树 (poplar) – 毛白杨 (Chinese white poplar)
树 (tree) – 杨树 (poplar) – 小叶杨 (Simon poplar)
衣服 (clothes) – 上衣 (upper outer garment) – 衬衣 (shirt)
衣服 (clothes) – 上衣 (upper outer garment) – 汗衫 (undershirt)
衣服 (clothes) – 上衣 (upper outer garment) – 外衣 (outerwear)
衣服 (clothes) – 裤子 (trousers) – 内裤 (under pants)

衣服 (clothes) – 裤子 (trousers) – 短裤 (shorts)
衣服 (clothes) – 裤子 (trousers) – 长裤 (long pants)

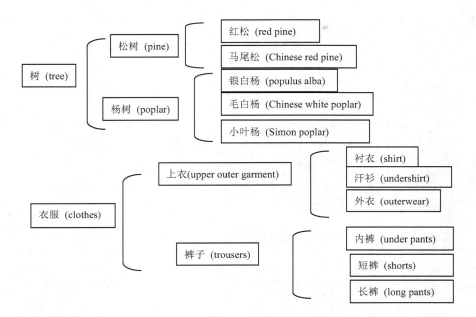

In all the above groups, the former are all concepts of genus followed by their respective concepts of species and the middle, which are concepts of species of the former, are in turn the concepts of genus of the words that follow them; this string of words are all clustered into a group by generic relation, in which the former one is the concept of genus of the latter one and the latter one is the concept of species of the former. Therefore, both the lexical meanings and concept correspondence of the words in each group designate a generic relation of concepts successively. This is the essential characteristic of generic words. Generic words are based on the generic relation of the objective things and their concepts, which is also a direct reflection of the close connection between lexical meaning and concept.

III Kinship words

Kinship words are words which indicate kinship relation. For example,

祖父(*zufu*, "grandfather"), 祖母 (*zumu*, "grandmother"), 父亲 (*fuqin*, "father"), 母亲 (*muqin*, "mother"), 哥哥 (*gege*, "elder brother"), 弟弟 (*didi*, "younger brother"), 姐姐 (*jiejie*, "elder sister"), 妹妹 (*meimei*, "younger sister"), 伯父 (*bofu*, "father's elder brother"), 伯母 (*bomu*, "wife of father's elder brother"), 叔父 (*shufu*, "father's younger brother"), 婶母 (*shenmu*, "wife of father's younger brother"), 姑姑 (*gugu*, "father's sister"), 姑父 (*gufu*, "husband of father's sister"), 堂兄 (*tangxiong*, "a son of father's brother who is elder than oneself"), 堂妹 (*tangmei*, "a daughter of father's brother who is younger than oneself"), 姥爷 (*laoye*, "maternal grandpa"), 姥姥 (*laolao*, "maternal grandma"), 舅舅 (*jiujiu*, "mother's brother"), 舅妈 (*jiuma*, "wife of mother's brother"), 姨妈 (*yima*, "maternal aunt"), 姨父 (*yifu*, "husband of maternal aunt"), 表哥 (*biaoge*, "a son of father's sister or of mother's brother or sister who is older than oneself"), 表妹 (*biaomei*, "a daughter of father's sister or of mother's brother or sister who is younger than oneself")

Kinship words in language are formed based on all kinds of kinships in society. The kinship system is diverse in languages of different ethnic groups: some are simple while others are complicated. Kinship words in Chinese are extremely ample and they formed a kinship word system. Quite a few people have investigated Chinese kinship word system and compared kinship word system in Chinese and those in foreign languages and a lot of significant researches have been done.

One can find from an observation of kinship words that the internal relation of kinship words can be classified into coordinate relation and generic relation; therefore lexical meaning and concept correspondence of kinship words can sometimes be realized as coordinate relation and sometimes as generic relation in dynamic application and sometimes even as a cross-cutting relation of the two.

With the development of the society and changes in the social relationships between people, kinship words begin to be extrapolated gradually in actual use and many kinship words are designating non-kinship relations at present. The increase in the number of single child in China will definitely result in various changes in the usage of Chinese kinship words and lead to changes and development in Chinese kinship word system.

Note

1 The definitions in *The Contemporary Chinese Dictionary* are used in the following discussion if not specified.

6 The evolution of word meaning and its laws

Section 1 Types of the evolution of word meaning

I One sense of a word and the meaning of a word

A word is the combination of sound and meaning and once combined it will be relatively stable. However, since language is constantly developing, words possess the property of variability as a component of language. The combination of the sound and meaning of a word is relatively stable; meanwhile, it is constantly changing and gradually developing in the process of evolution. Therefore, we can say that, just like other things, the static and still form of existence of word meaning is relative and the dynamic and changing one is absolute.

Like everything else, the development and evolution of word meaning is also extremely complicated, abundant and active. The changes can be synchronic or diachronic; they can also be historical or temporary and among all these, the initial change tends to start from a temporary, individual and extremely subtle one. However, no matter how word meaning changes, the variations always manifest in the combination of sound and meaning in the first place. Moreover, different changes gradually constitute different kinds of change types and laws.

Due to the fact that words can be classified into monosemes and polysemes, word meaning can be defined as the meaning of a monoseme or a sense item of a polyseme, which is one sense of the word; in either case, it is one sense of a word and the meaning of a monoseme and the meaning of the word is consistent with each other. As for the meaning of a polyseme, which designates multiple sense items and has different meanings, it can also be regarded as the meaning of a word at large, but they are sense items within the interior of the word meaning. Therefore, one sense of a word can only correspond to the meaning of a sense item, and the meaning of a word is the sum total of all the sense items of the polyseme; hence in this case, one sense of a word is only a part of word meaning and it is one sense item of the word, so they (one sense of the word and the meaning of the word) are quite different from each other. There are quite different manifestations for this case of word meaning as far as the evolution and development of word meaning is concerned; thus we must make sure what the ranges and situations are when discussing the evolution of word meaning. Meanwhile, we will and must distinguish one sense of a word from the meaning of a word.

II An analysis of the types of the evolution of word meaning

Since the evolution of one sense of a word is different from that of the meaning of a word, we must deal with them separately when analyzing the types of the evolution of word meaning.

(I) The evolution of one sense of a word

The evolution of one sense of a word can be classified into four types as follows.

TYPE ONE: ENRICHING AND DEEPENING OF WORD MEANING

The enriching and deepening of word meaning is the change and development within the scope of one sense of a word, which refers to the change and development of the connotation of a certain sense of a word from being simple, superficial and incorrect to being complex, profound and correct while its denotation is kept unchanging. There are mainly two reasons for this change: one is that although the objective thing is generally unaltered, with the development of human cognition, people's understanding about the objective thing had been changed and deepened; therefore the word meaning is changed and developed. For instance,

- 水 (*shui*, "water"): Originally it was colourless, odourless, and tasteless drinkable liquid; now we learn that a water molecule consists of one oxygen atom and two hydrogen atoms.
- 电 (*dian*, "electricity"): Originally it meant "阴阳激耀 (*yin yang ji yao*, 'the collision of *yin* and *yang*')"; now it means "a physical phenomenon arising from the existence and the change of electric charge, an important energy used extensively in production and daily life to provide light, heat and power, etc."
- 鬼 (*gui*, "ghost"): Originally people who died were called ghosts. The behaviours of people after death and the ghost into which people turned after death were all regarded as real things. Nowadays, it is a superstitious and unscientific statement.
- 鬼火 (*guihuo*, "devil-fire"): People often related the flaming fire in dislocated lands with ghost in the past, so it was called "devil-fire". But now they realize that it is "corpse light", which is the flame when phosphine burns. Because phosphine can be decomposed after the corpses of human beings and animals being putrid and combusted automatically, people can see white and glaucous wildfire in the wild land at night.

It can be seen from the above examples that when people's cognition changed and developed, it will affect the change and development of word meaning directly. In this case, some word meanings become more abundant than before and some of them are corrected out of being wrong.

Other examples like this include "人 (*ren*, 'human beings')", "石 (*shi*, 'stone')", "银 (*yin*, 'silver')", "上帝 (*Shangdi*, 'God')" and "神仙 (*shenxian*, 'immortal')" and so on.

The other one is that the objective thing has changed and developed, so people have new insights into it and the word meaning is enriched and deepened. Taking one sense item in "运动 (*yundong*, 'doing sports')" as an example: it originally meant "体育运动 (*tiyu yundong*, 'physical exercises')". Nowadays, the contents of physical exercises gradually become abundant and diversify along with the development of events and modes in physical exercises. For example, when we say "运动 (*yundong*, 'sport')" in "要参加运动，锻炼身体。 (*Yao canjia yundong, duanlian shenti*, 'Do some sports and take some exercises.')", it does not only refer to several monotonous activities, but means various physical exercises including running, jumping, gymnastics, martial art and swimming, etc. Thus it can be seen that the development of objective things per se can also enrich and deepen the content of word meaning.

TYPE TWO: ENLARGING OF WORD MEANING

When talking about the enlarging of word meaning, we should clarify "what is the enlarging of word meaning" in the first place. The enlarging of word meaning is usually taken to include both the enlarging of one sense of a word and the addition of sense items of a word in a certain academic writing at the present time. But here, we just confine ourselves to the former one. As a linguistic terminology, "the enlarging of word meaning" should have a specific content and scope in designation. How should we define it? We will make an analysis and interpretation from the manifestations and characteristics of word meaning change.

The reason that the enlarging of word meaning is defined as the broadening of word meaning within the scope of one sense of a word lies in the fact that it is the result that the scope of the same class of objective things designated by the word meaning has been widened, i. e., the change and development that a certain sense item of a word has been expanded from denoting the concept of species to denoting the concept of genus. The content designated by the original word meaning is included within the scope designated by the enlarged word meaning, i. e., the original meaning designating the concept of species is included in the scope of the meaning designating the concept of genus and the enlarged new meaning and the original meaning constitute a relation of that of genus and species. For instance, the word "嘴 (*zui*, 'mouth')" originally meant "鸟的嘴 (*niao de zui*, 'beak of bird')", but nowadays it refers to "口的通称 (*kou de tongcheng*, 'a general name of mouths of all species')". It is obvious that the latter one is a concept of genus, which covers the mouths of all animals, and its primary meaning "beak of bird" becomes a concept of species that is included in the denotation of the concept of genus "a general name of mouths of all species"; thus the new meaning and the original one form a relation of that of genus and species.[1]

Since the enlarging of word meaning is a matter of the development and evolution of one sense of a word, the enlarging is confined to the scope of this sense and the formation of a new meaning indicates the disappearance of the old one, because they cannot co-exist within the form of the same word at the same time. Consequently, once a word designates the enlarged meaning, it will not indicate the original meaning anymore when it exists independently. For this case, the original meaning will be designated by another new form: a new word or a phrase. For instance, when "嘴 (*zui*, 'mouth')" means "口的通称 (*kou de tongcheng*, 'general name of mouths of all species')", its original meaning must be expressed by a phrase "鸟的嘴 (*niao de zui*, 'mouth of bird')". Likewise, when the meaning of "江 (*jiang*)" changes into the general name of river, its original meaning will be designated by such neologisms as "长江 (*Changjiang*, 'the Changjiang River')" or "扬子江 (*Yangzi Jiang*, 'the Yangtze River')", etc.

It must be pointed out that although the original meaning cannot be used freely any more as an independent meaning in this case, it may well be used to designate the object designated by the original meaning in specific linguistic contexts because the original meaning has been included in the enlarged one. We take "嘴 (*zui*, 'mouth')" as an example again. In "嘴的功能可以饮食...(*Zui de gongneng keyi yinshi*. ... 'The function of mouth is drinking. ...')", it is obvious that "嘴 (*zui*, 'mouth')" refers to the enlarged meaning, i. e., "the general name of mouth"; whereas in "这只鸟很漂亮, 绿色的羽毛、黄色的嘴...(*Zhe zhi niao hen piaoliang, lüse de yumao, huangse de zui*. ... 'The bird is beautiful with green feather, yellow beak')", it certainly means "鸟的嘴 (*niao de zui*, 'beak of a bird')". Thus it can be seen that a certain word meaning can correspond to different specific things within the scope of its designation in different concrete contexts, which of course includes the correspondence to the specific things that its original meaning designated. This is determined by the characteristic of correspondence to the concrete objects of word meaning. However, it must be made clear that correspondence to concrete objects of word meaning is completely different from independent sense item of a word. Although the enlarged original meaning can be manifested by correspondence to concrete objects, it cannot exist as a sense item independently.

Of course, there also exists a phenomenon in language that when the word meaning enlarged, the original meaning would be preserved in some idioms, compounds or idiomatic linguistic forms as the old meaning of the word instead of existing as an independent sense item of it; therefore the original meaning will sometimes be listed as a sense item in dictionaries in order that one can conveniently understand the ancient meaning of that word. For instance, the definitions for such words as "江 (*jiang*)" and "琴 (*qin*)" in *The Contemporary Chinese Dictionary (Revised Edition)* are of this kind.

The development of word meaning is so subtle that many delicate and fine differences appear due to various reasons and the enlarging of word meaning is no exception. Therefore we generalize the enlarging of word meaning into two different cases as follows.

The first case is that even though the objective things are unaltered, word meaning will be enlarged because of the change of people's cognition and their language habits. For example, "肉 (*rou*, 'meat')" originally meant "鸟兽之肉 (*niao shou zhi rou*, 'meat of bird and beast')" while "人的肉 (*ren de rou*, 'human's flesh')" is designated by "肌 (*ji*, 'flesh')". Duan Yucai clearly said in his *An Annotation on the Origin of Chinese Characters (Shuo Wen Jie Zi Zhu)* that "人曰肌, 鸟兽曰肉, 此其分别也。 (*Ren yue ji, niao shou yue rou, ci qi fen bie ye*, 'Human's flesh is called 肌(*ji*, flesh) and the meat of bird and beast is called 肉(*rou*, meat): this is the difference)". However, the meaning of "肉 (*rou*, 'meat')" was widened later. Flesh and muscle of all animals can be called "肉 (*rou*, 'meat')" and "鸟兽之肉 (*niao shou zhi rou*, 'meat of bird and beast')" falls within the scope of "肉 (*rou*, 'meat')", so "肉 (*rou*, 'meat')" and "鸟兽之肉 (*niao shou zhi rou*, 'meat of bird and beast')" are in a relation of genus and species and when "肉 (*rou*, 'meat')" exists independently, it does not have the meaning of "鸟兽之肉 (*niao shou zhi rou*, 'meat of bird and beast')" any more.[2] It is obvious that the evolution of "肉 (*rou*, 'meat')" is a phenomenon of the enlarging of word meaning, which is caused by the change of people's cognition and language habits, because "鸟兽之肉 (*niao shou zhi rou*, 'meat of bird and beast')", "人之肉 (*ren zhi rou*, 'flesh of human beings')" and "一切动物之肉 (*yi qie dong wu zhi rou*, 'meat of all animals')" have already existed and do not change at all and it's the change of the names of objective things that makes the scope of word meaning widened. This is quite common in vocabulary. All the following examples are of this kind.

双 (雙) (*shuang*): originally meant "两只鸟 (*liang zhi niao*, "a pair of birds')", and the meaning after enlarging refers to everything that is "成双的 (*chengshuang de*, 'in double')".

皮 (*pi*): originally meant "兽的皮 (*shou de pi*, 'fur of beast')"; now it means "人或一切生物的皮 (*ren huo yiqie shengwu de pi*, 'skin of human beings or all creatures')".

睡 (*shui*): originally meant "坐着打瞌睡 (*zuo zhe da keshui*, 'sit there and doze off')", but after enlarging it is used as "睡眠的通称*(shuimian de tongcheng*, 'a general term for sleep')".

杂 (*za*): originally meant "五彩相会 (*wu cai xiang hui*, 'multicoloured')", now it has a enlarged meaning of "多种多样的东西相混 (*duozhong duoyang de dongxi xiang hun*, 'all kind of things mixed together')".

洗 (*xi*): originally meant "洗脚 (*xijiao*, 'footbath')", and the new meaning after enlarging becomes "洗涤的通称 (*xidi de tongcheng*, 'a general term of wash')".

红 (*hong*): originally meant "粉红 (*fenhong*, 'pink')", and the new meaning after enlarging becomes "红色的通称 (*hongse de tongcheng*, 'a general term of red')".

灾 (*zai*): originally meant "自然发生的火灾 (*ziran fasheng de huozai*, 'fire disaster happened spontaneously')", that is, so-called "天火 (*tianhuo*, 'natural fire')", but after enlarging it means "一切的灾难 (*yiqie de zainan*, 'all kinds of disasters')".

牙 (*ya*): originally meant "槽牙 (*caoya*, 'molar tooth which is in the back of mouth')", and the new meaning after enlarging becomes "牙的通称 (*ya de tongcheng*, 'a general term of tooth')".

Another case of the enlarging of word meaning is that the objective things have developed and so does human cognition correspondingly so as to cause the enlarging and development of word meaning. A word of this type usually designated certain specific objects originally and represented the concept of these specific objects. However, with the development of society, objects of the same kind appeared and their number gradually increased, and in order to distinguish the different objective things of the same class, people would use various new terms to designate them, including the original ones; thus the original word becomes a general term to designate the whole class of the objects. Meanwhile, word meaning is enlarged and developed. That is to say, the concept of species with coordinate relation appeared because of the appearance and development of things of the same class and the content originally designated by that word became one of the several concepts of species and obtained a new name whereas the original word became a word designating the concept of genus. Therefore the denotation of the word is expanded and its connotation becomes more generalized and the word meaning is thus enlarged. Examples of this type of enlarging of word meaning abound in language. For example, "灯 (*deng*, 'lamp')" originally meant "油灯 (*youdeng*, 'oil lamp')", but since lamps of various types appear afterwards, what originally referred to by this term is now designated by "油灯 (*youdeng*, 'oil lamp')". Meanwhile, many new words representing coordinate concepts of "lamp", such as "汽灯 (*qideng*, 'gas lamp')", "电灯 (*diandeng*, 'electric lamp')", "日光灯 (*riguangdeng*, 'fluorescent lamp')" and "矿灯 (*kuangdeng*, 'miner's lamp')", etc. appear and are appearing gradually and constantly. The original word "灯 (*deng*)" becomes a general term designating various "lamps" and becomes a word expressing the concept of genus to which all these lamps belong, thus the meaning of "灯" is enlarged. The following words also belong to this case. For example,

枪 (鎗) (*qiang*): originally meant a piercing weapon that had a point and a handle in ancient times, now it becomes a general name for "红缨枪 (*hongyingqiang*, 'red-tasseled spear')", "手枪 (*shouqiang*, 'pistol')", "步枪 (*buqiang*, 'rifle')" and "机关枪 (*jiguanqiang*, 'machine gun')", etc.

炮 (礟、砲) (*pao*): originally meant a weapon used to attack a city by launching stones in ancient times, but now it becomes a general name for "迫击炮 (*paijipao*, 'mortar')", "榴弹炮 (*liudanpao*, 'howitzer')" and "高射炮 (*gaoshepao*, 'archibald')", etc.

琴 (*qin*): originally meant a musical instrument that was long and narrow and had seven strings on it and it must be played by hands. Now it becomes a general name of "风琴 (*fengqin*, 'organ')", "钢琴 (*gangqin*, 'piano')", "提琴 (*tiqin*, 'violin')", "口琴 (*kouqin*, 'mouthorgan')" and "电子琴 (*dianziqin*, 'electronic organ')", etc.

布 (*bu*): originally meant "麻布 (*mabu*, 'flax')", but now it is a general name for all cloth woven by cotton and hemp, etc.

It can be seen from the above that the enlarging of word meaning is caused by various reasons. All phenomena of the enlarging of word meaning, however, share a common characteristic – i. e., they are all changes within the scope of one sense of a word, in which the word meanings denoting the concept of species evolved into that denoting the concept of genus and the original meaning is included within the new meaning and cannot be used as an independent sense item any more after the enlarging of word meaning. In general, the original meaning will be then expressed by a new linguistic form. We cannot deny, nevertheless, that the original meaning and new meaning of a limited number of words do not form a relation of the concept of genus and that of species after the enlarging of word meaning and the original meaning will disappear losing its function in designating object. The change of "脸 (*lian*)" is a case in point. The word "脸" originally meant "面部眼睛下面的部分 (*mianbu yanjing xiamian de bufen*, 'the part under eyes on one's face')"; now it designates "整个的面部 (*zhengge de mianbu*, 'the whole face')" after a process of enlarging and its original meaning does not exist anymore.

TYPE THREE: NARROWING OF WORD MEANING

The narrowing of word meaning also happens within the scope of one sense of a word. Its characteristic is that the denotation that the word meaning designated becomes smaller while the connotation becomes more profound. In fact, it is the evolution and development in which one sense of a word denotes a concept of genus instead of designating a concept of species. After narrowing, the original concept designated by the word will get a new name (a new word or a phrase) and the meaning that the new concept expresses will form a relation of genus and species with the narrowed meaning. For example, 金 (*jin*) originally meant "一切的金属" (*yique de jinshu*, 'all metals'), but now it has a narrower meaning of 黄金 (*huangjin*, 'gold'). Now the original meaning is indicated by "金属" (*jinshu*, 'metal'), and 金属 (*jinshu*, 'metal') and 金 (*jin*, 'gold') form a relation of genus and species. The following words are all of this kind. For example,

瓦 (*wa*): originally meant "一切用土烧成的器皿 (*yiqie yong tu shao cheng de qimin*, 'utensils made of baked clay')", but now it means specifically "用土烧制的用来铺盖屋顶的建筑材料 (*yong tu shao zhi de yong lai pugai wuding de jianzhu cailiao*, 'a building material burned by clay used to cover roofs')".

臭 (*chou*): originally meant "一切的气味 (*yiqie de qiwei*, 'all kinds of smells')", but now it means specifically "坏味 (*huai wei*, 'foul smell')".

坟 (*fen*): originally meant "一切高大的土堆 (*yiqie gaoda de tudui*, 'high and large mounds')", but now it means specifically "坟墓 (*fenmu*, 'grave')".

禽 (*qin*): It was originally the general name of "飞禽走兽 (*feiqin zoushou*, 'fowl and beast')", but now it refers only to "飞禽 (*feiqin*, 'fowl')".

子 (*zi*): The original meaning included "儿子 (*erzi*, 'son')" and "女儿 (*nü'er*, 'daughter')", but now it can only designate "儿子 (*erzi*, 'son')".

丈人 (*zhangren*): originally meant "老年男人的通称 (*laonian nanren de tongcheng*, 'the general name of oldman')", but now it only means "岳父 (*yuefu*, 'wife's father')".

勾当 (*goudang*): originally meant "各种事情 (*gezhong shiqing*, 'all behaviours')", but now it only means "坏事情 (*huai shiqing*, 'criminal or immoral behaviours')".

事故 (*shigu*): originally meant "各种事情 (*gezhong shiqing*, 'all kinds of things')", but now it only means "在生产上或工作上出现的意外的损失或灾难 (*zai shengchan shang huo gongzuo shang chuxian de yiwai de sunshi huo zainan*, 'accidents that happen in production and disaster')".

One can have a glimpse of the general situation of the narrowing of word meaning from the above examples. Meanwhile one can see that the semantic morpheme meaning can also be narrowed. For example, both "禽 (*qin*, 'fowl')" and "子 (*zi*, 'son')" only have semantic morpheme meanings from the perspective of the contemporary Chinese language.

The narrowing of word meaning also manifests that word meaning has gotten more and more precise and accurate. With the deepening of human cognition, people have to continuously create numerous new words and expressions to further distinguish objective things due to the generality and fuzziness of the original word meanings and they are narrowed down when the word meanings used to designate general things now designate more specific ones.

When word meaning is narrowed, its scope of reference becomes smaller, so the narrowed meaning cannot refer to the objects that it originally designated in general, except for those used in the original fixed linguistic forms.

TYPE FOUR: TRANSFER OF WORD MEANING

The transfer of word meaning is also an evolution and development of word meaning within the scope of one sense of a word. Its characteristic lies in that the scope of reference of the word meaning has changed, i. e., the concept designated by the word meaning has changed. With the word form unchanged, the new denotation and connotation designated by the word meaning have totally replaced the original old ones. The word no longer designates either the original object or original concept after word meaning transfer. For example, "走 (*zou*)" originally meant "跑 (*pao*, 'run')" in ancient times but now it designates "行走 (*xingzou*, 'walk')", which underwent a process of transfer in meaning. Other examples are:

事 (*shi*): originally meant "官吏 (*guanli*, 'official')", but it now means "事情 (*shiqing*, 'affair')".

权 (*quan*): originally meant "秤锤 (*chengchui*, 'poise')", but now it means "权利 (*quanli*, 'right')".

钱 (*qian*): originally meant "一种农具 (*yi zhong nongju*, 'a farm tool')", but it now means "钱币 (*qianbi*, 'money')".

斤 (*jin*): originally meant "斧子一类的工具 (*fuzi yi lei de gongju*, 'a tool like axe')", but now it is the unit of weight, i. e., "十两为一斤 (*shiliang wei yijin*, 'shi *liang* (50 grams) is one *jin*')".

精 (*jing*): Originally meant "上等的精米 (*shangdeng de jing mi*, 'fine rice')", but it now means "经过提炼或挑选的 (*jingguo tilian huo tiaoxuan de*, 'refined or selected')" and "精华 (*jinghua*, 'elite')".

脚 (*jiao*): originally meant "小腿 (*xiaotui*, 'lower leg')", but now it means "人和动物的腿的下端,接触地面支持身体的部分 (*ren huo dongwu de tui de xiaduan, jiechu dimian zhichi shenti de bufen*, 'the lower end of leg of human beings and animals, which is the part that touches the ground and supports the body')".

行李 (*xingli*): originally meant "两国往来的使者 (*liangguo wanglai de shizhe*, 'massagers who contact between two countries')", but now it means "出门时所带的包裹、箱子等 (*chumen shi suo dai de baoguo, xiangzi deng*, 'package and trunk which people bring with in travel')".

书记 (*shuji*): originally meant "秘书 (*mishu*, 'secretary')", but it now means "党团组织的负责人 (*dang tuan zuzhi de fuzeren*, 'leader of a party or a league')".

The transfer of word meaning is comparatively complicated and the primary reason that makes word meaning transferred lies in the development of the sense items of a word. For example, "年 (*nian*)" originally meant "谷熟 (*gu shu*, 'the grain is ripe')", but now it has a new meaning of "年月的年 (*nianyue de nian*, 'year')". Its original meaning has disappeared in the process of development and it makes the meaning of "年 (*nian*)" transferred. Secondly, the borrowing method (one of the Six Scipts, six catetories of Chinese character construction) also makes word meaning transferred. For example, "密 (*mi*)" originally meant "一种山 (*yi zhong shan*, 'a kind of mountain')" and it was used with the meaning of "精细 (*jingxi*, 'precise and accurate')" by the borrowing method later. Its original meaning has disappeared in the process of application with the borrowed meaning "precise and accurate" becoming more and more popular, and thus the word meaning transferred. Of course, the "精细 (*jingxi*, 'precise and accurate')" meaning of "密 (*mi*)" is hardly used independently now and has become a semantic morpheme meaning.

It can be concluded from the analysis on the above four types that the evolution and development of word meaning within the scope of one sense of a word has a common characteristic: the appearance of the new meaning means the disappearance of the old one; therefore, when this change completes, the new meaning and the old one cannot co-exist synchronically in the process of deepening, enlarging, narrowing and transfer of word meaning. If they still co-exist simultaneously, it means that the evolutionary process of one sense of a word has not finished yet and this change of word meaning belongs to the evolution issue within the scope of the meaning of a word. It thus can be concluded that the fact that the new meaning and the old one cannot co-exist synchronically in the change of one sense of a word is an important indication that the evolution of deepening, enlarging, narrowing or transfer of word meaning has finished.

II The evolution of the meaning of a word

The evolution of the meaning of a word falls approximately into two types: the addition of sense item and the reduction of sense item. As a matter of fact, the development and evolution of the meaning of a word is far more complicated. Within the range of one word, the evolution of word meaning can be realized as the addition and reduction of sense item and it can also be realized as the evolutionary process of the sense item itself as well. That is to say, at the same time with the development and evolution of the meaning of a word, one sense of that word may also be in the process of a dynamic change. Therefore, the change of one sense of a word is always intertwined with the change of the meaning of a word and both of them are changing at the same time.

Type one: the addition of sense item

The addition of sense item is also among the laws of evolution of word meaning. It is the evolution within the scope of a word, i. e., the addition and development of sense item within a word. Since word meaning designates concept, the addition of sense item means the addition of the concept expressed by the form of the same word, which leads to the addition, enriching and development of the new meaning of that word. However, the appearance of the new meaning only indicates the addition of a new sense item and it will not interfere with the existence of the original sense items, let alone leads to the extinction of the original meaning within the scope of the word. For the addition of sense item, the new sense item and the old one can co-exist simultaneously within the form of one word and keep the independence of their own. For example,

> The original meaning of 手(*shou*) is (1)"人体上肢前端能拿东西的部分 (*renti shangzhi qianduan neng na dongxi de bufen*, 'hand')", and later on the sense (2) "拿着 (*na zhe*, 'have in one's hand; take'): 人手一册 (*ren shou yi ce*, 'a popy for everyone')" and (3) "擅长某种技能的人或做某种事的人 (*shanchang mouzhong jineng de ren huo zuo mouzhong shi de ren*, 'expert at some occupation or job')": 能手 (*nengshou*, 'skilled hand')|拖拉机手 (*tuolaojishou*, 'tractor driver') are added.
>
> (P1161, *The Contemporary Chinese Dictionary (Revised Edition)* with sense items abridged)

It can be observed from the definition of "手 (*shou*)" in *The Contemporary Chinese Dictionary (Revised Edition)* that the senses of this word are totally different sense items included within the scope of the word, which are derived from the

The evolution of word meaning and its laws   179

original meaning and the original one still exists after the new ones emerged with the new and the old meanings co-existing within the form of "手" and keeping independence of each own to be respectively used freely by people. The senses that these sense items designate are all different from each other and every sense has its own correspondence to concept and correspondence to concrete object. The linguistic contexts that they appear are also different from each other and no sense item can be exchanged with others in any case.

There are basically two cases for the addition of sense item. The first one is that the original meaning and new meaning co-exist with the original one being still used as the primary meaning. This abounds in the addition of sense item. For example,

1   讲 (*jiang*):

   (1) speak; tell; say; talk; relate; deliver oneself of: ～故事 (*jiang gushi*, "tell a tale; relate a story").
   (2) explain; make clear; interpret; represent: 这本书是～气象的 (*zhe ben shu shi jiang qixiangde*, "The book is on meteorology").
   (3) discuss; negotiate; confer: ～价儿 (*jiangjiar*, "bargain").

   (P626, *The Contemporary Chinese Dictionary (Revised Edition)* with the sense items abridged)

2   老 (*lao*):

   (1) (as opposed to young) old: ～人 (*laoren*, "old people") |～大爷 (*lao daye*, "uncle; grandpa")
   (2) elderly person: 扶～携幼 (*fu lao xie you*, "take the old folk by the arm and lead the children along")
   (3) (as opposed to new) old: ～厂 (*lao chang*, "old factory") | ～根据地 (*lao genjudi*, "former revolutionary base area")
   (4) dated; antiquated: ～机器 (*lao jiqi*, "outdated machine") |房子太～了 (*fangzi tai lao le*, "(the) house is too old").
   (5) original, unchanged: ～脾气 (*lao piqi*, "the same old temperament") |～地方 (*lao difang*, "the same old place").

   (P757, *The Contemporary Chinese Dictionary (Revised Edition)* with the sense items abridged)

3   头 (*tou*):

   (1) head; part of the body that contains the eyes, ears, nose, and mouth at the front of the body in animals and on the top of humans.
   (2) hair; hairstyle: 梳～ (*shu tou*, "comb the hair") |梳什么样的～ (*shu shenmeyang de tou*, "what kind of hairstyle to comb").
   (3) (～儿) (*tour*) top; tip; end: 山～儿 (*shantour*, "hilltop; top of a hill") | 中间粗, 两～儿细 (*zhongjian cu, liangtour xi*, "thick in the middle, and thin at both ends").

180   *The evolution of word meaning and its laws*

(4) (～儿) (*tour*) beginning; end: 提个～儿 (*ti ge tour*, "give sb a lead") |什么时候才走到～儿 (*shenme shihou cai zou dao tour*, "When will one come to the end").

(P1270, *The Contemporary Chinese Dictionary (Revised Edition)* with the examples changed and the sense items abridged)

舌头 (*shetou*):

(1) tongue; organ attached to the floor of the mouth, used in the ingestion of food, the perception of tasted, and, in humans, the articulation of speech sounds.
(2) enemy soldier captured for the purpose of extracting information.

(P1114, *The Contemporary Chinese Dictionary (Revised Edition)*)

黑暗 (*hei'an*):

(1) dark; without light:山洞里一片～ (*shandongli yipian hei'an*, "It's pitch dark in the cave").
(2) <fig.> (of social conditions) corrupt and (of politics) reactive.

(P514, *The Contemporary Chinese Dictionary (Revised Edition)*)

Although the numbers of sense items of these words are not all the same, they share an apparent characteristic, i. e., their first sense item is the original meaning and the other sense items are derived from the original one. The emergence of new sense item, however, did not lead to the disappearance of the original meaning; on the contrary, the new and the original ones co-exist within the scope of the same word and retain their independence with their original meaning as the basic meaning of the word.

The other case after the addition of sense item is that although the original meaning co-exists with the new meaning, the new one has become the primary meaning while the original one turns into the secondary meaning. For example,

世 (*shi*): originally it meant "the time period of father to son" but now it means

(1) lifetime; life: 一生一～ (*yisheng yishi*, "one's whole life; throughout one's life; all one's life").
(2) generation, seniority in a family or clan generation hierarchy passed on through people of blood relationship: 第十～孙 (*di shishi sun*, "the 11th in descent; descendant in the 11th generation").

(P1151, *The Contemporary Chinese Dictionary (Revised Edition)* with the sense items abridged)

时 (*shi*): originally it meant "season, i. e. spring, summer, autumn and winter" but now it means

(1) time; times; days: 盛极一～ (*sheng ji yi shi*, "reach the zenith, be in vogue (for a time)").

(2) fixed time: 按~上班 (*anshi shangban*, "go to work on time").
(3) season: 四~ (*sishi*, "four seasons").

(P1143, *The Contemporary Chinese Dictionary (Revised Edition)* with the sense items abridged)

As far as "世 (shi)" and "时 (shi)" are concerned, although their original meanings have come to the secondary place, they are still independent sense items of the words; thus the new meanings and the original one co-exist with each other and they can keep their independence. Therefore they belong to the addition of sense item.

Type two: the deletion of sense item

The deletion of sense item is also the evolution and development within the scope of a word. Contrary to the addition of sense item, it refers to that some sense items have disappeared from the sense items of a word. Take the term "强 (qiang)", for example. Its definitions in *Ci Yuan (The Chinese Etymologicon) Revised Edition in 1980* are

1 强 (*qiang*):

   (1) a name of an insect. *Shuo Wen Jie Zi*: "强 (*qiang*), a name for earthworm. It belongs to the radical of 虫 (*chong*, "insect"), and reads like 弘 (*hong*)."
   (2) (as opposed to "weak") strong and powerful.
   (3) vigorous.
   (4) excel; surpass.
   (5) resolute; firm.
   (6) have a surplus; slightly more than.
   (7) a surname.

   The definition in *The Contemporary Chinese Dictionary (Revised Edition)* is as follows:

2 强 (*qiang*):

(1) (as opposed to "weak") strong; powerful; mighty; of great power or force: 工作能力~ (*gongzuo nengli qiang*, "very capable in work").
(2) excel; be demanding; be resolute; of a high degree demanded by one's feelings or will: 责任心~ (*zerenxin qiang*, "with a strong sense of responsibility").
(3) by force; forcibly: ~渡 (*qiangdu*, "force or fight one's way across a river" | ~占 (*qiangzhan*, "seize; forcibly take").
(4) (usu. used for comparison) better; stronger: 今年的庄稼比去年更~ (*Jinnian de zhuangjia bi qunian geng qiang*, "The crops are doing better this year than last year").
(5) (as opposed to 'a little than') slightly more than; a little over; plus; used after fractions or decimals to indicate a number a little more that the original

number: 实际产量超过原定计划百分之十二 (*Shiji chanliang chaoguo yuanding jihua baifenzhi shi'er qiang*, "The actual output has exceeded a little over 12 percent of the original plan").
(6) a surname.

Of course, we cannot expect that definitions in different dictionaries are absolutely the same, we can find, however, that they are basically alike after a close comparison. For example, the corresponding sense item from the second term to the seventh term in *Ci Yuan (The Chinese Etymologicon)* can be found in *The Contemporary Chinese Dictionary (Revised Edition)*, whereas the first item in the former is not listed in the latter. Another example is "喽啰 (*louluo*, 'underlying')"; its definitions in *Ci Yuan (The Chinese Etymologicon)* are:

喽啰 (*louluo*): (1) cuteness; alertness. (2)(*old*) a band of outlaws. (3) disturb; roar.

The definition in *The Contemporary Chinese Dictionary (Revised Edition)* is:

喽啰 (louluo): (*old*) rank and file of a band of outlaws; (*fig.*) underling; lackey.

It can be seen that both the first and the third sense of "喽啰" have also disappeared now by a comparison on the definitions of two dictionaries.

It can be concluded from the analysis of the above two types of evolution that the change of the meaning of a word and that of the meaning of the sense item of a word is quite different. It is obvious that either the addition or deletion of sense item only involves the addition/deletion of sense items, and it does in no way influence the existence of other sense items and that the emergence of a new sense item will never lead to the disappearance of the original sense item and the new and old sense items may well co-exist with each other; on the other hand, the disappearance of an original sense item will never cause the change of other sense items, and no matter how sense items change, the independence of their own can be maintained within the scope of that word. This is the common property and characteristic that different types of evolution and development of the meaning of a word share.

Section 2 Laws of the evolution of word meaning

I Types of word meaning evolution and the formation of laws of the evolution

We have discussed six types of meaning evolution, in which "type" is defined in the sense of the manifestations and results of the evolution. None of these types, however, comes into being all at once, and they proceed through a process of evolution and abide by certain laws. As far as the above-mentioned types are concerned, there exist manifold complex connections and relations between them and a basic pattern and law have been formed. On the whole, as far as the evolution of one sense of a word and the evolution of the meaning of a word are concerned, the former is one of the evolutionary processes of the latter, and it can be said to be the necessary method and way for one sense of a word to change; meanwhile, the evolution of one sense of a word is a result of the evolution of the meaning of a word with the addition of sense items being an ongoing stage and the deletion of sense items being a finished one. It can be said that the whole system of word meaning is continuously evolving and developing within this complex relation in accordance with various laws of word meaning evolution.

Language changes in a gradual way; therefore the evolution of word meaning generally undergoes quite a long time and eventually forms a certain trajectory of evolution. Now we start with the six types of evolution to analyze the trajectory of word meaning evolution.

As with the development and change of other components in language, word meaning evolution frequently stems from temporary changes in language use. People will create some new language elements in verbal communication out of the need of expression. For word meaning, these newly created elements can be classified into two classes. Firstly, neologisms are created to express new meanings. Secondly, new sense items are created within the original word to express new meanings through such ways as semantic extension, metaphor, metonymy and specific reference, etc. Once the two temporary changes are recognized and conventionalized by people, it will result in a certain evolution and development of the word meaning system.

Expressing new meanings by creating neologisms affects the development of word meaning system in two ways. On the one hand, the emergence of new meanings amplifies and enriches the content of the word meaning system and helps to enlarge the content of the old word clusters and create new word clusters thereby promotes the development of the word meaning system. Many word meanings designating new things are of this type. On the other hand, the emergence of new meanings leads to a certain change of the designation scope and content of the original word meanings. For example, the appearance of such new meanings as "轿车 (*jiaoche*, 'sedan car')", "面包车 (*mianbaoche*, 'minibus')", "吉普车 (*jipuche*, 'jeep')" and "卡车 (*kache*, truck)", etc. absolutely results in the expansion of the meaning of "汽车 (*qiche*, 'automobile')". Take "吃 (*chi*)" for another example: it had two senses of "食 (*shi*, 'eat')" and "饮 (*yin*, 'drink')" in medieval times; afterwards a new word "喝 (*he*, 'drink')" appeared and took over the meaning of "饮 (*yin*, 'drink')" from "吃", which resulted in narrowing the meaning of "吃". Thus it can be seen that the appearance of new meaning affects the evolution of word meaning in two ways: firstly, it affects the entire word meaning system; secondly, it has an influence on the meaning of a word or one sense of a word. Therefore, those evolutionary cases belonging to the second type are always related with a certain type of evolution that analyzed previously, and what happened in the first place is always the addition of sense item to the original word.

Expressing new meaning by using the form of an already existing word usually originates from rhetorical usage, and once it is settled down, nonetheless, it will take on the form of the addition of sense item to the original word in the first place. For instance, the word "包袱 (*baofu*)" had only two sense items originally, i. e., (1) cloth used to wrap and (2) a package wrapped in cloth. Afterwards, people compared "思想负担 (*sixiang fudan*, 'mental burden')" to "包袱" and it is gradually conventionalized. As a result, "包袱" has a new sense item "burden", which results in the addition of sense item to "包袱".

As can be seen from the above analysis, no matter which method is used to express new meanings, once it is related with one sense of a word or the meaning of a word, it will lead to the addition of sense item to the original word. In other words, out of all the six types of word meaning evolution, excepting the deepening of word meaning, all the other five types must go through the stage of the addition of sense item.

There will be various complicated situations after the addition of sense item.

Firstly, the addition of sense item either makes a monoseme become a polyseme or enriches the sense items of a polyseme. This becomes relatively stabilized for a comparatively long period in the process of the development of word meaning, which helps bring about the enrichment and development of polysemes in vocabulary. For example, "错 (*cuo*)" meant "stagger and mixed" at first and it came to mean "mistake" later on, so both these two senses exist in this word nowadays and become sense items of it. This belongs to one of the most obvious cases in which the addition of sense item is indeed a type and the result of word meaning evolution.

Secondly, the new sense item and the old one co-existed for a period of time after the addition of sense item, but the connection between them gradually became weak afterwards and eventually the sense items were differentiated under the same phonetic form and they became independent and different words. This change belongs to a case of the reduction of sense item of the original meaning of the word while it is a case of word coinage by word-meaning differentiation to the newly differentiated sense item. There are quite a few examples of this type in the development of Chinese vocabulary. For instance, "月 (*yue*, 'moon')" in "月亮 (*yueliang*, 'moon')" and "月 (*yue*, 'month')" in "日月 (*riyue*, 'day and month')", "刻 (*ke*, 'quarter')" in "一刻钟 (*yi ke zhong*, 'a quarter of an hour')" and "刻 (*ke*, 'cut')" in "雕刻 (*diaoke*, 'engrave')" are all differentiated in this way. Not only word meaning evolution and development are brought about but also a great number of homophones are produced by such differentiation.

Thirdly, both the new sense item and the old one gradually changed in the process of co-existence after the addition of sense item. For the two corresponding new and original sense items, the new one came to be the generally used sense and the old one was used less and less and even disappeared in the end. The disappearance of the old sense item is a result of the reduction of sense item and this result serves to finish such change as the enlarging, narrowing and transferring of word meaning so far as the two corresponding new and original sense items are concerned. Therefore we can say that such processes as the enlarging, narrowing and transferring of word meaning start with temporary changes of language and after that the changes are conventionalized and all these processes are finished after completing the two stages of the addition and the reduction of sense item. The addition and the reduction of sense item in the change of the meaning of a word are both resulted from the evolution of word meaning and belong to the process of the change of one sense of a word, while the enlarging, narrowing and transferring in the change of one sense of a word are all accomplished after such an evolutionary process as the addition of sense item and the co-existence of the two senses in the first stage and then the reduction of the sense item. For example, "江 (*jiang*)" in "《孟子·滕文公上》 (*MengziTengwengongShang*, 'Tengwengong Volume I, Mencius')": "决汝汉, 排淮泗, 而注之江。 (*Jue Ru Han, pai Huai Si, er zhu zhi Jiang*, '(Da Yu) made vents of the Ruhe River and the Hanjiang River and cleared up the sands in the Huai River and the Sishui River so as to make water flow into the Changjiang River.')" It is obvious that "江" in this example is a proper noun meaning "长江 (*Changjiang*, 'the Changjiang River')". Afterwards "江" has got a new sense item and becomes a general name for "river". For example, in "《世说新语·言语》 (*Shi Shuo Xin Yu·Yan Yu*, 'Speeches, A New Account of the Tales of the World')": "将别, 既自凄惘, 叹曰: '江山辽阔, 居然有万里之势。 (*Jiang bie, Ji zi qi wang, tan yue*: '*Jiang shan liao kuo, ju ran you wan li zhi shi*', Parting with friends, Yuan Hong was very sad and frustrated. He said: 'The world is so big and the vastness of land is unimaginable.')" Here "江 (*jiang*)" is used as a general name of river. We can find further evidence that "江" was used as a proper noun and a general noun at the same time in 《书经·禹贡》 "(*Shu Jing·Yu Gong*, 'Tribute of Yu, The Book of History')". For example, "江" in "江汉朝宗与海 (*Jiang Han zhao zong yu hai*, 'The Changjiang River and the Hanhe River all flow into sea.')" is a proper noun, while "江" in "九江孔殷 (*jiu jiang kong yin*, 'such a broad area as nine rivers')" is a general name. The sense "the Changjiang River" of "江" gradually disappeared later on in the development process, so its sense items were reduced and at the same time, such a sense as "a general name of river" is added to replace the disappeared sense thus the evolution of the enlarging of word meaning has been finalized at last. Another example is "臭": "《诗·大雅·文王》 (*Shi·Da Ya·Wen Wang*, 'Wen Wang, Da Ya in the Book of Poems')" said "无声无臭 (*Wu sheng wu xiu*, 'No sound and smell')". It was said in "《荀子·王霸》 (*Xunzi· Wang Ba*, 'Wang ba, Xunzi*')": "口欲綦味, 鼻欲綦臭 (*Kou yu qi wei, bi yu qi xiu*, 'People want to taste the best and smell the most fragrant smell')". Both "臭" in the two above examples mean "气味 (*qiwei*, 'smell')". However, the meaning of "恶气味 (*e qiwei*, 'stinky smell')" had existed in pre-Qin period (before 221 B. C.). For example, " 《庄子·知北游》 (*Zhuangzi· Zhi Bei You*, '*Zhi Bei You, Chuang-tzu*')" said "其所美者为神奇, 其所恶者为臭腐。 (*Qi suo mei zhe wei shen qi, qi suo wu zhe wei chou fu*, 'One regards what he likes as magnificent things and what he disgusts as rotten things.')". The word "臭" in this sentence means "恶气味 (*e qiwei*, 'stinky smell')". It can be seen that the two sense items of "臭" co-exist in this period. The using of "恶气味 (*e qiwei*, 'stinky smell')" became more and more frequent and the frequency of "气味 (*qiwei*, 'smell')" gradually reduced after Han Dynasty (206 B. C. –A. D. 220) until it lost the qualification to be an independent sense item. The sense item of "臭 (*chou*, 'stinky')" had gone through the process of the reduction of sense item.

In the meanwhile, the two respective sense items of "臭" alternated with each other and resulted in the narrowing of word meaning. This is also the case with the transferring of word meaning. Take "兵 (bing)" as an example: "《荀子·议兵》 (*Xunzi·Yi Bing, 'Yi Bing of Xunzi'*)" said "古之兵，戈、矛、弓、矢而已矣 (*Gu zhi bing, ge, mao, gong, shi er yi yi*, 'Weapons in ancient times included just dagger, spear, hand-bow and sagitta')". It's obvious that "兵" means "兵器 (*bingqi*, 'weapon')" here. Afterwards, "兵" got a new meaning "士兵 (*shibing*, 'soldier')" and a new sense item was added to the word; thus the two meanings co-existed for a period of time. For instance, "《孟子·梁惠王上》 (*Mengzi · Liang Huiwang Shang, 'Liang Huiwang (I), Mencius'*)" said "兵刃既接，弃甲曳兵而走。 (*Bing ren ji jie, qi jia ye bing er zou*, 'When the war broke out, some soldiers threw away their weapons and escaped')". It was said in "《庄子·盗跖》 (*Zhuangzi· Dao Zhi, 'Dao Zhi, Chuang-tzu'*)" that "勇悍果敢，聚众率兵 (*Yong han guo gan, ju zhong shuai bing*, 'someone who is brave and resolute can gather people together and lead the troops')". It is obvious that "兵" in the first example means "兵器 (*bingqi*, 'weapon')" and in the latter it means "士兵 (*shibing*, 'solider')". With the development of word meaning of "兵", the frequency of the two sense items changed and the original meaning disappeared and was not used independently, so the sense items of "兵" were reduced with the new meaning and the old one alternating with each other and the transferring of word meaning finished.

It is quite obvious from the above that after a sense item is added, the new meaning and the old one will co-exist with each other for a period of time before another sense item is reduced. The enlarging, narrowing and transferring of word meaning are all accomplished in this way. Meanwhile, the relations among the several types of the evolution of word meaning are clearly manifested by the specific evolutionary processes.

II *The function of polyseme in word meaning evolution*

It is obvious that polysemes play a significant role in the process of word meaning evolution. Because the addition of sense item is an indispensable type in the evolution of word meaning, the appearance of polyseme is the result of the addition of sense item and polysemes are the carriers of this type of evolution.

After a polyseme appears, the fact that its sense items co-exist with each other within the same word provides a concrete and easy foundation for the evolution of one sense of a word. People can employ all the sense items in a free and natural way in communication according to the need of society and the sense items are conventionalized gradually in this process. The result of the evolution will be settled down by the reduction of sense item when the change of a certain sense reaches a certain extent, thus the evolution of one sense of a word is accomplished. Thus it can be seen that the evolution of word meaning is difficult to happen without the addition and reduction of sense item and the existence of polysemes. It can be found from observing all types of word meaning evolution that all the other types of word meaning evolution, except for the enriching and deepening of word meaning, are all closely related with the addition of sense item because the reduction of sense item can only happen after the addition of sense item. Moreover, the enlarging, narrowing and transferring of word meaning all happen in such evolutionary processes as the addition and reduction of sense item. In the whole process of the evolution of word meaning, polysemes are always an indispensable component. Therefore, polyseme plays a decisive role in the process of word meaning evolution.

We have just made some analyses and interpretations on the trajectory of word meaning evolution in the above. As a matter of fact, the cases of word meaning evolution are extremely complicated and not all of them follow a linear way of development, but several states may usually be staggered with each other. For one sense of a word, sometimes it is enlarged, narrowed and transferred in succession. For instance, "臭", which was discussed previously, has gone through a process of transferring from the sense of "嗅 (*xiu*, 'to smell')" to that of "气味 (*qiwei*, 'smell')" before it completed the narrowing of meaning. Sometimes an evolutionary process of deepening may be coupled with the enlarging, narrowing or transferring of one sense of a word. It is more complicated, nevertheless, for the evolution and development of the meaning of a word. While the meaning of a word undergoes an evolutionary process of the addition or reduction of sense item, the senses of the word will inevitably change accordingly. Sometimes, the sense items in a mutual-conversion relation do not have a one-to-one correspondence within the scope of one word: it is possible that one original meaning may give birth to several different sense items. When a sense item is added, it may well be reduced at the same time, and vice versa. Because the conditions leading to the evolution of each word are different, the evolution that they underwent might be different from each other though they fell in the above-listed six types of evolution. For example, for some words, only sense items are added but for others several types of evolution may happen at the same time. Therefore, we must make a case-by-case analysis and interpretation for the evolution and development of word meaning.

The above is all about the evolution and development of lexical meaning. In addition, the evolution of word meaning can also be found in such aspects as meaning with special flavour and grammatical meaning. The meaning with special flavour of a word sometimes changes along with the change of its lexical meaning. For example, "乖 (*guai*, 'well-behaved')" originally meant "违背, 不协调 (*weibei, bu xietiao*, 'go against and out of tune')" and had a neutral and derogatory flavour, but now it means "伶俐、机警 (*lingli, jijing*, 'smart and alert')" and has a commendatory flavour. For another example, "喽啰 (*louluo*)", which was mentioned previously, with the development of lexical meaning, its flavour has been turned into derogatory from commendatory. Sometimes, the meaning with special flavour may also change with the lexical meaning remain unchanged. For example, "老爷 (*laoyye*)" originally was a term of address to "a person rich and powerful" with a neutral, sometimes, commendatory, flavour. But now when people use this word to address certain people, it has got a sarcastic and dissatisfactory flavour, e. g., "干部是人民的公仆, 不是人民的老爷 (*Ganbu shi renmin *de gongpu, bu shi renmin de laoye*, 'A government functionary is civil servant, not someone who lords over the people')". Therefore, "老爷" has a derogatory flavour nowadays. Other expressions like "少爷 (*shaoye*, 'young master')" and "少奶奶 (*shaonainai*, 'young mistress')", etc. are all of this kind. In contrast, such words as "工人 (*gongren*, 'worker')" and "劳动 (*laodong*, 'work')" were neuters and usually had a derogatory flavour in the past, but now often possess a commendatory flavour in actual usage. Such changes of word meaning with special flavour are inseparable with the changes in social system, people's cognition and moral standards.

The changes of grammatical meaning of a word have a close connection with that of lexical meaning and this connection is linked by the addition of sense item in most cases. For example, "领导 (*lingdao*)" originally was a verb meaning "率领并引导朝一定方向前进 (*shuailing bing yindao chao yiding fangxiang qianjin*, 'lead and guide the way; act as head and guide sb in specific direction')"; afterwards a new nominal sense item of "领导人(*lingdaoren*, 'leader')" was added. Another example is the above-mentioned word "乖 (*guai*)", which was an adjective originally, and now it can be used as an endearing name for "小孩 (*xiaohai*, 'little child')", which is obviously a noun.

In the development and evolution of word meaning, all the three aspects of word meaning will change and develop; nonetheless, we can observe from the above analysis that the evolution and development of lexical meaning is always the principal aspect and major part of the evolution of word meaning.

Furthermore, the change and development of word meaning may have more far-reaching effects: for example, the change of word meaning may affect the combination between words and the cluster of meaning, even the inner adjustment of the vocabulary system as a whole. These phenomena are inevitably interrelated and interacted with each other and they co-evolve and co-develop under this inter-relation and interaction. It cannot be denied at the same time that all these are part of the significant content of the developing language system as a whole. Observations and analyses from multiple perspectives and at different levels await us in the future for further and in-depth exploration and investigation of these problems.

Notes

1 P1681 of *The Contemporary Chinese Dictionary (Revised Edition)*. The word "嘴" is a polyseme, and we use "a general name of mouths of all species" because it is the correspondent sense item with "beak of bird" in the development of the word.
2 Sometimes the edible part of fruits can also be called "肉 (*rou*, 'plub')", such as "果肉 (*guorou*, 'plub')" "桂圆肉 (*guiyuan rou*, 'Longan plub')", which is another sense item of "肉 (*rou*, 'meat')" and it does not belong to "动物肌肉 (*dongwu jirou*, 'meat of animals')".

7 Exploring the dynamic form of vocabulary

Section 1 The dynamic form of vocabulary

I Vocabulary is an integrative unity in motion

Vocabulary is an integrative unity in motion due to the fact that language itself is an integrative whole in motion. Just like all other things, language is also in motion constantly and it is unceasingly changing and developing in the process of movement. Generally speaking, language has two forms of existence, one of which is a comparatively still form of static state and the other is a dynamic form in absolute motion. The still form refers to the situation in which language exists for a comparatively short period of time on the synchronic plane, which is transitory and relative, whereas the dynamic form refers to the eternal existing form of language, which is long-standing and absolute. It is due to the continuous interaction and alternation between the two forms that language renews and develops without intermission. New elements resulted from the synchronic dynamic change of language are constantly accepted and admitted into the static planes one after another, and the fact that these static planes line up in time order can fully illustrate that the whole language system is continuously undergoing diachronic dynamic changes and developments by successive passing-on and inheriting. It is under the interaction between the static form and the dynamic one that language and all its components move and develop forever. Therefore, language is always an integrative unity in motion on the whole.

We discussed briefly the static form and dynamic form of language in the above; the actual situations of language change and development, however, are quite complex. In short, the complexity is mainly reflected in two aspects. First, the dynamic form of language can be divided into diachronic change and synchronic change. Diachronic dynamic motion gradually forms the history of language development, for example, the appearance of the contemporary Chinese language differs from that of Chinese in the pre-Qin period (before 221 B.C.), which illustrates the dynamic developing process of Chinese from the pre-Qin period to the contemporary era; whereas the synchronic stage means a cross section such as the contemporary Chinese language stage and pre-Qin Chinese stage etc. Secondly, there is a distinction between speech elements and language elements in synchronic dynamic change. Since there exists a process of dynamic change between speech elements and language elements, there must be a dynamic motion process during a relatively short period of a synchronic stage. For instance, various dynamic change and development of language never stops in the contemporary Chinese language stage. All these cases result in the complexity that the static form and dynamic form of language are both linked with and differentiated from each other in the process of language movement and change.

This is the situation of language as a whole as well as various elements constituting language. Thus, as a component part of language, vocabulary is conditioned by the form of existence of language and the law of language development, and its situation is exactly the same as that of various representations of language. Consequently, just like language as a whole, vocabulary not only exists in both static form and dynamic form, but also is a complex integrative unity in motion.

Since various components making up vocabulary have different properties and characteristics, they differ in movement and development. On the whole, the development of basic vocabulary is comparatively slow while that of common vocabulary is more active and rapid. Despite all this, it is still absolutely undeniable that as component parts of vocabulary, basic and common vocabulary are constantly changing and developing as indispensible members of the integrative whole of vocabulary.

II The reasons for vocabulary development

Language is a social phenomenon; therefore language and vocabulary are in motion. All the movement of language and vocabulary, however, is socially constrained unlike that of natural objects that emerge and perish of themselves. Certainly, everything develops and changes with its own internal reasons and laws. For vocabulary, however, such characteristics as it being used in social communications by all the people and it reflecting various things, phenomena and relationships in the objective world through people's cognition do not only determine that vocabulary development is closely related to the development of society, but also form the social, cognitive and objective foundation of vocabulary development. It thus can be concluded from this perspective that vocabulary development is out of its internal causes, yet the internal causes and the external causes are connected with each other in an extremely close and indivisible way. Therefore, in order to find out the causes and conditions for the change and development of vocabulary, we must begin from the various aspects of society and the objective world.

(I) The development of society

Language, vocabulary in particular, develops with the development of society. Any change in society and the emergence of any novelty can be reflected in vocabulary. For example, since China's reform and opening-up, a great number of neologisms have emerged, e. g., "特区 (*tequ*, 'special zone')", "合资 (*hezi*, 'joint venture')", "托福 (*tuofu*, 'TOEFL')", "待业 (*daiye*, 'awaiting job

Exploring the dynamic form of vocabulary   191

assignment; unemployed')", "个体户 (*getihu*, 'self-employed households')", "专业户 (*zhuanyehu*, 'professional households')", "追星族 (*zhuixingzu*, 'idolaters; star fans')" and "关系网 (*guanxiwang*, 'relation net; web of relationship')", etc.; moreover, a great quantity of neologisms come into being in recent years, e. g., "酷 (*ku*, 'cool')", "作秀 (*zuoxiu*, "to make a show')", "上网 (*shangwang*, 'to surf the Internet')", "网址 (*wangzhi*, 'website')", "网友 (*wangyou*, 'net friend')", "光盘 (*guangpai*, 'CD')", "超市 (*chaoshi*, 'supermarket')", "上岗 (*shanggang*, 'to post; to be (re) employed')", "下岗 (*xiagang*, 'to be laid off')", "B超 (*bichao*, 'B ultra-sound')", "CT (*seiti*, 'CT')", "纯净水 (*chunjingshui*, 'purified water')", "三维画 (*sanweihua*, 'three-dimensional painting')", "VCD (*weiseidi*, 'VCD')", "DVD (*diweidi*, 'DVD')", etc. Furthermore, many words in existence such as "承包 (*chengbao*, 'to contract')" and "责任制 (*zerenzhi*, 'responsibility system')" are used more and more frequently than before due to the needs of social communication. All these suffice to prove the influence of social development on vocabulary development and the relationship between vocabulary development and that of language and society as well as the fact that the more numerous and complicated vocabulary is, the more developed language is and that vocabulary development does not only reflect vocabulary development to some extent but also reflects the development of society from many aspects. One may conclude, therefore, that language and vocabulary and our society can mutually illustrate and verify – we can not only study the extent of language development, that of vocabulary development in particular, in accordance with the situation of social development, but also understand the way in which society develops through the status of vocabulary development.

Take Chinese vocabulary as an example, its appearance changes completely with the social progress and the development of the Han nationality. Some Chinese words came into being very early in history. For example, "网 (*wang*, 'net')", "毕 (*bi*, 'a long-handled net for hunting')", "罗 (*luo*, 'a net for catching birds')", "罩 (*zhao*, 'a fishing cage')", "弓 (*gong*, 'bow')", "矢 (*shi*, 'arrow')" and "弹 (*dan*, 'ball')", etc. are all instruments or tools for catching birds or animals; "逐 (*zhu*, 'chase')" and "射 (*she*, 'shoot (with arrows)')", etc. are all ways of hunting, while "羊 (*yang*, 'sheep')", "虎 (*hu*, 'tiger')", "豕 (*shi*, 'pig')", "马 (*ma*, 'horse')", "鸟 (*niao*, 'bird')" and "鱼 (*yu*, 'fish')", etc. are the names of animals that are hunted. Such words as "特 (*te*)" and "骄 (*jiao*)" means "special" and "pride" respectively at present, while they both designated animals originally. The word "特" referred to "a bull" while "骄" "a horse tall in six *chi* (a traditional Chinese unit of length, one *chi* is about one third of a meter)" in ancient times. The obvious reason that these words came into being earlier was that in the early times, Chinese people engaged in fishing and hunting and animal husbandry. With the development of society, when agriculture was the principal means of social production, the words reflecting agricultural life appeared accordingly. For example, names of crops such as "黍 (*shu*, 'broomcorn millet')", "稻 (*dao*, 'rice')", "粱 (*liang*, 'fine grain')" and "粟 (*su*, 'millet')", etc., farming methods such as "耕 (*geng*, 'plough')", "耘 (*yun*, 'weed')", "种 (*zhong*, 'grow')" and "薅 (*hao*, 'pull up')", etc. and names of agricultural production tools such as "镰 (*lian*, 'grass hook')",

"铲 (*chan*, 'shovel')", "耒 (*lei*, 'fork')" and "耜 (*si*, 'plough')", etc. Most words in modern science and technology, such as "化学 (*huaxue*, 'chemistry')", "物理 (*wuli*, 'physics')", "光学 (*guangxue*, 'optics')", "力学 (*lixue*, 'mechanics')", "气流 (*qiliu*, 'airflow')", "真空 (*zhenkong*, 'vacuum')", "原子 (*yuanzi*, 'atom')", "电子 (*dianzi*, 'electron')", "导弹 (*daodan*, 'missile')", "激光 (*jiguang*, 'laser')", "电视 (*dianshi*, 'televison')", "化纤 (*huaxian*, 'chemical fiber')", "混纺 (*hunfang*, 'mixed spinning')", "空调 (*kongtiao*, 'air conditioner')", "计算机 (*jisuanji*, 'computer')", "超声波 (*chaoshengbo*, 'ultrasonic wave')", "电子表 (*dianzibiao*, 'electronic watch')", "太阳能 (*taiyangneng*, 'solar energy')", "微波炉 (*weibolu*, 'microwave oven')", etc., do not come into being until modern and contemporary times.

It goes without saying that such neologisms designating "激光 (*jiguang*, 'laser')", "电视机 (*dianshiji*, 'television set')", "尼龙绸 (*nilongchou*, 'ninon silk')" and "空调机 (*kongtiaoji*, 'air conditioner')", etc. will not come into language until there exist these novelties in society. It is impossible to find modern words and expressions in the vocabulary of the pre-Qin period (before 221 B. C.) due to the social essence that language develops with society.

The inter-communal contact is another aspect influencing vocabulary development. Loan words and dialect words in vocabulary are resulted from this contact. Neologisms can be created by the inter-lingual interaction which is promoted by mutual contact between different countries and ethnic groups while the mutual absorption of dialect words are resulted from mutual contact between different regions.

In the process of the historical development of Chinese vocabulary, the neologisms coined under the influence of foreign languages abound. Some of these words were created with the onomatopoeia method under the influence of the sound of foreign words; others were coined through the illustration method under the influence of the meaning of foreign words. In whichever case, it is closely linked with inter-communal contact. Chinese people have long been connected with other ethnic groups and the exchanges have been more and more frequent after the Western and the Eastern Han Dynasties with the development of China's politics, economics and culture. This leads to the emergence of a great number of loan words in vocabulary. For example, such Chinese words as "骆驼 (*luotuo*, 'camel')", "猩猩 (*xingxing*, 'orangutan')", "琵琶 (*pipa*, 'pipa, a four stringed musical instrument')", "苜蓿 (*muxu*, 'alfalfa')", "葡萄 (*putao*, 'grape')", "八哥 (*bage*, 'myna')", "胭脂 (*yanzhi*, 'rouge')", "琉璃 (*liuli*, 'coloured glaze')", "荽 (芫荽) (*sui* (*yansui*), 'coriander')" and "酥 (酥酪) (*su* (*sulao*), 'curds and whey')", etc. all came into being under the influence of the languages of Huns and Western Regions. Furthermore, such Chinese words as "佛 (*fo*, 'Buddha')", "僧 (*seng*, 'monk')", "魔 (*mo*, 'magic')", "钵 (*bo*, 'alms bowl')", "菩萨 (*pusa*, 'Bodhisattva')", "罗汉 (*luohan*, 'arhat')", "夜叉 (*yecha*, 'yaksha')", "金刚 (*jingang*, 'vajrabodhisattva, Buddha's warrior')", "忏悔 (*chanhui*, 'confess')", "现在 (*xianzai*, 'now')", "未来 (*weilai*, 'future')", "因缘 (*yinyuan*, 'hutupratyaya, primary and secondary cause')", "法门 (*famen*, 'dharmaparaya, gateway to the Law')", "地狱 (*diyu*, 'hell')" and "信仰 (*xinyang*, 'faith')", etc. were all generated with the introduction of Buddhism. Loan words come into Chinese in an even larger number

Exploring the dynamic form of vocabulary 193

with more and more frequent contact between China and foreign communities in the modern and contemporary times, for example, "几何 (*jihe*, 'geometry')", "比重 (*bizhong*, 'specific gravity')", "方程 (*fangcheg*, 'equation')", "积分 (*jifen*, 'integration')", "意识 (*yisi*, 'consciousness')", "抽象 (*chouxiang*, 'abstract')", "范畴 (*fanchou*, 'category')", "客观 (*keguan*, 'objective')", "民主 (*minzhu*, 'democracy')", "逻辑 (*luoji*, 'logic')", "浪漫 (*langman*, 'romance')", "模特 (*mote*, 'model')", "吉普 (*jipu*, 'jeep')", "坦克 (*tanke*, 'tank')", "芭蕾舞 (*baleiwu*, 'ballet')", "喀秋莎 (*kaqiusha*, 'Katyusha')", "巧克力 (*qiaokeli*, 'chocolate')", "VCD (*weiseidi*, 'VCD')" and "奥林匹克 (*aolinpike*, 'Olympics')" and so on.

The mutual exchange between different regions within a society is also one important aspect of inter-communal contact. Both the absorption of dialect words into *Putonghua* and the mutual absorption of words and expressions between dialects are the result of the contact between different regions of China.

In addition, the development of society is also reflected in the change and replacement of the social systems, which also can promote vocabulary development. For instance, when the Han nationality was in the slave society, there were numerous words designating slaves, e. g., "仆 (*pu*)" was a male slave while "妾 (*qie*)" was a female slave; "臧 (*zang*)" was a slave with weapon to protect and "臣 (*chen*)" was also a male slave trusted by the slave-owner to help him to supervise other slaves. Such words as "隶 (*li*)", "宰 (*zai*)", "奚 (*xi*)", "舆 (*yu*)" and "台 (*tai*)", etc. were also names for slave. When the Han nationality entered the feudal society, there emerged many words in Chinese reflecting the feudal system and life, for example, "皇帝 (*huangdi*, 'emperor')", "宰相 (*zaixiang*, 'prime minister')", "朝廷 (*chaoting*, 'court')", "封建 (*fengjian*, 'feudalism')", "割据 (*geju*, 'segmentation')", "地主 (*dizhu*, 'landlord')", "农奴 (*nongnu*, 'serf')", "农民 (*nongmin*, 'peasant')", "地租 (*dizu*, 'land rent')", "行会 (*hanghui*, 'trade guild')" and "状元 (*zhuangyuan*, 'Number One Scholar (title conferred on the one with the best score in the highest imperial examination)')" and "秀才 (*xiucai*, 'xiucai, one who passed the imperial examination at the county level in the Ming and Qing dynasties')" and so on. Today, when we look at the Chinese vocabulary, we will find a great number of words reflecting the socialist system. Some of these words and expressions were coined after the founding of New China; others became widely employed gradually after 1949 though they had existed long in the past, such as "土改 (*tugai*, 'land reform')", "公有制 (*gongyouzhi*, 'public ownership system')", "政协 (*Zhegnxie*, 'CPPCC')", "人代会 (*Rendaihui*, 'People's Congress')", "党委 (*dangwei*, 'Party committee')", "市委 (*shiwei*, 'municipal Party committee')", "总支 (*zongzhi*, 'general branch')", "劳保 (*laobao*, 'labour insurance')", "退休 (*tuixiu*, 'retire')", "离休 (*lixiu*, 'retire of veteran cadre')", "国营 (*guoying*, 'state-run')" and "双百 (*shuangbai*, 'Two Hundred Guidelines')", "四化 (*Sihua*, 'Four-Izations')", "消协 (*xiaoxie*, 'consumers' association')", "钉子户 (*dingzihu*, 'nail household; recalcitrant')" and "养老院 (*yanglaoyuan*, 'old people's home)" so on and so forth.

The development of society is manifold, so is its impact on vocabulary development; therefore it is extremely necessary for us to combine it closely with the development of society when analyzing and understanding vocabulary development.

(II) The development of people's cognition

The development of everything in human life is usually inseparable from the development of human being's cognition and vocabulary development is no exception. The development of people's cognition can promote vocabulary development from different aspects.

With the objective things unchanged, new words can be coined so as to promote vocabulary development due to the fact that people can come to know these objective things with the development of cognition, such words in physics as "电子 (*dianzi*, 'electron')", "中子 (*zhongzi*, 'neutron')" and "质子 (*zhizi*, 'proton')" and such abstract words as "思维 (*siwei*, 'thinking')", "认识 (*renshi*, 'cognition')", "空间 (*kongjian*, 'space')", "规律 (*guilü*, 'rule')", "悲观 (*beiguan*, 'pessimism')", "乐观 (*leguan*, 'optimism')" and "人生观 (*renshengguan*, 'outlook on life')", etc. are cases in point. The fact that people's thinking comes from superficialness to profundity may well promote the development of word meaning and the above-mentioned "水 (*shui*, 'water')", "电 (*dian*, 'electricity')" and "鬼火 (*guihuo*, 'wildfire')" are all good examples for this case. Moreover, with the development of cognition, people come to understand the objective things in a more refined and nuanced way thus leading to the development of synonyms, e. g., "看 (*kan*, 'look at')", "瞧 (*qiao*, 'watch')", "瞅 (*chou*, 'catch a glimpse of')", "盯 (*ding*, 'gaze at')", "瞪 (*deng*, 'glare at')", "瞄 (*miao*, 'aim at')" and "瞥 (*pie*, 'glance at')" and so on.

Owing to the changes in cognition and emotional attitude, people can also rename objects and the origin of "八大员 (*badayuan*, 'eight officers')" mentioned earlier is a case in point. A good number of neologisms are coined this way and such doublets as "戏子 (*xizi*, ' (derog.) opera jokery') – 演员 (*yanyuan*, 'player')", "邮差 (*youchai*, ' (derog.) mail carrier') – 邮递员 (*youdiyuan*, 'post man')", "店小二 (*dianxiao'er*, ' (derog.) bartender') – "服务员 (*fuwuyuan*, 'attendant')" and "老妈子 (*laomazi*, ' (derog.) amah') – 保姆 (*baomu*, 'nurse')" are vivid examples.

Another aspect of vocabulary development resulted from the development of cognition is that the development of cognitive and mental capacities can lead to the development of scientific research so as to lead to the generation of novelties and hence neologisms are created, e. g, such words as "卫星 (*weixing*, 'satellite')", "导弹 (*daodan*, 'missile')", "模压 (*moya*, 'mould pressing')", "塑料 (*suliao*, 'plastic')", "无影灯 (*wuyingdeng*, 'shadowless lamp')", "磁共振 (*cigongzhen*, 'magnetic resonance')", "电冰箱 (*dianbingxiang*, 'refrigerator')" and "计算机 (*jisuanji*, 'computer')" and so on. The fact that with the application of computer and the development of network information a great number of neologisms and new meanings spring up nowadays is also a forceful illustration in this regard.

(III) The contradiction and adjustment within the vocabulary system

Vocabulary is an aggregation the mutual relationship between the various elements of which are inevitably influenced by the emergence of the new elements and the extinction of the old ones and numerous contradictions within the vocabulary system are thus resulted in. The fact that these contradictions appear and are disposed of one after another promotes vocabulary development. For example, "江 (*Jiang*)" was originally a proper term designating the Changjiang River, while after it became a general term to refer to all rivers its original reference task was taken over by "长江 (*Changjiang*, 'the Changjiang River')". Taking "静 (*jing*, 'quiet')" and "净 (*jing*, 'clean')" as another example: they were homophones originally, in order to avoid confusion in meaning during communication, different disyllables appear: "安静 (*anjing*, 'quiet')", "背静 (*beijing*, 'quiet and secluded')", "平静 (*pingjing*, 'placid')", "清静 (*qingjing*, 'peace and quiet')", "幽静 (*youjing*, 'tranquil')" and "宁静 (*ningjing*, 'serene')", etc. are all related to "静" and "纯净 (*chunjing*, 'pure')", "洁净 (*jiejing*, 'clean')", "白净 (*baijing*, 'fair and clear')" and "明净 (*mingjing*, 'bright and clean')", etc. are all related to "净".

Absolute synonyms are also among continuous adjustment in the vocabulary system. The first method of adjustment for absolute synonyms in Chinese vocabulary is to reserve one of them and eliminate the other(s). For example, for the absolute synonymous doublets such as "爱怜 (*ailian*, 'love tenderly')" and "怜爱 (*lian'ai*, 'love tenderly')", "觉察 (*chajue*, 'be aware of')" and "察觉 (*juecha*, 'be aware of')", "代替 (*daiti*, 'replace')" and "替代 (*tidai*, 'replace')", "自行车 (*zixingche*, 'bicycle')" and "脚踏车 (*jiaotache*, 'bicycle')", etc., the former have been retained and later eliminated or are rarely used nowadays. The second way is to differentiate the absolute synonyms so each of them obtained a unique usage of its own. For example, "事情 (*shiqing*)" and "勾当 (*goudang*)" were originally absolute synonyms meaning "things" and they have become dissimilar in that "勾当" is used to refer to "bad things" more often than not due to differentiation.

Vocabulary is an integrated system the internal contradiction and adjustment in which will sometimes lead to chain reactions. Take "爱人 (*airen*)" for example: its original meaning was "boyfriend or girlfriend", but later it came to refer to "husband or wife" and its original meaning was then replaced by one new sense item of the word "朋友 (*pengyou*, 'boyfriend or girlfriend')" or one new sense item of the word "对象 (*duixiang*, 'boyfriend or girlfriend')" and as a result, "朋友" and "对象" in this context became absolute synonyms. The lexical system continues to adjust this doublet of absolute synonyms. Gradually, these two words are differentiated in meaning with special flavour and usage. From the perspective of the meaning with special flavour, "对象" has a stronger flavour of colloquialism than "朋友" and is more vernacular; from the perspective of usage, sometimes the two words can be used interchangeably in the same context, e. g., "那是他的对象 (*Na shi ta de duixiang*, 'That's his girlfriend')" can be substituted by "那是他的朋友 (*Na shi ta de pengyou*, 'That's his girlfriend')", but one can only say "他在搞对象 (*Ta zai gao duixiang*, 'He is dating')" instead of "*他在搞朋友 (*Ta zai gao pengyou*)". The meaning of "对象" is now further developed and thus different from that of "朋友": it now can also refer to "husband or wife" instead of designating only "boyfriend or girlfriend". Another aspect of the changing in the meaning of "爱人" lies in that its new sense comes to denote roughly the same with such words as "丈夫 (*zhangfu*, 'husband')" and "妻子 (*qizi*, 'wife')" that are already in existence in Chinese. Therefore the vocabulary system proceeds to adjust: these words are differentiated as far as the meaning with special flavour is concerned: compared with "爱人", "丈夫" and "妻子" are more solemn with a written flavour while "爱人" has a somewhat deeper "familiar" and "intimate" flavour. Some new words and expressions come to appear for the moment in this respect; for example, "老公 (*laogong*, 'husband')", which has a deeper emotive flavour, is becoming more and more popular among the young people and "老伴 (*laoban*, 'old gal')", which is more colloquial and emotive, is becoming more and more common among the elderly couples.

The multi-faceted and multi-dimensional contradictions and adjustments within the lexical system are very fascinating and vocabulary in language is constantly growing and flourishing under these contradictions and adjustments.

Section 2 The form of the diachronic dynamic motion of vocabulary

I The form of the diachronic dynamic motion and the history of vocabulary development

The diachronic dynamic motion of vocabulary is an essential and indispensable aspect of vocabulary development. In general, language is in constant motion so that it is always in a dynamic state; on the whole, one can only understand the trajectory of the various dimensions of the vocabulary in motion and have a clear look at the historical face of the development and change of vocabulary by comparisons of language in various different periods of time through the situations of diachronic movement. Although vocabulary, like language, is under gradual change, it is the process of the diachronic gradual change that forms the history of vocabulary movement and development. Therefore, we can see that the diachronic dynamic change of vocabulary not only makes possible the continuous development of language from the past to the present, but also links up the numerous synchronic states into various constituents of the diachronic stages through the dynamic operation. It is obvious that the historical existence of vocabulary can only be illustrated and the history of vocabulary change can only be formed through consolidating and linking up the numberless synchronic situations into an integrated process of the diachronic development and movement of vocabulary in its whole life period.

II The major dimensions of the diachronic dynamic motion of Chinese vocabulary

As one of the oldest languages in the world, Chinese has a long and rich history of vocabulary constituted by its diachronic forms of existence in dynamic movement. It is difficult to elaborate the complete picture of the development of Chinese vocabulary in detail and we just offer a brief illustration on the few major aspects of it as follows:

(I) The addition of neologisms

As mentioned earlier, language develops with the development of society and vocabulary is the most sensitive part in this process; therefore everything existing in society in various periods of history and in various domains of people's life are reflected in vocabulary, thus leading to the successive addition of neologisms. It can be seen from the entries in such Chinese dictionaries as *Er Ya* (a dictionary in ancient China), *Ci Hai* (the Revised Edition in 1989) and *Hanyu Da Cidian* (An Unabridged Chinese Dictionary) (finished in 1993): there are only 3,600 entries in *Er Ya*, 91,706 entries in *Ci Hai* and as much as 375,000 entries and more in *Hanyu Da Cidian*. The number of words in "*Er Ya*", though, may not reflect a complete picture of all the vocabulary in society at that time, it is evident from these several numbers of entries that differ greatly that the number of words has increased by hundreds times from ancient to contemporary Chinese.

The reasons for the increase of neologisms abound:

- The neologisms due to the emergence of novelties. For example, "上岗 (*shanggang*, 'to post; to be (re) employed')", "上网 (*shangwang*, 'to surf the Internet')", "彩电 (*caidian*, 'colour television')", "电脑 (*diannao*, 'computer')", "软件 (*ruanjian*, 'software')", "盒饭 (*hefan*, 'boxed meal')", "助听器 (*zhutingqi*, 'hearing aid')" and "肯德基 (*Kendeji*, 'KFC')", etc.
- The neologisms by renaming the objects with a new term. For example, "工资 (*gongzi*, 'salary')" at present for "薪水 (*xinshui*, 'salary')" in the past, "邮递员 (*youdiyuan*, 'post man')" at present for "邮差 (*youchai*, 'mail carrier')" in the past and "演员 (*yanyuan*, 'player')" at present for "戏子 (*xizi*, '(derog.) opera jokery')" in the past and so on.
- The neologisms created due to the evolution of word meaning. For example, after the enlarging of meaning of "河 (*He*)", the original object it referred to is expressed by the new word "黄河 (*Huanghe*, 'the Yellow River')"; when the meaning of "走 (*zou*)" changed from "running" to "walking", a new word "跑 (*pao*, 'run')" appeared in the lexical system to fill in the semantic gap; the appearance of the word "金属 (*jinshu*, 'metal')" is also due to the evolution of meaning of the word "金 (*jin*, 'gold')".
- The neologisms created under the influence of foreign languages. The words created under the influence of the phonetic forms of foreign words: e. g., "巴黎 (*Bali*, 'Paris')", "沙发 (*shafa*, 'sofa')", "苏维埃 (*Suwei'ai*, 'soviet')", "奥林匹克 (*Aolinpike*, 'Olympic')" and so on. The words created under the influence of the concepts designated by foreign words: e. g., "电话 (*dianhua*, 'telephone')", "煤气 (*meiqi*, 'coal gas')", "扩音器 (*kuoyinqi*, 'microphone')", "连衣裙 (*lianyiqun*, 'one-piece dress')" and so on.

In addition to the above cases, words can also be absorbed from dialects into the common language thus leading to the addition of neologisms. For example, "搞 (*gao*, 'make; do')", "垃圾 (*laji*, 'garbage')", "名堂 (*mingtang*, 'variety; item')" and "尴尬 (*ganga*, 'awkward')", etc. What is more, re-using archaic words and changing their meanings also belongs to the addition of new elements of language.

(II) The increase of disyllables

There has been always a distinction between monosyllables and polysyllables in Chinese vocabulary from the past to the present, while polysyllabic words are mainly composed of disyllabic ones. However, monosyllabic words were the majority in ancient Chinese, especially in Chinese of pre-Qin period (before 221 B. C.). For example, there are 2, 904 monosyllables but only 788 polysyllables in *Zuo Zhuan* (*Zuo's Commentary*).[1] With the development of Chinese, disyllables increase gradually in its vocabulary.

It is inevitable for Chinese vocabulary to develop from a monosyllable-dominant one to a disyllable-dominant one. Because with the development of society, the demand to communication becomes more and more complex and the numbers of the objects to be expressed becomes greater and greater, so limited monosyllabic forms result inevitably in the emergence of a large number of homophones in language, which in turn brings about much inconvenience and difficulties for people's communication, and it is under this circumstance that the disyllabification of Chinese develops. Therefore, the abundance of disyllables not only differentiates and solves the problem of homophones caused by monosyllabic words, but also effectively enriches Chinese vocabulary and greatly enhances the expressiveness of Chinese because disyllables are much more precise and accurate.

The development of disyllabic words in Chinese is mainly manifested in two aspects. One is that many originally monosyllabic words have been gradually replaced by disyllabic ones. Some are substituted by reduplication forms, e. g., "姑姑 (*gugu*, 'aunt')", "伯伯 (*bobo*, 'uncle')", "妹妹 (*meimei*, 'younger sister')" and "弟弟 (*didi*, 'younger brother')" and so on; others are replaced by coordinate compounds with synonymous semantic morphemes, e. g., "道路 (*daolu*, 'road')", "领导 (*lingdao*, 'leader')", "依靠 (*yikao*, 'rely on')" and "丢失 (*diushi*, 'lose')" etc. ; still others are taken place by another new form, e. g., "目 (*mu*, 'eye') – 眼睛 (*yanjing*, 'eye')", "耳 (*er*, 'ear') – 耳朵 (*erduo*, 'ear')", "冠 (*guan*, 'hat') – 帽子 (*maozi*, 'hat')" and "鹊 (*que*, 'pied magpie') – 喜鹊 (*xieque*, 'pied magpie')", etc. The other aspect is that most neologisms are disyllabic in form. For example, "卫星 (*weixing*, 'satellite')", "扫描 (*saomiao*, 'scan')", "同步 (*tongbu*, 'synchronization')", "彩电 (*caidian*, 'colour television')", "空调 (*kongtiao*, 'air conditioner')", "波段 (*boduan*, 'wave band')", "巧干 (*qiaogan*, 'work ingeniously')", "破格 (*poge*, 'break a rule')", "顶替 (*dingti*, 'replace')", "失足 (*shizu*, 'take a false step in life')", "劳军 (*laojun*, 'cheer troops')" and "家教 (*jiajiao*, 'teaching in home; family education')", etc. A great majority of neologisms in Chinese are disyllabic words.

Not only disyllabic words but also trisyllabic and four-syllabic words appear in great number in the contemporary Chinese language; nevertheless disyllabic words are still in dominance at present.

(III) The development of grammaticalization

There has long been a distinction not only between content words and function words, but also between root semantic morphemes and bound morphemes in Chinese vocabulary. In the process of vocabulary development, both Chinese function words and bound morphemes have developed with two specific ways of development, i. e., the creation of new elements and grammaticalization.

There are mainly two aspects of grammaticalization. One is the conversion from a content word class into a function word class in which a sense item designating functional meaning is added to the original substantive meaning, e. g., "因 (*yin*)" originally meant "reason; abide by" and a sense of "because" was added later on functioning as a conjunction. Other examples of this type include "的 (*de*, 'aux. [used after an attribute form]')", "夫 (*fu*, 'this; that; aux. [used at the beginning of a sentence]')", "耳 (*er*, 'only; just')" and "固 (*gu*, 'originally')", etc. There are also some words that the substantival meaning got lost in the process of development and can only be used as a function word, e. g., "然 (*ran*, 'but; however')", "所 (*suo*, "aux. [used before the verb in a subject-predicate structure to make it passive]')", "而 (*er*, 'and')" and "虽 (*sui*, 'although')", etc.

Another aspect of grammaticalization is that a content word which may function as a root semantic morpheme grammaticalized into a bound morpheme with the bound morpheme co-existing with the root semantic morpheme. For example, "了 (*liao*)", which was originally a content word meaning "finish; put to an end", can be used as a root semantic morpheme in compounding such neologisms as "了结 (*liaojie*, 'finish; put to an end')" and "了却 (*liaoque*, 'settle; finish')". Later on, it was grammaticalized into an ending pronouncing '*le*' to designate the grammatical meaning of "perfect" affixed to a verb, e. g., "看了 (*kanle*, 'have looked')", "做了 (*zuole*, 'have done')" and "睡了 (*shuile*, 'have slept')", etc. Such elements as "着 (pronouncing '*zhe*' after grammaticalization)" and "过 (*guo*, 'used after a verb to indicate the completion of an action')" are of this type. For another example, "头 (*tou*)" was a content word meaning "head" and later on it was grammaticalized into a suffix with the grammatical function indicating a noun, e. g., "石头 (*shitou*, 'stone')", "木头 (*mutou*, 'wood')", "想头 (*xiangtou*, 'hope')", "看头 (*kantou*, 'sth. worth seeing or reading')" and "甜头 (*tiantou*, 'benefit')" and so on. Others elements like "子 (*zi*)" (as in "房子 (*fangzi*, 'house')", "袜子 (*wazi*, 'sock')" and "家 (*jia*)" (as in "孩子家 (*haizijia*, 'kid')", "老人家 (*laorenjia*, 'oldster; the elderly')" are all the like. There exist still a small number of content words which can only be used as suffixes due to that their original meanings and functions faded gradually in the process of development, e. g., "然 (*ran*)" in "飘然 (*piaoran*, 'happy and relaxed')", "惨然 (*canran*, 'saddened')", "猛然 (*mengran*, 'abruptly')" and "默然 (*anran*, 'speechless; silent')" and "巴 (*ba*)" in "泥巴 (*niba*, 'mud')", "哑巴 (*yaba*, 'mute')", "结巴 (*jieba*, 'stammer')" and "砸巴 (*zaba*, 'break')", etc.

(IV) The development in word coinage and word formation

After analyzing the formation and structure of Chinese words one can find that in the early period of the development of Chinese language, a great number of

Chinese neologisms were created by arbitrary combination of sound and meaning and onomatopoeia. Such long-standing monosyllabic words as "山 (*shan*, 'mountain')", "水 (*shui*, 'water')", "日 (*ri*, 'sun')", "月 (*yue*, 'moon')", "鸟 (*niao*, 'bird')", "兽 (*shou*, 'beast')", "虫 (*chong*, 'insect')" and "鱼 (*yu*, 'fish')", etc. are created by arbitrary combination of sound and meaning while "猫 (*mao*, 'cat')", "鸦 (*ya*, 'crow')" and "蛙 (*wa*, 'frog')", etc. are coined by onomatopoeia. As far as word formation is concerned, monosyllabic words are in the majority and even in the double-syllable words, simple words are dominant, e. g., many of the alliterated disyllables and rhymed disyllables were created very early in Chinese. As for the ways of the combination of morphemes, coordinate compounds and subordinate words are more common, and verb-object compounds are much less, while the complement and subject-predicate compounds are rarer, which is quite clear in pre-Qin Chinese vocabulary.

Nowadays, word coinage and word formation in Chinese have seen a great development in that not only the methods of word coinage are diversified but also the ways of word formation have been enriched and become more and more precise and accurate, e. g., complement and subject-predicate compounds appear and different sub-types are differentiated within various ways of word formation. All these show that Chinese word coinage and word formation are under a continuous enrichment and development.

(V) The development of such word meaning clusters as synonyms, near-synonyms and polysemes and abstract terms

The continuous emergence of synonyms and the gradual increase of polysemes and abstract terms are the result of the development of people's cognitive ability and these phenomena also signify great enrichment and perfection of vocabulary. The development of Chinese vocabulary in this respect strongly indicates that Chinese is one of the richest and most developed languages in the world.

Synonyms and near-synonyms existed very early in Chinese vocabulary, and *Er Ya* was compiled according to the clusters of synonyms and near-synonyms. In the process of the development of Chinese vocabulary, the number of synonyms and near-synonyms is continuously increasing. As can be seen in various dictionaries of synonyms or books of differentiation and analysis on synonyms published nowadays that not only the number of the groups of synonyms and near-synonyms is obviously enriched and developed, but also the number of words within the group of synonyms and near-synonyms is constantly on the increase.

The development of polysemes is one of the inevitable trends of vocabulary development. Polysemes abound in Chinese because it is one with a long history. Most words that appeared early in time, especially monosyllabic ones, are polysemous. In addition, such word meaning clusters as antonyms and co-hyponyms etc. are also gradually multiplying.

The development of abstract terms depends not only on the development of people's cognition, but also on that of society, science and culture. People's rich imagination and concrete scientific practice can both promote the emergence of

Exploring the dynamic form of vocabulary 201

abstract terms. In the long process of historical development, the Chinese people created not only social civilization, but also a large number of abstract words, such as "灵魂 (*linghun*, 'soul')", "神韵 (*shenyun*, 'verve')", "幽灵 (*youling*, 'specter')", "精神 (*jingshen*, 'spirit')", "思维 (*siwei*, 'thinking')", "思想 (*sixiang*, 'idea')", "感情 (*ganqing*, 'sentiment')", "意识 (*yishi*, 'consciousness')", "抽象 (*chouxiang*, 'abstraction')", "概括 (*gaikuo*, 'generalization')", "规律 (*guilü*, 'rule')", "价值 (*jiazhi*, 'value')", "修养 (*xiuyang*, 'self-cultivation')", "世界观 (*shijieguan*, 'world outlook')" and "人生观 (*renshengguan*, 'outlook on life')" and so forth.

(VI) The development of word meaning

The development of word meaning is an important aspect of vocabulary development and it can promote the change and development of the vocabulary system from a great many different aspects. As was discussed in Chapter Six, the development of word meaning is extremely rich and complicated, so we won't go into much detail here.

(VII) The extinction of old elements

The development and change of vocabulary does not only manifest in the continuous increase of new elements, but also in the continuous extinction of old elements. The extinction of all old elements is a synchronic phenomenon: when an elementt existing in a previous synchronic plane disappeares in later synchronic stages, it can be regarded as extinct. The extinction of old elements can generally be classified into the following types:

1 THE EXTINCTION OF OLD WORDS

The reasons that cause the extinction of old words are manifold; therefore it falls into roughly the following different cases:

The extinction of old objects causes the extinction of old words. For example, "皇帝 (*huangdi*, 'emperor')", "状元 (*zhuangyuan*, 'Number One Scholar (title conferred on the one with the best score in the highest imperial examination)')", "巡抚 (*xunfu*, 'provincial governor')", "乡试 (*xiangshi*, 'provincial examination')", "八股文 (*baguwen*, 'eight-legged essay')", "丫鬟 (*yahuan*, 'servant girl')", "书童 (*shutong*, 'page-boy; a boy serving in a scholar's study')", "童养媳 (*tongyangxi*, 'child bride')", "巡捕 (*xunbu*, 'police or policeman (in former foreign concessions)')", "租界 (*zujie*, 'concession')" and "保长 (*baozhang*, 'the chief of 100 households')", etc. These words and expressions are generally termed as historical words and when people relating the bygone matters at any synchronic stage, they are still employed.

The change in the designation of objects causes the extinction of old words. For example, now one uses "眼 (*yan*, 'eye')" instead of "目 (*mu*)", "鞋 (*xie*, 'shoe')" instead of "履 (*lü*)", "观看 (*guankan*, 'watch')" instead of "观 (*guan*)",

"兴趣 (*xingqu*, 'interest')" and "兴建 (*xingjian*, 'build')" instead of "兴 (*xing*)", "害怕 (*haipa*, 'fear')" instead of "惧 (*ju*)", "睡觉 (*shuijiao*, 'sleep')" instead of "寝 (*qin*)", "医生 (*yisheng*, 'doctor')" instead of "医工 (*yigong*)", "工资 (*gongzi*, 'salary')" instead of "薪水 (*xinshui*, 'salary')" and "演员 (*yanyuan*, 'player')" instead of "戏子 (*xizi*, 'opera jokery')" and so on.

The development of society and the change of communicative demands cause the extinction of old words. For example, when livestock production played an important role in the social life of the Han nationality, people paid great attention to the name of livestock: there were a great variety of names designating "牛 (*niu*, 'ox')" in Chinese vocabulary, such as "牯 (*gu*, 'cow')", "特 (*te*, 'bull')", "犉 (*run*, 'ox with yellow hair and black lips')", "牬 (*bei*, 'two-year-old ox')", "犙 (*san*, 'three-year-old ox')" and "牭 (*si*, 'four-year-old ox')", etc. Later on, due to the diminishing of the function of husbandry in people's lives, these designations were gradually simplified and generalized to such an extent that various oxen were designated by only one word "牛" with the rest gradually dying out. A very limited number of words such as "特 (*te*)" are still being employed, though, but their meanings have been changed completely. Other examples are: "豝 (*ba*, 'two-year-old pig')", "豚 (*tun*, 'porket')", "騋 (*lai*, 'seven-*chi* high horse')", "駥 (*rong*, 'eight-*chi* high horse')", "駣 (*tao*, 'three-year-old horse')" and "髦 (*mao*, 'long-haired horse')", etc. were gradually replaced by "豕 (*shi*, 'pig')", "猪 (*zhu*, 'pig')" and "马 (*ma*, 'horse')" respectively and even "豕" gradually died off later on in the process of development.

The adjustment and standardization of the vocabulary system cause the extinction of old words. The development of absolute synonyms belongs to this type: the adjustment and standardization of a pair of absolute synonyms may well result in that one of the pair is preserved and the other is gradually worn out and dies out. Moreover, many words with foreign language flavour may gradually die away in the process of standardization and conventionalization. For example, "电话 (*dianhua*, 'telephone')" instead of "德律风 (*delüfeng*, 'telephone')", "煤气 (*meiqi*, 'gas')" instead of "瓦斯 (*wasi*, 'gas')" are preserved with the latter being eliminated, and now people are accustomed to using "扩音器 (*kuoyinqi*, 'microphone')", "连衣裙 (*lianyiqun*, 'one-piece dress')" and "青霉素 (*qingmeisu*, 'penicillin')" while "麦克风 (*maikefeng*, 'microphone')", "布拉吉 (*bulaji*, 'blayte; one-piece dress')" and "盘尼西林 (*pannixilin*, 'penicillin')" are now rarely used and they will also gradually die out from the view of development.

2 THE EXTINCTION OF SENSE ITEMS

The extinction of sense items also belongs to the extinction of old elements. For example, the original meaning of "牺牲 (*xisheng*)" was "beast slaughtered for sacrifice in ancient times", and "权 (*quan*)" designated "piptanthus" initially and later it meant "sliding weight of a steelyard", but all these sense items have already vanished in contemporary Chinese.

3 THE EXTINCTION OF SEMANTIC MORPHEMES

As constituents of words, semantic morphemes can be divided into root semantic morphemes and bound morphemes both of which undergo extinction in the process of development.

As far as root semantic morphemes are concerned, they tend to die out with the extinction of old words. Take "旌 (*jing*)" as an example: it originally had three sense items: (1) feather-decked banner hoisted on a mast in ancient times used to command soldiers or clear the way; (2) general term for banners and flags in ancient times; (3) commend. These sense items of "旌" were used as semantic morphemes to create neologisms in the past, e. g., "旌旗 (*jingqi*, 'banners and flags')", "旌麾 (*jinghui*, 'chief commanders banner')" and "旌表 (*jingbiao*, 'confer honours on the virtuous and the worthy')", etc. Nowadays, however, as an archaic word, "旌" is no longer employed by people and neither is it used as a semantic morpheme in word formation anymore under normal circumstances.

The extinction of bound morphemes: for example, "有 (*you*)" as a prefix in ancient Chinese forming "有夏 (*Youxia*, 'Xia Dynasty (2205–1766 BC) ')" and "有商 (*Youshang*, 'Shang Dynasty (1766–1122 BC) ')", etc. and "尔 (*er*)" as a suffix forming "率尔 (*shuai'er*, 'rashly')" and "卓尔 (*zhuo'er*, 'preeminent')" are both out of use at present.

It is a natural phenomenon that old elements in vocabulary wither away. As with the evolution of other elements in language, the extinction of an old element in vocabulary only means that this lexical element disappears in people's daily use, but it still exists in the totality of Chinese vocabulary. Even though some elements cannot be used independently as words, they can still be used as semantic morphemes: "观 (*guan*, 'watch; see; view; outlook')", "兴 (*xing*, 'start; rise')", "彩 (*cai*, 'colour; variety')" and "习 (*xi*, 'practice; custom; habit')" are all cases in point. Other elements are preserved in vocabulary as obsolete archaic words, but they can still exercise specific functions in specific occasions, and the use of classical Chinese words is a good example. Furthermore, these obsolete elements are precious materials for linguistic investigation. Thus it can be seen that although these obsolete elements are no longer serving people's communication, they are invaluable assets in vocabulary to be treasured and cherished.

The development of Chinese vocabulary is quite complicated and through the complicated phenomenon we can discern that there are two different fundamental trends of development with the endless increase of new elements and the continuous disappearance of old elements. One trend is from simplicity to complexity and the development of polysemes and that of synonyms etc. are of this type; the other trend is from complexity to simplicity and the generalization and simplification of the names of livestock and the elimination of absolute synonyms are of this kind. Therefore, when exploring and analyzing vocabulary development, we can not only see the trend from simplicity to complexity, but also should pay attention to the trend from complexity to simplicity so that we can have a better and more comprehensive understanding of vocabulary development.

Section 3 The synchronic mode of dynamic movement of vocabulary

I The inevitability and necessity of the existence of the synchronic mode of dynamic movement

The synchronic mode of dynamic movement of vocabulary, whose existence is both inevitable and necessary in that it embodies the absoluteness of the dynamic movement of vocabulary while manifesting the graduality and describability of vocabulary, is the foundation of the mode of vocabulary movement as a whole. Although the synchronic mode of dynamic movement of vocabulary is an objective existence, there exist good reasons for the fact that people are attaching more and more importance to the study of the synchronic dynamic status of vocabulary. On the one hand, language is gradually changing, therefore one can provide a relatively static description of language in a certain period in its dynamic changing process; on the other, in accordance with vocabulary development, one can artificially divide the whole process into different stages such as the stage of the Dynasties of Yuan, Ming and Qing, the modern stage and the contemporary stage and so on, so the synchronic study of vocabulary arises. Within a synchronic stage, one can observe the dynamic movement and change of vocabulary in a more detailed and concrete way. It must be made clear, nevertheless, that the synchronic stage and the static form are by no means in a one-to-one correspondence relation, let alone identical. The static form and dynamic form of vocabulary always co-exist within a synchronic stage and both of them illustrate the existence, movement and development of vocabulary from different angles. The synchronic static form of vocabulary does not only illustrate the content of the sign system of vocabulary, but also illustrates the real existence of vocabulary as an instrument for communication, while the dynamization of the static form makes possible the communicative function of vocabulary as an instrument for communication. Therefore, it should be accepted that within the mode of vocabulary movement as a whole, as one part of the system of linguistic sign, the static form of vocabulary is a necessary and fundamental one that makes possible the communicative behaviours for a certain communicative purpose; while the dynamic form of vocabulary is the one that performs the concrete communicative function by transmitting communicative information so as to achieve the communicative purposes in verbal communication. Without the static form of vocabulary providing necessary communicative elements for communicative behaviours, no communicative behaviour can be generated; while without the dynamic communicative behaviour, no communicative function of language elements can be realized and no new language element can be created. Therefore, within a synchronic stage, much of the dynamic movement of vocabulary is found in the emergence of speech elements and the mutual transformation between speech elements and language elements, and within this mutual transformation the phasic variation and development in the synchronic movement can be found and such phasic variation and development can further promote the change and development of vocabulary as a whole. It thus can be concluded that the static form and dynamic form of existence of vocabulary are two aspects of vocabulary movement as a whole and they are in a mutual dependence and mutual promotion relation realizing jointly the communicative functions of vocabulary and satisfying the needs of social communications, which is particularly apparent within the synchronic stage.

Within the synchronic stages, the extremely rich and ample dynamic movement of vocabulary can be classified into two aspects: Firstly, when people communicate with each other by using the speech which is constructed on the basis of language elements, these language elements begin to turn into speech elements from static language elements within the concrete contexts, and some of these speech elements may be brought about by the correspondence to concrete objects of word meaning and others may be determined by the subjectivity of people's using of words. Whatever the reason, there inevitably exist certain dynamic changes and differences between these dynamic speech elements and the static language elements. Secondly, in a specific context, people will always create a number of new elements on the basis of the original language materials to cater for the communicative needs. These two aspects are different, though they are both the result of the dynamic movement of vocabulary in people's speech behaviour and in the very beginning they both belong to the temporary speech elements which usually exist in their own specific context serving only the contingent speech behaviour and will no longer exist without the specific context and speech behaviour. Nevertheless, some of the temporary elements will be employed by people repeatedly in the same context so that they gradually turn into language elements from speech elements and go into the static vocabulary system and are consolidated as part of the historical development of vocabulary by diachronic change.

It is quite evident from the above that in the synchronic stage of vocabulary development there always exists a cycling process of movement in which the static language elements are employed resulting in dynamic speech behaviours through which speech elements are created and such speech elements are in turn conventionalized into language elements. In this process, the addition of new elements is always absolutely dominant although there exists the extinction of old elements. Thus vocabulary and other language elements continuously develop in such an endless cycling process.

It is also evident from the above that the synchronic stage of vocabulary development is a very fundamental stage for the dynamic movement and development of vocabulary, whose existence is the need of vocabulary development and whose emergence is also out of the necessity of the requirement of the social communication on language. It is the continuous cycling synchronic stages one after another that give a reason and possibility for the diachronic movement and development; therefore we can say that without the synchronic stage of movement there is no basis for development and in turn without the diachronic stage of movement there are no way and process in which the synchronic situations are consolidated and no possibility to illustrate the historical existence of vocabulary, let alone the formation of the history of vocabulary development.

From the above analysis we can see that, as with other aspects of language, the movement of vocabulary in the synchronic stage is realized through the continuous alternations between language elements and speech elements and vocabulary development on the whole is realized through the interactions between the diachronic movement and the synchronic movement. We therefore can conclude that vocabulary as a whole is always in the constant movement and development.

II The basics of the synchronic mode of dynamic movement

The representation of the form of the dynamic movement of vocabulary at the synchronic stage is quite complicated in that sometimes it is very clear and obvious and sometimes it is subtle and even obscure so that we need to observe and differentiate it seriously. The synchronic dynamic variation of contemporary Chinese can be analyzed in the following aspects:

(I) The creation of new elements based on the original language materials

It is a common phenomenon that people create new words and expressions and even new semantic morphemes based on the original language materials to cater for the communicative needs. Some neologisms are accepted and employed repeatedly by people once they come into being and are conventionalized as language elements in the end. In the meanwhile, certain semantic morphemes are also conventionalized accordingly. For example, the semantic morpheme "的 (*di*, 'taxi')" in the new expression "打的 (*da//di*, 'take a taxi')" has been accepted by all and is used to create such new compounds as "面的 (*miandi*, 'van taxi')" and "轿的 (*jiaodi*, 'sedan taxi')" and so on. Of course, other new elements are not accepted by the linguistic community and they are eliminated gradually as speech elements soon after their emergence or after being used for a short period of time. In the historical process of vocabulary development, the new elements in all ages undergo such a course of creation, development and change.

(II) The parolization of the phonetic form of words

Every society has its own common language, each of which has its own standard phonetic form, but when parolized in language application, everyone's speech sound carries the individual physiological and subjective characteristics of his/her own; for instance, the phonetic form of a man speaking *Putonghua* and that of a man speaking an interlanguage possess the characteristics of each own, which indicates that these speech sounds have parolized in verbal communication. Some of the parolized phonetic forms are extremely standard, nothing else but the language elements; others are deviated from the standard form to a certain degree, and being temporary in general, such parolized elements will be no longer in existence once falling out of the communicative environments. It is noteworthy that some parolized phonetic elements may be conventionalized gradually and once conventionalized, it will turn into a language element. For example, "呆" now is pronounced as "*dai*" instead of "*ai*". For another example, the word "特务 (*tewu*)" originally referred to "special military task (or duty), such as security, communications, transportation, etc., assigned on men, a company, or a battalion" with the pronunciation of "*te2wu2*", and later on its meaning has been extended to refer to "special (or secret) agent; spy; person having received special training for collecting secret information, carrying out subversive and sabotaging activities" with its pronunciation having been gradually changed into "*te2·wu*". Thus a new word is coined in Chinese community. It is obvious that this speech element has turned into a language element.

(III) The dynamic change and development of word meaning

Word meaning is quite active in verbal communication. The dynamic change of word meaning in speech communication can be roughly divided into the following four cases:

Firstly, because different people have different conditions, the meanings of language elements are apparently affected by subjective factors and this is reflected both in the discrepancy in the employment of the incomplete concepts between different people and in some modifications made intentionally to cater for the communicative needs.

Secondly, because of the correspondence to concrete objects of word meaning, the meaning of a language element turns into more explicit parole meaning within the specific context and this change usually narrows down the denotation of the word meaning and enriches its connotation.

Thirdly, within a concrete context, the original word meaning of a language element may change to designate otherwise and the specific meaning under this circumstance can only be understood by the hearer with the help of the context. This meaning is called generally deep meaning, the understanding of which usually undergoes a process of intention-comprehension.

Fourthly, there is the addition of new sense items. In verbal communication, it is extremely common that a certain new sense may be created due to semantic extension and/or association on the basis of the original meaning. For example, the word "包装 (*baozhuang*)" originally had two sense items: one is "wrap in paper, paper box or bottle" and the other is "packaging materials such as paper, boxes, bottles, etc.", and at present a new usage emerges: "make somebody look beautiful and exciting to appeal to the public or enhance marketability". For another example, the word "病毒 (*bingdu*, 'virus')" originally referred to "pathogen which is smaller than a germ and visible only under an electronic microscope" and nowadays "something in a computer that can destroy or disturb the operation of computer system" is also called "病毒". These two new senses have now already been fixed through the diachronic change and turned into language elements from speech elements because they are widely and frequently used.

Among the above-mentioned four cases of dynamic changes, the first three are generally temporary in nature because most elements of which cannot turn into language elements, except that they can enlive verbal communication. The fourth one, i. e., the addition of new sense items, is unique in that most of the added sense items have not only turned into language elements after being consolidated with the development of polysemes, but also play an active and indispensable role in the dynamic change of word meaning.

(IV) The flexible use of words and logically innovative collocations

In the actual speech activities words are inevitably combined with each other; therefore the grammatical properties of words are thus inevitably modified. The grammatical issues involved in the dynamic applications of vocabulary are mainly the following two aspects:

Firstly, the combination rules of words are modified. Adverbs cannot be combined with nouns in general, examples of adverb-noun combinations, however, are not uncommon at present, for example, when his wife talking of Ling Feng, a performing artist, she said: "我有时觉得他很台湾, 有时觉得他很内地, 有时觉得他既不台湾也不内地, 有时又觉得他既台湾又内地, 如果凌峰身上完全是台湾的思维, 我是不会接受的, ... (*Wo youshi juede ta hen Taiwan, youshi juede ta hen Neidi, youshi juede ta ji bu Taiwan, ye bu Neidi, youshi you juede ta ji Taiwan you Neidi, ruguo Ling Feng shenshang wanquan shi Taiwan de siwei, wo shi buhui jieshou de,* ... 'I sometimes feel that he is extremely Taiwan-like, sometimes feel that he is extremely Mainland-like, I sometimes feel that he is neither Taiwan-like nor Mainland-like and sometimes feel that he is both Taiwan-like and Mainland-like. If Ling Feng's thinking is completely Taiwan-like, it is unacceptable for me')". [2] There are several combinations of an adverb and the noun "台湾 (*Taiwan*, 'Taiwan')" and "内地 (*Neidi*, 'Mainland')" respectively, although the meanings of both the nouns "台湾" and "内地" are modified to a certain extent, people can not only accept but also completely comprehend the intended meanings of such combinations in speech. Other examples like "很青春 (*hen qingchun*, "very youth-like")" and "很德国 (*hen Deguo*, 'very Germany-like')" (both taken from television broadcasts) are very common nowadays in China.

It should be noted, however, that the usage of these combinations usually leads to further changes in word meaning, for example, the above-mentioned "台湾" and "内地", etc. no longer simply designate the objects per se, but begin to mean the properties of the way of thinking and living customs etc. that the objects concerned possess.

Secondly, logically innovative collocations. The logically innovative collocations in word combinations are quite frequent nowadays. For example, the combination of "灰色 (*huise*, 'grey')" and "挤进 (*ji jin*, 'squeeze ... into')" in "一切都是灰色的, 灰色的树, 灰色的房, 灰色的人群, ...似乎灰色要将一切都挤进大地中去。(*Yiqie doushi huise de, huise de shu, huise de fang, huise de renqun,* ... *sihu huise yao jiang yiqie dou ji jin dadi zhong qu,*'Everything is grey: grey trees, grey houses, grey crowds ... it seems that grey will squeeze everything into the Earth')" is an apparent parolized flexible usage and in this concrete context, "灰色" has already been assigned the ability to perform the action of "squeezing". The combination of "温暖 (wennuan, 'warmth')" and "洒 (sa, 'sprinkle')" in "温暖洒满人间 (wennuan sa man renjian, 'the world is sprinkled with the warmth')", that of "音符 (yinfu, 'musical note')" and "蹦 (beng, 'leap')" in "从钢琴中不断蹦出的杂乱无章的音符. . . (Cong gangqin zhong buduan beng chu zaluanwuzhang de yinfu, 'Rambling musical notes leap without intermission out of the piano')", and that of "建筑 (jianzhu, 'building')" and "流淌 (liutang, 'flow')" and that of "流淌" and "文化底蕴 (wenhua diyun, 'cultural deposits')" in "精致古老的建筑到处都流淌着中华民族博大精深的文化底蕴 (Jingzhi gulao de jianzhu daochu dou liutang zhe Zhonghua Minzu boda jingshen de wenhua diyun, 'The profound cultural deposits of the Chinese nation are flowing throughout the exquisite and ancient buildings')" are all cases in point. It is also obvious from the above examples that the grammatical meanings and even the meanings with special flavour of the words involved also change to a certain degree when the lexical meanings change in the dynamic flexible use.

Both the above-mentioned phenomena belong to the cases in which the language elements have turned into speech elements during the dynamic movement. Some of such elements may turn into language elements after conventionalization by the linguistic community, but most are of temporary nature in application and cannot turn into language elements. Though temporary, the elements resulted from the synchronic dynamic movement of vocabulary play an extremely active and important role in speech in that they can not only help to bring about vocabulary development in some respects, but also enhance the expressiveness of vocabulary by enriching the liveliness, vivacity and vitality in the expression of vocabulary.

The form of existence of vocabulary is discussed previously. As with all other language elements, there exists the differentiation between "static state" and "dynamic state" and that between "synchrony" and "diachrony" as well as the connections and relations between the four in the form of existence of vocabulary as a whole and thus we can see that there exist both static forms and dynamic forms in a synchronic plane and both static language elements and dynamic speech elements are included in the synchronic movement and that there not only exist the change and development of various synchronic language elements but also exist diachronic dynamic changes for a short period of time and the generation of new language elements in synchrony. The diachronic dynamic state, then, is equivalent to the superposition of the synchronic planes of various historical periods of language. Thus we can say that the range of the study of lexicology should include not only the traditional language and speech but also all the content of the synchronic and diachronic research of vocabulary. So and only so can we have a thorough command of the theories and methods of lexical studies macroscopically and make a refined, rigorous and thorough observation microscopically on any minute changes of vocabulary so as to widen and deepen the study of lexicology.

Section 4 The dynamic form of and the standardization of vocabulary

I On the standardization of vocabulary

As is well-known, the standardization of vocabulary is to artificially make standards which can be recognized and accepted by the members of a linguistic community on various aspects of vocabulary in accordance with the laws of vocabulary development per se under the constraint of conventionalization so as to standardize vocabulary. The established principles on vocabulary standardization such as "necessity", "universality" and "clarity", etc. are in fact concurrent with the recognisability and acceptability by all members of a linguistic community.

Because vocabulary exists in all domains of social life and involves various aspects of the utilization of vocabulary by all members of a linguistic community, the range of vocabulary standardization is extremely extensive and complex and various aspects of vocabulary are inevitably implicated, as demonstrated by: first, in a macroscopic view, vocabulary standardization involves various aspects such as the phonic form of words (speech sound), the written form of words (script), the meaning content of words (word meaning), the composition rules of words (grammar), and the application of words(pragmatics); therefore vocabulary standardization must take into consideration all the factors such as the standards and principles concerning speech sound standardization, writing standardization as well as grammar standardization; second, in a microscopic view, not only the standards must be made on the application and choice concerning neologisms, dialect words, loan words and archaic words, but also normative stipulations must be made on the standard form of the phonetic forms, the meaning content, the written form as well as the rules of the application and development of every word.

There are two types of vocabulary standardization: the first is the rigid standardization to which the standardization of person names, place names and agency names belong in general. For example, once the name of a person or that of a province, a city, a county or a street is settled and published, one cannot change the name, even including the form and rule of its written symbols, into other forms. Take "国家教育委员会 (*Guojia Jiaoyu Weiyuanhui*, 'The State Commission of Education')" as an example: it was shortened as "教委 (*Jiaowei*)" and now it has been transformed into "教育部 (*Jiaoyubu*, 'The Ministry of Education')", and the latter is normative at present. This is a case of rigid standardization because this official stipulation on the agency name determines that this is a normative usage and it cannot be modified at will in general. The second is compliant standardization, and this is the case for most words and expressions. Compliant standardization means that the standardization pattern complies with the social conventionalization and people's application habit of words and expressions and the artificially rigid stipulation is impracticable. For example, the two doublets of "大哥大 (*dageda*, 'mobile telephone')" vs. "手机 (*shouji*, 'mobile telephone')" and "邮码 (*youma*, 'post code')" vs. "邮编 (*youbian*, 'post code')" co-existed in speech within the same period of time, and even "大哥大" was once used more frequently than "手机", yet "手机" and "邮编" were accepted after the dynamic application for a while and can be identified as the normative pattern. Therefore it is impracticable to artificially stipulate which one is normative under such circumstances, and thus it can be seen that the standardization of such words must be carried out in a compliant way. What is more, correct conclusion for the standardization of these words can only be made after a delicate observation and analysis combined closely with the situations of the dynamic movement of vocabulary.

II The status of the dynamic movement of vocabulary as the core viewpoint of vocabulary standardization

As mentioned above, there are two forms of existence for vocabulary: the static and dynamic form with the static form of vocabulary being relative and the dynamic one being absolute so that vocabulary is always changing and developing in dynamic movement. Vocabulary standardization must consequently be carried out with the dynamic change and development of vocabulary and vocabulary specifications and standards must also change stage after stage with the situations of vocabulary change and development.

The dynamic forms of vocabulary can be classified into synchronic and diachronic ones while vocabulary standardization is more closely related to the synchronic state of the dynamic movement of vocabulary.

In the synchronic state of vocabulary, we would say that the static vocabulary system exists as a standardized instrument for communication and only when such an instrument goes into the dynamic form in communication can some elements of this system diverge. Vocabulary, however, is utilized all the time as an instrument for communication and it is through such utilization that the synchronic vocabulary movement is full of vitality and helps to bring about the progressive development of vocabulary. In the synchronic dynamic movement many new elements such as new words, new senses and new usages emerge; a great number of dialect words, loan words and archaic words are utilized by people; some old elements die out; while other extinct old elements are re-utilized; some of which re-appear in their original appearances while others re-appear with a somewhat modified sense. The cases are numerous, diverse and complicated, and in the meanwhile, many nonstandard elements emerge. Vocabulary standardization must keep up with these changes – that is to say, one must pay a close attention to and follow these changes so as to conventionalize and fix the elements that are needed and generally accepted by discarding the dross, selecting the essential, eliminating the false and retaining the true in accordance with the law of vocabulary development per se and abiding by the principle of conventionalization. When standardized elements are fed to the static system, we come to the last step of vocabulary standardization. The last step is definitely of the greatest importance to vocabulary development, and it is just because of the last step that not only the status of the synchronic state of the present static system is recorded, but also the development and change of vocabulary in the contemporary period of time are presented and illustrated.

The trajectory of vocabulary in the synchronic movement is as follows: in the first place, the appearance of a new individual element takes on an isolated and temporary state in general and with the application of it, there will be a variety of different situations, some are just a flash in the pan and will not appear again, others are employed within a small range and vanish before long, others will be gradually widespread and still others will have several different forms in use. It is quite obvious that a good many new elements cannot be otherwise than speech elements under these circumstances. As far as vocabulary standardization is concerned, confronted with the cases in the dynamic movement of vocabulary, one must first have a comprehensive command of the changing materials and highlight the vital and frequently used new elements which may go into the language system in the process of development and these are supposed to be the priorities of vocabulary standardization. Among these priorities, a variety of phenomena in the development and change of vocabulary will emerge, from the appearance of new words, new senses, new pronunciations and new usages to the various changes and developments of word meanings and the extinction and reappearance of old words and so on. Which should be fixed and which should be eliminated among these phenomena? The standardization staff should make new selection and standard in accordance with the laws of vocabulary development per se and the principle of conventionalization and turn the speech elements which meet the specifications and standards into language elements with the fixed form and send them on time to the static system of vocabulary. Thus it can be seen that it is not only possible but completely necessary to combine vocabulary standardization with the studies on the dynamic form of vocabulary and the studies on the change and development of vocabulary in dynamic movement will be the core viewpoint forever and ever.

It should be pointed out that the synchronic dynamic form of vocabulary is also a multi-dimensional one comprising diachronic factors of a certain period of time, which will also span a stretch of time with a certain process of development. Take the synchronic dynamic form of Chinese vocabulary in the period of Reform and Open-up for example, its movement process spans more than 30 years, though the processes for each individual element are different, yet it is inevitable that each of them undergoes a process; therefore in vocabulary standardization there must be a process for observation and reorganization in application for a period of time. The formation of a language element must undergo such different stages as creation, trial, conventionalization, popularization and being fixed as a language element in the end, and sometimes there are even reversions. Although the time needed maybe different for each element in each stage, no stage can be omitted for each new element. Hence there is enough time for observation and reorganization in vocabulary standardization. This also illustrates that a great deal of job in vocabulary standardization should be carried out within the dimension of the dynamic change of vocabulary, and it is the final part to finalize standards so as to turn speech elements into language elements, although the last part is of the greatest importance and indispensable.

III Several issues in vocabulary standardization

Vocabulary standardization is an extremely meticulous and complicated task, with meticulous indicating that one must track the change of every word, even that of a certain aspect of a certain word, and complicated indicating that one must attend to various aspects of vocabulary and even the connection and relation among such aspects. One must pay particular attention to the following issues in order to coordinate "meticulousness" and "complicatedness":

(I) To pay attention to the scope of the application of words

Because people in verbal communication in a community are different in their age, cultural standard and living environment etc., and the occasions and communicative purposes etc. are also distinct, they are dissimilar in the way and habit in which words are used in communication. Thus, it is necessary to differentiate which ones of the words and expressions employed are widely used by all the people and which ones belong to jargon or are of class and/or bloc parlance nature. The reason lies in that only when the scope of existence and the property of a word is clarified, can its usage, especially its frequency of use, be precisely mastered. For example, while a profession word has a very high frequency of use within its own trade and is to be treated as a normative word, the frequency of use in the parlance of all the people may well be different from that within the trade of its own. Accordingly, it is extremely necessary to pay attention to the scope of the application of words and whether a word is accepted as a language element or not should be decided in accordance with different situations and scopes.

(II) To reinforce the scientificalness of the standardization process

The issue of paramount importance is how to settle the normative pattern and standard and to establish accurately the standardized word form. People in the past mainly resorted to intuition to solve this problem. At present we can work out more scientific and more precise standards based on the word frequency after extensive corpus statistics with the help of computer. A lot of manual work should be carried out, however, to meet the accurate and scientific requirements. Word frequency counting with computer is rather complex and meticulous: in the first place, we must use right linguistic data to guarantee the right statistical results; secondly, the statistics must be multi-level and multi-angular ones in multiple domains, because the word distribution differs in actual use and different styles have different requirements for the application of words; therefore there is no easy way out.

(III) To establish the standardized model

The best embodiment of vocabulary standards is dictionary; thus a good dictionary is a model of vocabulary standards. All dictionaries are products of a synchronic stage, because any dictionary is created within a certain age whether it is a diachronic one or a synchronic one; therefore, a good dictionary does not only reflect the appearance of vocabulary development, but also possesses the bright normativeness and the characteristics of times. To take a standardized element into a dictionary is an extremely serious matter: for a word to be recorded in a dictionary does not only prove that this element is already a standardized element, but also proves that the property of the element has already turned from being a speech elements into being a language element and it has already become a member of the static synchronic system of vocabulary. The property of a number of entries in certain dictionaries published at present is rather obscure: some of them are language elements and others are speech elements. The all-embracing way like this is extremely destructive to the standardization of vocabulary, and if a dictionary incorporates elements of diverse nature, illustrations should be made on the property of each one.

Notes

1 Chen Kejiong: A Short Discussion on *Zuo Zhuan* (*Zuo's Commentary*) (Issue No. 1, 1982, *Journal of Central China Normal University*).
2 Ha Lei: From "Widow Village" to Cross-strait Intermarriage (http:// blog.sina.com.cn/s/blog_4dd44e550100egul.htm)l.

References

I Books

(1) Lexicography

[Han] Xu, Shen. *Shuo Wen Jie Zi (the Origin of Chinese Characters)*. Beijing: Zhonghua Book Company. 1963 (Reprint).
[Jin] Guo, Pu (Annote), [Song] Xing, Bing (Subcommentary), *Notes on Er Ya* [Qing], Ruan, Yuan (Proofread). *Notes on the Shi San Jing (Thirteen Classics)*. Beijing: Zhonghua Book Company. 1980 (Reprint).
[Qing] Duan, Yucai. *Shuo Wen Jie Zi Zhu (An Annotation on the Origin of Chinese Characters)*. Shanghai: Shanghai Classics Publishing House. 1981 (Reprint).
[Han] Yang, Xiong. *Fang Yan (Dialects)*, [Qing] Qian Yi (Ed.). *An Annotation and Commentary on Fang Yan (Dialects)*. Shanghai: Shanghai Classics Publishing House. 1984 (Reprint).
[Han] Liu, Xi. *Shi Ming (Explanations on Names)*, [Qing] Wang, Xianqian (Ed.). *A Supplement on the Annotation of Shi Ming (Explanations on Names)*. Shanghai: Shanghai Classics Publishing House. 1984 (Reprint).
Sun, Changxu. 1956. *Chinese Vocabulary*. Changchun: Jilin People's Press.
Cui, Fuyuan. 1957. *Lectures on Contemporary Chinese Word Meaning*. Jinan: Shandong People's Publishing House.
———. 1957. *Examples of Word Formation in Contemporary Chinese*. Jinan: Shandong People's Publishing House.
Lu, Zhiwei. 1957. *Word Formation in Chinese*. Beijing: Science Press.
Zhang, Jing. 1957. *Lectures on Vocabulary Instruction*. Wuhan: Hubei People's Press.
Gao, Mingkai and Liu, Zhengtan. 1958. *A Study on Loan Words in Modern Chinese*. Beijing: Language Reform Publishing House.
Wang, Li. 1958. *A History of Chinese Language (II)*. Beijing: Science Press.
Wang, Qin and Wu, Zhankun. 1959. *Modern Chinese Vocabulary*. Changsha: Hunan People's Publishing House.
Zhou, Zumo. 1959. *Lectures on Chinese Vocabulary*. Beijing: People's Education Press.
Sun, Xuanchang and Chen, Fang. 1965. *Polysemes, Synonyms and Antonyms*. Beijing: Beijing Press.
Ma, Guofan. 1973. *Idioms*. Hohhot: Inner Mongolia People's Publishing House.
Li, Xingjian and Liu, Shuxin. 1975. *The Knowledge and Application of Words*. Tianjin: Tianjin People's Publishing House.

Ma, Guofan and Gao, Gedong. 1979. *Two Part Allegorical Sayings*. Hohhot: Inner Mongolia People's Publishing House.
He, Jiuying and Jiang, Shaoyu. 1980. *Lectures on the Vocabulary of Ancient Chinese*. Beijing: Beijing Press.
Hong, Xinheng. 1980. *An Interpretation on Chinese Morphology and Syntax*. Changchun: Jilin People's Press.
Wang, Qin. 1980. *An Introduction to Proverbs and Two Part Allegorical Sayings*. Changsha: Hunan People's Press.
Wu, Zhankun and Ma, Guofan. 1980. *Proverbs*. Hohhot: Inner Mongolia People's Press.
Ren, Xueliang. 1981. *Chinese Morphology*. Beijing: Chinese Social Sciences Press.
Zhang, Shoukang. 1981. *Word Formation and Inflection*. Wuhan: Hubei People's Press.
Zhu, Xing. 1981. *A Brief Analysis of Chinese Word Meaning*. Wuhan: Hubei People's Press.
Gao, Wenda and Wang, Liting. 1982. *Vocabulary Knowledge*. Jinan: Shandong Education Press.
Ma, Guofan and Gao, Gedong. 1982. *Formulaic Expressions*. Hohhot: Inner Mongolia People's Publishing House.
Sun, Liangming. 1982. *Word Meaning and Definition*. Wuhan: Hubei People's Press.
Xiang, Guangzhong. 1982. *An Overview on Idioms*. Wuhan: Hubei People's Press.
Xie, Wenqing. 1982. *Synonyms*. Wuhan: Hubei People's Press.
Zhang, Yongyan. 1982. *A Brief Account of Lexicology*. Wuhan: Central China Institute of Technology Press.
Wang, Dechun. 1983. *Researches on Lexicology*. Jinan: Shandong Education Press.
Wu, Zhankun. 1983. *Vocabulary*. Shanghai: Shanghai Education Publishing House.
Wu, Zhankun and Wang, Qin. 1983. *A Brief Account of Modern Chinese Vocabulary*. Hohhot: Inner Mongolia People's Press.
Xu, Qing. 1983. *Informal Discussions on Vocabulary*. Hangzhou: Zhejiang People's Publishing House.
Liu, Shuxin. 1984. *Studies on Lexicology and Lexicography*. Tianjin: Tianjin People's Publishing House.
Fu, Huaiqing. 1985. *Modern Chinese Vocabulary*. Beijing: Peking University Press.
Guo, Liangfu. 1985. *Vocabulary*. Beijing: The Commercial Press.
Guo, Zaiyi. 1985. *On Explanation of Words in Ancient Books*. Shanghai: Shanghai Classics Publishing House.
Rondo, G. 1985. *Introduction to Terminology* (Liu Gang and Liu Jianyi, Tr.). Beijing: Science Press.
Jia, Yande. 1986. *An Introduction to Semantics*. Beijing: Peking University Press.
Wang, Ying. 1986. *Explanations on Words From Poetry, Ci and Lyrics*. Beijing: Zhonghua Book Company.
Leech, G. 1987. *Semantics* (Li Ruihua et al., Tr.). Shanghai: Shanghai Foreign Language Education Press.
Su, Baorong and Song, Yongpei. 1987. *A Brief Account of the Word Meaning in Ancient Chinese*. Shijiazhuang: Hebei Education Press.
Zhao, Keqin. 1987. *A Brief Account of Ancient Chinese Vocabulary*. Hangzhou: Zhejiang Education Press.
Li, Xingjian. 1988. *On the Learning and Use of Words*. Changchun: Jilin Literature and History Press.
Xie, Wenqing. 1988. *Antonyms*. Wuhan: Hubei Education Press.
Jiang, Shaoyu. 1989. *An Outline of Ancient Chinese Vocabulary*. Beijign: Peking University Press.

Pan, Yunzhong. 1989. *A Brief Account of the History of Chinese Vocabulary*. Shanghai: Shanghai Classics Publishing House.
Shi, Cunzhen. 1989. *An Outline of Chinese Vocabulary History*. Shanghai: East China Normal University Press.
Sun, Weizhang. 1989. *Chinese Phraseology*. Changchun: Jilin Education Publishing House.
Zhou, Guangqing. 1989. *A Brief Account of Ancient Chinese Lexicology*. Wuhan: Huazhong Normal University Press.
Guo, Liangfu. 1990. *Vocabulary and Dictionary*. Beijing: The Commercial Press.
Liu, Shuxin. 1990. *Chinese Descriptive Lexicology*. Beijing: The Commercial Press.
Xu, Liejiong. 1990. *Semantics*. Beijing: Language and Culture Press.
Shi, Youwei. 1991. *Loan Words: The Messenger of Foreign Cultures*. Changchun: Jilin Education Publishing House.
Zhou, Jian. 1991. *A Study on Synonyms*. Tianjin: Tianjin People's Publishing House.
Jia, Yande. 1992. *Chinese Semantics*. Beijing: Peking University Press.
Liu, Shuxin and Zhou, Jian. 1992. *Synonyms and Antonyms*. Beijing: The Commercial Press.
Su, Xinchun. 1992. *Chinese Lexical Semantics*. Guangzhou: Guangdong Education Press.
Xu, Weihan. 1992. *An Introduction to Chinese Lexicology*. Beijing: The Commercial Press.
Shi, Anshi. 1993. *Semantic Theory*. Beijing: The Commercial Press.
Wang, Li. 1993. *A History of Chinese Vocabulary*. Beijing: The Commercial Press.
Chen, Guanglei. 1994. *Chinese Morphology*. Shanghai: Shanghai Xuelin Press.
Gao, Shougang. 1994. *A General Survey on the Ancient Chinese Word Meaning*. Beijing: Language and Culture Press.
Liang, Xiaohong. 1994. *The Construction of Buddhist Words and the Development of Chinese Vocabulary*. Beijing: Beijing Language Institute Press.
Shi, Anshi. 1994. *Studies on Semantics*. Beijing: Language and Culture Press.
Zhang, Zhiyi and Zhang, Qingyun. 1994. *Words and Dictionaries*. Beijing: China Radio and Television Press.
Zhou, Jian. 1994. *The Meaning and Structure of Words*. Tianjin: Tianjin Ancient Books Publishing House.
Chang, Jingyu. 1995. *Chinese Vocabulary and Chinese Culture*. Beijing: Peking University Press.
Editorial Group of New Researches in Lexicology. 1995. *New Researches in Lexicology – Procedings of the First Modern Chinese Vocabulary Symposium*. Beijing: Language and Culture Press.
Li, Liangjun. 1995. *On Chinese Lexical Semantics*. Guilin: Guangxi Normal University Press.
Chen, Lizhong. 1996. *Yin Yang and the Five Elements and Chinese Lexicology*. Changsha: Yuelu Publishing House.
Fu, Huaiqing. 1996. *The Analysis and Description of Word Meaning*. Beijing: Language and Culture Press.
———. 1996. *A History of Chinese Lexicology*. Hefei: Anhui Education Publishing House.
Yang, Lin. 1996. *Chinese Vocabulary and Chinese Culture*. Beijing: Language and Culture Press.
Zhou, Dianlong and Li, Changren. 1996. *A History of Chinese Lexicology*. Beijing: China Overseas Chinese Press.
Xu, Guoqing. 1999. *On the System of Modern Chinese Vocabulary*. Beijing: Peking University Press.

Shi, Youwei. 2000. *Loan Words in Chinese*. Beijing: The Commercial Press.
Su, Baorong. 2000. *Studies on Word Meaning and Dictionary Definition*. Beijing: The Commercial Press.
———. 2000. *A Modern Annotation onShuo Wen Jie Zi (the Origin of Chinese Characters)*. Xi'an: Shaanxi People's Publishing House.
Zhang, Shaoqi. 2000. *A Study on Folk Etymology*. Beijing: Language and Culture Press.
Wang, Jihui. 2001. *A Study of Abbreviations in Modern Chinese*. Tianjin: Tianjin People's Publishing House.
Zhang, Zhiyi and Zhang, Qingyun. 2001. *Lexical Semantics*. Beijing: The Commercial Press.
Zong, Tinghu. 2003. *Zong Tinghu on Rhetoric*. Changchun: Jilin Education Publishing House.

(II) Others

Lü, Shuxiang and Zhu, Dexi. 1951. *Lectures on Grammar and Rhetoric*. Shanghai: Kaiming Book Company.
Wang, Li. 1951. *An Outline of Chinese Grammar*. Shanghai: Kaiming Book Company.
Stalin, Joseph. 1953. *Marxism and Problems of Linguistics* (Li Lisan et al.,Tr.). Beijing: People's Publishing House.
Chen, Wangdao. 1954. *An Introduction to Rhetoric*. Shanghai: New Literature and Art Publishing House.
Chicobava, A. C. 1954. *An Introduction to Linguistics*. Beijing: Higher Education Press.
Wang, Li. 1954. *Chinese Modern Grammar*. Beijing: Zhonghua Book Company.
———. 1954. *Chinese Grammar Theory*. Bejing: Zhonghua Book Company.
Hu, Fu and Wen, Lian. 1955. *An Exploration of Modern Chinese Grammar*. Shanghai: New Knowledge Press.
Lü, Shuxiang. 1955. *Papers on Chinese Grammar*. Beijing: Science Press.
Vinogradov, C. H. and Kuzmin, A. 1955. *Logic*. Beijing: People's Education Press.
Wang, Li. 1955. *Lectures on Chinese*. Beijing: Culture and Education Press.
Budagov, P. A. 1956. *An Introduction to Linguistics* (Lü Tonglun et al., Tr.). Beijing: Shidai Press.
Cen, Qixiang. 1956. *Basics of Grammatical Theory*. Beijing: Shidai Press.
Zhang, Zhigong. 1956. *A General Introduction to Chinese Grammar*. Shanghai: New Knowledge Press.
Cen, Qixiang. 1957. *General Linguistics*. Beijing: Science Press.
Gao, Mingkai. 1957. *On Chinese Grammar*. Beijing: Science Press.
———. 1957. *General Linguistics*. Shanghai: New Knowledge Press.
Lü, Shuxiang. 1957. *An Outline of Chinese Grammar*. Beijing: The Commercial Press.
Zhang, Huanyi. 1957. *An Outline of Rhetoric (Revised Edition)*. Shanghai: New Knowledge Press.
Wang, Lida (Tr. and ed.). 1959. *A Short History of Studies on Chinese*. Beijing: The Commercial Press.
Zhang, Zhigong (ed.). 1959. *Knowledge of Chinese*. Beijing: People's Education Press.
Hu, Yushu. 1962. *Modern Chinese*. Shanghai: Shanghai Education Press.
Wang, Li (ed.). 1962–1964. *Ancient Chinese (Four volumes)*. Beijing: Zhonghua Book Company.
Gao, Mingkai. 1963. *On Language*. Beijing: Science Press.

Gao, Mingkai and Shi, Anshi. 1963. *An Introduction to Linguistics*. Bejing: Zhonghua Book Company.
Gorsky, D. P. 1963. *Language and Thinking* (Xiong Yaoxiang et al., Tr.). Shanghai: SDX Joint Publishing Company.
Shanghai Education Publishing House (ed.). 1963. *Debates on Language and Speech*. Shanghai: Shanghai Education Publishing House.
Zhang, Gong. 1963. *Modern Chinese Rhetoric*. Shijiazhuang: Hebei Education Press.
Chen, Wangdao. 1978. *A Brief Introduction to Grammar*. Shanghai: Shanghai Education Publishing House.
Cai, Shangsi. 1979. *An Outline of Chinese Cultural History*. Changsha: Hunan People's Publishing House.
Chen, Zongming. 1979. *A Preliminary Study of the Logic of Modern Chinese*. Shanghai: SDX Joint Publishing Company.
Guo, Shaoyu. 1979. *A New Exploration into Chinese Grammar and Rhetoric*. Beijing: The Commercial Press.
Huang, Borong and Liao, Xudong. 1979. *Modern Chinese (I and II)*. Lanzhou: Gansu People's Press. 1991. Beijing: Higher Education Press (Revised Edition).
Jin, Yuelin. 1979. *A Concise Reader of Formal Logic*. Beijing: China Youth Press.
Lü, Shuxiang. 1979. *Issues on Chinese Grammatical Analyses*. Beijing: The Commercial Press.
Schaff, Adam. 1979. *An Introduction to Semantics*. Beijing: The Commercial Press.
Yin, Huanxian. 1979. *Essentials of Fanqie*. Jinan: Shandong People's Publishing House.
Lu, Zongda. 1980. *A Brief Introduction to Exegesis*. Beijing: Beijing Publishing House.
Lü, Shuxiang. 1980. *Platitudes on Chinese*. Shanghai: SDX Joint Publishing Company.
Saussure, F. 1980. *A Course in General Linguistics* (Gao, Mingkai et al., Tr.). Beijing: The Commercial Press.
Shi, Cunzhi. 1980. *Three Talks on Grammar*. Shanghai: Shanghai Education Publishing House.
Zhou, Dapu. 1980. *An Outline of Exegesis*. Wuhan: Hubei People's Press.
Cen, Qixiang. 1981. *Lectures on Historical Comparative Linguistics*. Wuhan: Hubei People's Press.
Wang, Li. 1981. *A History of Chinese Linguistics*. Taiyuan: Shanxi People's Publishing House.
Ye, Feisheng and Xu, Tongqiang. 1981. *An Outline of Linguistics*. Beijing: Peking University Press.
Yin, Huanxian. 1981. *Three Talks on Chinese Character*. Jinan: Qilu Press.
Guo, Xiliang et al. 1981–1983. *Ancient Chinese (Three volumes)*. Beijing: Beijing Publishing House.
Hu, Mingyang et al. 1982. *An Introduction to Lexicography*. Beijing: Renmin University of China Press.
Zhu, Dexi. 1982. *Lecture Notes on Grammar*. Beijing: The Commercial Press.
Cen, Qixiang. 1983. *Learning and Research of Linguistics*. Zhengzhou: Zhongzhou Painting and Calligraphy Press.
Chen, Yuan. 1983. *Sociolinguistics*. Shanghai: Xuelin Press.
Lu, Zongda and Wang, Ning. 1983. *Methodology of Exegesis*. Beijing: Chinese Social Sciences Press.
Lü, Shuxiang. 1983. *Lü Shuxiang's Analects on Chinese*. Beijing: The Commercial Press.
Zhao, Shikai. 1983. *Modern Linguistics*. Beijing: Knowledge Press.
Hong, Cheng. 1984. *Exegesis*. Nanjing: Jiangsu Ancient Books Press.

Liu, Ling et al. (ed.). 1984. *An Outline of Linguistics*. Beijing: Beijing Normal University Press.
Qi, Peirong. 1984. *An Outline of Exegesis*. Beijing: Zhonghua Book Company.
Chen, Songcen. 1985. *An Introduction to Sociolinguistics*. Beijing: Peking University Press.
Hong, Chengyu. 1985. *An Analysis of Ancient Chinese Word Meaning*. Tianjin: Tianjin People's Publishing House.
Sapir, Edward. 1985. *Language* (Lu Zhuoyuan, Tr.). Beijing: The Commercial Press.
Liu, Huanhui. 1986. *Verbal Communication*. Nanchang: Jiangxi Education Press.
Wu, Tieping. 1986. *New Explorations of the Relationship Between Language and Thinking*. Shanghai: Shanghai Education Publishing House.
Dai, Zhiyuan et al. 1988. *Principles and Applications of Communication*. Lanzhou: Lanzhou University Press.
Gregory, Michael and Carol, Susan. 1988. *Language and Situation*. Beijing: Language and Culture Press.
Luo, Changpei. 1989. *Language and Culture*. Beijing: Language and Culture Press.
Yin, Huanxian. 1990. *Yin Huanxian on Language*. Jinan: Shandong University Press.
Yuan, Hui and Zong, Tinghu (eds.). 1990. *A History of Chinese Rhetoric*. Hefei: Anhui Education Press.
Cen, Qixiang. 1992. *Selected Translated Papers in Foreign Linguistics*. Beijing: Language and Culture Press.
Wang, Zhanfu. 1993. *An Introduction to Studies on Context*. Hohhot: Inner Mongolia University Press.
Editorial Board. 1994. *Collected Essays on Celebration of Mr. Yin Huanxian's 50th Anniversary of Teaching*. Jinan: Shandong University Press.
Dai, Zhaoming. 1996. *An Introduction to Cultural Linguistics*. Beijing: Language and Culture Press.
Liu, Wenyi. 1996. *Contextual Studies*. Shijiazhuang: Hebei People's Publishing House.
Li, Xingjian. 1997. *New Papers on Language Learning*. Xi'an: Shaanxi People's Education Press.
Wang, Ning. 1997. *Principles of Exegesis*. Beijing: China International Broadcasting Press.
Zong, Tinghu. 2003. *Zong Tinghu on Rhetoric*. Changchun: Jilin Education Publishing House.

II Dictionaries

Zhang, Xiang. 1953. *An Annotation on Words From Poetry, Ci and Lyrics (I, II)*. Beijing: Zhonghua Book Company.
Fu, Dingyi. 1954. *A Dictionary of Two-character Compound Words (Four Volumes)*. Bejing: Zhonghua Book Company.
Yang, Shuda. 1954. *On Function Words*. Bejing: Zhonghua Book Company.
Chinese Language Department of Peking University. 1958. *A Little Dictionary of Chinese Idioms*. Bejing: Zhonghua Book Company.
(Qing) Zhang, Yushu et al. 1958. *Kangxi Dictionary (Photostatic Copy)*. Beijing: Zhonghua Book Company.
The Compiling Group of the Dictionary of Chinese Idioms of Gansu Normal University. 1978. *A Dictionary of Chinese Idioms (Revised in 1986)*. Shanghai: Shanghai Education Publishing House.

References

Lü, Shuxiang. 1978. *Function Words in Classical Chinese*. Shanghai: Shanghai Education Publishing House.
Wang, Li (ed.). 1979. *A Dictionary of Common Words in Ancient Chinese*. Beijing: The Commercial Press.
Dictionary Editing Group, Institute of Linguistics, Chinese Academy of Social Sciences. 1978–2002. *Modern Chinese Dictionary (All Editions)*. Beijing: The Commercial Press.
Editorial Department of the Commercial Press. 1979–1983. *Ci Yuan (The Chinese Etymologicon) (Vol. I–IV)*. Beijing: The Commercial Press.
Editing Committee of *Ci Hai*. 1980. *Ci Hai (Microcopy)*. Shanghai: Shanghai Lexicographical Publishing House.
Lü, Shuxiang (ed.). 1980. *Eight Hundred Words of Modern Chinese*. Beijing: The Commercial Press.
Zhang, Zhiyi. 1981. *Concise Thesaurus*. Shanghai: Shanghai Lexicographical Publishing House.
Editorial Office of Zhonghua Book Company. 1981. *The Great Chinese Dictionary*. Bejing: Zhonghua Book Company.
Department of Chinese Language and Literature of Peking University. 1982. *Explanation of Modern Chinese Function Words*. Beijing: The Commercial Press.
Fu, Guangling et al. (eds.). 1982. *Word Formation Dictionary of Common Words*. Beijing: Renmin University of China Press.
Wang, Li. 1982. *A Dictionary of Cognate Words*. Beijing: The Commercial Press.
Zhu, Qifeng. 1982. *Ci Tong (An Exhaustive Dictionary of Words)*. Shanghai: Shanghai Classics Publishing House.
Compiling Group. 1983. *A Handbook of Frequently Used Polysemes in Classical Chinese*. Hohhot: Inner Mongolia Education Press.
Editorial Board of the Dictionary of Logic. 1983. *A Little Dictionary of Logic*. Changchun: Jilin People's Press.
Editorial Department of Zhonghua Book Publishing House. 1983. *A Practical Big Dictionary*. Beijing: Zhonghua Book Company.
Hu, Pu'an. 1983. *A Dictionary of Folk Adages*. Shanghai: Shanghai Bookstore.
Mei, Jiaju et al. 1983. *A Forest of Synonyms*. Shanghai: Shanghai Lexicographical Publishing House.
Qiu, Chongbing. 1983. *Five Thousand Folk Adages*. Xi'an: Shaanxi People's Publishing House.
Tong, Huijun. 1983. *A Discrimination of Common Words With Identical Components But Different in Order*. Changsha: Hunan People's Publishing House.
Editing Group. 1984. *A Dictionary of Ancient Allusions*. Nanchang: Jiangxi People's Publishing House.
Liu, Zhengtan et al. 1984. *A Dictionary of Chinese Loan Words*. Shanghai: Shanghai Lexicographical Publishing House.
Wang, Anjie. 1984. *A Concise Thesaurus*. Harbin: Heilongjiang People's Publishing House.
Wen, Duanzheng et al. 1984. *A Dictionary of Two Part Allegorical Sayings*. Beijing: Beijing Publishing House.
Yang, Shengchu. 1984. *Reverse Order Entries of Modern Chinese*. Chengdu: Sichuan People's Publishing House.
Cheng, Xiangqing (ed.). 1985. *An Explanation and Discrimination of Content Words in Ancient Chinese*. Jinan: Shandong Education Press.
Li, Yihua and Lü, Deshen. 1985. *A Dictionary of Chinese Idioms*. Chengdu: Sichuan Dictionary Publishing House.

Long, Qian'an (ed.). 1985. *A Dictionary of Language in Song and Yuan Dynesties*. Shanghai: Shanghai Lexicographical Publishing House.
Lü, Caizhen et al. (eds.). 1985. *A Dictionary of Difficult Words in Modern Chinese*. Yanbian: Yanbian Education Press.
Shi, Dong. 1985. *A Concise Dictionary of Ancient Chinese*. Kunming: Yunnan People's Publishing House.
Wang, Jinzheng et al. 1985. *A Concise Dictionary of Linguistics*. Hohhot: Inner Mongolia People's Publishing House.
Wang, Lijia and Hou, Xuechao. 1985. *A Dictionary of Classified Idioms*. Guangzhou: Guangdong People's Publishing House.
Institute of Language Teaching of Beijing Language Institute. 1986. *Modern Chinese Frequency Dictionary*. Beijing: Beijing Language Institute Press.
Zhong, Jialing. 1986. *A Dictionary of Modern Chinese Abbreviations*. Jinan: Qilu Press.
Luo, Zhufeng (ed.). 1986–1993. *Hanyu Da Cidian (An Unabridged Chinese Dictionary) (Vol. I–XII)*. Shanghai: Hanyu Da Cidian Press.
Lin, Xingguang and Fei, Bai. 1987. *A Concise Chinese Thesaurus*. Beijing: The Commercial Press.
Liu, Shuxin. 1987. *A Dictionary of Modern Chinese Synonyms*. Tianjin: Tianjin People's Publishing House.
Min, Jiaji et al. 1987. *A Dictionary of Chinese Neologisms*. Shanghai: Shanghai Lexicographical Publishing House.
Wang, Wanren. 1987. *Explanations and Examples of Onomatopoeia*. Nanning: Guangxi Education Press.
Ji, Xianlin et al. 1988. *Language and Writing of Encyclopedia of China*. Beijing: Encyclopaedia of China Publishing House.
Li, Xingjian et al. (eds.). 1989. *A Dictionary of Neologisms*. Beijing: Language and Culture Press.
Liu, Jiexiu. 1989. *A Dictionary of Investigation and Explanation of Chinese Idioms*. Beijing: The Commercial Press.
Cen, Qixiang. 1990. *A Dictionary of Chinese Loan Words*. Beijing: The Commercial Press.
Zhou, Hongming. 1990. *A Dictionary of Chinese Formulaic Expressions*. Beijing: The Commercial Press.
Wang, Ying and Zeng, Mingde. 1991. *A Collection of Explanations on Words From Poetry, Ci and Lyrics*. Beijing: Language and Culture Press.
Luo, Zhufeng (ed.). 1994. *Hanyu Da Cidian (An Unabridged Chinese Dictionary) (Appendix and Index)*. Shanghai: Hanyu Da Cidian Press.
Yu, Genyuan (ed.). 1994. *A Dictionary of Modern Chinese Neologisms*. Beijing: Beijing Language Institute Press.
Wang, Ailu. 1995. *A Dictionary of Chinese Motivation*. Beijing: Beijing Language Institute Press.
Li, Xingjian (ed.). 2004. *A Dictionary of Standardized Modern Chinese*. Beijing: Foreign Language Teaching and Linguistic Studies Press and Language and Culture Press.

III Papers

Wang, Li. 1953. Problems with the boundary between words and word groups. *Studies of the Chinese Language*, 9.
Cao, Bohan. 1954. The contradiction between characters and words must be solved, in *A Symposia of Problems on Chinese Language*, Dongfang Bookstore.

Hu, Fu and Wen, Lian. 1954. The scope, form and function of words. *Studies of the Chinese Language*, 8.
Lin, Tao. 1954. Some questions on basic vocabulary in Chinese. *Studies of the Chinese Language*, 7.
Cen, Qixiang. 1956. Some questions about word formation in Chinese. *Studies of the Chinese Language*, 12.
Lu, Zhiwei. 1956. The object and procedure of word formation. *Studies of the Chinese Language*, 12.
Shi, Cunzhi. 1956. What is a word revisited. *Studies of the Chinese Language*, 9.
Wei, Jiangong, 1956. Synonyms and antonyms. *Chinese Language Learning*, 9–11.
Wu, Zhankun. 1956. Overlapped synonyms and their characteristics. *Chinese Knowledge*, 12.
Xing, Gongwan. 1956. Inflectional morphology and word formation in Modern Chinese. *Journal of Nankai University*, 2.
Zhang, Shilu. 1956. The relation between word meaning and parts of speech. *Chinese Language Learning*, 7.
Engels, Friedrich. 1957. The role of labour in the process of changing from ape to man. *Dialectics of Nature*. Beijing: People's Publishing House.
Ren, Mingshan. 1957. Synonyms and the polysemy of words. *Chinese Language Learning*, 4.
Sun, Liangming. 1958. The relation between the polysemy of words and the evolution of their meanings. *Studies of the Chinese Language*, 5.
Zheng, Dian. 1958. Japanese words in Modern Chinese. *Studies of the Chinese Language*, 2.
Zhou, Zumo. 1958. Vocabulary and lexicology. *Chinese Language Learning*, 9.
Lin, Tao. 1959. On standardization of Modern Chinese vocabulary. *Essays on Linguistics*, 3. Shanghai: Shanghai Education Publishing House.
Pan, Yunzhong. 1959. The formation and development of Chinese basic vocabulary. *Journal of Zhongshan University*, 1–2.
Sun, Liangming. 1959. Some problems in the study of Chinese morphology. *Humanities Journal*, 5.
Zhao, Zhenduo. 1959. Can a function word not be included in the basic vocabulary? *Humanities Journal*, 3.
Zheng, Dian. 1959. Essays on the history of vocabulary. *Studies of the Chinese Language*, 6-9, 11-12.
———. 1960. Essays on the history of vocabulary. *Studies of the Chinese Language*, 3.
———. 1961. Essays on the history of vocabulary. *Studies of the Chinese Language*, 6.
Zheng, Linxi. 1959. On the objective laws of word formation. *Studies of the Chinese Language*, 9.
Bo, Ming. 1961. On the relation between word meaning and concept. *Studies of the Chinese Language*, 8.
Cen, Qixiang. 1961. On the nature of word meaning and its relation to concept. *Studies of the Chinese Language*, 5.
Huang, Jingxin. 1961. On several problems in vocabulary. *Studies of the Chinese Language*, 6.
Shi, Anshi. 1961. On word meaning and concept. *Studies of the Chinese Language*, 8.
Yin, Huanxian. 1962. On the standardization of written forms of words. *Studies of the Chinese Language*, 6.
Chen, Jianmin. 1963. Abbreviation in modern Chinese – Also on general terms and the reduction of words. *Studies of the Chinese Language*, 4.

Lü, Shuxiang. 1963. A primary exploration to the problems of single syllable and double syllable in modern Chinese. *Studies of the Chinese Language*, 1.
Wang, Weixian, 1963. The relation between word meaning and concept revisited. *Zhejiang Tribune*, 4.
Zhang, Gong. 1964. Some problems of synonyms in modern Chinese. *Journal of Hebei University (Philosophy and Social Sciences Edition)*, 5.
Guo, Liangfu. 1981. Problems of Chinese vocabulary standardization. *Linguistic Research*, 2.
Li, Xingjian. 1981. Conceptual meaning and general meaning – Beginning with the meaning of the word "*Guojia*". *Lexicographical Studies*, 2.
———. 1981. On the definition of words – Beginning from "*jiuhuo*". *Lexicographical Studies*, 4.
Wang, Qin. 1981. On the archaic words in modern Chinese. *Journal of Xiangtan University (Philosophy and Social Sciences Edition)*, 1.
Yin, Menglun. 1981. On the division of historical periods in Chinese vocabulary research. *Literature, History and Philosophy*, 2.
Zhang, Yongyan. 1981. On the internal form of words. *Studies in Language and Linguistics*, 1.
Dai, Zhaoming. 1982. Nouns of a special construction. *Journal of Fudan University*, 6.
Jia, Yande. 1982. Several paradigmatic relations between word meaning within a semantic field. *Journal of Xinjiang University*, 1.
Song, Yongpei and Su, Baorong. 1982. Pay attention to ethnic characteristics and adhere to the comprehensive study of Chinese vocabulary in form, sound and meaning. *Journal of Sichuan Normal University*, 4.
Wang, Zhenkun and Xie, Wenqing. 1982. The componential analysis of antonyms. *Journal of Tianjin Teachers College*, 3.
Zhou, Zumo. 1982. The study of modern Chinese vocabulary. *Linguistic Research*, 2.
Fu, Huaiqing. 1983. The analysis of the meaning of words indicating actions and behaviours. *Journal of Peking University*, 3.
Shi, Anshi and Zhan, Renfeng. 1983. The general character, categories and imbalance of antonyms. *Essays on Linguistics*, 10. Beijing: The Commercial Press.
Liu, Shuxin. 1985. The Characteristics and categories of the internal forms of Chinese compound words. *Studies of the Chinese Language*, 3.
Chang, Jingyu. 1986. Context and semantics. *Chinese Study*. Tianjin: Nankai University Press.
Lin, Wanjing. 1987. On the synonymous disyllables with identical componenets but different in order. *Collected Papers of Academic Writing*, 2.
Lü, Jiping et al. 1987. The delimitation and interpretation of formulaic expressions. *Studies of the Chinese Language*, 6.
Sun, Yongchang. 1987. On the social factors of the change of word meaning. *Journal of Social Sciences of Hunan Normal University*, 4.
Wang, Shaoxin. 1987. On the interal semantic formation of Chinese compounds. *Language Teaching and Linguistic Studies*, 3.
Shen, Mengying. 1988. The infiltration of rhetoric methods and the creation of neologisms. *Journal of Shandong University*, 3.
Zhang, Zhi Gong. 1988. Vocabulary is important and vocabulary is difficult. *Studies of the Chinese Language*, 1.
Zhao, Keqin. 1988. On neologisms. *Linguistic Research*, 2.
He, Jiuying. 1989. On word meaning. *Research in Ancient Chinese Language*, 3.

Jiang, Shaoyu. 1989. Reflections on Chinese vocabulary system and its development and change. *Studies of the Chinese Language*, 1.
Sun, Yongchang. 1989. On the language factors of the change of word meaning. *Journal of Social Sciences of Hunan Normal University*, 5.
Xu, Weihan. 1989. On Chinese vocabulary system. *Research in Ancient Chinese Language*, 4.
Zhang, Yongyan. 1989. On Chinese loan words. *Language Teaching and Linguistic Studies*, 2.
Liu, Shuxin. 1990. The lexical attributes of the structure of compounds. *Studies of the Chinese Language*, 4.
Shi, Youwei. 1991. Ten aspects of the study of loan words. *Linguistic Research*, 1.
Zhou, Guangqing. 1991. New reflections on the structure of Chinese word meaning. *Journal of Jingzhou Teachers' College*, 3.
Cao, Congsun. 1992. On Chinese argots. *Studies of the Chinese Language*, 1.
Cheng, Rong. 1992. A tentative study on abbreviations. *Language Planning*, 7.
Jia, Yande. 1992. The development of semantics. *Language Planning*, 3.
Su, Xinchun. 1992. On the deep meaning in Chinese word meaning. *Journal of Guangzhou Teachers College*, 4.
Zhang, Lianrong. 1992. Inheritd semantic components in word meaning extension. *Journal of Peking University*, 4.
Zhou, Guangqing. 1992. Cultural psychology in the extension of Chinese word meaning. *Journal of Central China Normal University*, 5.
Chang, Jingyu. 1993. The relatioin of Chinese culture and the vocabulary of modern Chinese. *Chinese Language and Culture Studies*, 3. Tianjin: Nankai University Press.
Ying, Yutian. 1993. Types and definitions of figurative words and expressions. *Studies of the Chinese Language*, 4.
Wu, Tieping. 1994. On the word meaning, denotatum motivations of word-formation. *Modern Foreign Languages*, 1.
Sun, Liangming. 1995. On modernized researches of modern Chinese vocabulary. *New Research in Lexicology*. Beijing: Language and Culture Press.
Wang, Ning. 1995. The exploration and explanation of Chinese etymology. *Chinese Social Sciences*, 2.
Zhou, Jian. 1995. The morpheme choices of compound words. *Journal of Chinese Linguistics*, 7. Language and Culture Press.
Zhou, Hongbo. 1996. The prediction of neologisms. *Applied Linguistics*, 2.
Xu, Yaomin. 1997. The delimitation, setting and definition of idioms. *Studies of the Chinese Language*, 1.
Zheng, Yuanhan. 1997. In word semantic opposition question. *Studies of the Chinese Language*, 5.
Zhou, Jian. 1997. A study on synonymous words and expressions. *Studies of the Chinese Language*, 4.
Fu, Huaiqing. 2000. Some problems in the study of synonyms. *Studies of the Chinese Language*, 3.

Index

abbreviation 77–79
absolute antonyms 162
absolute synonyms 195
abstract words 200–201
adjectives, inflections of 104–107
adverb-noun combinations 208
affixation 99–100
affixes 52–54
age flavour 147
allegorical sayings, two-part 21–22
antonymous semantic morphemes 84
antonyms 159–163; absolute 162; characteristics of 159–161; definition of 159; relative 162–163; temporary 163; types of 161–163
antonymy 127
appositive relations 91–92
arbitrary combinations 67–68
archaic words 7–8
attributive relations 94–95

base form, of word 59–63
basic vocabulary 2–6, 14
basic words 2–5
bound morphemes 199

cadres 13
children's speech 13
classifiers 104
cognition 56, 64, 89–90, 97, 122, 170, 173–174, 194
co-hyponyms 163–166
coincidence relations 96–97
collocation of words 159
colloquialisms 112
common vocabulary 5–14
communication needs 64
complement compounds 85–86
complete synonyms 142–143, 152

compounding semantic morphemes 45–50; formation of 47–48; function of 48–50; properties and characteristics of 46–47
compound words 83
concepts: cognition and 122; coordinate 163–166, 174; grammatical meaning and 119–120; lexical meaning and 118–119, 121–122, 125–126; meaning with special flavour and 120; word meaning and 115–122, 174
concrete objects, word meaning and 116, 207
content words 199
contractions 77–79
contradictory relations 92–93, 161–162
coordinate compounds 84
coordinate concepts 163–166, 174

derivational affixes 53
diachronic dynamic motion 189, 196–203
dialects: regional 8–9, 12, 193; social 12–13
dialect words 8–9, 154, 193, 197–198
dictionaries 214
disyllabic words 75–77, 80–81, 198, 200
disyllabification 75–77, 103, 155
dynamic clusters 127
dynamic vocabulary 189–214; development, reasons for 190–196; diachronic dynamic motion 196–203; standardization of 210–214; synchronic dynamic change 204–209, 211–213

elderly persons 13
emotive flavour 145–146
enlargement, of word meaning 171–175
enrichment, of word meaning 170–171
ethnic groups, word meaning and 115
exotic flavour 146

fables 16–17
fixed structures: formulaic expressions 17–19; formulaic speech 22–23; idioms 14–17; proper nouns 22; proverbs 19–20; two-part allegorical sayings 21–22
foreign languages 9–12, 192–193
foreign words 32, 154
form-phonemic loans 9–10
formulaic expressions 2, 17–19
formulaic speech 22–23
four-syllabic words 198
function words 199

generic words 166–167
government relations 95–96
grammar 24, 25, 57
grammaticalization 199
grammaticalized elements 33
grammatical meaning 104, 105, 108, 111; of antonyms 160; concepts and 119–120; evolution of 187–188; of near-synonyms 155–156; word meaning clustering and 124–125, 126; *see also* word meaning
grammatical rules 90
graphic-semantic loans 10

homographs, polysemes and 139–140
homophones, polysemes and 138–139

identical relations 90–91
idioms 2, 14–17, 172
illustration 70–74; with addition of functional elements 73–74; from colour 72; from number 72; from possession 71–72; from properties and characteristics 71; with specification 72–73; from state of affairs 70; from usage 71
image flavour 146–147
incomplete synonyms 144–148, 152
infixes 53
inflection 99, 102–109
inflectional morphology 55, 61, 99–109; affixation 99–100; in Chinese 99–102; form and 107–109; meaning and 103–107; superposition 100–102; word formation and 102–109
inflectional suffixes 53
inflectional units 44

jargon 12–13

kinship words 167–168

language 55; dynamic 189–214; nature of 59; origin of 56; static 189; thought and 89–90
language elements 23–24, 57–59
language style 144–145
lexical meaning 33, 103–108, 110–112; of antonyms 160–161; cognition and 122; concept and 118–119, 121–122, 125–126; of near-synonyms 155–159; word meaning clustering and 124–126; *see also* word meaning
lexical morphology 80–87; nature and composite relations of semantic morphemes 83–87; number of semantic morphemes 82–83; phonetic form 80–82
linguistic function, of semantic morphemes 51–52
linguistic meaning 26
loan words 9–12, 58, 61
local flavour 147–148
logic 97
logically innovative collocations 208–209

meaning *see* word meaning
meaning-indicative phonetic transcription 10–11
metaphors 74, 133
metonymy 133–134
modifiers 32
monosemes 128, 169
monosemy 124; of polysemes 137–138, 150
monosyllabic words 80, 200
multiple-category membership 136–137

natural sound, as base form of word 63
near-synonyms 155–159, 200; characteristics of 155–157; definition of 155; types of 157–159
neologisms: in contemporary Chinese language 6–7; creation of 4, 6, 11, 55, 63–79, 197–198, 200; meaning of 91–92; origination of 13–14
non-reduplication words 81–82
nouns: adverb-noun combinations 208; proper 22

objectivity, of word meaning 113
onomatopoeia 68–69
onomatopoeic words 63
opposite relations 92–93, 161–162

parolized elements 206–207
partial-reduplicated words 81
phonemes 1
phonemic loans 9, 11–12
phonemic-semantic loans 10, 11
phones 1
phonetic change 69–70
phonetic form 28, 50, 80–82, 154, 206–207
phonetics 26
phrases: as base form 61–63; conventionalization into words 55; distinguishing words from 39–44
polysemes: definition of 128–129; development of 200; homographs and 139–140; homophones and 138–139; meanings of, and their relationships 135–136; metaphors 133; metonymy of 133–134; monosemy of 137–138, 150; multiple-category membership and 136–137; polysemous morphemes and 129–132; semantic extension 132–133; sense items of 132–140; specific reference 134; word meaning and 169; word meaning evolution and 186–188
polysemous morphemes 129–132
polysemy 124, 136–137
polysyllabic words 80–81
pragmatics 25
predication relations 96
prefixes 53
primary meanings 135–136
proper nouns 22
proverbs 19–20

reduplication compounds 87, 97
reduplication structures 34–36, 81, 103–104, 107–109
regional dialects 8–9, 12, 193
related semantic morphemes 84
relative antonyms 162–163
rhetoric 58
rhetorical comparison 74
rhetorical usage 183–184
rhetoric synonyms 151–152
rhotacization 69–70

rhymed disyllable words 82
root semantic morphemes 52, 83, 199

scientific terms 154–155, 194
segregatory words 41
semantic components 126
semantic extension 74–75, 132–133
semantic morphemes 1, 4, 44–54; affixes 52–54; antonymous 84; classification of 50–54; compounding 45–50; definition of 44–45; extinction of 203; formation of 47–48, 206; function of 48–50; internal structure 50; linguistic function 51–52; logical relationship between 97–98; monosyllabic 50; nature and composite relations of 83–87; number of 82–83; polysyllabic 50; properties and characteristics of 46–47; properties and meaning expression 52–54; related 84; root 52, 199; simple 48, 50; synonymous 84; types of 54
semantics 26
sense-corresponding synonyms 148–151
sense items: addition of 178–181, 184–186, 207; deletion of 181–182; emergence of 132–140; extinction of 202
sentence-making 29, 30, 36–38, 44
sentences 1–2, 25
simple semantic morphemes 48, 50
simple words 82
social dialects 12–13
societal development 190–193
Song Dynasty 6
sound-meaning arbitrary combination 67–68
specific reference 134
specifying compounds 85–86
speech sound 24, 26, 28, 57
stability, of basic vocabulary 4
Stalin, Josef 1
standardization, of vocabulary 210–214
static clusters 127
stems 53, 103
students 13
subjectivity, of word meaning 114
subject-predicate compounds 87, 90
subordinate compounds 84–85
subordination compounds 55
subordination relations 93
suffixes 53, 83

superposition 100–102
syllables 1, 32
synchronic dynamic change 189–190, 204–209, 211–213
synonymous semantic morphemes 84
synonyms 140–155; absolute 195; antonyms and 163; complete 142–143, 152; criteria and characteristics of 141; definition of 140; emergence of 153–155, 200; incomplete 144–148, 152; near-synonyms 155–159, 200; rhetoric 151–152; sense-corresponding 148–151; types of 141–153
syntactic constituents 27
syntax 2

Tang Dynasty 6
temporary antonyms 163
thinking activities 56, 64, 89–90; *see also* cognition
trisyllabic words 81, 198
two-part allegorical sayings 21–22

universality, of basic vocabulary 4, 5

verbal communication 25; co-hyponyms in 165–166; rhetoric synonyms and 151–152; word meaning evolution and 183
verb-complement compounds 86, 96
verb-object compounds 86–87, 95–96
verbs, inflections of 105
vocabulary: basic 2–6, 14; common 5–14; components of 2–23; contradiction and adjustment within system of 194–196; definition of 1; development, reasons for 190–196; diachronic dynamic motion of 196–203; dynamic form of 189–214; as element of language 24; extinction of old elements 201–203; as integrative unity in motion 189–190; properties of 1–2; standardization of 210–214; status and function of 23–26; synchronic dynamic change 204–209, 211–213; word formation and 57

word coinage 44, 55–58; activities 64–66, 89–90; appositive relation and 91–92; attributive relation and 94–95; in Chinese 67–79; coincidence relation and 96–97; development in 199–200; government relation and 95–96; identical relation and 90–91;

logical foundation of 89–98; opposite relation and 92–93; overview of 63–64; predication relation and 96; subordination relation and 93; synonyms and 154; vs. word structure 79–80
word formation 4, 44, 66–79; abbreviation 77–79; in Chinese 67–79; cognition and 89–90; conditions for 55–59; definition of 66–67; development in 199–200; disyllabification 75–77; form and 107–109; illustration 70–74; inflection and 102–109; with phonetic change 69–70; word morphology and 88–89
word meaning 28, 33, 36–37, 56, 93, 110–122; addition of sense item to 178–181, 184–186; characteristics of 112–116; cognition and 122, 194; communical nature of 114; concept and 115–122, 125–126, 174; concrete objects and 116, 207; contents of 110–112; deletion of sense item from 181–182; developmental nature of 114–115; development of 201, 207–208; dynamic change and 207–208; enlarging 171–175; enriching and deepening of 170–171; ethnic nature of 115; evolution of 154, 169–188; generality of 113–114; generally used sense 135–136; grammatical 111, 119–120, 124–126, 155–156, 160, 187–188; laws of evolution of 182–188; lexical 110–112, 118–119, 121–122, 124–126, 155–161; narrowing of 175–176; neologisms 91–92; objectivity of 113; one sense of word and 169, 170–178; overview of 110–116; polysemes and 186–188; primary 135–136; relationships between various 135–136; with special flavour 112, 120, 124–127; subjectivity of 114; transfer of 176–177; word formation and 103–107
word meaning clustering 123–168, 200–201; antonyms 159–163; co-hyponyms 163–166; criteria and principles of 123–127; division of 124–127; generic words 166–167; grammatical meaning 124–125, 126; kinship words 167–168; lexical meaning 124–126; meaning with special flavour and 124–127; monosemes 128; near-synonyms 155–159, 200; polysemes 128–140, 200; from static

and dynamic perspectives 127; studies on 123–124; synonyms 140–155, 200
word morphology 88–89
word order 155
words 27–44; abstract 200–201; aggregate of 2–23; archaic 7–8; base form of 59–63; basic 2–5; collocation of 159; compound 83; conditions for formation of 55–59; content 199; definition of 27–30; dialect 8–9, 154, 193, 197–198; distinguishing from phrases 39–44; disyllabic 75–77, 80–81, 198, 200; emergence of 55–63; extinction of 201–202; as fixed constructions 28–29; flexible use of 208–209; foreign 9–12, 32, 154; four-syllabic 198; function 199; generic 166–167; hierarchical analysis of 89; identification and division of 31–39; independent use of 29; kinship 167–168; language elements as foundation of 57–59; lexical morphology 80–87; loan 9–12, 58, 61; meaning of 28, 33, 36–37, 56, 93; as minimal units 30; monosyllabic 80, 200; onomatopoeic 63; passed down from history 5–6; phonetic form of 28, 50, 80–82, 154, 206–207; polysyllabic 80–81; reduplication structures 34–36; reduplication vs. non-reduplication 81–82; scope and application of 213; segregatory 41; simple 82; simplex form 34; trisyllabic 198; as unit for sentence-making 30, 36–38
word structure: appositive relation and 91–92; attributive relation and 94–95; coincidence relation and 96–97; government relation and 95–96; identical relation and 90–91; logical foundation of 89–98; opposite relation and 92–93; overview of 79–80; predication relation and 96; subordination relation and 93
writing system 25, 57–58

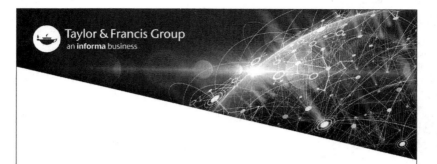